Creating a Life of Meaning and Compassion

The Wisdom of Psychotherapy

Creating a Life of Meaning and Compassion

The Wisdom of Psychotherapy

Robert W. Firestone, Lisa A. Firestone, and Joyce Catlett

With a Foreword by Daniel J. Siegel

American Psychological Association • Washington, DC

Published by
American Psychological Association
750 First Street, NE
Washington, DC 20002
www.apa.org

To order
APA Order Department
P.O. Box 92984
Washington, DC 20090-2984
Tel: (800) 374-2721
Direct: (202) 336-5510
Fax: (202) 336-5502
TDD/TTY: (202) 336-6123
Online: www.apa.org/books/
Email: order@apa.org

In the U.K., Europe, Africa, and the Middle East, copies may be ordered from
American Psychological Association
3 Henrietta Street
Covent Garden, London
WC2E 8LU England

Typeset in Goudy by World Composition Services, Inc., Sterling, VA

Printer: United Book Press, Baltimore, MD
Cover designer: Naylor Design, Washington, DC
Project Manager: Debbie Hardin, Carlsbad, CA

The opinions and statements are the responsibility of the authors, and such opinions and statements do not necessarily represent the policies of the American Psychological Association.

Library of Congress Cataloging-in-Publication Data
Firestone, Robert.
    Creating a life of meaning and compassion : the wisdom of
psychotherapy / Robert W. Firestone, Lisa A. Firestone, Joyce Catlett.
        p. cm.
    Includes bibliographical references and indexes.
    ISBN 1-59147-020-X (alk. paper)
    1. Psychotherapy.   I. Firestone, Lisa A.   II. Catlett, Joyce.   III.
Title

    RC480.F5558 2003
    616.89'14--dc21   2002043888

British Library Cataloguing-in-Publication Data
A CIP record is available from the British Library.

Printed in the United States of America
First Edition

For Louis:
Born with a brilliant mind to a world unkind.
A good man, a good friend.

CONTENTS

FOREWORD

DANIEL J. SIEGEL

I did not want this book to end. Like a close friend whose company fills you with joy and whose authenticity challenges you to be real, this book offers both comfort and companionship in the quest for truth about life.

Creating a Life of Meaning and Compassion: The Wisdom of Psychotherapy is about the wisdom of living. It offers the accumulated knowledge and insight of Robert W. Firestone's professional and personal search for an understanding of what it means to be human, to be real. Beyond a traditional focus on individual development, the book reveals powerful insights that have come from his 22 years of experience as a clinical psychologist in private practice as well as his life of reflection in a unique social group that has spanned more than three decades of friendship and exploration.

Robert W. Firestone, Lisa A. Firestone, and Joyce Catlett have collaborated to provide us with a banquet of insights into the nature of our inner lives and emotional relationships. Their mutually supported journeys—sailing around the world and exploring the core of their own minds—have created an opportunity for self-discovery that has been carefully documented and generously shared for our benefit. In this volume, we learn not only of the psychotherapeutic applications of this knowledge but also of its potential value in the lives of people everywhere.

At the same time that I was entering my adolescence in Los Angeles, this group of friends began meeting as adults and as teenagers just a neighborhood away from my family home. Our journeys have been quite different

Daniel J. Siegel, MD, is associate clinical professor of psychiatry, University of California at Los Angeles, and author of *The Developing Mind* and *Parenting From the Inside Out*.

and yet we have ended up with overlapping perspectives on life. Although our travels started in similar geographies, theirs was made as a social unit with deep respect for individual sovereignty; mine was carried out through personal reflection, a more traditional "nuclear family," and professional exploration. I wonder how different my life might have been if I had become a part of their teenage discussion groups, just a stone's throw from my home, back in those formative years. I am grateful that our paths finally did cross.

My path led me to set out alone to discover things about myself and eventually to focus on the mind, the brain, and human relationships through professional training and endeavors as a psychiatrist and educator. Drs. Firestone and Ms. Catlett share my passion for sailing, and this is perhaps a metaphor for our journeys through life. The wind and water force you to live fully in the present. Sailing also requires an awareness of where you have been and a vision of where you are going. Sailing, and living a meaningful life, both require and nurture our integration of the past, the present, and the imagined future. As we sail the landscape of our internal lives, such an integration of time may be at the heart of living a full and coherent life.

Another parallel in our views is the perspective that deeper self-understanding and authentic interpersonal relatedness go hand in hand, reinforcing each other as they deepen and become unburdened by restrictive adaptations from the past. Through research in attachment and convergent findings from neuroscience, we can learn how the development of the neural circuitry for self-knowledge overlaps with that for emotional communication and empathy. This feature of our social brains is beautifully revealed in the experiences described in this book.

I find myself now with the honor of writing a foreword to a work in which the authors have the generosity of heart to share with us their insights into the human experience. The vision of this volume illuminates the dilemma of fighting off the defenses that attempt to protect us from the pain of the past while trying to stave off the anxiety of the human realization of mortality that comes with a feelingful, awake life. That balance is not easily struck—the effort to find a way to feel real while at the same time not becoming overwhelmed by the existential pain of our awareness of death. Such awareness may be our uniquely human legacy, emerging from our cortical capacity to represent the future and be aware of the movement of time and our limited place in its passage. Within this challenge to live with eyes and heart wide open rests the ultimate goal: how to be fully human. With bravery and clarity, the authors lay out the blueprint of their collective wisdom to live a full life. It is our honor to receive it with open minds and a deep sense of gratitude.

PREFACE

The search for meaning is the search for expression of one's real self.
—James F. Masterson (cited in deMause, 2002, p. 238)

Our purpose in writing this book is to elucidate and demonstrate manifestations of the defensive process that limit the possibility of making positive changes in one's life. Relinquishing habitual defenses inevitably increases one's vulnerability to a world that is abrasive and destructive to the undefended person. People today are living within a social structure that deprives them of their special human qualities: their capacity for sustaining feelings of compassion for self and others, their drive to search for meaning, and their ability to live in harmony with others.[1] Indeed, the self seems under siege in almost every aspect of an individual's life. It is imperative at this stage in human evolution to consider new perspectives and to develop alternative ways of thinking and living that could transcend these destructive environmental and cultural influences. One of our goals is to provide such a perspective through an uncompromising view of the myriad forces existing within family and social systems that contribute to people's distress and suffering. Another goal is to outline methods for countering these inimical forces.

This book is addressed to people who believe that striving for a life of meaning and compassion is still possible and worthwhile. We delineate, for clinicians and other interested readers, the combined insights of clinical psychologists and our associates and friends as we grappled with forces, from within and without, that were limiting our lives. We provide a summary of the wisdom and self-knowledge we acquired as we sought a solution to the

---

The first author, Robert W. Firestone, originated the theoretical concepts, developed the therapeutic methodology delineated, and functioned as facilitator in the discussions with individuals in the friendship circle. The coauthors, Lisa A. Firestone and Joyce Catlett, organized and helped write the clinical case material and the personal accounts from participants in the group of friends and referenced the basic concepts and findings.

xi

destructiveness of society by developing a more decent and respectful way of living.

This book is the outcome of more than 40 years of explorations into the problem of resistance. This work broadens the concept of resistance in psychotherapy to include an understanding of people's fundamental resistance to a better life. It demonstrates the relationship between the structure and organization of psychological defenses and the fear of change, individuation, and personal power. In our investigations, we have found that most people tend to avoid experiences that are warm or constructive (Firestone, 1985). Most of us reject or manipulate our environments to evade emotional interactions that would contradict our early conceptions of reality. This phenomenon may be the single most limiting factor for all psychotherapies.

Psychological defenses predispose an inward, self-protective lifestyle that is the basis of a core resistance to change or improvement in one's life circumstances. These defenses originated in a social process and can potentially be altered in a social milieu. In the pages that follow, we describe the experiences of approximately 100 friends and acquaintances who, with no preconceived plan, created such a social environment. We are fortunate to have had the opportunity to participate in this friendship circle from the beginning. This book focuses on the process of change and the courage and dedication demonstrated in the struggle to overcome resistance to accepting an emotionally richer and more fulfilling way of living.

Over the past three decades, we have developed personally, enriched our relationships, and deepened our friendships by sharing business ventures, child-rearing, and adventure on the high seas. Success in these areas was made possible primarily because we have pooled our resources and have maintained an open forum for honest communication in which expressions of opinions and feelings are accepted and highly valued. In the process of talking together, we have gradually evolved a new way of living, based on an implicit code of ethical principles that focuses on avoiding behaviors that hurt other people—behaviors that are toxic to personal development, especially to that of children. The people in this group are strongly individualistic and originally came from diverse backgrounds, but we share a common interest in psychology. This book offers a view of this unique sequence of events that serves as an intriguing experiment in applied psychology.

In describing the experiences and our efforts to overcome defensive barriers to a fulfilling life, we are not suggesting that readers imitate their social milieu or pursue the same pathway but rather that they might learn from our insights. Although we share the beliefs of many philosophers that living the "good life" requires conscious reflection, we do not agree that this requires a prescribed adherence to a code derived from divine sources— or from human beings accorded near-divine status. To the contrary, we recognize that to pursue a more meaningful existence, one must seek to develop one's own potentialities in a unique manner. Our approach is centered on supporting the people we care about—clients, friends, and acquaintances—as they strive to fulfill their own vision of a better life.

On a more personal note, our inspiration to write this work came in part from a remark that R. D. Laing made shortly before his death. When visiting with our group of friends, Laing affectionately challenged the first author saying, "You should take a chance on preaching what you practice." The remark was complimentary, although ironic, in the sense that both men disapprove of preaching. But we knew what Laing meant. This book, in a sense, is an attempt to fulfill his wish.

INSIGHTS AND DISCOVERIES

The people described in this book learned that it is possible to live a meaningful, satisfying life if they are willing to challenge the defenses developed in childhood as a protection against anxiety and emotional pain. They found that facing painful feelings they had spent a lifetime avoiding allowed them to achieve a life far beyond what they thought possible. Their struggle to achieve a better life revolved around certain core issues.

An Openness to Experience

All people exist in a state of conflict between active pursuit of goals in the real world and an inward, self-protective defense system characterized by fantasy gratification and self-nurturance. A crucial step toward living a life of meaning and compassion involves moving away from inward self-parenting habit patterns to live one's current life rather than relive the past.

In fact, living a meaningful life requires the openness and vulnerability of experiencing one's inner life of emotions, thoughts, fantasies, and dreams, all the while seeking gratification of one's needs through an active outer life. When people are fully alive to their experiences in life, they inevitably suffer pain as well as joy. Unfortunately, the dominant social and cultural forces of Western society favor intellect over emotion, outer success over inner aliveness, and defensive over nondefensive living. From this perspective, one can understand why so many young people turn in despair to drugs, hostility, and violence.

The death of feeling and compassion in contemporary culture is a subject of powerful importance. Nothing illustrates this new trend more poignantly than the changes that have taken place in the field of psychotherapy over the past 30 years. Psychology in post–World War II America was an exciting movement dedicated to helping millions of people improve their personal lives and enhance their ability to work and love. Few of its pioneers dreamed in their worst nightmares that it would become a "psycho-pharma-cological" profession, as we see it, offering short-term cures through clever marketing and gimmicks.[2] This book describes one approach that could potentially counter what we perceive as a depressing trend and, it is hoped, help revitalize the disciplined study and practice of depth psychotherapy.

Autonomy and Social Affiliation

To be fully alive to experience, one needs to seek and experience both autonomy and social affiliation. To preserve feeling for oneself, an individual must confront the internalized destructive thoughts or internal voices that accuse the person of being inadequate, destructive, or bad, thereby undermining the ability to value his or her own experience. Facing the enemy within is liberating. As people become more autonomous they tend to experience a changing, rather than a fixed, identity. The goal is to find, not define, oneself, to be constantly open to growth and evolution, both in the moment and over time.

This is not a "selfish" vision, because the self cannot exist in a vacuum. Human beings have both the need and the desire for social affiliation. Individuals who are truly centered in themselves naturally develop empathy, a sense of compassion toward other people, and a desire to work for the good of the larger society. However, people cannot achieve such societal goals through guilt, rules, and prescriptions. A harmonious society becomes a possibility only when each individual becomes truly him- or herself and develops his or her own set of values. It is particularly worthwhile to create an environment with other people who share one's ideals and search for meaning.

Love and Transcendent Goals

The experience of love counters existential pain and despair. Loving others, and being loved by them, helps compensate for the anguish and torment inherent in the human condition. In pursuing a richer emotional life a person gradually develops the capacity to offer and accept love. Love requires outward expressions of affection, kindness, and consideration as well as internal feelings of tenderness, love, and warmth. However, many couples maintain a fantasy of love or an imaginary connection (fantasy bond) while their external behavior fails to correspond to any reasonable definition or meaning of the word "love." Finally, to be fully alive to all of life's experiences means to live a life that satisfies transcendent human needs: to love, to feel, to create, to help others, and to ponder the mysteries of existence—needs that are as important as the basic drives for food and shelter.

The preconditions for embarking on this lifelong enterprise are (a) committing ourselves to life and (b) learning to value ourselves. The process of wholeheartedly embracing life, regardless of the circumstances in which we find ourselves, is an ennobling project that lifts us out of the mundane routine of everyday life and raises us to a higher level of existence. Learning to value one's self is a difficult task because the ability to see ourselves as having worth and our life as having value is often damaged early on. There-fore, it becomes an ongoing endeavor to liberate ourselves from the residuals of damaging childhood programming and to learn to exchange restrictive, conventional modes of thinking for a kinder and less judgmental perception of ourselves and the world.

ORGANIZATION OF THE BOOK

This book is based on the psychological principle that the major obstacles to achieving a more fulfilling life are the defenses that each individ-ual develops in childhood against emotional pain, frustration, and anxiety. Although these defense mechanisms serve the function of helping children survive psychologically, they pose a serious limitation in an adult's life. Recognizing and challenging these defenses make it possible to move toward a freer, less defended life. When a group of people, such as the group described in this book, combine their resources and maintain a public arena for expressing feelings and opinions, they can achieve far more than any individual or family could accomplish alone.[3]

Our psychotherapeutic approach clearly is not meant to help the individ-ual adjust to a social structure; rather, it is meant to alter the social process so that it enhances the individual. By encouraging people to go beyond them-selves, we believe individuals can structure a way of life and a community that reflect in a healthy way on others. Our approach supports individuation as a goal, and we suggest that this allows human beings to develop their special qualities and to lead adventurous lives within their own value systems.

Although it is neither possible nor desirable to dictate how to accom-plish these goals, we are able to describe a variety of methods that clinicians can adapt to their practice to help their clients overcome their resistance to pursuing and accepting a more fulfilling life.

In the introduction and in chapters 1 and 2 (Part I), the authors introduce ideas to enhance the understanding of both professional and nonprofessional readers regarding how psychological defenses function to limit one's life experience and cause distress and considerable suffering. Chapter 1 describes a vision of a better life, a more fulfilling and meaningful existence, and introduces the concepts of the fantasy bond (an imagined connection to another person) and the voice (destructive thoughts antithetical to self and others). Chapter 2 sets forth the overall theory and discusses the etiology of defensive processes that are barriers to pursuing a better life.

Each chapter in Parts II and III (chapters 3 through 13) is divided into two sections: The first section describes psychotherapy methods, including the procedures of voice therapy, that clinicians can adapt to their practice. In this section, the first author is referred to as "Dr. Firestone" to indicate his professional role as a psychotherapist. The second section discusses the corrective experiences that were used and the insights that were achieved by individuals in the friendship circle that facilitated positive change or improvement. In this section, the first author is referred to as "Robert Firestone" to indicate his role as a participant–observer in the group discussion.

Chapters 3 through 9 (Part II) contain in-depth explanations of methods, guidelines, and suggestions for challenging and counteracting specific defensive behaviors and lifestyles, including addictive habit patterns and other self-destructive manifestations, a diminished ability to experience one's emotions, withholding behaviors, and defenses against death anxiety.

Chapters 10 through 13 (Part III) discuss problems arising in relationships based on the defenses each partner brings to the relationship and provides methods for recapturing closeness and intimacy in couple and family relationships. The chapter on child-rearing documents how the people in the group of friends have shared child-rearing functions in the context of an extended family constellation.

In Part IV, chapter 14 discusses human rights issues in interpersonal relationships and in society. Chapter 15 contrasts malevolent and benevolent societies, with the friendship circle as an example of a benevolent social process. Chapter 16 discusses the direction that the field of psychotherapy has taken in recent years. Chapter 17 describes the therapeutic value of friendship. Chapter 18 summarizes the authors' attitudes toward spirituality, mystery, and the search for meaning.

NOTES

1. In *Man's Search for Meaning*, Viktor Frankl (1946/1959) asserted that "every age has its own collective neurosis. . . . The existential vacuum which is the mass neurosis of the present time can be described as a private and personal form of nihilism; for nihilism can be defined as the contention that being has no meaning" (p. 152).
2. See *A History of Psychiatry* (Shorter, 1997); *Of Two Minds: The Growing Disorder in American Psychiatry* (Luhrmann, 2000); *Blaming the Brain* (Valenstein, 1998); and *They Say You're Crazy* (Caplan, 1995).
3. Martin Seligman (1990) has expressed a similar sentiment. He suggested that "when learned optimism is coupled with a renewed commitment to the commons [family, friends, community], our epidemic of depression and meaninglessness may end" (p. 291).

ACKNOWLEDGMENTS

We express our appreciation to Tamsen Firestone, Jo Barrington, Susan Short, and Jo Linder-Crow for their inspirational efforts in editing the manuscript. We are also grateful to Anne Baker, who worked closely with us to complete the final draft and to Tracy Larkin for her administrative support. We also thank Robert Romanelli and Jerome Nathan, who helped locate relevant works in the literature, and Jina Carvalho, for helping with the manuscript and for dissiminating a growing body of written works and films.

Our appreciation goes to Susan Reynolds, acquisitions editor at the American Psychological Association, for her ongoing encouragement and support, and to Judy Nemes, development editor, for her insightful suggestions regarding editorial and organizational changes.

We express our gratitude to the men, women, and children whose stories illustrate the various dimensions of the good life. We acknowledge their openness and honesty in revealing their personal truths. We thank them for sharing the insights they achieved as they tried to accommodate to a new way of being and living that gradually evolved. They were strongly motivated to make the knowledge and understanding that they gained along the way available so that others might benefit from their experiences. Finally, we thank Fred Branfman for his contribution to and ongoing support of this project.

The names, places, and other identifying facts contained herein have been fictionalized and no similarity to any people, living or dead, is intended. In some instances—for example, in the epilogue—certain names were not fictionalized, because these individuals specifically requested that their names remain unchanged.

Creating a Life of
Meaning and Compassion

The Wisdom of Psychotherapy

INTRODUCTION

Although hundreds of books are published each year dealing with theories about how to live a fuller life, achieve better relationships, raise happier children, succeed in business, and realize personal and spiritual goals,[1] this book relates the experiences of people who actually put these ideas into practice. These people, who range in age from infants to those in their 70s, are long-time friends and associates of the first author. This circle of friends may well be unique in a number of ways, including that it has functioned in an urban setting, is composed of professionals and business people, and has withstood the test of time. The people involved are committed to compassion and feeling; lead honest, open lives, and are not afraid to challenge the status quo when it seems appropriate. Despite the uniqueness of this group of people, however, we believe that many of the lessons learned can be valuable to all those seeking to develop themselves, just as the ideas and experiences described in this book have helped the people who developed them.

HISTORICAL DEVELOPMENT OF THE FRIENDSHIP CIRCLE

The history of this group of friends is a story about an unusual American subculture. First-time visitors to a gathering of this group often experience a kind of culture shock not unlike what they would experience on a visit to an unfamiliar country. Yet this story is about a group of men, women, and children who are ordinary people. What is different is their lifestyle of freedom, openness, and sharing, which represents for them the ideal state.

During the early 1970s, we and several associates who were interested in psychological issues began participating in seminars and discussions in which we revealed our innermost secrets, shared our pain and grief, and expressed powerful feelings. In sharing these painful experiences, both existential and interpersonal, we became acutely aware of forces within society and the nuclear family that were detrimental to human development and conducive to the formation of negative psychological symptoms. As a result, we became strongly motivated to try to minimize these destructive elements in our personal lives. Perhaps even then, on some unconscious level, we were beginning to formulate the elements of an implicit morality based on our mutual insights.

Nearly 30 years later, we are sharing the knowledge we accumulated through books, articles, and documentary films. We are committed to the ongoing project of discovering and putting into practice the essential ingredients of a more humane way of life, a lifestyle that places great value on each human being and is concerned with each person's individuation and autonomy. In the following pages, we trace the evolution of this unusual aggregation of people from its inception to the present day.

The story begins with a childhood fantasy, perhaps a latent fantasy that all people have, to share a better world with friends. This desire was particularly strong in us, as well as in many of our friends and colleagues: We wanted to live in a place where we could be honest with one another, where we could really be ourselves, and where we could be kind and generous. We dreamed of a truly democratic place where each person would be acknowledged and respected.

No person or group of people set out to create this lifestyle. It emerged naturally, the extension of a small nucleus of individuals and their families that now has expanded significantly.[2] The growth of our group of friends centered primarily around three areas of endeavor. The first was the rebuilding of a sailing schooner, which led to gradually expanding sea voyages and eventually to a circumnavigation; the second was the sharing of several business ventures; and the third involved a strong desire to understand ourselves. Each of us had a keen focus on our personal development, that of our families, and especially that of our children. The essential ingredient prevalent within these endeavors was our truthful communication with each other and the compassionate atmosphere that prevailed in our ongoing discussions.

Beginnings

By the late 1960s, the people in the families of our original group were spending much of our leisure time socializing, traveling together, playing sports, boating, motorcycling, and most important, exchanging psychological and philosophical ideas. This small group of people, which initially consisted of seven families, were unusually good friends who had a strong desire for social and personal contact. Some of the friendships were long-standing even then, averaging 10 to 15 years, and one friendship had been ongoing for more than 35 years.

One of the distinguishing characteristics of the friends' social lives is humor. We shared anecdotes forged from personal experiences together and spent considerable time in laughter and good-natured joking. If there was a crisis, everyone helped out. We gave each other a great deal of support and contributed to one another's goals. The parents in this small circle of friends involved themselves in helping take care of each other's children and took an active interest in each child's psychological well-being.

The individuals who were the founding members of the friendship circle, as well as others who were drawn to the group, seemed to have several basic characteristics in common. They were intelligent, sensitive people who had an abiding interest in self-fulfillment and mutual regard and tolerance for others. They were nonjudgmental in their attitudes and focused on self-knowledge in the Socratic sense. Typically nonjoiners, their individualism and independence played a significant part in the attraction they held for each other. It was this unique group of individuals that ultimately formed the core of what later became quite a large collection of people.

Discussion Group With Colleagues and Friends

Backtracking to the early 1970s, many of the first author's colleagues and close friends had already been talking together informally and sharing their feelings and perceptions for a number of years. When they heard about what was happening in a psychotherapy group he had formed in 1969, they were inspired by the insights and the shared interactions and wanted to form a similar group that would meet on a regular basis.

Before that time, the first author had conducted individual psychotherapy for about 12 years. He had been hesitant about expanding his work into the field of group therapy for several reasons. For one, he had an inherent dislike of groups and of the group process. He had seen the effects of conventional group pressure, which people so often conform to at the cost of their individuality and independence. On the other hand, he believed that because neuroses and emotional disorders had originated in a social setting, the pain and psychological problems of neurosis could be dealt with effectively in a new kind of social atmosphere that the group could provide.

However, considering a discussion group for his colleagues and friends that would meet on a regular schedule required much serious thought. For example, what type of responsibility would he be assuming? He spent several weeks coming to a decision about their request for an ongoing discussion group to deal with personal issues. There were many factors to be considered. Would his friends and associates react to him as a therapist instead of a friend, regardless of the fact that he wished to be an equal participant?

In the ensuing discussions, his friends assured him that they could look after themselves. In truth, these men and women were highly intelligent, responsible individuals, well-respected in their professions. Among them were engineers, systems analysts, lawyers, teachers, psychologists, and businesspeople. Still, the first author approached the project with caution and informed everyone that they would begin with a trial period. He planned to start with the small group of psychologists who had been consulting with him for several years and then add one or two people at a time over the following two to three months.

The Experiential Weekends

The late 1960s and early 1970s was the era of encounter groups and experimental workshops. In those days, leadership seminars and marathons were commonplace in the practice of psychotherapy. During this period, participants in the expanding discussion group of associates and friends became interested in participating in an experiential weekend to facilitate deep emotional expression. We anticipated that the prolonged contact would help break down our defenses and permit us to reach a deeper sense of ourselves. During the first weekend, people from this group gathered in the living room of a large A-frame cabin in the midst of a pine forest overlooking Lake Arrowhead. During the meetings, which lasted for as long as five or six hours, we gradually became less defended and more open with one another, and the atmosphere grew progressively more accepting and sensitive.

A number of people relived painful episodes from their childhoods. At one point, a man had a vivid image of himself as a small, innocent boy who loved his mother and father. He remembered how he had protected his parents by never telling them that he had overheard their heated arguments as he lay awake in bed every night or that these fights had caused him so much unhappiness. Even though he had had years of therapy, this man had never allowed himself to experience these deep feelings of sadness before the weekend. A number of others also began to express strong feelings, recalling painful events they had endured while growing up. At times, they cried or moaned or vented explosive anger. Afterward, they felt relieved and had clear insights about how these suppressed emotions were affecting their current lives.

As the weekend progressed, an amazing transformation took place. If one had photographed people's faces before and after the event, one would have found them nearly unrecognizable. Faces initially etched with stress and anxiety and lined with the cumulative effect of character defenses were gradually changing. Later the same faces were flushed with feeling and aliveness.

Afterward, many people spoke of their appreciation for what they felt had been a remarkable experience. They realized that during this weekend they had been living an entirely different lifestyle. In reflecting on the way people had briefly lived and interacted, we concluded that this was a fitting way for people to spend their lives.

However, when the participants returned home, the majority gradually lost this edge of feeling and communion with themselves and became defended once again. They were disappointed, as we were, that they had reverted to so-called normal life in such a short time. It was clear that during the marathons these people had been emotionally alive, whereas in their everyday lives they regressed to a familiar, nonfeeling existence, characterized by role-playing, toughness, paranoia, and other cut-off states. They were not in touch with themselves or their real experience.

FURTHER DEVELOPMENTS

In an effort to preserve the enriched and authentic way of being they had experienced during the experiential weekend, these people began to change their routine, habitual lifestyles. They discussed these changes openly in their group meetings and were encouraging of, and receptive to, feedback from their friends and family members. During these discussions, they often heard important information regarding the ways they were defending themselves and learned how their defenses were hurting both themselves and their loved ones.

Over the years, these people gradually gave up many of their addictive habit patterns and defensive styles of interacting with their mates and family members. They began to challenge negative ways of evaluating and categorizing themselves and became more open to the possibility of change. Increasingly responsive to their own feelings, they developed more sensitivity and compassion for others. The dishonest and intrusive responses that had characterized many of their "normal" interactions were diminished to a considerable extent. Disrupting defenses that had given them a false sense of security enabled them to become more spontaneous and energetic. They began to look more alive, and their appearances changed for the better, sometimes radically. Motivated by their experiences in the mountains and other group interactions, these men and women have, to a large degree, achieved their goal of bringing the warmth and aliveness of those weekends into their everyday lives.

The Young People's Discussion Group
and the Circumnavigation of the World

In 1971, we discovered that some of our children had begun experimenting with dangerous drugs. We were all deeply concerned that they might be involving themselves in the destructive pattern of addiction so prevalent among young people at the time. It seemed that several teenagers in the neighborhood had become addicted, and there were reports of some who had overdosed. We were also concerned with the overall psychological well-being of our offspring. As a result, we asked one of the fathers, a jewelry importer who had a natural rapport with the teenagers, to lead a discussion group for them. The children, who were mostly between the ages of 10 and 13, met once a week to talk about their thoughts and feelings, their goals, their alienation from their parents, their competitive feelings, and their emerging sexual feelings.

After several months of meeting together, the teenagers invited their parents to join their talks. These talks had a powerful effect on parents and children alike. Because these parents were concerned and because the content of their talks was reminiscent of their own childhood pain, they experienced considerable sadness. The democratic exchange of perceptions and the sincere expression of feelings that occurred during these meetings between parents and children gradually dissolved the generational boundaries. Parental roles began to be discarded and the adolescents related to their parents on a more equal basis. Incidentally, the discussion group succeeded in its original goals: The young people gave up their experimental use of drugs and the dishonest, rebellious life it predisposed. They began to challenge many of the hypercritical, judgmental attitudes they had grown up with and spoke out against condescending and disrespectful treatment.

In 1973, the parents in the five original families purchased an unfinished, 85-foot schooner. In the years that followed, as we completed work on the boat, it became a vehicle that helped us to learn to work together on a shared project. It also became a vehicle for adventure and travel and a means for the teenagers to increase their self-confidence and sense of independence and develop their leadership skills. In November 1976, the schooner set sail on a 17-month voyage around the world. Because of the adults' work schedules, parts of the journey were made by the 11 teenagers alone, without adult supervision. During the years of preparation and sailing, they had learned the basics of boat-handling, engine mechanics, electronics, navigation, and medical procedures, skills that would be necessary at those times when they assumed total responsibility for the ship. During several fierce storms in the Gulf of Aden, Indian Ocean, and the North Pacific, the teenagers were completely on their own. They found that talking together about their fears and other concerns was essential under conditions where their survival might well depend on their morale and team spirit.[3]

While the young people were on the voyage, many of their parents and other adults entered into business together. Although we were advised by bankers and established business acquaintances that friendship and business rarely mix and that our businesses would fail and ruin our friendships, we nevertheless decided to embark on three small business ventures. At that time, none of us had had any formal business training; in addition, the fledgling businesses were started with an unusually small amount of capitalization.

On their return from the circumnavigation, several of the teenagers became involved in the companies and rapidly rose to leadership positions. The businesses flourished and grew, leading to extraordinary financial successes. The energy and high morale created by open discussions between management and employees (modeled on the earlier teenagers' discussions and on the style of communication that prevailed in their parents' talks) played an important role in people's ability to resolve conflict and contributed to our outstanding accomplishments in these enterprises.

Creating a Better Life

As our friends and associates relinquished many of the deadening routines and painkillers that had been limiting their lives, we found ourselves talking at a deeper level and even more candidly than before about relationships, sexuality, competitive feelings, and interactions with our children. Out of these conversations, a set of implied values began to emerge, based on an understanding of what had hurt us in childhood and characterized by ongoing attempts to remove unnecessary obstacles to straightforward communication.

In 1979, this group of people asked the first author to relinquish his private practice and devote himself to be an observer–participant and to continue consulting with them in their discussions. Once again, there was an emphasis on him not conducting psychotherapy nor assuming responsibility for the well-being of the people involved. He would simply pursue his own creative work, which involved further elaborating his theories and ideas. On a strictly personal level, he felt the situation would be the most fulfilling part of his life, a crucible for further developing an understanding of himself and for making explicit, in writing, the implicit values he had practiced all his life.

His overall goals were to explore those aspects of daily living that are conducive to mental health—that is, the attitudes, actions, activities, and conditions that are necessary for enhancing people's lives. He wanted to examine the dimensions of the meaningful life that his friends and colleagues had created, gather the relevant data, and find out how people can put these principles and values into practice in their everyday lives.

DISCOVERIES AND INSIGHTS

Our observations have been rewarding in terms of an accumulated pool of knowledge regarding what constitutes a more fulfilling life and what impediments emerge as people seek to embrace a life characterized by authenticity and compassion. By both observing and participating in this unique psychological laboratory, we made discoveries about individuals and society that indicated a direction to take that would lead toward a better way of living. Our long-term involvement with this group of people afforded us valuable information about people's resistance to having experiences that are warmer and more constructive than what they had previously experienced. In addition, the wealth of information available from our observations of the children as they grew up led to insights about the kind of family life and child-rearing practices that are the most favorable for raising emotionally healthy children.

This book is filled with examples from the experiences of these people and the practical and philosophical wisdom that has come from our 30-year dialogue, spanning three generations. We believe that the basic ideas generated during the evolution of this miniculture may be generally valid for human behavior in the larger society. We do not wish to imply that a person should follow any particular pathway in attempting to achieve a better life, nor must people necessarily pursue their goals within a group context. We merely hope that the insights gained from our experiences might inspire readers to give more value to their own lives, to pursue their own form of self-realization, and to search for their own personal meaning in life.

It is important to reemphasize that the ideas contained in this book about how to live a meaningful life do not exist in a vacuum; they were developed by people who contended with and then overcame deadening defenses and tendencies to maintain the status quo. These ideas have been put into actual practice with good results by people who were determined to fulfill their dreams of creating a better world for themselves and their children. We believe that the knowledge acquired during this extended study can be adapted to a wide range of circumstances and environments. Giving up defensive habit patterns, living more sociably, and learning to be more authentic and honest in communicating are all courses of action open to most people in their everyday lives. With a full realization of these possibilities, this work describes both the vision of the good life and the challenges over which an individual must triumph to achieve it.

NOTES

1. Books on this topic include *The Human Quest for Meaning* (Wong & Fry, 1998); *Flow: The Psychology of Optimal Experience* (Csikszentmihalyi, 1990); *Going on Being* (M. Epstein, 2001); *Living the Mindful Life* (Tart, 1994); *Transforming the Mind* (Dalai Lama, 2000); and *A Small Treatise on the Great Virtues: The Uses of Philosophy in Everyday Life* (Comte-Sponville, 1996/2001). In the wellness literature, see *Love and Survival* (Ornish, 1998), and in the self-improvement genre, *The Power of Now* (Tolle, 1999) and *Anatomy of the Spirit* (Myss, 1996). For perspectives on positive psychology, see *Handbook of Positive Psychology* (Snyder & Lopez, 2002); *Optimism & Pessimism: Implications for Theory, Research, and Practice* (Chang, 2001); *The Science of Optimism and Hope: Research Essays in Honor of Martin E. P. Seligman* (Gillham, 2000); and the special issue on the topic in the *American Psychologist* (Fowler, 2000).

2. The fact that the friendship circle evolved naturally with no preconceived plan differentiates it from other extended family arrangements or "shared households" that were preplanned. See *Shared Houses, Shared Lives: The New Extended Families and How They Work* (Raimy, 1979), and *Is It Utopia Yet? An Insider's View of Twin Oaks Community in its 26th Year* (Kinkade, 1994).

3. The circumnavigation was documented in a film, *Voyage to Understanding* (Parr, 1983) and in a video documentary, *Friendship: A Life of Meaning and Compassion* (Parr, 2002).

I

THE CHALLENGE

1

A VISION OF A MEANINGFUL LIFE

The aim of life is to live, and to live means to be aware, joyously, drunkenly, serenely, divinely aware.

—Henry Miller (1941, p. 2)

Andrea (50): I consider life to be a tremendous gift and a tremendous opportunity. It's an opportunity to be something that never was before and will never be again. There's something unique in each person that's made up of the things they love, that they're interested in, their funny little quirks. So I think the good life is for a person to realize as much as they can about who they are. Doing so, however, requires the courage to challenge the defenses we developed as kids that keep us from being fully alive.

Lia (21): In living the good life, not being defended is very important. By that I mean to always be open to the next happening, even if you get hurt. I don't like the actual process of getting hurt, but I like that I stay open and I forgive. I might be angry or upset, but I'm always open to change. I feel that if you're not open, you're not really living. And it's really important to let people in because that's what's going to make life full.

Life in the twenty-first century poses a number of challenges as increasing numbers of people spend more time in front of computer screens working on abstract intellectual or technological tasks (Anderson, Bikson, Law, & Mitchell, 1995; Cooper, Scherer, Boies, & Gordon, 1999; Kandell, 1998; Kraut et al., 1998; Sproull & Kiesler, 1991; Turkle, 1997; Young, 1998).

15

Indeed, the isolation and comfort of contemporary society carry with it the risk of reinforcing psychological defenses that contribute to an inward, self-protective, and somewhat emotionally deadened way of being and living.[1] It appears that as people move toward a more materialistic, mechanistic outlook, many of them are neglecting their emotional growth, personal relationships, and family life (Berke, 1988; Hewlett, 1991; Kozol, 1995; Lasch, 1984; R. Putnam, 1995; Vitalari, Venkatesh, & Gronhaug, 1985). The question arises: Can people devote themselves to further developing their capacity to feel compassion for themselves and empathy toward others, or does this outlook preclude their successful functioning in the modern world?

The individuals in the friendship circle have a vision of a better life, one that transcends these dichotomies. They have struggled to find a way to live that is emotionally fulfilling in terms of personal and family life that has at the same time allowed them to achieve success in the practical world of business. They have discovered that it was not necessary to choose between emotionally rich inner lives and outer successes.

The "good life," as they define it, is not a specific outcome but rather an ongoing psychological journey. The goal never has been to arrive at a particular plateau in one's personal development, enjoy a certain level of status or wealth, or engage in a specified set of activities. It has been to embark on a lifetime venture that challenges defenses against early emotional pain and death anxiety. This process has enabled these individuals to feel increasingly alive, to remove obstacles to truthful communication and love, and to find success in the real world. They have found that a more fulfilling life cannot be achieved by seeking to be "happy" in the sense that this word is often used: a state of being characterized by an absence of unpleasant experiences such as fear, anxiety, or pain. To the contrary: They have discovered that pursuing a life of compassion and meaning requires becoming vulnerable to all dimensions of living—sadness as well as joy, pain as well as comfort, fear as well as confidence. It also involves a commitment to an ongoing search for personal meaning and transcendent goals—of which happiness is often a byproduct.

THEORETICAL APPROACH

The essence of this psychological journey involves a continual effort to confront and relinquish self-protective methods of dealing with early emotional pain, the awareness of death, and other painful realities of the human condition. These defenses keep people from realizing the human potentialities that are their birthrights.

The Fantasy Bond: A Primary Defense

The primary defense against the pain of childhood deprivation and knowledge of death is the fantasy bond, an imaginary fusion or illusion of connection with one's family, ethnic group, nation, or religious and ideological cause (Firestone, 1984, 1985). Maintaining this fantasy bond offers short-term relief against anxiety and fears but diminishes long-term vitality. Disrupting it creates an initial increase in fear and anxiety but is essential to living fully. Bear in mind that in defining a fantasy bond, we are not referring to genuine affection, love, or loyalty within a couple or family. We are describing a destructive way of relating to another person based on an imagined connection, a fantasy of love that is a substitute for real love and closeness.

The fantasy bond is formed originally in early childhood as a substitute for love and care that may be missing in the infant's environment. It is highly effective as a defense because a human being's capacity for imagination provides partial gratification of needs and reduces tension. The illusion of being connected to the mother (or primary caregiver), together with self-gratifying, self-soothing patterns such as thumb-sucking, nail-biting, and excessive masturbation are an attempt to heal the fracture in separation experiences and compensate for emotional deprivation. Such behaviors lead to a posture of pseudoindependence in the developing child, an attitude that "I don't need anyone, I can take care of myself." The irony is that the more an individual relies on this fantasy process, the more helpless or ineffective he or she becomes in the real world. The more seriously children are deprived, the more they depend on the fantasy bond as a compensation and reject genuine closeness and affection from others.

Several theorists, beginning with Hellmuth Kaiser, have dealt with the modes of relating based on fantasy processes or a delusion of fusion (Karpel, 1976, 1994; Wexler & Steidl, 1978). Indeed, Kaiser (Fierman, 1965) asserted that the universal psychopathology was "the attempt to create in real life by behavior and communication the illusion of fusion" (pp. 208–209). Kaiser's germinal idea that this illusion represents the "universal symptom of neurotic disturbance" is analogous to our conceptualization of the fantasy bond or self-parenting process as the primary defense mechanism in neurosis.

People go to great lengths to maintain the illusion of connection. Many select mates who remind them of their parents to try to recreate their past. They ignore their children's individuality and try to mold them into an image of themselves in an attempt to achieve a kind of immortality. Others work compulsively, take refuge in routines, or choose addictions to avoid real experiences that threaten their illusions. In contrast, individuals living a self-actualized existence discover what lies beyond defenses and illusions of connection. They make real contact and establish genuinely loving relationships with actual people in real life in spite of the awesome specter of existential aloneness and interpersonal pain.

The Voice Process: A Secondary Defense

Within each person there exists an essential dualism, a primary split between forces that represent the self and those that oppose the self. These elements can be conceptualized as the "self system" and the "antiself system" (Firestone, 1997a). The two systems develop independently; both are dynamic and continually evolve over time. In other words, people possess conflicting points of view and beliefs about themselves and others, their relationships, and events in the world, depending on which aspect of the personality, self or antiself, is dominant at any given time. The former point of view is rational, objective, and life-affirming. The latter is made up of a destructive thought process or "voice," an overlay on the personality that is opposed to the ongoing development of the self.

The voice, as we have defined it, is the language of the defensive process (Firestone, 1988). It refers to a well-integrated system of thoughts and attitudes, antithetical toward self and cynical toward others, that is at the core of an individual's maladaptive behavior. The voice functions as a secondary defense that supports the fantasy bond (or primary defense) and self-parenting, inward behavior patterns. It is a form of intrapsychic communication that ranges from minor self-criticisms to major self-attacks and fosters self-soothing habit patterns, isolation, and a self-destructive lifestyle. We propose that the voice represents the introjection of destructive thought patterns and attitudes based on an identification with negative attitudes and defenses of one's parents.

The voice may at times parallel one's value system or moral considerations. However, rather than motivating one to alter behavior in a moral or constructive manner, the voice tends to occur *after* the fact and is generally harsh and judgmental. The definition of the voice excludes those thought processes concerned with values or ideals, as well as those thoughts involved in creative thinking, constructive planning, and realistic, compassionate self-appraisal. It does not refer to mental activity that is generally described in fantasy or daydreams. Voice attacks are directed toward others as well as toward oneself. Both types of voices, those that belittle the self and those that attack other people, predispose alienation and provide the individual with rationalizations for retreating to a more defended, pseudoindependent posture.

Our specific orientation and approach to psychotherapy has come to be known as "voice therapy." Voice therapy is a cognitive–affective–behavioral methodology that brings internalized destructive thought processes to the surface, with accompanying affect, in a dialogue format that allows a client to confront alien components of the personality. The method helps clients develop insight into the sources of their discomfort, assists them in gradually modifying behavior in the direction of their stated goals, and aids them in opposing the dictates of the negative thought process.[2]

THE FRIENDSHIP CIRCLE

In the past 50 years in America, many groups of people have tried to create more satisfying lives by challenging traditional solutions (Raimy, 1979). If this friendship circle has grown and flourished where many others have not, it is because of three basic principles that have guided the members' efforts over the past quarter century: (a) kindness, (b) honesty, and (c) the maintenance of a forum that insures freedom of speech and emotional expression.

These people operate with an explicit ethic of kindness, generosity, and friendship. Many encounter groups disbanded in the 1960s and 1970s because of hostility and aggressive behavior. In contrast, these individuals have from the beginning encouraged the expression of all feelings, while discouraging the acting out of angry feelings in unkind ways. Over the years, people have come to realize that they will not be rejected if they reveal themselves.

They place the highest value on honesty, while confronting and challenging manipulations, lies, and melodrama. People in the friendship circle do not shrink from expressing anger, frustration, or disappointment when they feel it, but they do so in a way that conveys the genuine caring and compassion that underlies these reactions. These people have found that their lives have been significantly expanded by working through their defenses and painful emotions, both individually and in discussions where they openly share their feelings with each other.

Because they were willing to face their pain and to talk honestly with others about their feelings, these people have built enduring friendships. The essential feature of their friendships is not simply the fact that they spend time together, but that they do so in a truthful, feelingful, and undefended way. They have come to understand the value of friendship, and this has become a vital element of their philosophical approach.

> *Chris (28):* To lead the good life, you have to be vulnerable, and I think that is one of the hardest things for anybody to be consistently, to really be open and vulnerable to anybody, everybody.

> *Mallory (18):* I feel the good life is to live in the moment always, and to really feel the things that are happening to me

no matter what they are, the happy things and the sad things, and everything. To really feel my life.

Justin (18): Having the good life is to have people around you who you really like, who care about you, who are honest with you. The way my friends treat each other is much sweeter, much nicer, and much friendlier than people do in most places that I see, or most people in general.

Natasha (19): I feel like I can say anything to my friends. I think we all trust and care for each other. If something is getting in the way of our friendship, it's worth talking about.

Michelle (38): I think most people would say that they care about the people closest to them, but this way of life is caring in a real way, where a person's thoughts and feelings matter each time they have them; where people are sensitive to one another's interests, to what brings them joy, the things that make them sad, the kinds of things they want to pursue; where real issues are dealt with; where kids aren't protected from real life issues like death or aging, or any of the real parts of life that I think a lot of kids are kept from. Parents think they are protecting their children, but it keeps them from experiencing something that might touch them very deeply.

There is no rigid formula for what constitutes a meaningful life for a given individual (nor should there be). However, it is possible to ground one's goals for a better life in sound mental health principles that include an understanding of what it truly means to be a human being (B. Schwartz, 2000).

The vision of a better life, as portrayed in this chapter, is the result of our observations of the individuals of the friendship circle as they transformed their lives in ways that allowed them to develop their human potential. The essential human qualities crucial to this development include the search for meaning, the ability to love and to feel compassion for self and others, the capacity for abstract reasoning and creativity, the ability to experience deep emotion, the desire for social affiliation, the ability to set goals and develop strategies to accomplish them, an awareness of existential concerns, and the potential to experience the sacredness and mystery of life.[3] Choosing challenge over the comfortable and familiar is essential if people are to realize these inherent aspects of human nature. People must be willing to take the risks necessary for self-actualization and suffer through the accompanying anxiety.

One fundamental mental health principle is that although human beings have demonstrated aggressive behaviors, they also have an enormous capacity to live altruistic, complex, and meaningful lives and are not instinctively destructive, as Sigmund Freud (1925/1959) suggested. Human beings act out aggressive patterns and hostility because they experience a good deal of pain and frustration in their development and are damaged early in life, not because of innate drives for self-destruction (Bandura & Walters, 1963; Berkowitz, 1989; N. Miller & Dollard, 1941). If frustration is reduced and unnecessary interpersonal suffering in children's lives is minimized, human beings will experience growth both as individuals and in society.

This is in no way meant to downplay humanity's display of aggressive behavior, sadistic tendencies, or predilection for warfare (Firestone, 1996). The human destructiveness manifested throughout the twentieth century, combined with today's nuclear, biological, and chemical technologies and the ongoing threat of terrorism, has raised serious questions about the ability of the species to survive even in the short-term. And humankind's long-term well-being is equally in question, as new technologies have been developed to manipulate both the biosphere without and the gene within. For the first time, humans now have the power to govern the process of evolution itself, thus threatening not only all those now alive but all life to come.[4]

On an individual level, people are often far more cruel toward themselves and others than they realize. Although human beings have unprecedented power to destroy life, they also have a wide variety of positive qualities that make each person potentially admirable and lovable. If the majority of people chose to develop their potential for love and decency, they might collectively alter the course of history.

When we refer to "life-affirming" human potentialities in our writing, we mean those capacities and personal qualities that enhance life for oneself and others, both qualitatively and materially. These qualities cannot be simplified or measured in quantitative terms alone. The process of developing these attributes is unique to each person's ability and circumstance. It involves having a desire for self-knowledge and self-understanding as well as a vision of one's future. Although we acknowledge that many people do not seem to value this form of personal enterprise, we also recognize that there are virtually no limits to humans' potential to achieve more productive, feelingful lives if they are so determined.

If a meaningful life is fundamentally one in which we fully develop our human potentialities, describing these potentialities is central to our understanding of how to proceed.

The Search for Meaning

Human beings have an innate sense that there is "something more" to life than material success. As Victor Frankl (1946/1959) noted, human beings are meaning-seeking creatures. They cannot pursue happiness in and of itself. Rather, they need to seek authentic personal meaning in their lives—through their relationships, children, work, and creativity. By doing so, they will experience happiness as an outgrowth of their journey. Members of the friendship circle have put this concept to work for them.

Charles ran a prosperous direct-mail business in the 1970s and early 1980s. He was a political consultant influential in both state and national elections. In the mid 1970s, Charles made friends with people from the friendship circle. As he became increasingly involved and participated in talks, he began questioning the deeper meaning of his work. To maintain profit, his firm sometimes supported causes that he actually opposed in principle. He began to realize that he was compromising his basic values whenever he worked for these causes. After considering the core issues, he decided to only work for those whose views supported his ethical values. Although this decision initially resulted in some loss of business revenue, Charles felt more at peace with himself.

The desire for meaning is a basic component of achieving a better life as people go beyond their basic needs to engage in activities that they regard as having greater meaning for themselves, society, and the future. Life itself may have no hidden meaning or intrinsic significance. Individuals find meaning for themselves when they invest their own feeling and personal energy in activities that express their special wants and priorities. The artist, musician, or novelist finds meaning in self-expression. Some people experience it primarily through interaction with friends and family. Others do so by contributing to a humanitarian cause or improving the lot of future generations. As Ernest Becker (1973/1997) wrote, "The most that any one of us can seem to do is to fashion something—an object or ourselves—and drop it into the confusion, make an offering of it, so to speak, to the life force" (p. 285).

Love, Compassion, and Empathy

Perhaps the single-most important life-affirming human quality is the ability to love—to feel compassion and empathy for, and express kindness, generosity, and tenderness toward, other people. Learning to love others requires first valuing oneself. There are few experiences in life that make people feel more alive, that are more critical to a life of meaning and compassion, than genuinely loving or caring for another person.

The word "love" has become so banal that to a large extent it has lost a clear sense of meaning. Love can be defined as feelings and behaviors that enhance the emotional well-being of oneself and the other. Loving operations can be characterized as affection, respect for each person's boundaries, generosity, tenderness, and a desire for close companionship in life. Loving someone in one's thoughts and feelings is a necessary but insufficient component in creating a loving relationship. Love must also be expressed through loving behavior to optimally affect one's partner, family member, or friend.

Sexual love is vital to one's sense of fulfillment in an intimate relationship in which erotic feelings and sexual responses are simply an extension of affection and communication. The combination of sexuality and close personal communication represents an ideal in a couple's relationship.

Genuine love also requires valuing the other person's goals in life separate from one's personal needs and interests, and respecting the autonomy of the other. Empathy and compassion are based on the ability to understand another person's perspective—that is, to understand how we would feel if we were that person in any given situation. Empathy originates in an ability to reflect on one's thoughts, feelings, and intentions and to find common ground in the experiences of others. The ability for self-reflection—that is, being able to examine one's own feelings and having an intuition regarding other people's intentions—is an ability that children develop at an early age.

In summary, internal feelings of love and compassion are fully represented only when they are expressed outwardly in loving operations—that is, in actions that affect others. Love is a powerful antidote to the existential despair inherent in the human condition. When mature love exists between two people, its expression can approach the level of a spiritual experience.

Abstract Reasoning and Creativity and the Ability to Experience Deep Emotion

Human beings have the unique capacity for abstract thought. The creation of language, the development of complex mathematical systems, and the evolution of culture began with the ability to think abstractly, in symbols. However, many people are so damaged in their emotional development that they lose their capacity to function creatively and intellectually and are forced to deal with life in a shallow, concrete, or rigid fashion. Therefore, a fundamental aspect of an emotionally fulfilling life is using one's mental capacities to the fullest, in a way that supports rather than denies or degrades life.

While many people believe that the capacity for thought is a human being's most distinguishing feature, it is actually the interaction between thoughts and feelings that separates us from other animals. People have used their miraculous brains for both good and evil, to enhance life and to destroy it, to make scientific breakthroughs in medicine and produce weapons of mass destruction. Men and women can choose to use their intelligence in a moral manner. The progress that has been made in civil rights; respect for differences in gender, religious background, ethnicity, and sexual orientation; and helping those in need are examples of people using their intelligence in combination with their feelings of empathy and compassion. Humans have an astonishing ability to feel deeply, to reflect on their feelings, and to use both thought and feeling to create a full, alive, and meaningful life.

Human progress can best be measured not by material success but by our long and slow progress in learning to accept, understand, and appropriately express our feelings. Only by leading a feelingful existence can individuals come to relate to each other in a rational, peaceful, lawful manner. In contrast, when they are cut off from their feeling selves, they are the most destructive to themselves and others. Most people relive rather than live their lives by remaining locked into compulsively repeating outdated, destructive behavior patterns. When this is true, their emotional reactions are inappropriate and maladaptive. A major difference between an emotionally enhanced life and an emotionally deprived existence is the ability to fully feel and reflect on one's experiences in the present.

Social Affiliation

Human beings have a far greater capacity than any other animal for social affiliation—the ability to share thoughts, feelings, and experiences with others, as well as to nurture, support, and enjoy the company of their fellow beings. Developing this characteristic is vital to the achievement of a better life because people live, survive, learn, and grow through interactions with others. Although it is of course possible to enjoy solitude and to use it creatively, it is the rare human being who lives in total isolation from others, and the even more unusual soul who is able to do so successfully.

Social affiliation is generally crucial for growth, but because defenses so often impair one's ability to relate to others, it is particularly important to learn how to develop friendships. It is also important to create and sustain meaningful relationships with one's mate and children. Living in harmony with family and friends in an atmosphere of congeniality is the professed goal of most people.

Stan (39) was a friendly, outgoing youngster until he was 11 and suffered the devastating loss of his mother. He recalls that after she died, he gradually narrowed down his social life and focused almost exclusively on his studies and later on his career as an architect. By the time he reached his late 20s, he had built a highly profitable architectural firm, at considerable cost, however, to a social and personal life.

> After my mother died, I began to avoid all my friends. I think it must have caused me too much pain to be social, to get out of the house, to continue being friends with the kids at school. Over the years, I had fewer and fewer friends. I spent most of my time alone. Looking back

I realize that I was a very solitary person, almost completely isolated from human contact, except for the long hours I spent at work; even there I tended to work alone.

Last year, I happened to meet someone who was a participant in this group of friends. I decided that I wanted to change my pattern of seclusion and isolation. Since then, I feel like I've slowly been able to recapture many of the experiences that most kids experience during their teens: exciting adventure, sports, just having fun in socializing with people. I've also recaptured the feelings that go along with having friends—rivalrous, competitive feelings, and even negative feelings like envy, jealousy, and anger—all the emotions I missed during my years of self-imposed isolation. On some level, I feel almost like a child again, having all these feelings.

I believe that children, as a rule, are more honest and spontaneous than adults, and these qualities characterize my friends and really appeal to me. It seems to me that as most people get older, they build sophisticated defenses against being close to other people, even their husbands or wives. They seem to cut down on the number of people who they would call "friends." I feel like I'm doing away with those sophisticated defenses simply from being more social, from talking with people, from sharing projects. This is the way of life that I lost touch with in the aftermath of my mother's death.

Imagination, Goal-Setting, and Planning for the Future

The ability to imagine, to conceptualize something new, and to plan for the future are uniquely human traits. Out of the potential for inventiveness and imagination comes achievement, aesthetic and innovative pursuits, and material success. The telephone, airplane, and computer all existed in the human imagination long before they were translated into reality. Every great painting, symphony, or sculpture sprang from the artist's imagination more than from his or her hands or even mind. Developing the ability to conceptualize the possibility of change is vital to both personal satisfaction and social progress. Unfortunately, the ability to "dream" or picture the future can be damaged in the developing child by inadequate or destructive parenting (Brazelton & Greenspan, 2000).[5]

Closely related to imagination is the ability to set goals and develop strategies to attain them. An important dimension of a meaningful life involves envisioning goals that express one's unique identity and interests and then taking the actions necessary to realize these goals in the real world. Actively striving and competing for one's objectives rather than seeking satisfaction in fantasy alone is crucial to a fulfilling life. It is possible to reach one's full potential only when one's inner dreams and desires result in real accomplishments in the external world. Indeed, it is clear that success and achievement will have little personal value to an individual who has not developed his or her other human potentialities—that is, the capacity for feeling, loving, and social affiliation.

An Awareness of Existential Realities

The ability to imagine has not only afforded humankind great accomplishments, it has also burdened us with the horror of being able to conceptualize our own death. Nothing has shaped civilization and how we live, for better or worse, more than our realization of our finite existence. The defended individual, faced with the fact of mortality, will tend to progressively retreat from living in a futile attempt to take control over death and avoid the anxiety of the ultimate separation from self and loved ones (Firestone, 1994). On the other hand, facing issues of mortality can give life a poignant meaning in relation to its finality. Imagining the end of life in an undefended state of mind makes people aware of the preciousness of each moment, and they are more likely to invest more of themselves in their relationships. It can spur them to greater creativity and make them more compassionate toward other people who share their fate.

In 1996, Bill, a 35-year-old business executive, was piloting a small plane from Los Angeles to San Diego. He was a new pilot, as yet unable to fly by instruments. Suddenly, he found himself in a dark cloud and became completely disoriented. He lost track of where he was, of up and down, and became terrified that he would crash. He struggled to maintain control of the plane. After 15 long minutes, he finally emerged from the cloud, found his bearings, and landed safely.

The experience, he says, changed his life. Realizing how fragile life really is led him to value it far more highly. Soon he began thinking of having children, which led to the birth of his son Mitchell in 1999. "It feels like having Mitchell has changed my whole perspective on life," he says.

> On an emotional level, I think I've always resisted growing up, partly I guess because if I could remain a teenager, I could believe I would never die. But the near plane-crash and now having Mitchell has helped me realize that it is time to become an adult. Life is too precious and I have too many responsibilities to be able to pretend to myself anymore that I can remain a child. This realization has made me more focused in my work, while also leading me to place a higher value on recreation and travel, and on my family and friends.

Spirituality and Mystery

Human beings possess the ability to have spiritual experiences that transcend the satisfaction of material needs and to sense mysteries that elude human understanding. At many points on the journey through life people encounter events that bring out a deep appreciation of nature and the unknown and generate spiritual experiences that evoke deep emotional responses. It is when this search for meaning and spiritual awareness takes people to the edge of human understanding, where they accept the ultimate mystery of their lives and the limitations of science and rationality, that they know at the most profound level what it means to be fully human.

When individuals accept the uncertainty and ambiguity of life, they may come to believe that there are no absolute "truths" to be discovered. They may determine that wherever there is an absence of fact, they have the right to choose and embrace their own beliefs regarding the origins and nature of life. Such individuals tend to seek the "god" within themselves rather than outside themselves and develop their own belief system rather than accepting more formal religious teachings.

CHARACTERISTICS OF AN UNDEFENDED INDIVIDUAL

Because of defenses formed early in life, very few people ever fully develop the life-affirming potentialities described earlier. Breaking with the past and overcoming defensive behaviors allows people to continually enhance their human potential.

People who are vulnerable and undefended are exposed to a world that is perpetually new and continually changing, a world where life is an open-ended adventure. They develop a depth of compassion and a basic trust in other people that have powerful effects on all their relationships. The hurtful behaviors they may have manifested in earlier relationships decrease, and as a result they are able to have a constructive effect on friends and family members.

The undefended individual looks very different from his or her more defended counterparts. When people are vulnerable, their lack of defensiveness is apparent in their faces and expressive movements. Their vitality and energy are evident in a warm, friendly glance, a softness in expression, a way of making direct eye contact, a style of relating personally, and a state of relaxation, in contrast to an agitated or emotionally deadened state. They retain their excitement about living primarily because they are still connected to their emotions and experience both the pleasure and sorrow of life.

People striving to lead a more fulfilling life attempt to find a balance between work and their personal lives and place a high value on play, leisure, and recreation. They try to create a home environment for themselves and their loved ones that is optimal for the realization of each person's full potential. They are very much aware of their wants and aspirations and direct their actions toward fulfilling these goals rather than living out their parents' wishes or directives for their lives. They have developed their own value system and choose to challenge themselves in their relationships. In pursuing their own path, they have their own compass, so to speak, and have set their own course in life rather than remaining passengers on a rudderless ship. They face death straightforwardly and feel sad about the future loss of themselves and their loved ones. Understanding that all people ultimately share the same fate, they see no person as inferior or superior to them, nor do they invest any person with greater or lesser status.

A PROFILE FROM THE FRIENDSHIP CIRCLE

Nothing conveys the meaning of the concept of a better life more than understanding how normal, ordinary people live it on an everyday basis. For example, Dean, 49, has two children, ages 14 and 19, and a close relationship with a woman he has known for 20 years. He is involved in a highly profitable business enterprise with many of his friends. In his spare time, he writes poetry and composes lyrics and music for a band that he leads. He plays baseball every weekend and enjoys sailing and power-boating.

Dean defines the "good life" primarily as being "awake"—that is, open and aware to all of life's experiences:

> What do I think a good life is? One thing I would like to be is self-aware, not self-conscious, and I think there's a huge difference between the two. And to be an individual within a culture. It's like in that book, *The Unbearable Lightness of Being*, where you are looking at the balance of being connected to a culture, which you need, and being free to be yourself. Being too free, you fly away; being too connected, you're weighted down. And trying to find that balance is a lifelong journey.
>
> To me, the good life is being awake, it's being aware of what's happening, not being lulled into sleep by your negative thinking, by your hatreds, by your prejudices, by your routines.
>
> I think one aspect of our life that may be the most unique is the talks. In some sense, the talks are wake-up calls, wake-up calls to the self, saying "Wait, there's something really going on here." It's not what happened in the past, it's not projecting that past on to the now. Something is really going on here and now. There are real things to deal with, things to feel.

Personal History

The product of a traumatic childhood, Dean grew up insecure and feeling a deep sense of shame about his family. As he describes,

I was one of nine kids and my parents were always pretty poor. For most of my childhood, my parents had a very violent relationship. My mother was pretty crazy, so there was never a sense of peace in the household. And we were ostracized in the community because of my mother's craziness. Kids in the neighborhood were told by their parents, "You can't play with those kids." We were considered the "bad family" in the community. My father moved a lot, changed jobs a lot, and we moved from town to town.

I was very angry as a kid. I learned to be pretty private and quiet and never really trusted anything or any calmness; I really took everything inside myself. I would go to the library a lot. I would get on my bike and just go to the library and spend hours reading books. I became infatuated with Mark Twain. I read everything by him. *Tom Sawyer* and *Huckleberry Finn*, especially, evoked a feeling of just wanting to be away. Wanting to be on an island somewhere. Wanting to just be on a river.

After leaving home at 18, Dean lived in Hawaii for three years with his girlfriend. When he returned to the mainland, he began studying journalism at San Francisco State College.

At the time I met my friends here, I was very open to learning about myself. When I was in Hawaii I had gone through a bit of a depression, and it frightened me because I didn't understand what was going on; I had never gone through that before. So I started to be interested in psychology and started to read books to try to understand what was happening with me.

In retrospect, Dean believes he probably would have led a relatively conventional life had he not become involved with this circle of friends.

In some way I guess I was hungry for something different than what I was experiencing myself in the world. In 1976 I visited an old friend in L.A. and met his friends. They were going to get together, and I guessed that they met once or twice a week to discuss personal issues. It was an unusual experience for me, and it just struck me, "this is what life should be." The talking seemed so real, about things that bothered people as children and currently. The things that bothered them now were often echoes and mirrors of what had happened to them as children, and how that would get in the way of what was happening currently. The real things in people's lives.

I met a lot of people I was very interested in. The women, I thought, were very attractive, which was interesting to me. They were very friendly and seemed to be very nice. And in their interactions, there was a lot of eye contact. This was something that stood out to me. So the weekend was very stimulating to me on a number of fronts. One was that the sense of community I saw there was different. Also I was very interested in their sense of fun. After that visit, I decided to move to Los Angeles and get to know these people better.

Over the years, Dean has gradually become less self-protective and inward, primarily, he believes, because he has learned to understand and accept his feelings, especially his feelings of anger. The learning process consisted of a long-term struggle to uncover the layers of defenses that he had laboriously built to suppress the fear and rage he experienced early in life.

> One night, when I was around 12 or 13, I went into the kitchen and my father was in a rage at my mother, and he had picked up a knife. I went running between them and got him to come to his senses. It was a dramatic event, but it was typical of what would happen. My anger as a kid was a killing rage. I was so furious. So hurt. So I had to bury it.
>
> Later, I was trying to understand the time I became enraged at my girlfriend in Hawaii. At that moment, a brief image of stabbing her with a knife flashed across my mind. The whole thing was such a devastating experience for me. Years later, in talking to my friends and in trying to come to grips with that incident and with my reactions, I discovered there was an anger in me that was healthy. It was a real response to things that had provoked me as a child, things that were frustrating to me, that were frightening to me. But I associated that anger with my father's insane anger and with my mother's insane anger. I felt that my anger was a kind of anger that would destroy the world.
>
> To be provoked by my girlfriend, even though it was minor, and then to remember that image of the stabbing, me stepping between my father and mother, was such an echoed image, that *any* anger I feel I immediately associate with the rage that I had as a kid. And so when it's provoked, I don't want to go near that. I began to realize that my anger frightened me and humiliated me. It made me very afraid of confrontation, of conflict.

Dean soon became an active participant in the group discussions. In these talks, he asked his friends to give him feedback about defensive behaviors that he wanted to change, including the maladaptive ways he dealt with anger. Dean recalls one group in particular, where a young woman had confronted him. She referred to a recent situation where Dean had made a sarcastic remark at her expense. She added that she was often offended by his cynicism and sensed a kind of low-key anger in him.

> In that particular talk, Stacy said she felt really hurt and also very provoked by a sarcastic remark I had made to her about what she was wearing at a party. I thought the comment was funny, a joke, very innocuous. But she retorted that she didn't think it was funny at all. As she talked, she went on to say that she also believed I was hurting myself in some way by being cynical and sarcastic. At that point, I had a lot of feelings.

After apologizing to Stacy for my comments, I went on to explore some of the feelings that were right under the surface. As I talked in sort of a rambling style, just saying all my thoughts out loud, I had the realization that I was still very anxious in my personal life and in my work in regards to any kind of conflict and also in competitive situations. The situation with Stacy had been competitive, there were other guys there and I had felt awkward, so that remark just came out of my mouth. But then I was struck by how many times a day I said those kinds of things, and how often I felt cynical towards certain people, women especially. It all boiled down to the fact that my anger was something that hadn't healed. And I had found a convenient, sort of acceptable way to suppress the rage by being cynical and keeping people at a "safe" distance.

Over the years and from talking about some of the other defenses I used to keep down my rage, I've learned that I can understand this anger. Maybe it doesn't heal completely, but I can understand it. It definitely makes me more comfortable with it when it comes up. So I withdraw less. I've also learned to separate my own internal feelings from how people perceive me. Most important, I've learned to not project my angry feelings onto the world at large, onto my friends, and then to think that they're angry at me. I've learned over the years that a lot of these things don't change overnight. Being with my friends, talking with them in our group discussions, getting feedback, has afforded me the chance to continually learn about myself. Learning about myself around people who are congenial. And compassionate. And direct.

The transformation that has occurred in Dean's life over the years was possible because of his continually challenging defensive habit patterns that had helped him cope with the trauma and anxiety of his childhood.

For me, I think that there's a certain inertia, the inertia of falling into patterns based on early childhood experiences, the defenses you create. They're comfortable even though they may be painful. They're familiar even though they may be painful. And they work best in a vacuum. And that vacuum could be by yourself, it could be with one other person, it could be in the "nuclear family." But still it's those defenses that hurt you. And I think it takes a lot of introspection, as well as developing yourself with other people. You get outside validation about the kinds of things that enhance your experiences and your well-being and the things that detract from your life.

So you have to know yourself and hopefully have people around you that you trust who can point out the times when you may be falling back into your old patterns. For myself, when I think of why I chose to live around the people I've been friends with, those relationships and that social setting have given me a chance to slow the inertia toward the defended aspects of my personality that would have continued to deaden my experience.

Dean feels that his ongoing battle is largely about learning to feel more compassionate toward himself:

> The way I've learned to see people is how I wish I could see myself. I see people with compassion. I see when they're struggling, and I've learned not to judge them. It's been harder for me not to be judgmental toward myself. However, the way my friends are with me makes it much harder for me to be judgmental toward myself.

Creative Pursuits

Dean's interest in psychological and philosophical ideas has grown steadily over the years, and he is valued for his creativity in writing, his editing skills, and his music. Dean's friends have had a definite effect on his developing his music interests.

> My song writing would not have occurred to the degree it has without the support and inspiration of the people I've known for the past years. As sort of a joke, I once wrote this song called "The Love Diet." It was a silly song. But I got such a good response from it that I revealed more songs I had written. And they got a good response. So somehow I was inspired to play in public, and to think that I could actually write and perform a song.
>
> Being here with my friends was the difference between being in my room and kind of playing a guitar in fantasy, and bringing that fantasy out into the real world. Otherwise, I would never have been able to picture myself getting up in front of people and actually strumming a guitar and actually singing. From a musical perspective, many of these songs were written during the period of time when I was the most stimulated. I was falling in love, I was having a child, and I was learning more about myself. It was a very exciting time for me and it came out in a creative burst.

Current Life

Over the past 25 years, Dean has gradually become acculturated to a warmer, more constructive way of living and has given up many defensive ways of interacting. The personality characteristics that Dean possesses embody many of the human potentialities described earlier. His creativity, imagination, ability to cope with life effectively, sense of adventure, and practical successes are evident. He is highly individualistic and his personal search for meaning has led him to develop his own set of values and philosophy of life. When asked about what life meant to him, he responded,

> I think the meaning in life is really making someone's life a little bit better, in little or big ways. Helping one another get from point A to

point B. If someone's got a problem they want to talk about, listen to them. Or if they need $20, give it to them, being generous with whatever you have, meeting a need.

Dean's current life appears to represent the realization of his particular vision of a better life. Friends and coworkers describe him as a warm person, a loyal friend with special rapport with people and a deep concern and love for children, which has made quite a difference in many of their lives. They say he is not vain or focused on image and status, and describe him as a person who is emotionally honest and direct and who takes pleasure in the projects he shares with them. He values experiencing his feelings, especially feelings of sadness. In being aware of his own mortality, he has strong desires to make the most of each moment and of each exchange that he has with other people.

For Dean, what matters the most is the opportunity to develop personally, to speak his mind and talk about his perceptions and feelings. He attributes his accomplishments in business and the creative arts primarily to what he has gained from meaningful interactions with his friends in one-to-one conversations and in the group discussions.

During his "creative burst" of song writing described earlier, Dean wrote a song expressing his troubled reactions to the turbulence of his childhood. Titled "Never Going Back," it contained the lines: "But the truth is in his eyes, that's where the fear and anger lies, and the pain of all the lessons that he learned." Today there is an absence of fear and anger in Dean's eyes. Sharing life with his friends and devoting himself to ideas, adventure, work, loving relationships, and children have erased most of the shame of the past.

CONCLUSION

The crucial elements involved in fulfilling one's potentialities as a human being, as outlined in this chapter, lie in becoming aware of the defenses that one developed as a protection against the pain of childhood deprivation, rejection, and the fear of death, and in identifying how they limit one's present-day life. People can fulfill their potential for finding transcendent meaning in their lives if they are willing to question and alter rigid views and negative programming from the past. As defenses break down, an individual can experience deep feeling toward self and others. It *is* possible to live a relatively undefended, open, and free life in this world. But, as the following chapters describe, doing so requires becoming aware of, identifying, and overcoming psychological pain and the associated defenses.

NOTES

1. See findings from Kraut et. al's (1998) study of 169 people in 73 households during their first one to two years of Internet use that support this statement. In her book, *Caught in the Net*, Young (1998) noted that "25 percent of all respondents [to her survey] reported getting hooked in their first 6 months on-line" (p. 27).
2. Voice therapy methods are similar in some respects to Beck's (A. Beck, Rush, Shaw, & Emery, 1979) cognitive therapy and Ellis's (Ellis, 1973; Ellis & Harper, 1975) rational–emotive therapy; however, there are a number of basic differences. Ellis proposed that human beings have powerful innate tendencies to think irrationally, whereas we believe that disordered thinking is a function of deficient child-rearing practices. Beck's reports, describing "automatic thoughts," appear to coincide with certain aspects of the voice process. However, our therapy methods are concerned with the dynamic origins of the voice rather than attempting to argue the client out of his or her false beliefs or schema using logic, humor, or questioning. We also focus more on accessing the emotions associated with the destructive thought process.
3. In describing these universal human attributes, there are problems, because in much of contemporary writing and in the media, words that portray these characteristics, such as "self-actualizing," "authentic," "self-fulfilling," "life-affirming," "love," and so forth, have been overused to the point where their meaning has become banal.
4. Suicidologist Edwin Shneidman (1973) referred to this possibility of global destruction in *Deaths of Man*:

   > For the first time in six centuries (since the great European plagues) a generation has been born and raised in a thanatological context, concerned with the imminent possibility of the death of the person, the death of humanity, the death of the universe, and, by necessary extension, the death of God. (p. 189)

5. See *The Irreducible Needs of Children*, in which Brazelton and Greenspan (2000) asserted, "Brain scans of older individuals show that . . . deprivation or alteration of needed experiences can produce a range of deficits" (pp. 1–2).

2

FACTORS THAT IMPEDE
PERSONAL DEVELOPMENT

To grow up at all is to conceal the mass of internal scar tissue that
throbs in our dreams.
                                        —Ernest Becker (1973/1997, p. 29)

It is a sad fact that most people are damaged psychologically in their
capacity to reach their human potential (Briere, 1992; Hassler, 1994; A.
Miller, 1980/1984a).[1] They are the victims of generally well-meaning parents
who themselves suffered unnecessary damage in their own developmental
years. Unintentional abuses experienced during child-rearing, compounded
by existential dread, negatively imprint the individual in a manner that is
passed on to succeeding generations. When children are emotionally deprived or psychologically damaged, they form powerful maladaptive defenses
that preclude the possibility for a richer, more fulfilling life. Tragically, when
they grow up they are inadvertently obligated to pass on the "wisdom" of
their defensive apparatus to their offspring, most often to their detriment.

Although in our work we deal primarily with psychological or environmental factors that affect the emotional development of children, we do
not deny or minimize other influences on the personality of children or
adults. Biological tendencies, inherited temperamental differences (Chess
& Thomas, 1999), and genetic predispositions combine with environmental
influences to form unique and complex phenomena.[2] Indeed, all human
experiences are psychosomatic—that is, inclusive of mind and body. In
addition, there is no singular cause of specific symptoms or emotional disorders, because all psychological functions are multidetermined.

35

It is clear that psychological or environmental as well as biological factors are critically important in the development of psychopathology. The heritability for a vulnerability to manic depression, substance abuse, depression, and even some cases of suicidal behavior has been demonstrated. At the same time, research has established the presence of environmental or psychological factors in these disorders as they recur in successive generations within families (Brown, Cohen, Johnson, & Smailes, 1999; Cicchetti & Toth, 1995; Dinwiddie & Bucholz, 1993; Fleming, Mullen, & Bammer, 1997; C. Walsh, MacMillan, & Jamieson, 2002). We believe the process of identification and imitation may well be an even more powerful factor than genetic heritability in the intergenerational transmission of negative parental traits, behaviors, and defenses (Firestone, 1997b).

HOW PEOPLE ARE DAMAGED IN THEIR HUMANNESS

There appear to be several primary factors that cause parents to affect their children adversely. Many parents have a proprietary interest in their offspring. They have a mistaken sense of ownership that allows them to intrude on their children's personal boundaries. They imagine, on a deep level, that this "belonging" ensures their survival, that their children are their legacy to be left in the world after the parents' death as evidence that their lives were meaningful. One reason for having children is that it provides parents with a framework for this fantasy of immortality (Firestone, 1994; Rank, 1936/1972). This defense against death anxiety works only as long as the children remain carbon copies of their parents. One cannot live on through a child who has fundamentally different characteristics. In that sense, one must imprint sameness on the child; for example, a Democrat or agnostic could not imagine living on through a child who was a Republican or a religious fundamentalist, respectively.

The need to project one's image onto one's progeny has serious negative implications for the child striving to achieve independence and autonomy. Indeed, any attempt on the child's part to deviate from his or her parents' approach to life is likely to be misinterpreted to mean that he or she is defiant, rebellious, or rejecting and therefore requires being "brought back into line" (Richman, 1986). In addition, many parents use their children as waste receptacles for their projections (Bowen, 1978; Brazelton & Cramer, 1990; Kerr & Bowen, 1988). They dispose of traits they dislike in themselves by projecting them onto their children and are critical and punitive in relation to these characteristics. In summation, parents' proprietary interest in their children has a stultifying effect on the individuation process and significantly limits their children's opportunities in life.

Another process by which parents unknowingly cause their children pain is the refusal to allow a loving relationship with their child to intrude on their own defense system. Parents' defenses are often threatened by the liveliness and spontaneity of their children, whose innocence and vulnerability remind parents of the hurts in their own childhood (Bloch, 1978; Laing, 1990; D. Stern, 1995; Welldon, 1988). When there is a choice between the welfare of the child and preserving their own defense system, the child's best interest is usually expendable. In their inability to accept love and closeness without discomfort or pain, parents block out the child's love for them as real people and play out roles rather than relate with real feeling (Bugental, 1986). The most important thing a parent can do is to be a lovable, responsible adult role model, to come out from behind the parental facade and relate to the child as a real and authentic human being.

The third process detrimental to successful parenting lies in each parent's defensive idealization of his or her own parents (Arieti, 1974; Firestone, 1990b; Oaklander, 1978). Parents who themselves were unloved as children or who suffered parental abuses blame themselves and grow up with a negative perception of their own personal worth rather than a clear view of the immaturity, weakness, or hostility of their parents. This whitewashing of the parents at the child's expense acts as a survival mechanism for the helpless, dependent young person, because recognizing the full impact and meaning of the negative characteristics of one's parents predisposes severe anxiety states and a sense of hopelessness in the child.[3] Paradoxically, if the child perceives him- or herself as bad, there is hope that if he or she changes, he or she may eventually win the love of his or her parents.

Unfortunately, these feelings of inadequacy and badness prevail as a significant part of each adult's self-concept and, as noted, are generally projected onto children, with painful consequences. For parents to maintain their defensive equilibrium, they are compelled to act out patterns of abuse that they themselves experienced during their formative years (Kerr & Bowen, 1988; Minuchin, 1974; Palazzoli, Boscolo, Cecchin, & Prata, 1975/1978). It is known that parents who as children were beaten or violated sexually are likely to repeat the pattern and physically abuse their children (Blumberg, 1974; Conte, 1988; Conte & Schuerman, 1987; Emerson & McBride, 1986; Garbarino, Guttmann, & Seeley, 1986; Steele, 1990). But few people realize how more subtle emotional abuses, such as criticality, name calling, domination, and the like are also repeated compulsively (Boszormenyi-Nagy & Spark, 1984; A. Miller, 1980/1984a).[4] All of this is true in spite of parents' best intentions. Many parents inadvertently take back part of the life and spirit that they offered the child at birth and seriously impact each child's ability to pursue the good life.

PSYCHOLOGICAL DEFENSES

Psychological damage is threefold: parental abuses imprint the child, which leads to defense formation, and defenses then pose limitations in later life. The most serious limitation to achieving a self-affirming, meaningful life lies in the self-nurturing, self-protective defenses that people resort to in the process of growing up in an effort to insulate themselves from pain and anxiety. Solutions that once were the best means to cope with uncomfortable, debilitating circumstances that were inescapable in the child's world eventually become imprisoning agents.

Defenses function in a maladaptive way, very similar to the way the body reacts in cases of pneumonia or allergies. The presence of bacteria, viruses, or irritants in the lungs arouse protective responses in the immune system to meet the invasion of foreign elements. However, the strength of the body's defensive reaction often leads to congestion and other symptoms that are potentially more dangerous to the person than the original assault.

Destructive forces existing within the family and in society necessitate the formation of defenses that later fracture each person's ability to fully experience his or her life. If we conceptualize human existence as feelings, sensations, perceptions, and thoughts that flow through us and affect our unique personal qualities and predispositions, we can recognize how important it is not to damage any aspect of our capacity to fully feel and experience our lives. If we find it necessary to repress or distort our experience, we lose much of what is vital. If we face threatening situations that cause us to defend ourselves by cutting off feeling for ourselves and others, we are deprived of much of what is most alive and human.

SOURCES OF PSYCHOLOGICAL PAIN

It is important to understand why people need to embrace a defensive posture in responding to their early environments. What are the factors that cause them to form defenses that later restrict their lives? There are two primary sources of psychological pain, *interpersonal* and *existential*, that impinge on infants and young children and lead to the development of self-protective defenses.

Interpersonal pain is caused by the frustration, aggression, and mistreatment that children experience in their earliest relationships with parents or caretakers. Existential pain refers to the pain of aloneness; inevitable separation experiences; potential loss of love objects; environmental threats such as crime, poverty, and war; and the inevitability of aging and death.[5]

By the time they are three or four years old, most children have come to realize that the life they thought was permanent is, in fact, temporary

(S. Anthony, 1971/1973; Kastenbaum, 1974, 1995; Lester, 1970; Nagy, 1948/1959; Rochlin 1967). Their whole world is turned upside down by their dawning awareness of death. The defenses that they developed first in relation to interpersonal distress are now crystallized. From this point on, both kinds of pain, interpersonal and existential, trigger the defensive process, contribute to people's tendencies to retreat from life, and diminish the expression of those special attributes that are fundamentally human (Firestone, 1994, 1997a; J. Greenberg et al, 1990; S. Solomon, Greenberg, & Pyszczynski, 1991).[6]

INTERPERSONAL PAIN AND THE FORMATION OF THE DEFENSE SYSTEM

There are several sources of interpersonal pain and frustration that necessitate the formation of defenses. These include the inevitable separations that occur in each child's life, as well as experiences of emotional deprivation, rejection, or parents' overt or covert hostility.

Emotional or Psychological Abuse

In an earlier work, R. Firestone (1997a) defined emotional child abuse as:

> Damage to the child's psychological development and emerging personal identity, primarily caused by parents' or primary caretakers' immaturity, defended lifestyle, and conscious or unconscious aggression toward the child. We must consider it an abuse when imprinting from early interactions with family members has long-term debilitating effects on a person's conception of self and personal relationships, leads to a condition of general unhappiness, causes pain and anxiety in one's sexual life, and interferes with and stifles development of career and vocational pursuits. Although personal deficiencies and limitations in adult functioning are at times a result of biological or hereditary factors, in our experience they have been more closely related to, or even overdetermined by, abuses suffered in the process of growing up. (pp. 19–20)

Each person experiences varying degrees of emotional pain in his or her earliest relationships. Even in ideal families, there is inevitable frustration, and most family situations are less than ideal (Beavers 1977; Beavers & Hampson, 1990; Tedeschi & Felson, 1994). With respect to physical or emotional child abuse, virtually no family can withstand close scrutiny (Briere, 1992). At the same time, to castigate or blame mothers and fathers or to be moralistic or punitive about damaging child-rearing responses only compounds the problem and causes additional and unnecessary suffering.

There is a great deal of difference between accounting for and understanding the roots of psychopathology and focusing blame.

The amount of frustration, stress, and pain that children experience varies widely, of course. The more parents were deprived, rejected, or misunderstood during their own formative years, the greater the impairment of their parental functions, regardless of their stated commitment or concern for their children. Parents who have not faced and made sense of what happened to them as children seem compelled to repeat the treatment they received as children (Main & Hesse, 1990; A. Miller, 1980/1984a; Straus, 1994).

Although incidents of physical and sexual abuse[7] are reprehensible and tragic, not enough attention has been paid to other forms of maltreatment that also have adverse effects on the child's personality, spontaneity, and sense of self. Emotional or psychological child abuse is virtually inevitable in the context of the traditional nuclear family. This form of mistreatment is the daily fare of the large majority of children in our society and yet it leaves no visible scars (Garbarino & Gilliam, 1980; Kempe & Kempe, 1984; Laing, 1969/1972; Rohner, 1986, 1991; Shengold, 1989). Alice Miller (1979/1981, 1980/1984a) has written outstanding works describing the numerous forms of torment children are exposed to.

More recently, Barber (2002) has delineated various forms of parental intrusiveness or psychological control and discussed research findings regarding its effects on children and adolescents. These forms of psychological maltreatment are far more damaging in terms of stifling children's human potentialities than most people realize. So many children in our society are the victims of parents' immaturity, neglect, hostility, or outright sadistic treatment; their suffering can exceed the distress caused by physical beatings (Blumberg, 1974; Briere, 1992; Emerson & McBride, 1986; Ferenczi, 1933/1955; Finkel, 1987; Garbarino et al., 1986; A. Miller, 1979/1981, 1980/1984a, 1981/1984b; Schakel, 1987; Shengold, 1989).

At birth and for several months afterward, the infant is unusually sensitive and vulnerable to sensory inputs and very reactive to its immediate surroundings (Stern, 1985; Stratton, 1982). Infants can be observed responding with their whole being to loud noises and other painful intrusions from the outside world. Moreover, certain events or situations that from a parent's perspective may seem innocuous may appear life-threatening to the baby. For example, an infant may feel completely abandoned and suffer a form of anxiety, referred to by Winnicott (1958) as annihilation anxiety, when its caregiver leaves the room for a few minutes to prepare a bottle. Because the baby has not as yet developed a future time perspective and is so reactive, its "reactions interrupt the 'going on being' of the infant. An excess of this reacting produces not frustration but a *threat of annihilation*. This . . . is a very real primitive anxiety" (p. 303).

It is important to mention that children of all ages tend to be more reactive to painful experiences than to positive ones and therefore tend to form their defenses at these times of undue stress and tension (Baumeister, Bratslavsky, Finkenauer, & Vohs, 2001; Ferenczi, 1933/1955; A. Freud, 1966; Gilbert, 1989). Baumeister et al. (2001) stated, "Bad emotions, bad parents, and bad feedback have more impact than good ones, and bad information is processed more thoroughly than good" (p. 1).

D. Siegel (1999) stated, "The relationship between emotion and memory suggests that emotionally arousing experiences are more readily recalled later on" (p. 48). An aversive event (painful event) often becomes conditioned to a fear response (LeDoux, 2002), and this conditioning may have had survival value in the evolutionary sense. Gilbert (1989) noted,

> Emotional states ensure than an animal continues its behaviour long after an immediate threat is out of the sensory field. Emotional states tend to change more slowly than cognitive processes. For example, following a near-miss car accident we may remain in a shaken-up or anxious state long after we cognitively realise that we have survived. Sometimes these kinds of experiences can ignite other kinds of psychopathological difficulties. (pp. 28–29)

Surveys, clinical studies, and our own experiences have led us to conclude that *normative* child-rearing practices in our society have pathogenic properties and effects (Felitti, 2002; Felitti et al., 1998). As one example, a national survey of disciplinary practices reported by J. Kaufman and Zigler (1987) showed that 97% of all children in the United States have been physically punished. Straus (1994) found that parents who administered daily or weekly spankings were more reflective of a cultural norm than a deviation.

Perhaps the most compelling evidence regarding the prevalence of abusive or dysfunctional child-rearing practices and their long-term effects can be found in longitudinal research conducted by Felitti et al. (1998). Findings from this investigation, the Adverse Childhood Experiences (ACE) study, with 17,421 adult Kaiser Foundation Health Plan members as participants, revealed "a powerful relation between our emotional experiences as children and our adult emotional health, physical health, and major causes of mortality in the United States" (Felitti, 2002. p. 44).

Findings from the ACE study showed that "23.5% of participants reported having grown up with an alcohol abuser . . . contact sexual abuse was reported by 22% of respondents (28% of women and 16% of men" (Felitti et al., 1998, p. 252). "More than half of respondents (52%) experienced $\geq$ 1 category of adverse childhood exposure; 6.2% reported $\geq$ 4 exposures" (p. 249).[8] In the conclusion of an article that described this ground-breaking study, these researchers asserted that "because adverse childhood experiences are common and they have strong long-term associations with adult health risk behaviors, health status, and diseases, increased attention to primary, secondary, and tertiary prevention strategies is needed" (p. 254).

In commenting on the increasing normalization of psychopathology in the Western world, Laing (1990) declared, "Pathology has, or has almost, taken over, and has become the norm, the standard that sets the tone for the society . . . [we] live in" (p. xi). Emphasizing that emotional maltreatment and neglect are inevitably involved in acts of physical or sexual abuse, Garbarino et. al. (1986) asserted,

> Rather than casting psychological maltreatment as an ancillary issue, subordinate to other forms of abuse and neglect, we should place it as the centerpiece of efforts to understand family functioning and to protect children. In almost all cases, it is the psychological consequences of an act that define that act as abusive. (p. 7)

In listening to parents describe their own upbringing, we noted several forms of emotional maltreatment that have significant effects on children's personalities. These included (a) behaviors based on parents' hostility toward the child—sarcastic, derisive, or condescending comments, harsh mistreatment in the name of "discipline," lack of respect for the child's boundaries, threats of abandonment or loss of love, and the stifling of a child's aliveness, spontaneity, and curiosity; (b) child-rearing practices based on indifference or neglect—deprivation or outright rejection, lack of genuine physical affection, interest, or concern, lack of sensitivity to a child's needs, excessive permissiveness, and parents' inconsistency; (c) behaviors based on ignorance—overprotection of the child and isolation from social contacts; (d) overly restrictive or harsh moral codes and values; and (e) parents' negative qualities, addictive habit patterns, and defended lifestyles that the child is exposed to and imitates (Berger & Thompson, 1995; Black, 1981; McClearn, Plomin, Gora-Maslak, & Crabbe, 1991; Seixas & Youcha, 1985).

Parents' defenses are invariably damaging to their offspring. One destructive form of psychological abuse is that which is acted out by parents who are emotionally hungry toward their children, who take *from* their children rather than give *to* them. Parents tend to confuse actions based on their own strong dependency needs from the past with behaviors based on true regard for their children. Immature or emotionally hungry parents exert a strong pull on their offspring, which drains the child's emotional resources (Belsky, Taylor, & Rovine, 1984; Firestone, 1990b; Levy, 1943; Parker, 1983; K. Rosen & Rothbaum, 1993; Stern, 1985; Tronick, Cohn, & Shea, 1986; West & Keller, 1991).[9]

Another damaging type of emotional abuse can be seen in the nonfeeling physical contact that emotionally deadened parents tend to have with their children. Research has shown that infants raised by these "emotionally unavailable" parents often develop symptoms of a "failure to thrive" syndrome (older children who have been consistently related to without feeling show considerable apathy, lethargy, and developmental delays).[10] Egeland and Sroufe (1981) found that "having a mother who is chronically unavailable and unresponsive has devastating consequences on the child that touch every aspect of early functioning" (p. 89).

In addition, recent findings in neurological studies of the brain have confirmed what psychologists have known for decades—that the effects of unfeeling contact and emotional neglect often last a life time. Extensive research conducted by Perry, Schore, and Siegel shows that damage incurred by children from this form of emotional deprivation, especially before the age of 3, is "hard-wired" into the brain. Perry (1999), Perry and Marcellus (1997), Schore (1994), and D. Siegel (2001) explain that the human brain is not fully developed at birth. Its further development, especially development of the right hemisphere during the early years of life, is environmental or use-dependent. In other words, healthy development of the part of a young child's brain that is responsible for self-reflective thinking, the regulation of emotions, and the capacity for experiencing empathy is for the most part dependent on the environment provided for the child.[11]

Schore (1994) emphasized that:

> The external environment is a social environment specifically contained in the dyadic interaction [between parent and infant] and if psychotoxic it can literally induce increased synapse destruction in the internal environment of the child's growing brain. (p. 413)

Perry (1996) contrasted the impact on the child of a nurturing environment with that of an emotionally or physically hostile one:

> When the child's development is characterized by structure, predictability, nurturing, and enriching emotional, social and cognitive experiences, a vulnerable and powerless infant can grow to become a happy, productive, insightful and caring member of society—contributing to us all. Sadly, few families and communities can provide this idealized early life. Indeed, it is in the familial incubator that children are the most frequently manipulated, coerced, degraded, inoculated with destructive beliefs. (p. 1)

It is important to stress that many of the behaviors that hurt children occur on the periphery of parents' consciousness. There are a number of reasons that parents are seemingly oblivious to the ways they damage their children; however, two reasons are relevant: (a) most parents have forgotten or rationalized their own parents' mistreatment of *them* (Ensink, 1992; A. Miller, 1980/1984a); and more importantly, (b) many parents are insensitive to themselves, relating to, mistreating, and punishing themselves in much the same style that they were treated as children.

Finally, children imitate their parents' repression and denial by suppressing unacceptable feelings such as anger and fear. Because of their lack of awareness and their intolerance of certain feelings, parents not only damage their children but also unwittingly prevent their recovery by not allowing them to cry or feel sad. To recover from trauma, it is necessary for children to express their sadness, anger, and grief, and talk about their feelings. An environment that does not permit this type of expression prolongs children's misery and suffering.

Physical and Sexual Abuse

In situations in which emotional abuse is compounded by incidents of physical and sexual maltreatment, the child's initial response to pain may become almost automatic. In severely mistreated children, it does not take much additional stimulation from the external world to reactivate internal signals of fear and tension, and this sets up a cycle of retraumatization (Herman, 1992; Post, 1992; van der Kolk, Greenberg, Boyd, & Krystal, 1985). Under these conditions, children develop many defenses that help numb their pain, that allow them to escape emotionally from terrifying situations through depersonalization or dissociation, or that provide a fantasy world as an alternative to unremitting fear.

Under conditions of physical or sexual abuse, where the person to whom the child naturally turns for protection is also the frightening or punishing agent, the child usually fails to develop a secure attachment (Lyons-Ruth & Jacobvitz, 1999; Main & Solomon, 1986).[12] Again, as in cases of emotional abuse, the continual fear, together with the lack of human contact and social interaction, can damage certain circuits in the brain that are responsible for the development of basic trust and a desire for social affiliation.

Witnessing violence between parents and being the victim of physical, emotional, and sexual abuses are probably the most serious forms of trauma that can occur in the life of a young child. Perry (1997) noted that "both lack of critical nurturing experience and excess exposure to traumatic violence will alter the developing central nervous system, predisposing to a more impulsive, reactive, and violent individual" (p. 131). The traumatic fear states aroused by these events cause the brain to release certain toxins that actually change the structure of the brain and central nervous system, destroying cells and synapses that are responsible for the regulation of emotions and the development of compassion and empathy.[13]

Moreover, LeDoux (2002) has demonstrated that early learning is also dependent on the child's emotional state:

> Because emotion systems coordinate learning, the broader the range of emotions that a child experiences the broader will be the emotional range of the self that develops. This is why childhood abuse is so

devastating. If a significant proportion of the early emotional experiences one has are due to *activation of the fear system* [italics added] . . . the characteristic personality that begins to build up from the parallel learning processes coordinated by the emotional state is one characterized by negativity and hopelessness rather than affection and optimism. (p. 322)

Lacking the ability to regulate emotions or the capacity for empathy, children substitute defensive and destructive ways of handling stress and pain that can persist for a lifetime (Schore, 1994). When a child who is damaged in this way enters adolescence, he or she finds that he or she is literally controlled by his or her feelings, much as a 2-year-old is when in the throes of a temper tantrum. Their emotions are like a runaway roller-coaster, and they cannot get off.

More children than we would like to acknowledge are currently growing up in these circumstances (Briere, 1992; Straus, 1994; Straus & Gelles, 1986). According to Perry (1997), "In the United States alone, at least 5 million children are either victims of and/or witnesses to physical abuse and domestic or community violence" (p. 125). Finkelhor (1986) summarized the prevalence of sexual child abuse in the United States and reported rates ranging "from 6% to 62% for females and from 3% to 31% for males" (p. 19) [comparable with the Felitti et al. (1998) findings cited previously]. The interventions needed to help them break down their maladaptive, defended ways of coping with the pain caused by these events are difficult at best.

The Core Defense: The Fantasy Bond

The primary method that children use to cope with emotional or physical deprivation and rejection early in life is to imagine themselves as one with the parental figure. As described in chapter 1, the core defense is the fantasy bond, an imaginary connection formed by the infant with his or her mother or primary caretaker.

Observations of the parents in the friendship circle with their infants reaffirmed a theory formulated by the first author early in his career as a psychologist. He concluded that ideal mothering would consist of nurturing the baby in a manner that reduces stress to a minimal level. The product of this ability on the part of the mother or caregiver was termed "love-food," which means having both the strength of character and the desire to meet the baby's needs and help him or her develop into a comfortable social being (Winnicott, 1960/1965). Love-food is necessary for survival in both the physical and psychological sense.

When deprived of love-food, infants experience intense anxiety and pain. During periods of deprivation, they attempt to adapt by forming a fantasy bond of being merged with the mother or parenting figure. Infants and young children who feel empty and starved emotionally come to depend more and more on this process because it partly relieves their hunger and reduces their anxiety (Firestone, 1984).[14] They also tend to compensate for the lack of nurturance by using various forms of self-nourishment, such as thumb-sucking and excessive masturbation. Later, as adults, they use other persons and substances as soothing agents.

Children experience a false sense of self-sufficiency because they have taken into themselves the image of the "good and powerful" parent. Unfortunately, at the same time, they must also take on their parent's rejecting attitudes toward them. These internalized parental attitudes form the basis of their negative self-image and a destructive thought process. In effect, children simultaneously develop a feeling of being the strong, good parent and the weak, bad child. In denying their needs and wants in relation to other people, they become a system unto themselves. The more seriously deprived children are, the more they depend on the fantasy bond as a compensation and resist genuine closeness and affection from outside.

To illustrate, a mother who was a patient in our clinical practice several years ago revealed that she had been feeding her infant daughter, Kay, with a bottle for approximately 18 months when relatives began to put pressure on her to discontinue bottle feeding. One night, in giving in to their pressure, she refused to give the bottle to Kay. The child cried most of the night until at one point, the mother could no longer stand it and offered her the bottle. Kay's response was to throw the bottle from the crib and put her thumb into her mouth. In other words, she now refused to accept gratification from the outside and instead was involved in gratifying herself. In attempting to cope with the frustration, pain, and anguish in her early life, Kay suppressed her feelings, found partial gratification in the imagined connection expressed through the sucking of her thumb, and rejected the other means of gratification. The mother reported that Kay never took the bottle again.

This incident was reflective of a general pattern of rejection and deprivation in Kay's family that contributed to her becoming increasingly inward, self-nourishing, and self-protective as she grew older. As an adolescent, Kay was aloof and distant from friends and family members and gained considerable weight. For a number of years she used laxatives in a self-destructive manner to try to control her weight. In effect, she was nourishing and punishing herself, having substituted a form of internal gratification for taking a chance on closeness in interpersonal relationships where she would feel vulnerable again.

The fantasy bond is the child's attempt to parent him- or herself.[15] It is made up of both self-nourishing thoughts and habits as well as self-punishing attitudes and behaviors. Once a fantasy bond is formed, people often choose to protect it at all costs. Their major goal becomes that of maintaining the safety and security of the internalized parent. They come to prefer fantasy and internal modes of gratification to seeking and finding real satisfaction and love from others in a relationship. For example, parents' efforts to relieve distress in their offspring can deprive children of even the minimal frustration experiences needed for normal development and teach them self-soothing, self-nurturing habit patterns that may later limit them as fully functioning adults. In many instances, the excessive use of drugs for infants suffering from colic; overfeeding children to quiet them; or bouncing, rocking, or walking endlessly with the child to calm him or her may predispose a child to continue to rely on these methods as a form of self-gratification. Later as adults, they continue to regulate and parent themselves in adult life in essentially the same way that they were originally treated by their parents. They often develop rationalizations for avoiding close associations or pursuing goals that would bring them real satisfaction or become cynical about other people or relationships in general.

The extent to which people eventually come to rely on fantasized connections and addictive behaviors is determined by the degree of frustration, pain, and emotional deprivation they experienced early in life. For children who are seriously deprived, the self-parenting process (made up of the fantasy bond and self-nurturing behaviors) eventually becomes addictive in itself. Children and adults have at their disposal an immediately rewarding method of escaping circumstances that are anxiety-provoking.

As adults, most individuals extend this self-parenting process into their intimate relationships. They tend to develop modes of relating wherein they rely almost completely on their partner for their sense of self-worth or use the relationship to achieve a feeling of ultimate safety and security. In the process of forming a fantasy bond, they substitute a fantasy of love, closeness, and connection in place of the real friendship, sexuality, and affection that may have originally characterized the relationship.

Once an illusion of connection with the partner has been formed, experiences of genuine love and intimacy interfere with its defensive function, whereas symbols of togetherness and images of love strengthen the illusion. Any event that arouses an awareness of separateness can be anxiety-provoking and give rise to hostile feelings. For example, when either partner moves away from an addictive mode of relating toward more independence or autonomy, symptoms similar to those manifested in withdrawal from chemical dependency, including intense anxiety, reactive depression, irritability, anger and often rage, feelings of "falling apart" or disintegrating, and overwhelming sadness and grief may be aroused in the other person.

To summarize, the primary defense or fantasy bond arises to fill a gap where there is environmental deprivation; it "nourishes" the self and becomes the motivating force behind self-limiting, self-destructive behavior. No child has the ideal situation; thus all people depend to some degree on internal gratification from the fantasy bond.

The Core Conflict

As a result of forming defenses early in life, people live in conflict. They are torn between real feeling and experience in their lives and leading inward, self-protective lifestyles, cut off from feeling and emotional involvement. In attempting to resolve this basic conflict and establish some kind of equilibrium, most people eventually come to live on a defensive level, existing within a narrow, restricted range of experience. They often choose addictive ways of gratifying themselves internally—nurturing, comforting, and soothing themselves—rather than trying to satisfy their wants through the active pursuit of personal goals and interests. The psychological equilibrium they achieve can be threatened by loving or constructive events that contradict their early childhood experiences. To protect the fantasy bond from these "positive" intrusions, most people recreate the original conditions within their family through three methods: selection, distortion, and provocation.

People tend to select partners who are similar to the individuals in their early lives because those are the people that their defenses are appropriate to. They distort their mates as well as others and see them like the people in their past. If all else fails, they try to provoke responses in others that will duplicate their past. Using these methods, they recreate the negative aspects of their original family in their new relationships, thereby preserving the internalized parent. In effect, they relive rather than live their lives.

The fantasy of being connected to another person, together with self-nourishing habits, cuts off feeling responses. This, in turn, interferes with developing a true sense of self. People tend to seek the seeming calmness or tranquillity of their defensive solution rather than the self-actualization and satisfaction that might come from the active pursuit of what they want out of life. They are often willing to give up positive, goal-directed behavior to preserve internal sources of gratification.

Many people develop a facade or shell of toughness and hardness that precludes the very closeness they desire. Attempting to protect themselves against being hurt again, they bring on the distress they are trying to avoid. In developing attitudes of mistrust and cynicism based on early hurts, they act in ways that put distance between themselves and others. By becoming self-protective and self-nurturing, they fail to take the risks necessary for self-actualization and hide behind the safety of conformity instead of pursuing their own individuality.

The Defense of Identifying With the Aggressor and Formation of the Self and Antiself Systems

R. D. Laing (1960/1969) proposed a division within the personality that reflected a discrepancy between the "false self," or social facade, and the "real self," or authentic personality. As noted in chapter 1, we conceptualize a more fundamental division as representing a split between the part of the personality that is harmonious with the individual and his or her goals and another part that is alien, opposed to the individual's best interests, and ultimately self-destructive (Firestone, 1997b). The degree to which people are divided within themselves depends on the kind of parenting and environment they experienced as children as well as their exposure to illness, accidents, and loss, such as a loved one leaving or dying.

Even if infrequent, incidents in which parents express their anger punitively or punish the child harshly make a significant impression on the child. Under conditions of extreme stress and abuse, the child disengages from the self—the weak, helpless child—identifies with the aggressive parent, and incorporates the parent's hostility as part of his or her own personality. This unconscious maneuver of splitting from the self partially alleviates the child's terror and provides a sense of relief. In the process, however, the child takes on not only the parent's aggression directed toward him or her but the guilt, the fear, and in fact the total complex of the parent's defensive structure (Bettelheim, 1943/1979; Ferenczi, 1933/1955; A. Freud, 1966).[16]

In other words, in the face of emotional pain or intolerable anxiety, the child tries to preserve some level of rationality and sense of wholeness, no matter how primitive (Noyes, Hoenk, Kuperman, & Slymen, 1977). Efforts to maintain logic under stressful conditions lead to the specific defense of identifying with the aggressor. Rather than suffer complete ego disintegration, children make a powerful identification with the same forces that produce the torment they are trying to escape. Adopting this defense leads to a basic split in the personality between the self and antiself. Both parts of the personality are dynamic and are continually evolving and changing. Thus, people carry within themselves tendencies to both actualize and obliterate the self.

The Self System

The positive side of the division within the personality originates in the unique propensities and potentialities innate in each person. These include physical abilities and attributes, temperament, inherited genetic abilities, and the natural assimilation of the positive, desirable traits that the parents possess. The self system also consists of positive experiences resulting from parents' or other caring adults' nurturance and love and other experiences that facilitate the child's growth and development.

The Antiself System: Voices That Predispose Alienation

The antiself is made up of a system of destructive thoughts and associated angry feelings that are opposed to the self and cynical toward other people. Destructive thoughts against ourselves as well as cynical attitudes toward other people predispose alienation and distance in our closest relationships. They represent a form of internal communication, ways of talking to ourselves that lead to distrust, restrict emotional transactions, and contribute to an inward, self-protective lifestyle.

All people tend to carry on some form of internal dialogue as though another person were talking to them: criticizing, accusing, imparting negative information about significant others, and encouraging them to engage in self-defeating, addictive habit patterns. These negative thoughts or voices range from unconscious or subliminal to fully conscious. Internalized voices, including those that take the form of imagined rejection, negative anticipations, and cynical views of others can be thought of as secondary defenses that protect the primary defense of self-parenting. The voice process is the mechanism that regulates self-limiting, defensive behavior and causes the person to reject positive experiences. It is, in effect, the language of the defensive process.

In being divided, people have two opposing points of view about themselves, other persons, and events in their interpersonal world. One represents the self system and reflects their real point of view, their natural wants and their desires and needs. The other represents the antiself system and is made up of internalized voices (negative parental introjects) that are antithetical to people's best interests and opposed to the fulfillment of their wants and needs.[17] These negative thoughts exist on a continuum that includes mild self-criticisms, thoughts that encourage addictive behavior, thoughts influencing self-destructive behavior, and at the extreme end of the continuum thoughts of suicide.

Case Study

> When Don was 19, he suffered from a major depressive episode and persistent thoughts of suicide precipitated by the loss of the relationship with his high school girlfriend. After two years of psychotherapy, he developed a stronger sense of self, embarked on a career in engineering, and eventually started his own business. Now, 20 years later, as his business expanded and brought him financial success and a sense of accomplishment, he became aware than he had surpassed his father, who at the time was on the brink of bankruptcy. Don began to experience malicious self-recriminations and suicidal thoughts that frightened him and threatened to undermine his accomplishments. His subsequent retreat into an immature, regressive state and the self-defeating behaviors he began to act out served the defensive function

of helping him avoid direct competition with symbolic rivals and escape the guilt reactions he experienced in surpassing his father.

Don's regression was triggered in part by irrational fears and suspicions he developed in relation to his employees and his male friends. By participating in group psychotherapy and recording his thoughts and feelings in a journal, he began to challenge these projections from the past. Gradually he came to realize that he was distorting his present-day competitors based on remnants of his father's hatred toward him as a rival in the family. In identifying with his father, Don had taken on his father's rage in the form of voices telling him to do away with himself. Now, in competitive situations, he was experiencing strong self-destructive urges.

Later, Don developed additional insight into the reasons he had retreated from competitive situations, both in business and interpersonal relationships. He traced the source of his guilty reactions to success, malicious self-accusations, and suicidal ideation to situations in his childhood where he had been severely punished by his father. He came to understand how his self-destructive tendencies and his punitive, belligerent attitudes toward himself had been transmitted through three generations within his family constellation. He recorded some of these insights in a journal entry:

> For as long as I can remember I would often catch my father looking at me as if I had committed a horrendous crime and, because of some loophole, escaped the severe punishment I deserved and was set free into his family instead. It was a powerful gaze that never failed to fill me with guilt for a misdeed I assumed I had done in a time before memories.
>
> My father's first job at 14 was at my grandfather's garage. One day, on his way to work from school, he made the mistake of first joining some of his friends at the drug store to have a soda. My grandfather came out of the garage and saw him through the store window. He marched across the street and into the store. I picture my father looking up for a minute and seeing my grandfather storming across Main Street like murder on legs. I feel what he felt because similar moments are carved in my bones. Unbridled fury coming down the path. My grandfather burst into the store, lifted him off his stool by his collar, and dragged him, stumbling awkwardly, back across the street.
>
> I was around ten when my father told this story and I knew the complete humiliation of what he had endured. It was the first time that I was aware that my father, in recounting these events in his past, had no feeling for himself. If anything, there was a hint of his siding with my grandfather against himself. I knew then that deep inside, he maintained, and accessed on a daily basis as verification of his character, a detailed record of what my grandfather collected as the indisputable evidence of his badness. It was as if a part of him thrived on hatred toward my father.

From a young age, my father hungered to get away from that life. Most of all, away from my grandfather. He longed to be rid of the shackles of my grandfather's eyes. He was motivated by his desire for freedom and dreamed of someday creating a family that would be different from his. But my father continued to treat himself in the same manner his father had treated him. He may have moved away, found another lifestyle completely lacking in the surroundings he had been raised in, but he never escaped my grandfather. He left home not knowing he was infected with his upbringing. In a way, my father became his father, and I was born into the role that had once been acted by my father.

Anger from my father was the verification of my existence. All other avenues contained a black emptiness. I learned to live in the format of the only way he could have seen a son, in the same template of how he had once been viewed. My relationship with him was through his anger. Without ever consciously admitting it to myself, I exerted caution and respect for the potential of his rage and buried what I feared was his thinly veiled restraint to end my existence.

In filling the part of the lazy son, I cleared my father of all wrong-doing and provided, to myself, the evidence of my unlovability, my badness. A solid case which verified that it was not that my father was incapable of love, it was that I was unlovable. My badness the root of his fury. The structure of my security depended on the basic facts that I was bad, he was good, and the turmoil in our household was due strictly to my evil.

It was as if I found camaraderie with my father in sort of mentally standing next to him, kind of looking with him down at me. His saying, "you know, he really is a terrible kid," and part of me, standing next to him, looking down at me and saying, "you know, he certainly is."

After I had these insights, I understood my father's numbness when he discussed the incidents between him and his own father. He had buried the facts, along with his innocence, by handing down tradition in his relationship with me. The act of beating me for the first time had all but eradicated what little hope there was of his ever knowing his own innocence. The same would hold true for me unless I stepped out of tradition and allowed myself the benefit of a doubt.

EXISTENTIAL PAIN: THE IMPACT OF DEATH ANXIETY ON DEFENSES

Children develop the core defense or fantasy bond before they learn about death. They experience separation anxiety at every phase in their development as they gain in independence and self-assertion. Often the anxiety of being separate from their parents precipitates a fear of loss and a dread of annihilation. To ease their fears, they retreat to the imagined merger with their mother or caregiver. The fantasy connection is a desperate attempt on the child's part to deny his or her true state of aloneness, helplessness, and vulnerability. By the time children develop a concept of their personal death, they already have at their disposal a complex system of defenses against separation anxiety. Indeed, death symbolizes the ultimate separation.

Children become aware of death in successive stages (S. Anthony, 1971/1973; Kastenbaum, 1995; Nagy 1948/1959): first that people die, then that their parents will die, and finally that they themselves will not live forever. This discovery literally destroys their illusion of being self-sufficient. They are unable to bear the prospect of losing themselves through death. On some unconscious level, they deny the reality of their personal death by returning to an earlier stage of development before they knew about death. We have observed children who reverted to immature behavior, for example, bed-wetting or tantrums, and withdrew from close personal contact with other family members. Even when there have been no early losses through death or separation in a child's life, there often is a gradual loss of spontaneity, a retreat from the pure joy of play, and a denial of other pleasures of life after children become aware of death.

In their desperation to escape a situation from which there is no escape, children cling even more tenaciously to the fantasy bond or self-parenting process. S. Anthony (1971/1973) commented on children's tendencies to defend against their evolving knowledge of death by imagining a union with the parent or sibling after death:

> In all these instances, anxiety is clearly about death as separation from the love-object, and the defence has taken the form of a belief or hope of union in death; indeed unconsciously of a closer union in death than was possible in life. (p. 151)

Many children imagine that even though their parents are mortal, they (the children) can still take care of themselves, can still "feed" themselves. Many make resolutions or vows to never trust others or to never become deeply invested emotionally in another person or in life. In this way, the core defense and a pseudoindependent way of being are strengthened and become more deeply entrenched *after* children learn about death.

Children's nightmares appear more frequently during this crucial stage, that is, between the ages of 3 and 7 (Firestone, 1994). These terrifying dreams are filled with dangers, monsters, themes of punishment, indicating a deep-seated preoccupation with death and the vulnerability of their bodies. These nightmares appear to decrease in frequency during later childhood and early adolescence, a fact that may indicate the child's increased ability to deny death on an unconscious level.

In summary, defenses that children form in early childhood are significantly reinforced as they develop a growing awareness of death. The most powerful and effective denial of death lies in the fantasy bond that the child develops originally as a compensation for what is missing in his or her early environment. After children become aware of death, they are faced with the choice of living with the awareness of death, existential aloneness, and people's inhumanity to others, or escaping into emotional deadness and denial.

CONCLUSION

The ideas presented in this chapter point the way toward a richer, less defended way of life. A major part of overcoming defenses lies in learning the truth about oneself, about one's family, and about society. Understanding destructive factors that affect people opens up the possibility of adopting alternatives to a defended way of life. Achieving insight into the division within oneself also enables one to take action to counteract the prescriptions of the voice. The alternative path presented throughout this book indicates a direction that runs counter to the path most people have chosen. It appears that most of us have spent our lives protecting ourselves with defenses we were forced to adopt as children. These defenses are not only unnecessary but indeed, they are harmful to us, to our loved ones, and especially to our children. It is our belief that living with minimal defenses and maximum vulnerability is the only feasible way to live a truly vital, meaningful life.

Defenses that were appropriate to children who were at the mercy of their environment are no longer appropriate to adults who can control their world to a considerable degree. Unfortunately, the fear of change often causes people to persist in holding on to their defenses long after the original situation that aroused their fear has passed. However, by giving up many of their most treasured negative ways of looking at themselves and at the world, people *can* regain feeling for themselves as well as a sense of dignity and self-respect. As they begin to experience more of themselves and the reality of their lives, they can envision the possibility of living an adventurous, life-affirming existence.

NOTES

1. Briere (1992) asserted that "the majority of adults raised in North America, regardless of gender, age, race, or social class, probably experienced some level of maltreatment as children" (p. xvii).

2. Chess and Thomas (1999) suggested that the etiology of emotional disorders and dysfunctional behaviors lie in the "patient's *specific vulnerability* and the interaction with the *specific environmental stress*. The pathology will not be in the person's psychological structure but *in the interactional process*" (p. 208).

3. See Bloch's (1978) *So the Witch Won't Eat Me*, in which she stated "That a distorted parental image may be essential to the psyche's defensive system has emerged with great clarity from both my work with children and my psychoanalytic treatment of adults" (p. 162).

4. See *The Psychologically Battered Child* (Garbarino et al., 1986), *Understanding Abusive Families* (Garbarino & Gilliam, 1980), and *Emotional Abuse* (Loring, 1994) for cogent descriptions of the effects of emotional child abuse and its intergenerational nature. Also see Rohner's (1991) findings that parental rejection appears to have a universal effect on children.

5. The first author's (R. Firestone) approach to early defense formation in the individual integrates psychoanalytical and existential systems of thought, which contributes to a more comprehensive view of human behavior (Firestone, 1997a).

6. See research findings regarding the effect of death awareness on people's defenses reported by "terror management" theorists Simon, Greenberg, Solomon, Pyszczynski, and others. Their studies are reviewed (Simon et al., 1997) in "Terror Management and Cognitive-Experiential Theory: Evidence That Terror Management Occurs in the Experiential System."

7. We agree in substance with Garbarino and Gilliam's (1980) broad definition of abuse or maltreatment as "acts of omission or commission by a parent or guardian that are judged by a mixture of community values and professional expertise to be inappropriate and damaging" (p. 7).

8. The Adverse Childhood Experiences (ACE) Study used seven categories of childhood exposure to abuse and household dysfunction: psychological abuse, physical abuse, contact sexual abuse, exposure to substance abuse, mental illness, violent treatment of mother or stepmother, and criminal behavior in the household. The study verified "the relationship between childhood exposures and disease conditions that are among the leading causes of mortality" (Felitti et al., 1998, p. 248).

9. See Stern's (1985) description of "overattunement" on the part of some caregivers, which he perceived as a "counterpart of physical intrusiveness" (p. 219).

10. Some children who have suffered emotional neglect and who were raised by "psychologically unavailable" parents may exhibit symptoms of "nonorganic failure to thrive" such as apathy, lethargy, developmental delays, or a failure to grow—in other words, "deprivation dwarfism" (Drotar, 1985; Drotar, Eckerle, Satola, Pallotta, & Wyatt, 1990; Kotelchuck, 1980).

11. Schore (1994) cited Trevarthen's (1990) argument that "the epigenetic program of brain growth requires brain-brain interaction and occurs in the context of a positive affective relationship between mother and infant" (Schore, 1994, p. 104).

In "Bonding and Attachment in Maltreated Children," Perry (1999) noted that "holding, gazing, smiling, kissing, singing, and laughing all cause specific neurochemical activities in the brain. These neurochemical activities lead to normal organization of brain systems that are responsible for attachment" (p. 4).

12. Interpreting Main and Solomon (1986), researcher D. Siegel (1999) noted that "disorganized attachment develops from repeated experiences in which the caregiver appears frightened or frightening to the child. . . . Repair in such a dyad after these interactions does not occur" (p. 117).

    Research has shown that exploitation of the child as a sexual object can lead to ego fragmentation and later to addictive behavior and dissociative disorders (Briere & Runtz, 1987; Chu & Dill, 1990; Sanders & Giolas, 1991), multiple personality disorders (Coons, 1986; F. Putnam, Guroff, Silberman, Barban, & Post, 1986; Ross et al., 1990), and other disorders (Cavaiola & Schiff, 1988; Conte & Schuerman 1987).

13. See Perry (2000), "Violence and Childhood: How Persisting Fear Can Alter the Developing Child's Brain." The "alarm reaction" (similar to a persistent state of fear) has been studied extensively, according to Perry (1996): "The brains of traumatized children develop to be hypervigilant and focused on non-verbal cues, potentially related to threat" (p. 4). Also see Herman's (1992) descriptions of the profound effects of traumatic events on physiological arousal, emotion, cognition, and memory in *Trauma and Recovery* and in van der Kolk, McFarlane, and Weisaeth's (1996) edited volume, *Traumatic Stress*.

14. Research has shown that fantasy can be rewarding under conditions of physical deprivation (Keys, Brozek, Henschel, Mickelsen, & Taylor, 1950). Also see Silverman, Lachmann, and Milich (1982) and Orbach, Shopen-Kofman, and Mikulincer's (1994) paper, "The Impact of Subliminal Symbiotic vs. Identification Messages in Reducing Anxiety."

15. Bollas's (1987) description of the "self as object" is similar in some respects to our conceptualization of the self-parenting process. Bollas stated, "It is my view that each person transfers elements of the parent's child care to his own handling of himself as an object" (p. 59). "If we look closely at our patients we would probably all agree that each has his or her own sense of existence but that, by virtue of the persistent pathology of their defenses, they live by disowning the self" (p. 63).

16. Ferenczi (1933/1955) was the first to describe identification with the aggressor: "The weak and undeveloped personality reacts to sudden unpleasure not by defence, but by anxiety-ridden identification and by introjection of the menacing person or aggressor" (p. 163).

17. Findings from empirical studies related to the internalization of childhood trauma were reported in "Studies in Self-Representation Beyond Childhood" (Bocknek & Perna, 1994). Also see Bornstein's (1993) studies investigating the hypothesis that dysfunctional parental introjects predict an individual's risk for psychopathology.

II

OVERCOMING BARRIERS TO PSYCHOLOGICAL DEVELOPMENT

3

DISRUPTING FANTASY PROCESSES

> It is certain that in adult life gratification through fantasy is no longer harmless. As soon as more considerable quantities of cathexis are involved, fantasy and reality become incompatible: it must be one or the other.
>
> —Anna Freud (1966, p. 81)

The capacity of human beings to imagine and symbolize is at once a strength and a weakness.[1] The ability to produce in fantasy an image of oneself and others, as well as the capacity to partially gratify oneself with such images, is functional as a defense in the face of early environmental deficiencies. However, as with any defense, the continued reliance on fantasy processes as a substitute for a painful reality and as a replacement for seeking gratification in the external environment sets the stage for psychological disturbance.

All people exist in conflict between an active pursuit of goals in the real world and a dependence on fantasy gratification. In the course of the developmental sequence, psychological equilibrium is achieved when an individual arrives at a specific solution to the core conflict. This equilibrium is often attained at the expense of satisfying object relations and is threatened by warm or constructive events that contradict earlier painful experiences. The defensive solution to the conflict acts as a powerful resistance to changing one's life for the better. The attempt to live in a world that is more rewarding or more congenial than the world one knew as a child disturbs one's psychological equilibrium.[2]

Portions of this chapter adapted from Firestone, R. W. (1993). The psychodynamics of fantasy, addiction, and addictive attachments. *American Journal of Psychoanalysis, 53,* 335–352. Adapted with permission of Kluwer Academic/Plenum Publishers.

The child's resolution to the basic conflict is not a philosophical decision in which the advantages and disadvantages, pros and cons, are rationally weighed. The particular solution is determined while experiencing painful and often conflicting emotions that are at the least difficult and uncomfortable for the vulnerable child. To ascertain what factors predispose a positive or negative resolution, one must examine the psychological dimensions of each child's life experience and come to understand how the defenseless child learns to cope with life within the early relationship constellation.

If the child is fortunate enough to have mature and loving parents who provide the necessary love-food required for adequate sustenance, he or she would be able to live in a real world and would have less need to depersonalize or develop defenses that function to deny reality and avoid psychological pain and frustration. On the other hand, if the child is the victim of immature, inadequate, or hostile parenting, the traumatic impact of extensive frustration on the all-encompassing reactivity of the infant or small child causes intolerable psychological pain, and a defended posture is the only escape. Fantasy processes and a marked tendency to suppress or repress painful experiences take over in an attempt to ease the suffering.

As described in the previous chapter, the helpless child joins symbolically with the powerful parent, and this imaginary fusion reduces anxiety and provides partial relief of the tension associated with the frustration of basic needs. He or she develops an illusion of self-sufficiency in which he or she is both the parent and the object of parenting.[3] The greater the rejection or deprivation, the stronger the imaginary attachment in fantasy, and the greater the loss of reality testing. The most significant issue is that fantasy gratification and self-nourishing behaviors can come to be preferred over seeking fulfillment in the interpersonal world. Furthermore, the process of gratifying oneself with internal images or self-parenting mechanisms and the pursuit of gratification in the external world are mutually exclusive. Therefore, real satisfaction jeopardizes the fantasy process and results in anxiety.

The degree to which a person depends on fantasy for psychological survival will determine the extent to which he or she will have to invent or provoke rejection where there is none. For example, a woman who falls in love, then finds herself suddenly believing that her lover is pulling away from her for no apparent reason, or without any behavioral change on his part, is in all probability protecting the self-parenting process. Because she cannot tolerate the intrusion of genuine love into her fantasy of self-sufficiency, she must eventually push her lover away, all the while believing that she is being rejected. Or a man who avoids his wife sexually may at the same time support an illusion of pseudoindependence through compulsive masturbation. Many of the problems within relationships indicate the powerful effect of each partner's dependence on both the primary and secondary fantasies and the defenses that sustain them.

RESISTANCE IN PSYCHOTHERAPY

Resistance to change in psychotherapy, as well as people's fundamental resistance to a better life, takes the form of protecting the individual against anxiety states that arise whenever fantasy processes and the associated self-nurturing behaviors are threatened.[4] Most people tend to reject or manipulate their present-day environment to avoid emotional interactions that would contradict their early conception of reality or disturb the self-parenting process, despite the fact that this means continuing to suffer. This paradoxical aspect of human behavior may be the single most delimiting factor in psychotherapy; it is an obstacle to anyone attempting to make positive changes in his or her life (Ghent, 1990/1999; Leahy, 2001; Rank, quoted in Kramer, 1996; Wachtel, 1982).[5]

Ernest Becker (1973/1997) explained the problem of resistance in psychotherapy as follows:

> The patient is not struggling against himself, against forces deep within his animal nature. He is struggling rather against the loss of his world, of the whole range of action and objects that he so laboriously and painfully fashioned during his early training. (p. 170)

The more that people are able to break with fantasy processes and self-parenting behaviors, the greater the opportunity they have for finding satisfaction in real relationships and fulfillment through goal-directed behavior. Therefore, an integral part of the therapeutic process involves exposing the primary defense or self-parenting process and the secondary defenses (internalized thoughts or voices) that protect it. At the same time, the therapist attempts to make reality more inviting indirectly by responding with compassion and sensitive understanding. In the framework of this therapeutic alliance, he or she encourages the client to challenge distortions of reality and relinquish self-parenting, addictive habit patterns. Developing insight into the dimensions of the defensive process facilitates clients' movement toward pursuing external sources of gratification in the interpersonal environment.

DIMENSIONS OF THE DEFENSIVE PROCESS

Firestone (1988) has defined neurosis as an inward, defensive process that leads people to seek satisfaction more in fantasy than in the real world. It is the attempt to recreate, both in fantasy and action, a parent or parents in other persons or institutions, or if all else fails, in oneself. There are three major dimensions of the defensive process, each of which represents an adaptation to deficiencies and pressures in the early environment. These defense mechanisms become abnormal because of their intensity or degree and their misapplication to new persons or situations (Searles, 1979).

The interrelated dimensions of the defensive apparatus include those that primarily involve fantasy processes: (a) developing an idealized image of parents and family; (b) maintaining a negative self-image; and (c) displacing negative parental traits onto other people and the world at large, disrupting one's capacity to function in the real world.[6] Therapeutic interventions that are directed toward altering one dimension necessarily challenge the entire defensive process. The components of the defense system are not discrete entities or specific defenses, but tend to overlap to a considerable extent.

Idealization of Parents and Family

The idealization of parents and family is a necessary part of the self-parenting system. In an attempt to partially alleviate the pain and anxiety of emotional deprivation in a climate where their needs are not met, children fantasize an image of the parent or parents as good and loving. As noted in chapter 2, because of the child's extreme dependency during the early years, he or she must perceive the parent as benevolent or powerful rather than recognizing parental weaknesses or rejection. If in reality the parents are punitive and anxiety-provoking, in the child's mind it is not because they are hostile or inadequate but because he or she is bad. As Fairbairn (1952) succinctly put it: "It becomes obvious, therefore, that the child would rather be bad himself than to have bad objects" (p. 65)—that is, "it is better to be a sinner in a world ruled by God than to live in a world ruled by the Devil" (pp. 66–67; see also Arieti, 1974; Blatt, Auerbach, & Aryan, 1998; Kempe & Kempe, 1978; Oaklander, 1978).

The preservation of the idealized image of the parent is made possible because of the unconscious process by which unpleasant traits of the parent are blocked from the child's awareness and projected onto the biosocial environment. This removal from consciousness is made easier by the acceptance at face value of parental verbal protestations of love and concern and by a process of selective inattention whereby the child remains unaware of the parents' rejecting behavior. Thus, the child retains two images of the parent: the good image, which is conscious, and the bad image, which remains largely unconscious and is projected onto other people in the interpersonal environment. To be able to successfully parent oneself in fantasy, one must maintain an image of one's parent as being powerful, good, or adequate.

The fact that an individual is critical of his or her parents may not necessarily indicate that he or she has overcome an idealized view of them. Even people who disparage and blame their parents for their own unhappiness may be masking an idealization process. They may be holding on to exaggerated images of parental power and benevolence while refusing to accept the fact that their parents were people with defenses and limitations who were unable to provide love and nurturance.

Maintenance of a Negative Self-Image

The idealization of the parents leads to converse feelings about the self.[7] A system of negative thoughts, feelings, and attitudes toward the self is an integral part of the self-parenting process and is inextricably tied to the internalized idealized image of one's parents. This self-hatred originates from the introjection of the parent's negative attitudes toward the child during times of extreme stress through the process of identifying with the aggressor (Ferenczi, 1933/1955; Firestone, 1997a; A. Freud, 1966). The aggression and anger that the parent directs toward the child at these times is introjected in conjunction with the internalized, idealized parental image. The resultant negative attitudes toward self become a prominent part of the self-concept and are regulated by a negative thought process or voice. For example, clients who were abused verbally or physically as children tend to depreciate themselves and often repress memories of being punished or claim that their parents were justified in being punitive (A. Miller, 1980/ 1984a; Shengold, 1989).

People react to a negative self-image in paradoxical ways. They can be extremely critical and attacking of themselves, or they can defend against the negative self-image with compensatory processes. Some children develop attitudes of superiority and an inflated image of self to compensate for their negative self-image and feelings of inferiority. Vanity and narcissistic feelings of specialness represent a fantasized image of the self. These are remnants of the child's imagined invincibility and omnipotence that have been reinforced by parents' build-up of his or her performance and selected positive traits. Unable to offer their offspring genuine appreciation and love, many parents substitute flattery, praise, and special treatment for real affection, or they try to live vicariously through their children's accomplishments. Vanity is also a powerful defense against death anxiety; the unconscious belief is that even though other people die, one is immune to death because one is special in some way. Images associated with feelings of exaggerated self-importance represent a fragile adjustment to reality; when the fantasized image of self is shattered by failure or by direct competition with a rival, the underlying feelings of self-depreciation, shame, and reactive rage emerge.[8]

Projection of Negative Parental Qualities and Behaviors Onto Others

The displacement of negative parental traits onto the interpersonal environment is a result of the child's blocking from awareness the parents' weaknesses and their negative qualities. To preserve the self-nourishing system by maintaining the idealized parental image, the damaged individual projects the parents' weaknesses and undesirable traits onto others. By judging their parents as right or superior and others as wrong or inferior, children (and later, adults) preserve their illusions about the family.

If the general atmosphere of the home environment is hostile and the parents inadequate or untrustworthy, the child's feeling reactions to these conditions will later be transferred to new situations and to the world at large (A. Miller, 1980/1984a; Shengold, 1989). As an adult, the individual will distort events and other people and respond to them in terms of these negative expectations. In addition, children have strong tendencies to deny and project their angry reactions to parental rejection. When present-day circumstances arouse their anger as adults, they are reminded of early experiences that frustrated or hurt them. Their anger is directed either inwardly toward themselves or projected outwardly onto others. Denying hostility toward their parents allows children to maintain the fantasized connection with them. Redirecting these aggressive impulses allays the fear of losing the actual parents or of a breakdown in the imagined fusion.

To the extent that individuals generalize these fantasized images to new people and new situations, they are reluctant to trust again and instead tend to move toward an isolated, inward state. The good parent–bad child dyadic image appears to persist into adulthood, insuring the repetition of painful and unsatisfying relationships comparable to the experiences in the early relationship constellation. People externalize the self-parenting process by acting out either the "good parent" or "bad child" image in new associations. Secondary fantasies of rejection, negative anticipations, and cynical views of others in the form of internalized voices regulate these distancing behaviors in adult attachments, thereby supporting the primary defense and illusions of pseudoindependence.[9]

On a behavioral level, increased reliance on fantasy processes tends to be progressively incapacitating because it interferes with real planning, creativity, and tangible actions directed toward the actual accomplishment of one's goals. A negative spiral of frustration, fantasy, and addiction, followed by increased frustration, is set into operation. Eventually the self-parenting process can become addictive in itself; it can persist for long periods after deprivation has ceased and predisposes negative behavioral responses (Firestone, 1984, 1993). For example, people who exist primarily in an inward state of fantasy drastically reduce their emotional exchanges with others.

In summary, people who have been hurt in their earliest relationships are fearful of taking a chance again and tend to lead restricted lives in which risks are limited and achievements are curtailed. However, as people develop a more realistic, objective appraisal of their parents and learn to tolerate ambivalent feelings toward themselves and others, there is generally marked improvement in their adjustment. Challenging clients' exaggerated images of parental goodness and the corresponding negative views of self and helping them to cope with the ensuing anxiety are important aspects of an effective psychotherapy program.

HEALTHY FUNCTIONING VERSUS RELIANCE ON SELF-PARENTING FANTASY PROCESSES

Theoretically, the self-parenting process can be understood as an addictive psychonutritional system in which the individual imagines that there are limited quantities of nourishment available in the interpersonal environment and therefore chooses to nourish him- or herself. It is possible to develop a comparative model of emotional health versus maladaptive functioning in terms of the self-parenting process. The degree to which an individual comes to rely on self-nourishing mechanisms and fantasy processes can be conceptualized as a progression ranging from external object gratification to complete autistic involvement in self-gratification. The distinctions between healthy functioning and serious psychological disturbance are generally quantitative rather than qualitative. However, as the continuum progresses and there is extensive damage to ego functioning and more serious regression, there are qualitative changes, such as delusions, hallucinations, and thought disorders.

Healthy psychological functioning and addictive propensities can be represented on a continuum, ranging from an outward lifestyle of pursuing goals in the real world to an inward lifestyle characterized by fantasy, passivity, and isolation, as delineated in Table 3.1.

THREE STATES OF FANTASY INVOLVEMENT

The attitudes and behaviors listed previously exist on a continuum from healthy functioning to serious pathology. For purposes of elucidation, they can be arbitrarily divided into three categories that describe an individual's resolution of the core conflict: (a) the individual who lives a realistic committed life, whose actions correspond to his or her aspirations and abilities; (b) the individual who, to varying degrees, uses elements of reality to reinforce and support an ongoing fantasy process rather than really investing in relationships and career; and (c) the individual with extreme propensities for fantasy and imagined fusion who moves toward increased isolation and withdrawal from other people.

TABLE 3.1
Outward Lifestyle Versus Inward Lifestyle

Outward	Inward
Social involvement	Isolation
Relatedness to others	Depersonalization
Maintaining a separate identity	Merged identity and fusion
Feeling state	Cutting off or withdrawal of affect; impersonal relating
Goal-directed behavior; self-fulfillment; self-affirmation	Seeking gratification in fantasy; self-denial; self-destructiveness
Lack of self-consciousness; realistic self-appraisal; self-assertion	Hypercritical attitudes toward the self; passivity; victimized stance
Adaptability	Nonadaptability
Facing up to pain and anxiety with appropriate affect and response	Using routinized habits, addictive personal relationships, and substances as painkillers
Self-fulfillment	Self-denial
Genitality	Masturbatory or addictive sexuality
Searching for meaning and transcending goals	Narrow focus

Note. Copyright © 2003 by The Glendon Association.

Individuals in category a exhibit considerable personal integrity—that is, their words are consistent with their actions. In contrast, people in category b tend to be self-denying to a large extent, and lack integrity in relation to their motives and desires. When they fail to take action in relation to their wants, they find it difficult or almost impossible to communicate honestly. When they deny their needs or desires, they are deceiving themselves and others; on the other hand, when they have desires that they inhibit or fail to pursue, their outward behavior contradicts their spoken motives.

Individuals in category b tend to react with discomfort or even anger to real love, recognition, or success. The source of these negative emotions is generally suppressed or rationalized because these reactions are inappropriate and irrational. The repressed feelings are redirected and either internalized in the form of self-criticism or elaborated into paranoid attitudes toward the source of gratification—that is, the person or persons responsible for the positive experience. Rejecting behavior may take the form of simple dismissal of compliments, unresponsiveness, coldness, withholding responses (holding back of affection or work performance), or misinterpretation of kindness or approval. Individuals in category c may actually become suspicious about other people's motives or develop paranoid ideation. Acting out these responses is the most important factor influencing the deterioration and breakdown in intimate relationships over the course of time.

Individuals in category b may give the outward impression that they are attempting to find satisfaction in relationships and real achievement. Instead, they use real events as a means of reinforcing or "feeding" their fantasies. They tend to value form over substance in interpersonal relationships. For example, many married couples place a strong emphasis on the symbols of love and on ritual or role-determined responses, such as remembering birthdays and anniversaries or routine sex, while otherwise treating each other indifferently or disrespectfully. Being able to maintain the form of the relationship, the roles, conventions, and routine practices, is proof that they are still in love, when in fact the substance of the relationship, the genuine affection, friendship, and love has diminished or disappeared altogether.

Many people in this category tend to mistake an internal image or feeling of love for the outward expressions of affection, respect, and concern for another person. For example, many parents assume that their inner fantasies and feelings about loving their children are comparable to outward expressions of warmth and tenderness. They feel that their children can read their minds and somehow know that they are loved. The familiar cliche repeated by a parent or a well-meaning relative to the effect that "Your father (mother) really loves you—they just don't know how to show it," confuses children rather than reassuring them. Feelings of love retained in parents' fantasies and not expressed outwardly do not reach their offspring and tend to fail to provide their children with the necessary emotional sustenance. Parents may be describing their internal state accurately; nevertheless their external actions toward their children very often contradict their internal state.

In general, it is difficult to convince parents or marital partners who are trying desperately to preserve a fantasy of love that they do not have a loving relationship. They believe that they feel love and attraction; they may spend considerable time thinking about love or daydreaming about their partner, yet their outward expressions of affection are limited or even contradicted by hostile or rejecting behavior toward their mate.

THREATS TO SELF-PARENTING FANTASY PROCESSES

Once an individual has achieved a stable, albeit limiting, balance between depending on fantasy processes or pursuing satisfaction in the real world, anything that threatens his or her solution to the conflict arouses anxiety or fear. "Positive anxiety" (Whitaker & Malone, 1953) can be precipitated by unusually rewarding experiences, personal growth, and achievement that threaten an individual's early perception of self and disturb the primary defense of self-parenting. "Negative anxiety," on the other hand, results from personal failure, excessive frustration, rejection and hurt, physical illness, separation or loss, and an awareness of one's personal mortality.

In this section, we describe four situations in life that disturb the fantasy process and arouse anxiety: (a) intrusions on self-feeding behaviors, tension-reducing routines, or addictive attachments; (b) exposure of the contradiction between people's actions and their stated goals; (c) the achievement of an unusual success or satisfaction in a relationship; and (d) threats posed to a fantasized image of greatness or exaggerated self-importance brought about by real comparisons. It is important that clients recognize that their progress toward developing realistic goals and taking steps toward these goals pose a threat to the fantasy process and self-nurturing behaviors.

Intrusions on Self-Feeding Habit Patterns and Routines

Addictive patterns of behavior, whether they involve substances, routines, or obsessive attachment to another person, often come to be preferred over genuine feeling interactions with others. The disruption of these self-parenting patterns brought about by efforts to give up an addictive substance, a compulsive routine, or fantasies of fusion that lead to an impersonal, addictive style of relating tends to arouse considerable anxiety. The rise in anxiety results in both aggressive and regressive reactions (Firestone, 1990a).

Etiology

Clinical observations have shown that even young infants avert their gaze in response to specific patterns of behavior on the part of the primary caretaker. They turn their heads away or look beyond or "through" another person (Brazelton & Greenspan, 2000; Broussard, 1979; Field, 1987; Fraiberg, Adelson, & Shapiro, 1980; Main & Solomon, 1986; Stern, 1985; Tronick, 1980). A young child can sense the parent's unwillingness to make real contact because of the parents' feelings of discomfort and anxiety, which are transmitted to the child unconsciously on a nonverbal level. They learn early on to adjust their responses accordingly (Lyons-Ruth & Zeanah, 1993; Tronick, 1980; Tronick et al., 1986).[10] As they grow older, they become refractive to warm, affectionate contact, connect to others without feeling, tend to be overly dependent, and eventually may turn to substances or compulsive routines to eliminate pain and reduce tension.

Many parents find that their infant's cries arouse painful emotions in them, bringing to the surface suppressed feelings from their own childhoods. The attempts of these parents to allay painful emotions in their offspring can deny children even the minimal frustration experiences necessary for normal development. They unwittingly teach their children self-nurturing behaviors, rituals, and routines that eventually limit them as fully functioning human beings. In cases in which there is considerable early emotional deprivation, these routines and painkilling behaviors can eventually become addictive for the child.

In the following case example, therapeutic interventions, based on the first author's theoretical position, were directed toward intruding on ritualistic behavior exhibited by a 2-year-old girl, a process that precipitated a heightened state of anxiety and powerful expressions of anger and rage.

Case Study

As she approached her second birthday, Melinda, an appealing, dark-eyed little girl, began to exhibit numerous signs of depression and withdrawal. She appeared listless, lacked energy and vitality, and often appeared lost in a world of her own. In addition, she had begun to have temper tantrums over the past six months. Only one technique seemed effective in calming her. If her mother held Melinda while standing up and walking around the room, Melinda would bury her head in her mother's shoulder, her body would become limp, and she would stop crying. She would lie silent and lifeless in her mother's arms with her eyes partly closed and glazed over. At these times, she had the appearance of a person on drugs.

Background

At the age of three weeks, Melinda began crying for long periods of time, and showed other signs of distress. Her misery seemed endless despite her parents' constant attention and concern. Melinda's mother, Mrs. S., appeared to be extremely nervous when in contact with her infant. She held her tightly and paced the floor while bouncing her up and down vigorously in a futile attempt to quiet her. Mr. S. was more passive and indulgent but took his cue from the mother and participated in the bouncing routine.

For the first year of her baby's life, Mrs. S. had exhibited symptoms of a postpartum disturbance and seriously doubted her ability to nurture her baby. In a later interview, she revealed that her mood swings at the time were the

> most severe in my life. I went from joy and happiness to complete depression. I had suicidal thoughts and feelings for the first time in my life. My internal pain was unbearable. I've been through a lot of difficult times in my life, but I

had never felt the depth of the depression I experienced being a mother.

When Melinda was six months old, Mrs. S. asked her sister-in-law to help her take care of the infant. Almost immediately, Melinda showed noticeable improvement. The extremely tense, hyperactive baby appeared calm and relaxed. It appeared that partial separation from the disturbing parental environment was a key factor in relieving Melinda's tension and incessant crying. However, all was not well.

As she entered her second year, Melinda showed signs of an inward, self-protective orientation and became increasingly refractive to physical affection. She exerted considerable effort in trying to avoid affectionate contact: she would grimace and actually recoil from affection. Typically, in a reunion situation, Melinda's face would light up with excitement and she would run straight toward the familiar figure, then veer away at the last moment. She responded to women with an automatic, impersonal clinging and rejected men, including her father.

Melinda's demands for rituals and specific activities became a major part of her social interactions. Her play was constricted and rigid, and there was considerable perseveration in her handling of toys or ordinary household objects. Her compulsivity did not allow her much freedom for interactive or even parallel play with her peers. Her bedtime routine consisted primarily of a specific pattern of songs, bedtime stories, and her favorite ritual—the familiar journey on an available shoulder with her head turned away from the world. She repeatedly requested one particular song or story; if another tune or story were suggested, she would stiffen her body and scream, "No! No! Same song! Same song!"

The little girl's voice became soft and subdued and was at times barely audible. Unless she was engaged in an activity that held her interest for the moment, her affect was somewhat flat and her face unexpressive. Melinda also manifested eating disturbances, characterized by frequent angry refusals to accept food from others, even candy, ice cream, or other favorites. The overall impression was of a little girl who seemed to have lost her natural desires. Her generalized wants were transformed into a desperate search for *something* to fill an emptiness. When she found "it," though, she was never satisfied. For example, she often cried pathetically for her mother or aunt to hold her. When her cries were complied with, she continued to wail, "Hold me, hold me," refusing to be reassured by the reality that she was being held. Her dazed state precluded contact with reality.

Melinda's parents' and aunt's efforts to nurture the small child and gratify her wants and needs appeared to be counterproductive. Each time her wishes were granted or her demands to repeat a particular activity were met, her symptoms became more pronounced. It became obvious that a different approach was necessary to prevent Melinda's further deterioration.

Treatment Strategy

At this point, Melinda's parents consulted a child psychologist, who began play therapy with her. The little girl seemed drawn to the female therapist's warm, easy-going manner and began to form an attachment to her after two or three sessions. However, it was not long before her symptoms began to manifest themselves in this new relationship. In an attempt to interrupt Melinda's compulsive, ritualistic behavior and alleviate her other symptoms, K, the therapist, intervened by (a) directly challenging her tension-reducing rituals and routines and other self-nourishing habit patterns, and (b) encouraging her to move toward nonaddictive attachments and increased autonomy.

In the playroom, Melinda soon became focused on a wind-up music box that played one of her favorite tunes. When K suggested other activities to the child, offered to read to her or simply talked with her, Melinda immediately degenerated into an uncontrollable tantrum or persisted in crying pitifully for the duration of the session.

K's primary goal at this stage of the treatment was to break the addictive, repetitive aspects of Melinda's behavior. K recounts her interventions with Melinda at this point in the therapy:

> By the third session, I became aware that Melinda was relating to me like an object rather then as a person and using me as a means for obtaining her "fix," similar to the behavior of an addict. So during the next session, when Melinda indicated that she wanted me to wind up the music box, I anticipated that she was headed for a serious tantrum. So I said "I'll play with you, but I'm not going to play the music box for you." Melinda screamed, "Play music box!" She was getting more and more into her tantrum, so I decided to let her tantrum run its course and stay with her until she got through it. I sat down next to her on the rug where she lay screaming and kicking.
>
> Melinda began screaming louder, "Play music box! Play song!" I responded: "Melinda, I would love to play with you. I'll read you a story, but I'm not going to wind up the music box."
>
> Melinda's tantrum escalated to the point where she seemed to be on the verge of complete ego-disintegration. She could barely speak, but managed to scream again and again, "Play music!"
>
> I responded by saying, "I'm so sorry to see you feeling sad." Any time I reflected what I thought she was feeling, she was furious. I had the impression that she didn't want to feel anything real—that's what she was trying to cut off with her rituals. I said again, "I'm so sorry you're feeling sad. I'd love to make you feel better."
>
> Between wails, Melinda said, "*Not* sad." I said, "Melinda, I'm sorry that you are so angry."

Melinda angrily wailed, "*Not* angry!" and continued to repeat the same words over and over: "Play song!"

I reassured her by saying, "I would love to make you feel better, but I won't play the song." Her tantrum continued for nearly 45 minutes, at which time she crawled to the edge of the rug and lay very quiet. I didn't say anything. She knew I was there beside her. Then she suddenly lifted her head and turned to look at me. She seemed to be a totally different person. She looked straight at me and asked in a normal, bright voice, "K, read story?"

She came and sat beside me, and I read her a story. During subsequent sessions, I repeated this intervention several times, and each time her tantrum was noticeably less intense and of briefer duration. She would cry for only a minute or two at the most and then come out of her angry state in a more relaxed, happy mood.

Over the next few months, the therapist continued to help Melinda to break addictive routines, supported her in "sweating through" the anxiety aroused as she gave up each favorite routine, and constantly moved her away from repetitive habit patterns. As Melinda's parents collaborated with the therapist and developed insight, they refused to indulge the child or cater to her demands but instead offered her kindness, affection, and humor, which helped bring the little girl back to life. The crisis was over.

During the therapeutic interaction, Melinda progressed through many of the withdrawal symptoms that drug abusers endure: intense anxiety, rage, depression, sadness, and mourning, and finally the recovery of affect and motivation to pursue her wants in a more appropriate and outward manner. She emerged from the series of sessions far more relaxed, happy, and centered in herself. The break with her addictions released considerable energy, and she became lively and spirited. In contrast to her previous shyness and quiet reserve, she spoke in a loud voice, clearly stating her wants, likes, and dislikes. Her isolated, ritualistic play appeared to be a thing of the past; she spontaneously initiated activities with other children and actively sought affection from her parents, relatives, and other adults.

Follow-up at age 8 indicated that Melinda is an energetic, spontaneous, happy child. She is lively and excited by her life and has positive social relationships with her peers and family members. She is highly intelligent and creative and has composed a number of poems that capture, in clear, simple language, universal themes of childhood and her unique perspective on the world around her.

Discussion

Melinda had responded to the pain and anxiety caused by her hypersensitivity and her parents' inability to cope effectively with the resulting behaviors. Her mother's depressed state also contributed to Melinda's attempts to parent herself through fantasy. This gave her an illusory sense of independence and fusion. She made the best adaptation possible under the circumstances. However, her self-parenting mechanism involved a reliance on addictive, self-feeding behaviors and routines that led to serious maladjustment at an early age. This case study illustrates that until Melinda's addictive attachments and repetitive habits were addressed and challenged, there was continual regression and depersonalization. When she was allowed to sweat out her addiction rather than being indulged, she recovered her vitality and was able to benefit from positive environmental influences that were previously of little value to her.

We contend that this treatment strategy is essential in all cases of addiction and furthermore hypothesize that there are addictive elements in each person's adjustment, based on self-gratifying fantasy processes, that limit his or her life and vitality. If the therapist or client fails to deal with the addictive processes related to symptom formation, the client will be to varying degrees restricted in his or her capacity to function in the interpersonal world and may never approach fulfillment of his or her potential for love and feeling.

Exposure of the Discrepancy Between People's Actions and Their Stated Goals

In observing both clinical and nonclinical populations, we have found that people are often dishonest about their motivations and aspirations. In other words, there is an enormous discrepancy between what most people say they want and what they can actually tolerate having. When a prized fantasy or life-long dream becomes a reality, the fantasy or dream is no longer under the person's control; one can no longer conjure up the satisfaction of one's wants in fantasy and obtain partial gratification or relief from psychological pain. It appears that many people are more adapted to being relatively unsuccessful, to *not* getting what they want, than they are to achieving success or having their dreams come true. Any disruption of anticipatory fantasies or visions of future success, as well as any disruption of the ability to blame failures on external circumstances, is typically avoided. When the discrepancy between a person's actions and his or her stated goals is pointed out or otherwise becomes apparent, his or her resistance and hostility is likely to be aroused.

Achievement of an Unusual Success or Satisfaction in a Relationship

Closely related to the threats to fantasy processes described previously—exposure of the fact that most people do not really want what they say they want—is the phenomenon of adverse reactions to and regressions that follow an atypical success or achievement of happiness in a close relationship. In general, any positive event that indicates a change in a person's identity, that disturbs his or her psychological equilibrium, that emphasizes his or her difference from the family, or that fulfills an important personal or career goal creates anxiety and fear and has the potential for precipitating a long-term regression.

It appears that the probability of regression is highest for individuals who achieve personal goals that are especially meaningful to them or who approach the attainment of the kind of life "they have always dreamed of." In general, any event that fulfills a significant personal goal has the potential for precipitating an anxiety state and subsequent regression. Serious, long-term regression can occur in relatively well-adjusted individuals when they achieve in reality a cherished fantasy they have been using as an internal source of self-gratification and for the alleviation of emotional pain and frustration.

In the business world, numerous examples of incompetency, inadequate performance, and the onset of self-destructive behavior following acknowledgment of an important achievement, a significant promotion, or the assumption of a leadership position have been documented in the literature (Clance & Imes, 1978).[11] These seemingly paradoxical reactions are understandable when one recognizes how real accomplishments disrupt fantasy processes that people have used since early childhood as a means of psychological survival. Regressions precipitated by unusual positive events can also be understood in the context of death anxiety. "Any experience that reminds an individual that he possesses strength, independence, personal power, or acknowledged value as a person will make him acutely conscious of his life and its eventual loss" (Firestone, 1990a, p. 127).

It is important to recognize that fantasy processes protect an individual from death anxiety as well as early interpersonal pain. Viewing the self-parenting process as the primary defense against both sources of pain facilitates an understanding of the full range of people's resistance to change. It clarifies why people cling to a negative self-concept learned in the family or persist in holding on to feelings of vanity and omnipotence and explains their overriding need to form illusions of fusion in their closest associations.

Threats Posed by Realistic Feedback to a Fantasized Image of Greatness or Vanity

Disruptions in self-aggrandizing fantasies occur when individuals receive realistic feedback, face direct competition in areas that hold important real or symbolic significance for them, or experience a failure. Many people have fantasies about being exceptional, special, and imagine themselves capable of performing at unrealistically high levels (Kernberg, 1980). When performance falls short of perfection, or when they receive real feedback regarding their performance, severe self-castigation and demoralization can result.

A compensatory image of exaggerated self-importance often extends to beliefs about marriage and the family. People believe their families to be superior to others and look down on different approaches to living. Marital partners believe that being specially chosen or preferred over all other rivals guarantees them immortality through specialness. Society's conventions, mores, and institutions support a myth of exclusive and enduring love in couples. Couples who vow to "forsake all others" as a way of promising fidelity often also renounce old friends, and systematically exclude new friends—potential rivals—to preserve the illusion that they are preferred forever. If this illusion is destroyed, there are dire consequences. Many times this fantasy of specialness is interrupted by the discovery of the partner's unfaithfulness, leading to catastrophic consequences for the relationship.

THE ROLE OF INTERNALIZED VOICES IN MAINTAINING SELF-PARENTING FANTASIES

Secondary fantasies of rejection, negative expectations, and cynical, hostile attitudes toward other people support a defensive function that protects the self-parenting process and illusions of self-sufficiency. These views are maintained by voices, negative thought processes that regulate behavior and cause the individual to reject positive experiences.

The voice may be experienced as partly conscious self-critical thoughts, for example, "You're unattractive. Why would anyone care for you?" "You're don't deserve love. You're just not a lovable person," or "You're not as interesting as other men (women). How can she (he) be attracted to you? You're going to be rejected." In addition, negative cognition regarding one's body and sexual performance such as, "You're not touching him (her) right. You're not excited enough, you're not going to be able to maintain your erection," often intrude into a couple's lovemaking, interrupting the flow of feeling and emotional closeness and causing partners to retreat to a less personal, more mechanical style of sexual relating.

Self-depreciating attitudes and cynical derogatory thoughts toward others are closely related in the defensive apparatus; both predispose alienation from other people, fostering a retreat to an inward, self-protective lifestyle. Warnings, admonitions, and suspicious voices about others appear to be in one's own self-interest, but they actually hinder the achievement of happiness and satisfaction in one's relationships and impair the pursuit of one's goals. "You're such a sucker to get involved with him (her). Don't get too attached." "You need your space." "No one understands you." "Only your family cares about you." "People are out to take advantage of you." "You don't need anyone." Sexual stereotypes often dictate people's behavior in relation to the opposite sex, even though these attitudes may not be subscribed to on an intellectual level: "All men want is sex. They won't commit to marriage or a loving relationship." Or "Women are unreliable and overemotional. They're childish and need to be taken care of." These negative, stereotypical attitudes influence each partner's distancing and withholding behaviors and are detrimental to relationships, particularly when they remain only partly conscious. In general, people tend to use their cynical and hostile attitudes toward other people as rationalizations for their withdrawal from intimacy and as a confirmation of their belief that they can only depend on themselves.

Individuals experience strong feelings of guilt when they act in a manner that goes against their stated goals and aspirations and, in the process, hurt others or disrupt their relationships. However, focusing on their guilt merely exacerbates the process of self-recrimination and intensifies their voice attacks, causing them to continue to act out the same harmful patterns. On the other hand, if they understood themselves and identified the destructive thought processes, they could improve their relationships or move on toward better choices in future associations.

These self-attacks and hostile attitudes toward other people are part of a self-destructive process that exists to varying degrees in each person. Seriously disturbed individuals actually hear voices as though they originate externally, as in auditory hallucinations. These extreme manifestations of the voice play an important role in the schizophrenic process and in criminal behavior.[12]

People maintain their defensive posture by holding on to negative hypotheses toward themselves and others, especially those who love them. These internalized voices can be formulated and brought clearly into consciousness through the methods of voice therapy procedures, which will be described later in this chapter and again in chapter 8.[13] By exposing negative thoughts and their antecedents, people can disrupt the idealization of the family and alter their self-image in a positive direction.

IMPLICATIONS FOR PSYCHOTHERAPY

Without exception, all of the clients from our psychotherapy practices as well as our colleagues and friends revealed they had suffered a certain amount of trauma during their formative years. Despite the best intentions of their parents, unconscious destructive forces were at work, hurting them at a time when they were most vulnerable. As a result of developing defenses and relying on fantasy processes to protect themselves against pain, anxiety, and stress, they had to struggle against the compulsion to lead defensive, addicted, inward lifestyles.

In being defended and relying on fantasy as a compensation for gratification, people generally tend to become hardened, tough, and refractive to affection and emotional exchanges, which causes incidental hurt to the people closest to them. For example, Sheila found it intolerable to accept love from the man who had made her feel that she was a lovable woman. According to Sheila:

> This new identity would have made a lie of everything I have believed about myself until now. If I had allowed Doug to love me and had not pulled away, I would have to accept his reality, that there was nothing really wrong with me, the exact opposite of how I felt in my family. It seems like such a perverse choice, but I rejected him rather than shake everything up by questioning my old identity.

Sheila's insights about the origins of her tendencies to punish people who loved her and appreciated her real qualities enabled her to develop more tolerance for love and intimacy in a subsequent relationship. In challenging her defensive pattern of not allowing love in her life, she discovered that one reason she had rejected Doug was because of her fear of being hurt again the way she had been hurt in her family. She found that, paradoxically, the same defenses and distorted beliefs about herself and others that had shielded her from overwhelming pain and distress when she was small now restricted her life and prevented her from finding happiness in a meaningful love relationship.

Our primary goal in working with clients has been to help them move away from their defenses, negative views of self, and self-gratifying behaviors so that they can expand their lives and tolerate more gratification in reality. A secondary, related goal is to help the client remain open to experience and feelings and maintain the ability to respond appropriately to both positive and negative events in life. We have found that the procedures of voice therapy significantly enlarge the client's boundaries and bring about a more positive sense of self.

THE METHODS OF VOICE THERAPY

Voice therapy is a cognitive–affective–behavioral methodology. It is cognitive because it helps to elicit and identify, on a conscious level, a person's negative thoughts and attitudes toward self. It is affective in that it brings these thoughts into consciousness, along with the accompanying feelings such as anger and sadness associated with these thoughts. It is behavioral because there is focus on changing the behaviors that are self-limiting or self-destructive. Voice therapy procedures are composed of three components: (Step I) the process of eliciting and identifying negative thought patterns and releasing the associated affect; (Step II) discussing the resultant insights regarding the sources of the voice and making connections between destructive thoughts and self-destructive behaviors; and (Step III) collaboratively planning corrective experiences to counteract self-destructive behaviors regulated by the voice. These three components are not necessarily undertaken in this order. Voice therapy is not interpretative or analytical in the sense that clients form their own conclusions about the sources of their destructive thinking.

In Step I, clients verbalize their negative thoughts *toward* themselves in the second person, "you," as though they were talking to themselves, instead of the first person, "I," statements *about* themselves. Statements such as "I'm so incompetent, I always make mistakes" become *"You're* so incompetent. *You* always make mistakes."* Putting self-attacking statements in this form often releases strong affect followed by spontaneous insights, which are then discussed with the therapist during Step II. In Step III, clients formulate the interests that are part of their identity (the self system) and the unique values that give their lives special meaning. Then, with the therapist, they plan steps to take toward fulfilling these goals. As they take risks in changing well-established behaviors and move toward a new level of vulnerability, they learn to tolerate the anxiety involved in positive change.

In a number of the chapters that follow, we describe the procedures of voice therapy in more detail and delineate other methods that clinicians can use in helping their patients deal with limitations imposed by the formation of defenses. Becoming aware of one's defensive behaviors and self-protective lifestyles is a first step in disrupting the defensive apparatus. Patients can come to realize that most of their defenses are no longer necessary for survival in adult life. It is also important that they recognize that their fears of changing long-standing patterns is understandable because these defenses were formed during childhood when they had little or no control over their lives.

With clients entering therapy, the therapist would be aware that the feelings of anxiety, pain, and sadness that motivated them to seek professional help are, in all probability, indications of an awakening; they are actually healthy signs that painkilling defenses are breaking down. As therapy proceeds, the process of identifying the dictates of the voice and regaining feeling for oneself lead the development of countermeasures—ways of living and being that challenge the tendency to relive the past rather than one's current life. In tracing the source of their destructive thoughts and beliefs to early interactions in the family, clients also tend to develop more compassion for themselves regarding how they were damaged in the process of growing up. In addition, by stressing the importance of each client valuing him- or herself simply for being alive, the therapist communicates his or her belief that each person has worth as a unique human being and that a person's worth is not dependent simply on performance.

CORRECTIVE SUGGESTIONS IN PSYCHOTHERAPY TO FACILITATE MOVEMENT TOWARD REAL SATISFACTION

Collaborative interventions that effect changes in an individual's behavior in his or her everyday life are a necessary part of any effective therapeutic procedure. As noted, they are the third, and perhaps the most important step in voice therapy methodology. Therapist and client cooperate in planning corrective experiences[14] that bear a direct relationship to the addictive or maladaptive behaviors that are being influenced by the client's negative cognitions. These fall into two broad categories: (a) corrective suggestions that help interrupt the client's self-feeding habits and his or her reliance on fantasy and addictive attachments for gratification; and (b) corrective suggestions that expand the client's world by encouraging him or her to take risks and gradually overcome fears related to pursuing wants and priorities.

Even in the beginning phases of psychotherapy, corrective suggestions can be used to encourage clients to avoid the addictive substances and habit patterns they use to suppress feeling. Implementing a suggestion that breaks a self-nourishing behavior or painkilling routine is often a first step toward change on a deep character level. Although it is often difficult for the alcoholic, drug user, or client with an eating disorder to maintain the resolution to alter his or her addictive patterns throughout the course of treatment, it is necessary for a successful prognosis.

Breaking into addictive patterns of relating can be as difficult as disrupting an addiction to a physical substance. The difficulty is partly a result of the fact that people are often unaware that they have sacrificed their individuality to become one half of a couple for purposes of security, or that their original feelings of friendship, love, and sexual attraction may have diminished. Thus, a suggestion that could benefit couples involved in a fantasy bond is to admit the true state of their relationship, recognize they are in a fantasy of closeness, and stop denying the fact that they have become distant and that their actions are no longer loving.

To help clients understand the origins of their fears related to pursuing gratification in interpersonal relationships, it is worthwhile to suggest that they write a personal history, including a description of significant childhood events; as well as their current relationships; personal and career concerns; and special desires, goals, and aspirations. Through the process of recording early painful experiences of deprivation, clients also come to understand that early experiences in the family necessitated a retreat into fantasy and dependence on self-nurturing behaviors. In making a sharp distinction between past and present, they often begin to challenge beliefs that they cannot survive if they have to face again the primitive longings and the rejection they experienced early in life. This realization helps them overcome their fears of taking a chance again on seeking satisfaction in a new relationship. They recognize that they no longer have to respond to situations as though they were still utterly dependent on their parents for survival.

The information gathered from the history also helps therapists assess their clients' special wants, priorities, and goals. The process of identifying a client's particular wants and aspirations facilitates therapists' awareness, in subsequent sessions, of the client's body language and other behavioral cues (increased rate of speaking, eye contact, a fleeting smile, or a light in his or her eyes) indicative of his or her specific interests, goals, or aspirations. This awareness is vital as clients begin to uncover their unique points of identity and move toward their stated goals. Gradually they allow the self system to emerge and take precedence over the antiself system.

An important corrective suggestion involves the client's setting definite goals for what he or she wants in interpersonal relationships or career pursuits. Clients are encouraged first to record their goals in writing in a journal and second to write down the actions they need to take to accomplish their goals.[15] Then therapists encourage the client to increase his or her participation in chosen activities, projects, or friendships and take risks that reach out to others and leave them open to new experiences.

USE OF CORRECTIVE SUGGESTIONS IN THE FRIENDSHIP CIRCLE

Corrective suggestions have also been used by people in the friendship circle.[16] Over the past 25 years, we have arrived at some basic hypotheses about people's fundamental resistance to change, based on observations of individuals in this milieu. The most interesting finding was the fact that people exposed to a better life are refractory to it because it threatens core psychological defenses. The intolerance of real acknowledgment, affection, and love was observable in individuals' career pursuits and their closest relationships. Despite these difficulties, over the years most of the people gained insight into these adverse reactions and have gradually come to accept more acknowledgment and affection.

The procedures they developed to alter their defenses began informally, as general trends, but later became more specific in their application to diverse problem areas. These suggestions and methods mitigated against the use of addictive substances, social isolation, deadening routines, and role-determined behavior that cut off feelings. Individuals found that altering routine habit patterns released energy that previously had been used in the service of an inward, self-protective lifestyle.

In their interactions with their families and friends and in their group discussions, these people placed a high value on honesty and compassion. As a result, they learned to look at themselves realistically by talking openly about themselves and sharing their perceptions with their friends. By listening to feedback, they developed a more realistic and often a more congenial attitude toward themselves. Learning to accept constructive criticism without becoming defensive helped them identify self-defeating behaviors that had sabotaged the achievement of their stated goals, and as a result, they were able to make their actions correspond more closely to their expressed desires.

Challenging the Idealization of Parents and Negative Self-Image

In the forum of open discussion that evolved, these people succeeded in breaking down the defensive idealization of their own parents and helped their children develop a more objective, realistic picture of themselves and other family members. Parents did not attempt to disguise their limitations; rather, they spoke honestly and forthrightly about their shortcomings. In the accepting atmosphere of their talks, parents were not blamed or castigated. Instead, insights were used to develop an objective view of parents and family members that included both the good and the bad.

In the discussions, all opinions were respected, including those of children. No one interrupted or interfered when children and adolescents described their perceptions of their parents and other adults. In addition, there were opportunities for children to observe their parents interacting with other adults and children in a wide range of situations. This relatively objective view of each person's unique personal qualities was conducive to disrupting internalized negative self-attitudes as well as compensatory attitudes of vanity and superiority.

In the group meetings, people learned to identify their hostile views of themselves by verbalizing their self-critical thoughts in the second person, "You're incompetent, you're worthless," as though someone else were talking to them. They identified these destructive thoughts and attitudes as originating from interactions within their original family that had been particularly painful or anxiety-provoking. Uncovering these negative attitudes toward self gave people a perspective on their parents' point of view toward them, which, in turn, helped them to modify these views and develop a more positive self-image.

Within the couple, individuals developed insight into the ways they were symbolically holding on to idealized views of parents and family. By disclosing or giving away distorted views that either idealized or denigrated their partner, they developed a more objective and empathic perspective on one another. They came to understand that maintaining an idealized view of their partner represented a projection of the idealized image of their parent or parents onto the substitute parental figure and, similarly, that holding on to a depreciated view of their partners often reflected the projection of the parent's negative traits onto the other. The process of identifying these distorted views enabled partners to take back these projections and assume responsibility for their own behavior, which reduced tension in their interactions.

Overcoming Fears and Moving Toward Real Satisfaction

Disclosing their fears about being close in a relationship allowed people to face their anxiety about rejection and move toward their goal of achieving personal fulfillment in their intimate associations. By listening to the stories of other couples, partners learned how compulsive routines that had given them a certain level of comfort and security had detracted from the happiness and satisfaction they could achieve together. For example, many found that they had developed certain rituals and habitual ways of communicating and interacting that detracted from the spontaneity that had once characterized their relationship. Some couples revealed that they had fallen into a routine of making love only at certain times, and others had established habitual patterns of scheduling mealtimes, weekend activities, and vacations so that there was little variation, uncertainty, or spontaneity in their everyday lives. These patterns had effectively drained much of the vitality and excitement from their relationship. They discovered that by giving up these deadening routines and becoming open to new experiences, they became more vulnerable, which had a positive effect on other aspects of their relating.

In discussions in which many couples participated, partners often faced the unpleasant truth that their self-protective inward behaviors had gradually eroded the original feelings of love between them and that their relationship was based more on a fantasy of love and connection than on real feeling. Exposing the destructive elements of the fantasy bond and behaviors that supported their sense of a merged identity opened up the possibility for genuine relating on a more personal basis.

In their business ventures, the same atmosphere of direct communication existed, and there were frank discussions between management and other personnel. Psychological defenses underlying poor work habits were identified and worked through as people talked together in the straightforward, compassionate style that they had developed in other areas of their lives. The energy and vitality resulting from breaking withholding defenses, habits of procrastination, victimization, vanity and status-seeking, and being able to speak candidly without fear of retaliation led to high productivity for the business ventures and individual successes for the employees. In recognizing the importance of identifying and pursuing one's own unique desires and priorities, management encouraged employees to explore their interests and aptitudes and to seek their own particular niche in the companies.[17]

Individuals in the friendship circle who planned and put into action these corrective suggestions became more vital and lively, responded with more appropriate affect to events in their lives, and became more centered in themselves. We found that corrective suggestions, used within this social context, acted as catalysts to help individuals approach new, unfamiliar, or open-ended situations in which they were more vulnerable, less defended, and in which their actions were based more on reality considerations rather than fantasized images.

CONCLUSION

Early in life, satisfactions achieved by the deprived child in fantasy and self-parenting mechanisms eventually come to be preferred over real gratification because they help to alleviate painful emotions and allow the child to maintain an illusion of control. Once the fantasized connection is formed and the parental introjects well-established, people have a strong resistance to investing emotionally in genuinely satisfying relationships. The principal goal, then, is to maintain the imagined safety and security of the fantasy bond at the expense of personal fulfillment.

Until people learn to take definitive actions in opposition to the prohibitions of the internalized voice, they will continue to live in a narrow range of experience with significant limitations. Developing an awareness of destructive voices that preserve the idealization process and attack the self, disrupting habitual routines and addictive styles of relating, and challenging compensatory feelings of vanity and superiority, all help to break down self-parenting fantasy processes and enhance an individual's capacity to cope with the real world. Corrective suggestions that function to challenge internalized thoughts or voices facilitate the process of change and contribute to the development of a greater tolerance for an emotionally richer, more fulfilling life.

We believe that the ultimate goals of psychotherapy are to help people achieve a free and independent existence, find satisfaction in interpersonal relationships, remain open to experience, and respond with appropriate affect to both positive and negative events in their lives. The aim is not to change people but to offer each person the maximum possibility for growth consistent with their own desires or motivations. Voice therapy techniques do not represent an onslaught on defenses or an attack on the way people choose to live; rather, they imply a sensitive interrelationship characterized by respect for individuals and their right to make choices, even when they choose to be defended.

While recognizing the pervasiveness and essential destructiveness of defenses, therapists must understand that people come by their defenses honestly in the sense that events in their early lives led to the necessary adaptation for psychological survival. For example, although therapists point out significant blocks to a client's overall development, they respect the fact that the ultimate decision to challenge or disrupt fantasies of fusion, addictive habit patterns, and anxious attachments rests with each individual.

A person's potential for future development should not be compromised by treatment processes that focus on the amelioration of symptoms and relief of anxiety to the exclusion of understanding and coping with character defenses and powerful inimical forces within the personality. If these forces are not dealt with successfully and defenses remain intact, the therapeutic relationship may inadvertently deprive the person of his or her opportunity to live fully. Voice therapy encourages people to live life as a continuous process of discovery and adventure, with uncritical acceptance of their most irrational thoughts and feelings. The therapeutic venture, through counteracting the dictates of the voice and disrupting fantasies of connection to internal images and external objects, offers people the opportunity to fulfill their human potentialities.

NOTES

1. In *By Force of Fantasy*, Person (1995) provided descriptions of the creative uses of fantasy both on an individual level and in terms of generating cultural myths. Person also emphasized that fantasy processes encompass much of conscious and unconscious mental activity.
2. See Blatt and Erlich's (1982) discussion of a form of resistance that "is against change per se and the disruption of an established equilibrium. There are intense pressures to inhibit growth, a fear of the future, of change and the unknown" (p. 74).
3. Bollas (1987) cited a case history in *The Shadow of the Object* that illuminates the dynamics discussed in this section. Bollas's patient:

   Somatized conflict in order to regress into a mother–child relation, where she was the object of a mothering part of her that was always presenting herself with medicines and comforting words. . . . She would quite literally have a conversation with herself in which the mothering part would say, "Don't listen to him [the therapist]); he's just trying to upset you," and the little girl part of her would feel fearful and hurt, and quite angry with me. (pp. 57–58)

4. Movement in any direction—a retreat further into fantasy and self-parenting or movement toward external goal-directed behavior—is accompanied either by negative or positive anxiety. See Whitaker and Malone's (1953) discussion of positive and negative anxiety in *The Roots of Psychotherapy*.

5. See Leahy's (2001) discussion of the seven dimensions of patient resistance in *Overcoming Resistance in Cognitive Therapy* (pp. 283–287); Blatt and Erlich's (1982), "A Critique of the Concepts of Resistance in Behavior Therapy"; and Ghent's (1999) chapter, "Masochism, Submission, Surrender," where he makes the important distinction between submission and surrender in discussing resistance. Also see Neborsky and Solomon's (2001) description of complexity theory (D. Siegel, 1999) as a means for understanding resistance and Otto Rank's (Kramer, 1996) concept of "constructive resistance."

6. The other major components of the defensive process are discussed in subsequent chapters: inward, self-nourishing habit patterns and routines; a progressive loss of feeling for self and others; a passive, victimized orientation toward life; and withholding—a holding back or withdrawal of positive responses from others and passive–aggressive manifestations.

7. The correlation between an idealized image of the parent and the "bad" self-image has been investigated empirically by Blatt et al. (1998), using the Differentiation–Relatedness Scale (Diamond, Blatt, Stayner, & Kaslow, 1991). These researchers discussed the development of schemas of self and others—in other words, "internal working models" that "are constructed in interpersonal transactions that begin with the infant–caregiver relationship" (p. 65).

8. See Auerbach's (1993) discussion of "The Necessity of Narcissism and a Possible Transcendence Through Intersubjectivity" (pp. 88–93).

9. Internalized voices may be hypothesized as part of the multisystems of internal working models as well as the "segregated systems" first described by John Bowlby (1980): "The generalizations about mother, father and self enshrined in what I am terming working models or representational models will be stored semantically (in either analogical, propositional or some combined format)" (p. 62). "Within the framework proposed we can best conceive the self and how it may be possible also to conceive of a person having more than one self" (p. 63). "The information [of one working model] likely to be defensively excluded is of a kind that, when accepted for processing in the past, has led the person concerned to suffer more or less severely" (p. 69).

   Also see Fonagy's (2001) chapter, "How Can Attachment Theory Benefit From Psychoanalytic Insights?" and Bornstein's (1993) research related to the correlation between internal working models and adult psychopathology. See additional research regarding internal working models or mental representations in J. Solomon and George (1999) and George, West, and Pettem (1999).

10. Tronick (1980) reported that "when mothers held a frozen posture and a still face while looking toward their infants, the babies looked away and eventually slumped away with a hopeless facial expression" (p. 7). Lyons-Ruth and Zeanah (1993) also found that in these instances, "Several self-regulatory behaviors are at the infant's disposal, including looking away from a disturbing

event, self-soothing as seen in thumb sucking, or self-stimulating behaviors" (p. 21).

11. For example, Welldon (1988) reported the case of a woman for whom:

    professional success was unconsciously linked with killing her mother. The latter was literally experienced by her as an "internal saboteur" who would undermine all her efforts to succeed. We can clearly see in this patient the splitting between her "libidinal ego" and the "internal saboteur" described by Fairbairn. (p. 25)

12. See *A Concept of the Schizophrenic Process* (Firestone, 1957) and "Assessing Violent Thoughts: The Relationship Between Thought Processes and Violent Behavior" (Doucette-Gates, Firestone, & Firestone, 1999).

13. Voice therapy was so named because it is a process of giving spoken words to the negative thought processes that regulate an individual's maladaptive and self-limiting behavior (Firestone, 1990c).

14. The term *corrective emotional experience* was first suggested by Franz Alexander (cited by Arlow, 1989) to describe procedures applied to cases that had been generally refractory to treatment.

15. Regarding maintaining a daily log, see Jerome Singer's (1998) report on the MacArthur Foundation-sponsored Program on Conscious and Unconscious Mental Processes.

16. As noted in the preface, we have divided each of the chapters in Parts II and III (chapters 3 through 13) into two sections. The first section focuses on methods, including voice therapy, that therapists can use in their psychotherapeutic practice; the second section focuses on corrective suggestions used and insights gained by participants in the friendship circle. Therapists may also find these suggestions and insights useful in helping facilitate change in their clients.

17. The companies included a jewelry importing business, a computer distribution company, a commercial interior design company, and more recently, a telecommunications corporation. The application of psychological principles to these business organizations has been documented in video documentaries, *Of Business and Friendship* (Parr, 1987) and in *Friendship: A Life of Meaning and Compassion* (Parr, 2002).

4

CHALLENGING ADDICTIVE, SELF-NURTURING LIFESTYLES

Addiction is an emotional relationship with an object or event, through which addicts try to meet their needs for intimacy.
—Craig Nakken (1996, p. 8)

One of the most important challenges facing individuals who are motivated to live a more vulnerable, less defended lifestyle is learning to give up addictive habit patterns they have used to cope with psychological pain. Children develop their self-nurturing behaviors to help them survive a less than ideal parental environment. Unfortunately, the methods that they adopt to numb their pain or reduce their emotional distress become habit-forming and, to varying degrees, generalize to an addictive lifestyle.

THE DEVELOPMENT OF SELF-NURTURING LIFESTYLES

In this chapter, we focus on a specific component of the defensive process that helps preserve the core defense of self-parenting: self-nurturing behavior patterns, including addictive modes of relating to another person. Self-nourishing behaviors begin early in life, in the form of thumb-sucking or masturbatory activity, for example. As children grow older, they develop increasingly sophisticated habits and techniques with which to parent or "feed" themselves. Activities such as nail-biting, smoking, drinking, excessive masturbation, addictive sex, and drug abuse are relied on for self-gratification, relief of tension, and partial fulfillment of needs (Firestone, 1993).

87

An increased involvement with addictive substances, habitual responses, and rituals interferes with goal-directed activity in the real world and limits gratification in one's personal relationships. These addictive habits and lifestyles are closely linked to patterns of withholding, self-denial, and fantasy involvement in that they function to reduce emotional transactions with other people.

The self-parenting process is often extended to include other persons, taking the form of addictive attachments. Many couples form a fantasy bond in which they maintain an illusion of being fused as a substitute for real love and closeness, which may be difficult to tolerate. The gradual decline in personal relating, sexual attraction, and desire that occurs in so many relationships has its basis in one or both partners' tendencies to hold on to their core defense of self-parenting and in their pseudoindependent orientation to life.

Addictive behaviors associated with a self-nurturing lifestyle can be divided into three groups: (a) addiction to physical substances; (b) addiction to compulsive, ritualistic behavior; and (c) addictive attachments, in which one or both partners uses the other primarily to relieve feelings of anxiety and insecurity.

ADDICTION TO PHYSICAL SUBSTANCES

Many people suffer from eating disorders as a result of the addictive substitution of food as a source of emotional gratification. Eating often becomes a primary focus for children who are starved for affection, attention, and care. In these cases, people's eating habits take on a meaning other than simple enjoyment or gratification of physical hunger. When food is repeatedly used to minimize or numb emotional hunger, it can result in cycles of overeating and dieting, or binging and purging. These inward, self-feeding patterns are seriously maladaptive.

In this chapter, we relate the story of Trish, an attractive, articulate 40-year-old accountant, who as a teenager had been heavily involved in drugs and binge-eating. She felt progressively more self-hating and eventually made two serious suicide attempts. Over the course of therapy, she gradually altered her dependence on physical substances and made progress in her personal relationships. As noted in the preface, in the following segment, the first author is referred to as "Dr. Firestone" to indicate his professional role as psychotherapist in the session.

In a session, Trish talked about her decision to give up the last remnant of her long-standing eating disorder: her pattern of eating alone. She described her reactions to altering this habit in the interview:

Trish:	Thanksgiving was the other day and it was the first time—I hate to use the word first time, it sounds so dramatic—but literally the first time in my life that I wasn't thinking about what was going to be served. I looked forward to the occasion. It made me so sad that night just to be there with my family and friends, but I know I couldn't really touch what I was feeling. I'm afraid to be without that fascination of food in my life.
Dr. Firestone:	Why do you think the food became so important to you in the context of what we're talking about?
Trish:	Well, I know I was starved as a child. I don't know if that has anything to do with why it was important. I don't know.
Dr. Firestone:	How do you mean starved?
Trish:	Well, literally. My mother was very fat. She was about five foot two and weighed 210 pounds when I was young. And she always said, "I'm going to keep you thin no matter what." I remember that from when I was tiny. So she controlled everything I ate, very strongly, to the point where I couldn't sleep because I was so hungry. That led to a whole secretive thing of sneaking food and eating horrible food, because you can't eat anything healthy when you're sneaking it fast, on the run sort of.
Dr. Firestone:	So you were tampering with a life-long pattern actually, to give that up.

Trish had revealed earlier that as a child, she would smuggle food from the kitchen, take it to her closet, and consume it quickly. She usually took an entire box of cookies from a grocery bag, hoping that her mother would not remember purchasing it. When she had eaten the cookies, she would tear up the package and hide the pieces in the toes of her shoes. After her mother left the house, Trish would take the pieces of the package outside to the trash.

Trish:	I've always thought it was just the food, but now I know the isolation was as meaningful to me as the actual food.
Dr. Firestone:	A safe place, in other words.
Trish:	(sad, tearful) A safe place. That's right. A safe place. Like warm, like a good-feeling place. Sort of what my closet was when I was growing up, because that's where I would eat, and it was small and warm. It felt actually like being held because it was small. Also after I stopped eating alone, I think that I started to want things that

	I don't usually want, but I'm very uncomfortable with that feeling.
Dr. Firestone:	You mean when you gave up eating that way in isolation.
Trish:	Yes. My boyfriend went away, and I missed him so much, but I couldn't communicate that to him. I'm very uncomfortable with wanting because it feels too strong, and it feels inappropriate in that sense.
Dr. Firestone:	So breaking that addiction really made you feel real wanting.
Trish:	Yes, it did.

In the case of anorexia nervosa and bulimia, the self-feeding may actually pose a threat to the general health and life of the individual (Chernin, 1985; Claude-Pierre, 1997; Sandbek, 1993). A number of studies indicate a correlation between other addictive behaviors and eating disorders. For example, Zerbe (1993) cited findings from a study showing that "at least 30% and perhaps as many as 50% of patients with bulimia nervosa also have a history of current or prior substance abuse" (p. 224). These disorders are also associated with self-parenting in that the person is feeding him- or herself instead of accepting emotional resources from outside.

Patients with serious eating disorders, the large majority of whom are young women, are generally cut off from their feelings and lack a clear awareness of the sensation of hunger. The anoretic patient's refusal of food often reflects a desperate attempt to ward off the extreme anxiety or panic associated with early feeding experiences. In her book, *The Hungry Self*, Kim Chernin (1985) pointed out that inconsistent maternal care[1] is found in the childhoods of many women diagnosed with eating disorders: "This sense of the mother's actual or impending breakdown has burdened the childhood and adolescence of women with eating disorders. Again and again we find a vision, carefully hidden, of the mother's inner collapse and emotional crisis" (p. 77).

In relation to deficits in paternal caregiving, Kasl (1989), in *Women, Sex, and Addiction*, discussed the comorbidity of sexual addiction, codependency, and substance abuse that she had observed in many of her clients: "Many sexually addicted and codependent women have traits of or diagnosable cases of anorexia and bulimia" (p. 184). In her description of factors that may contribute to this particular constellation of addictive symptomatology, Kasl called attention to a specific form of paternal rejection: the "sudden withdrawal from daughters when they reach adolescence," and noted that:

This is extremely common, especially with fathers who can relate to a daughter as genderless until she develops a woman's body. Uneasy about his own sexual feelings for her and unable to deal with his discomfort or shame, a father may withdraw from her. (p. 262)

According to Herman (1981), incest or seductive behavior on the part of fathers is also correlated with addictive behavior, depression, and suicide attempts in adolescent and adult women. In her study of 40 women, she found that:

The pathological effects of overt and covert incest were similar in nature and differed mainly in degree, the daughters of seductive fathers exhibiting in milder form many of the same symptoms that in the incest victims were developed to great severity. (p. 125)

DRUG ABUSE AND ALCOHOLISM

The same issues of self-parenting that are operating in eating disorders are central in drug abuse and alcoholism.[2] Experts who have studied addiction emphasize the ability of drugs "to obliterate mental anguish and provide primitive need gratification" (E. Kaufman, 1974, p. 364). In a review article, Blatt, McDonald, Sugarman, and Wilber (1984) showed that most addicts are

reluctant or unable to seek satisfaction in normal interpersonal relationships and instead remain aloof and independent and use the drug to induce a blissful, symbiotic, narcissistic state. The drug replaces interpersonal relationships as a primary source of achieving satisfaction and pleasure. (p. 168)

Clinicians and researchers have explored the link between drug abuse and early deprivation or trauma. Khantzian, Mack, and Schatzberg (1974) conceptualized heroin addiction as a compensatory "self-caring" and self-regulating mechanism. They concluded that the drug becomes the only means for achieving the security and satisfaction that would ideally have been experienced in the early relationship with the mother. Their formulations are closely related to our views of the defensive function served by the self-parenting process.

The negative thought process or voice plays an important role in eating disorders and addictive behaviors, including excessive drug use and alcoholism. First, the person is exhorted to indulge in the habit and later punished for submitting to this weakness. For example, the alcoholic tells him- or herself: *"Why don't you have a drink? What harm will it do? You really need it to relax with these people tonight."* Later, after capitulating to the voice, the attack becomes, *"You're a hopeless drunk! You never live up to your resolutions. You've let your family down again!"* In an effort to alleviate the pain of these vicious self-recriminations, the person invariably resorts to more painkillers, and the cycle continues.

It is difficult to break these patterns, because the anxiety allayed by the use of substances resurfaces during withdrawal. There are painful emotions of sadness or rage that are complicated by childlike or regressive behavior when people attempt to abstain from the use of these substances.

ADDICTION TO ROUTINES AND HABITUAL RESPONSES

Routines and rituals dull people's sensitivity to painful feelings by lending an air of certainty and seeming permanence to a real life of uncertainty and impermanence. Behaviors or rituals that temporarily reduce anxiety have the potential of becoming compulsive, as they did in the case of Melinda, described in chapter 3. Patients with obsessive–compulsive disorder who also have an anxiety disorder often experience panic attacks when unable to perform their rituals (Kozak & Foa, 1997; Levenkron, 1991). The anticipatory anxiety related to the threat of a panic attack reinforces the need to engage in the ritualistic, habitual behavior. When these habits intensify, they become seriously maladaptive, consuming increasing amounts of the person's time and energy and limit his or her life.

Obsessive–compulsive disorder (OCD) is "characterized by recurring, intrusive thoughts (obsessions), usually accompanied by repetitive, seemingly purposeful behaviors (compulsions), such as ritualistic washing" (Zohar & Insel, 1987/1997, p. 277). According to Zohar and Insel, "the symptoms are often refractory to psychodynamic treatments . . . and thus several new approaches to the syndrome have evolved" (p. 277). Jeffrey Schwartz (1996) asserted that the disorder "is related to a biochemical problem in the brain . . . [in which] four key structures of the brain become locked together, and the brain starts sending false messages that the person cannot readily recognize as false" (p. xv).

In his outline of a four-step treatment strategy, Schwartz recommended first relabeling the "intrusive thought or urge to do a troublesome compulsive behavior" (p. xxi); second, reattributing the origin of the symptom, saying "I have a medical condition called OCD. I am having the symptoms of a medical problem"; third, refocusing "your attention on another behavior and doing something useful and positive" (p. xxi); and fourth, revaluing— learning "to devalue unwanted obsessive thoughts and compulsive urges as soon as they intrude" (pp. xxi–xxii). Several elements of Schwartz's intervention are similar in certain respects to voice therapy procedures that are used to identify and then separate out self-destructive thoughts from a realistic point of view.

On a subclinical level, people can become addicted to habitual activities and compulsive behaviors that are considered to be acceptable or even desirable, such as overworking, watching television, video and computer games, browsing the Internet, reading, gambling, shopping, and exercising. These types of activities are potentially addictive because they are primarily inward, self-involved, and narcissistic.

Excessive masturbation to reduce tension is generally a symptom of emotional deprivation. The child discovers that touching his or her genitals not only leads to pleasant sensations but tends to neutralize emotional distress. This activity can develop into a self-soothing, isolated method of taking care of oneself. When habitual masturbation persists in the extreme, becoming preferable to sexual activity with another person, it is representative of a self-feeding process and inward lifestyle.

SEXUAL PROBLEMS IN ADULT RELATIONSHIPS BASED ON THE SELF-PARENTING PROCESS

Sexual relationships can also function as painkillers when they are used as a means of partially gratifying primitive longings and deeply repressed oral needs (Carnes, 1991, 1992; Kasl, 1989).[3] Many couples develop a routinized, mechanical style of love-making. At the same time, they may hold back their affection or a full sexual response. There is an emphasis on control and fantasy to increase excitement when self-gratifying, withholding modes of sexual relating come into play. Whenever sex is being used primarily for control, power plays, manipulation, security, self-soothing—that is, for purposes other than its natural functions of pleasure, procreation, and as an emotionally rewarding exchange between two people—there is generally a deterioration in the sexual relationship (Firestone & Catlett, 1999).

An understanding of how fantasy and the self-parenting process operate in addictive sexual relating and disorders of low sexual desire is important in helping people overcome these problems. Sexual problems are often manifestations of an individual's retreat from offering gratification to or seeking gratification from other persons. This may be expressed through sexual symptoms in the male of premature ejaculation, retarded ejaculation, or impotence; or in the female through unresponsiveness and an inability to achieve orgasm. Many women unconsciously avoid being attractive, for example, by putting on weight, thereby discouraging men from approaching them. In this example, they are directly feeding themselves and acting out the self-parenting process. It is generally not the actual weight as such (except in extreme cases of obesity) that puts the man off, but rather the woman's negative attitude and feeling about her body that discourage her from wanting sex and inevitably affect her partner's attraction to her.

A man may also feel resentful of needing a woman sexually and may, through masturbation, sustain the infantile fantasy that he can take care of himself, that he does not need her. When a man feels unlovable, inadequate, or empty emotionally, he is often restricted in his ability to give. He may feel that he is unable to care for or satisfy a woman and may avoid her sexually or become uncommunicative and distant. If he perceives her as being emotionally hungry and desperate toward him, he may experience her desire for sex as a demand. He may be afraid that she will drain him, will take everything from him. Therefore, he may become especially withholding and unresponsive. In general, the majority of sexual problems in relationships can be traced back to the core defense of self-parenting and the secondary fantasies or internalized voices that sustain it (Firestone, 1990d).

ADDICTIVE ATTACHMENTS—THE FORMATION OF A FANTASY BOND IN COUPLE RELATIONSHIPS

The process of forming a fantasy bond or addictive attachment with one's partner greatly reduces the chance of achieving a satisfying relationship or marriage. Most men and women are unaware of their tendency to give up their individuality to become one half of a couple, to merge themselves with another person for purposes of security. The feelings of love, friendship, and sexual attraction that exist in the initial phases of a relationship tend to arouse painful emotions of sadness and grief from the past, as well as fears of potential rejection or abandonment. In an attempt to avoid reexperiencing these feelings, one or both partners generally retreats to a defended posture and reestablishes psychological equilibrium, thereby maintaining the familiarity of the past and creating emotional distance in the relationship.

Early symptoms of deterioration include diminished frequency of eye contact; a sense of obligation; a decrease in spontaneity, playfulness, and honest communication; and a waning of feelings of sexual attraction. Partners usually try to preserve their original feelings of attraction and love while they hold on to habitual methods of self-gratification and a pseudoindependent posture. The two conditions are mutually exclusive. The dilemma is obscured by a fantasy of love and closeness, while real love, friendship, and concern are gradually replaced by intrusive, possessive styles of relating or by avoidance and withdrawal. People try to cover up the reality of their diminished love and affection with a fantasy of enduring love and substitute *form* for the *substance* of the relationship. The human capacity for self-deception enables the partners to maintain an internal image of closeness and intimacy, while acting in ways that contrast with any recognizable definition of love.

When either partner attempts to move away from the addictive attachment toward independence or autonomy, symptoms similar to those manifested in withdrawal from chemical dependency are aroused in the other. These symptoms include feelings of desperation, emotional hunger, disorientation, and debilitating anxiety states. The intensity of these emotional reactions indicates the powerful nature of the imagined connection or fantasy bond existing between the partners.

A PSYCHOTHERAPEUTIC APPROACH TO ADDICTIVE, SELF-NURTURING BEHAVIORS AND LIFESTYLES

The goal of psychotherapy is to help individuals move away from addictive lifestyles so that they can expand their lives and tolerate more gratification in real interactions and relationships. A necessary objective is to provide them with an authentic relationship during the transition from relying on addictive substances to seeking and finding satisfaction in genuine relationships outside the office setting. Therapists need to actively confront the person's self-nourishing habit patterns without being judgmental or parental. At the same time, the transitional relationship with the therapist makes reality more rewarding. The approach is twofold in its focus: (a) it challenges and disrupts the addictive patterns, and (b) it encourages movement toward real gratification and autonomy in the external environment.

An addicted person's lack of self-control and compulsive involvement in self-nurturing behaviors point up an important prerequisite for therapy: It is necessary for the person to give up addictions before any real therapy takes place (Black, 1981; Seixas & Youcha, 1985). This creates a paradox. The alcoholic or drug abuser needs to give up these substances to get well, yet this is the presenting problem. Nevertheless, no substantial progress can take place as long as these patterns are being acted out. In spite of this dilemma, a therapist or counselor of strong character, concerned and sensitive, can establish a preliminary contract with the patient on this issue.

In early sessions, the therapist points out, in nonjudgmental, nonmoralistic terms, the serious consequences of the patient's addiction. It is vital that patients become aware on a feeling level of the harm they are inflicting on themselves through the continued use of substances. The therapist's warmth, strength, and maturity are essential in gaining and holding a patient's respect and trust so that he or she will continue to be motivated to give up the addiction. If the patient refuses to enter into such an agreement at this time, prognosis is poor. This approach is not limited to working with patients where addiction and drug abuse are primary. Contracts with respect to abstinence as a prerequisite for therapy have been shown to be effective in all types of therapeutic endeavors. There is accumulating research showing the efficacy of contingency management procedures for alcohol- and drug-dependent clients (Feeney, Young, Connor, Tucker, & McPherson, 2001; Kaminer, 2000; Petry, 2000; Petry, Tedford, & Martin, 2001).[4]

It appears that the prohibition against commonly used self-nourishing habits as a precondition for therapy may be a powerful treatment method in and of itself. Interference with these addictive patterns fosters a state of deprivation, which in turn arouses anxiety and renders repressed feelings more accessible. For example, in working with intense feeling release therapy, we found that as a result of these preconditions, patients felt close to their underlying pain, which led to deep catharsis and development of their own crucial intellectual insights. Patients and research participants who continued to control the acting out of habitual addictive patterns progressed rapidly and made important behavioral changes, whereas those who reverted to addictions and acting out were limited in their therapeutic gains.

Identifying Negative Thoughts That Control Addictive Behavior

In the case of Trish, described earlier, the process of consistently identifying her self-attacks and working on corrective suggestions over an extended time period eventually freed her from the addictions and self-destructive habit patterns she had maintained for the major part of her life. As she refrained from engaging in overeating and dieting, her self-attacks at first escalated and her anxiety intensified. Later, in an interview, she described the process:

> Trish: At one point, I realized that I'd always had the feeling that I didn't exist in my family. I had a feeling of never existing there as a person. I had a lot of feelings after realizing that, and I felt really anxious.
>
> One thing is I like to be slim, but it's been a real fight. I've been very heavy at times and I've gone up and down with it a lot and I wanted to binge that day, strongly, but I didn't do it.
>
> Dr. Firestone: What would you have said to yourself if you had?
>
> Trish: I would have annihilated myself. First in going to eat, I would have told myself: "Look, you don't need anybody, so what if you have a bite? You feel anxious, you want to calm down, you want to feel better, just have something to eat, you'll be relaxed. Just calm down. What's going on in your life? What're all these words anyway? What are you talking about? What does it all mean? What does it mean in your life? It means nothing. Just relax, just eat something, just sit down, relax."
>
> That would have been what would have led me to it (eating). Then I would have eaten and then the voice would have said: "You fat pig! You don't care about any person in your entire life. You've never cared about anybody.

You're not loyal." This causes more pain. *"You're not loyal, you're not committed to anything, you're a weak piece of shit!"* (cries) *"You can't hold on to one thing you commit to. You're nothing. Just get out of here. Just get out of people's lives, you're a burden to people. Just get out of here."* Just a real strong feeling of *"Run! Get out!"*

After identifying her negative thoughts, Trish experienced considerably less distress, became increasingly more cheerful, and modified her feelings of self-depreciation. It is interesting to note that her symptoms progressed from actual suicidal behavior to temporarily deserting her family (conceptualized by many clinicians as being a substitute suicide) to actions that were destructive to her physical health (cycle of overeating and dieting); and eventually they were reduced to a subclinical level. Follow-up at three years indicated that Trish's fluctuations in mood were well within the normal range, and there was stability in her relationships.

Encouraging the Expression of Wants and Needs

Many individuals engage in self-denial, limit their personal and career goals, and otherwise inhibit themselves because this type of self-restriction or rationing is under their control. They are only comfortable about expressing a need when they feel that they are guaranteed it will be met. However, they are afraid of indicating their wants honestly and having them refused or rejected. They react to this situation as if it were life-threatening. They respond as though they are still as vulnerable as they once were when they were completely dependent on their parents for their survival.

Clients must become aware of their ongoing needs and desires and use the therapeutic situation to ask directly for what they want. The inevitable limits to personal gratification inherent in the boundaries and discipline of ethical psychotherapy practice lead to frustration of the client's infantile wishes. Therefore, individuals learn that they can survive without the therapist's gratification of their primal needs and come to terms with their anger at being frustrated. This is the crux of an effective therapeutic process with addicted individuals, because in the course of facing their anger at the inevitable frustration, they strengthen their independence and relinquish the fantasy bond with their parents, as well as their dependency on internal sources of gratification.

Corrective Suggestions for Breaking Addictive Behaviors

There are a number of corrective suggestions that people can institute to disrupt long-standing addictions and self-nourishing routines and that will assist them in learning to tolerate the ensuing anxiety of change.

It is important for the client to become aware of the habit patterns and routines that he or she may be using as painkillers to avoid experiencing anxiety, anger, or other feelings of emotional distress. Identifying the specific defenses against feeling places them more under the client's conscious control. Gradually, through effort and understanding, her or she can gain control of the defensive behavior. Exploring the origins of a defense or addictive habit pattern that was once functional, and recognizing that it is now limiting one's life, is an important step in disrupting the defense and regaining feeling.

Clients can be encouraged to be aware of occasions where they feel compelled to indulge their addiction and focus on the anxiety, anger, or depressed feelings that emerge. They can keep a journal or daily log of the thoughts and feelings that arise as they relinquish the addictive pattern. In general, the process of recording emotional reactions at these times helps people maintain their resolution to abstain.

Individuals can also reveal, to an understanding person, the contents of the internalized voices they experience when tempted to engage in an addictive behavior or activity. It is crucial in challenging self-nurturing habits that clients learn to be open and nonsecretive because deception, secrecy, and fears of being stigmatized can short-circuit the process of change. The identification and expression of voice attacks and feelings of shame to another person is a self-discipline that breaks into this pattern of secrecy and duplicity. This type of exposure or externalization enables clients to gain a measure of control over these behaviors.

Disrupting Addictive Attachments and Moving Toward Genuine Relating

When working with clients who relate in an impersonal, addictive style, it is essential to address fears that have interfered with their pursuit of satisfaction in real relationships. In many cases, people have acted on the dictates of internalized voices and as a result are demoralized in relation to pursuing personal goals. Seemingly self-protective thoughts warn people against investing themselves emotionally in caring for another person. They emphasize the possibility of being hurt or victimized if they become "too involved." For example, clients attempting to initiate a new friendship or relationship often report voice attacks such as: "Why would he (she) want to go out with you? You're so uninteresting, unattractive, etc."

Maintaining a daily journal can be beneficial because it helps people identify specific events or circumstances that precipitate social fears and self-attacks (Firestone, Firestone, & Catlett, 2002). Recording these thoughts in a journal or revealing them to a congenial listener represents a form of reality-testing. Objective and supportive responses from another person often help counter inaccurate and unrealistic views of self previously used as rationalizations for not pursuing a new relationship. Finally, it is of the utmost importance that clients learn to anticipate a temporary increase in anxiety and negative thoughts or voices as they modify addictive behaviors and attachments and move toward attaining real satisfaction in their lives.

Resistance to Corrective Suggestions

Implementing a suggestion that breaks a self-nourishing habit pattern is often a first step toward change on a deep character level, yet clients' resistance to instituting these changes is powerful. Most self-nourishing behaviors are directly related to the neurotic process of symbolically satisfying oral needs. The use of addictive substances has functioned to numb the client's feelings of pain, sadness, and fear. Suggestions, or in serious cases, mandates, to stop addictive behavior leave clients vulnerable to the painful feelings they have been suppressing, often for years. For this reason, most clients find it difficult to give up the symbolic substitutes for the love they were deprived of as children. They dread the prospect of facing withdrawal with its psychologically distressing and sometimes physically painful symptoms. The rationale and purpose underlying the use of therapeutic suggestions that trigger anxiety and other painful emotions is to assist clients in gradually accommodating themselves to the tension involved in constructive change. As they learn to tolerate sensations of discomfort and anxiety without regression or reversion to old behavior patterns, they are free to progress.

In many cases, the client's progress may be marked by anxiety, regressive trends, and increased voice attacks. Nevertheless, if they persist in their determination to give up an addiction, their reactions generally subside and their ability to experience both the joy and pain of living is enhanced.

Trish found that there was a tremendous amount of tension and fear in breaking a powerful defense that had once helped her survive psychologically. At the time she made the decision to give up her habit of eating in isolation, Trish received a disturbing phone call in which her mother revealed that she had cancer. The phone call triggered malicious, self-critical voices that Trish verbalized:

Dr. Firestone: It seems like you haven't felt this bad in years.

Trish: I really haven't. After the conversation with my mother, I tried to make my actions appropriate to my life, but my heart wasn't in it. I felt so on the outside of my life, but I knew it wasn't right.

Dr. Firestone: That doesn't work. You have to deal with the real feelings.

Trish: And over the last month I made up my mind that one thing I wouldn't do was eat alone. But the feeling is like, now you have nothing, absolutely nothing. And even though I know it's not true, it's a very depressing feeling. Because whatever that isolation meant to me, it felt like I had something. It's something I've done ever since I was so little. It's hard to shake the feeling but that's like a big source of why now I have nothing. It's almost like you have nothing to live for now.

Dr. Firestone: Say it as a voice.

Trish: *What's your new deal? Your new deal, you're not going to eat alone. What is that shit? Now what do you have? You have nothing to look forward to. Now you're just going to die! You're just going to die like me. A sick death. You're going to die of cancer. Just wait til you get it! Just wait. Get checked because you're going to get it and you're going to die just like me!* (cries) (long pause)

Dr. Firestone: It seems like that was the final attack, the final upper hand.

Trish: Because that's what she said in the phone call.

Dr. Firestone: What did she say?

Trish: She said, "It's my responsibility to tell you that I have colon cancer and that you'll probably get it, so have yourself checked right away so they can catch it early." I said, "Well, if there's anything I can do...." I couldn't even get the words out of my mouth. Before I could finish my sentence, she said, "I don't need *anything* from you! I have people who love me. I'm beautiful. I'm a blond now. I have people who worship the ground I walk on. I have family." But that family was never me. Her family was her brothers and sisters, it was never me. (cries) I felt old after that, and before that conversation I had felt young, alive sexually, very happy, wanting more with my boyfriend.

Dr. Firestone: Looking back at these past weeks, it seems like you gave up your life.

Trish: I felt so much like giving up.

Dr. Firestone: You really gave up your life and feeling, even though you went through the motions.

Trish: I didn't feel happy. I felt tortured, so tortured, sleepless nights, which I haven't had in so many years. And I couldn't feel good. I just couldn't feel good and I've been so emotional.

Dr. Firestone: It seems like there really were two parts to this, the traumatic attack that your mother made on you, and the tone and feeling toward you reminded you of the feelings that you had growing up, through most of your life, actually. But these were accentuated by the fact that you were giving up an addictive style of living, which was an attempt to help yourself. Giving up that alone would have created a depression. Just challenging an addictive pattern and not giving in to the pattern would have led to your feeling sad or feeling hyperemotional. But the two things combined created tough conditions for you and caused you to feel like you did before.

Trish: Without the old defense.

Dr. Firestone: Right. So that's why you have been so tortured this week. It seems like you took on an awful lot at the same time. It was an unfortunate coincidence. The incident with your mother came up at a time when you were trying to really change your life for the better and were feeling optimistic, but your hurt and anger toward your mother caused you to turn against yourself.

Following this session, Trish reported experiencing "almost no voices in my head" and her depression lifted. When her mother died a year later, she experienced a temporary resurgence of guilty self-recriminations. Identifying the destructive thoughts underlying her guilt reactions allowed her to once again pursue her own wants and priorities, and she continued to develop in each area of her life.

Although corrective suggestions are often initiated by clients and develop out of their own motivation to alter addictive, self-defeating behaviors, the situation still lends itself to the arousal of strong feelings of resistance. On an intrapsychic level, corrective suggestions for behavioral change represent a separation from parental introjects. On an interpersonal level, clients often plan specific changes to break behavior patterns that have been modeled after addictive or compulsive behaviors exhibited by their parents. This is particularly evident in cases where a parent or parents had problems with substance abuse. Studies have shown that there are at least 22 million adults in the United States who have lived with an alcoholic parent (Seixas & Youcha, 1985). Claudia Black (1981) reported that "fifty to sixty percent of all alcoholics (a low estimate) have, or had, at least one alcoholic parent. Alcoholism is a generational disease" (p. 4). This differentiation from parental figures, both symbolically and in reality, often brings the client to a crucial point in his or her therapy (Firestone, 1988).

Otto Rank (1936/1972) understood that this symbolic separation/individuation process was related to the patient's resistance and was an expression of the patient's "counter-will." "The 'being separated' is appre-hended [by the patient] as compulsory and is responded to with counter-will, which can manifest itself not only as resistance, or protest, but also in the form of love fixation and gratitude" (p. 81). Although initially collaborat-ing on planning corrective measures as an equal partner with the therapist, a client may subsequently reverse his or her point of view concerning the desire to change. At this time, clients tend to distort the situation and deal with it in a paranoid manner. For example, they may believe that the therapist is telling them how to conduct their lives or accuse the therapist of making decisions for them. They project their desire to change onto the therapist and perceive him or her as having a stake in their progress. Espe-cially in cases in which addictive processes are being interrupted, even relatively mild-mannered clients can become uncharacteristically angry and paranoid.

CORRECTIVE SUGGESTIONS USED IN
THE FRIENDSHIP CIRCLE

In recounting the historical roots of the friendship circle (see the introduction), we noted that many people relinquished self-nourishing habit patterns and routines they had previously used to alleviate or diminish painful emotions of sadness, anxiety, and frustration. For the most part, they gave up smoking and drinking, disrupted repetitive behaviors that had reduced their tension and stress, and challenged habitual styles of relating in their closest associations.

These individuals found that breaking an addiction immediately opened them up to focusing on their wants and needs in their present situations. They developed more integrity in their lives, because in moving away from addictive behavior, they were no longer secretive, dishonest, or duplicitous in their communications.

Breaking Self-Nourishing Behaviors

People in the friendship circle learned to take into account stressful events in their everyday lives that might affect them during the transition to a more outward, fulfilling life. They became more aware of their strengths and weaknesses and adopted a gradual, step-by-step approach to changing well-established addictive behavior patterns.

When attempting to alter any dimension of the self-parenting process, they tend to move slowly and consistently toward their personal goals, keeping in mind their level of tolerance for the anxiety and the temporarily increased voice attacks inevitably aroused by the process of change. First, through talking together, they came to recognize that they often rationalized their use of alcohol, drugs, or food by believing that they needed these substances to relieve tension states or other forms of distress. As noted previously, there is the unavoidable paradox involved in the necessity to relinquish one's reliance on a particular drug or substance before real progress or personal growth takes place. Many individuals in the friendship circle began by identifying a specific addictive behavior that they believed was emotionally deadening to them or that limited them in their career or in their personal and family relationships.

Second, as noted earlier, individuals learned to uncover the destructive thoughts that were playing a role in their maintaining the particular behavior. Third, they identified triggering events or situations that intensified their urge to engage in their addiction and talked about the feelings aroused by these events. Fourth, they adopted various strategies that strengthened their sense of self and allowed them to move toward pursuing their real interests and goals in life.

As people gave up compulsive or addictive behaviors dictated by the voice, their real self (the self system) increasingly emerged and took precedence over the enemy within. They began to regain the multitude of feelings they had suppressed for years, and became more aware of the wants and desires that were a fundamental part of their unique identity. In the group discussions, they revealed many of the reasons they had been afraid to pursue their goals and priorities in life. They described events in their childhood that they felt had made it necessary to cut off their feelings by using fantasy and addictive behaviors. Talking about these events and experiencing the emotions they had suppressed at the time enabled them to make a clear distinction between past and present circumstances. As a result, they were able to challenge the belief that they could not survive if they had to face again the painful longings and rejection they had experienced early in life. The recognition that current situations were different than those in the past helped them deal with their fears of taking a chance again on seeking satisfaction in reality through goal-directed behavior.

Disrupting Repetitive Behavior Patterns Through a Life of Adventure and Travel

As we have seen, the addictive quality of repetitive activities and routinized habit patterns lies in the fact that human beings have a strong propensity to use them to reduce anxiety. They can provide an illusion of continuity—of life going on in the same way year after year, without end. This false sense of eternal life and permanence may be one of the primary attractions of living in an inward state of dulled awareness. Over the years, we have found that taking advantage of opportunities to break these habit patterns and routines releases energy and creates a more intense awareness of separate and distinct events as they occur.

The ocean voyages undertaken by the group of friends were effective in disrupting the daily routines that characterized their lives on land. For example, the four-hour watches interrupted habitual patterns of working, eating, and sleeping. Unfamiliar physical activities, eating in shifts, sleeping in bunks rather than in one's bed, all interfered with the "normal" pattern of everyday life. Switching watches at intervals also prevented these four-hour-on, eight-hour-off stretches from becoming routine.

When sailing, the separation from land, from home, and from the imagined security provided by familiar scenery arouses powerful feelings each time the voyagers head for the open ocean. There seems to be more involved in this experience than the simple fear of being alone in the midst of a sea devoid of recognizable landmarks. Symbolically, to many people, land means home, security, safety, and protection against the harsh outside world. Home signifies a connection with one's past, a sense of belonging to a place and a family. Any separation severs one's ties, threatens illusions of security, and thus creates anxiety, the degree depending on one's need to preserve emotional ties with home and family. However, we found that after this initial anxiety is endured, certain changes occur in the "wanderer" that are subtle, yet significant. Some changes are a result of unfamiliar surroundings, and others are the psychological effects of separation.

After two or three days at sea, people find themselves totally involved in a daily existence far different from what they lead on land. The pace of life is noticeably slowed down. Thoughts and feelings undergo a metamorphosis. There are fewer distractions from the trivial details of everyday life to attend to; people's minds and perceptions become clear; and there is time to sense and feel the variations of nature.

An interesting phenomenon occurs each time there is an ocean crossing: The people onboard experience a profound sense of being in a world all their own—separated entirely from the rest of the world. Without any reasonable expectation of rescue should there be trouble, they are completely interdependent and therefore sensitive and cooperative. People know they share a common fate should anything happen to their ship. Here, on the wide expanse of the ocean, life and death are thrown into sharp focus, and people come to value their own lives and the lives of others more than they ordinarily do at home.

Separation from mates and loved ones also breaks into an illusion of connection with another person that characterizes many relationships. In their early voyages, because of their partners' work schedules, some of the men and women traveled without their mates. During these brief periods of separation, there were remarkable changes in the behavior of many of these individuals. They appeared happier; felt more free to express their own opinions and in general seemed to have more dimensions to their personalities. However, within hours of being reunited with their mates, most lost their liveliness, their alert and happy faces, and slipped back into their patterns of arguing and subtle manipulations that were typical of their interactions with their spouses before the trip. These observations were discussed in our groups, adding to our understanding of psychological defenses and how they operate in relationships. Through these discussions, men and women were able to begin a process of improving their relationships. (See chapter 10.)

A number of benefits were derived from these extended voyages. (a) They effected important changes in many people. For example, people were involved in a way of living onboard that considerably minimized their tendencies to complain, worry, or feel victimized. They learned that many of the so-called comforts of home that they had believed were essential to their well-being and happiness were in fact nonessential and unnecessary. They discovered that many of their possessions were cumbersome and limited their mobility and sense of freedom. (b) The ocean crossings, which often necessitated separation from loved ones, contributed to an expanding body of knowledge regarding the propensity of people to form imaginary connections with significant persons in their lives to protect themselves against separation and death anxiety. And (c) the journeys were the source of practical suggestions that helped individuals disrupt behaviors, rituals, and routines that had supported this form of anxious attachment and style of relating. For example, while at sea, members of a couple often found themselves talking more openly to friends about problems they were experiencing in their relationship. The overall social atmosphere was conducive to spending less time alone in private conversations that at times could be destructive. This, in turn, led to improvement in their relationship over the course of the voyage. When they returned to land, many couples attempted to replicate these conditions in their everyday life. They chose to limit the frequency of their problematic interactions or dialogues in favor of including a third party in their conversation or talking about the problem in a group meeting.

CONCLUSION

In working with addicted clients, their lack of self-direction and self-control, combined with an unusually self-protective, self-nurturing style, points to one important requirement: It is usually necessary that they make inroads in giving up their addiction before improvement or real personal growth takes place. When their addictions are more under control, clients gain insight into the origins of their addictive behaviors, and they inevitably reexperience the painful feelings and deep frustration that originally caused them to seek gratification inwardly. In the addictive state, they tend to believe that they would not survive if they were to once again experience their primitive wants or needs and the associated pain. It is important that clients learn that as adults, the fulfillment of these infantile needs is no longer essential for their survival, or even for their happiness, and they can learn to tolerate frustration as an inevitable part of living. This insight, when experienced on a deep emotional level, can serve as a catalyst as they progress toward a point in their development where they are able to enjoy a life with close relationships and maintain their separateness and independence.

NOTES

1. Zerbe (1993) noted that "the common denominator underlying many cases of anorexia nervosa and bulimia nervosa is the amount of maternal over- and underinvolvement that influences the child's ability to grow psychologically, establish personal boundaries, and regulate her own body" (p. 54). Also see S. Johnson, Maddeaux, and Blouin's (1998) review of studies of bulimia.
2. Researchers Hall, Havassy, and Wasserman (1990) have shown that seemingly diverse forms of addiction are actually interrelated.
3. See Patrick Carnes's (1992) formulation of the steps in sexual addiction, which are similar in many respects to the cycle of addiction described in this chapter.
4. See Beutler and Harwood (2000), *Prescriptive Psychotherapy*, which describes interventions that include contingency-contracting with respect to abstinence. With most patients, Beutler and Harwood recommended,

> At some point in the first six sessions, if substance use is problematic, the patient should be asked to make a commitment to remain drug free. There are procedures that have been used to help the patient explore this decision. For example, a therapist can use the *advantages-disadvantages analytic* procedure to explore the patient's beliefs, enhancing motivation, and identify goals to support new skills. (p. 93)

Other methods include guided imagery, participation in a 12-step program, relaxation training, thought substitution, and the use of the *Daily Thought Record* (DTR; A. Beck, Wright, Newman, & Liese, 1993). Also see the journaling exercises from chapter 6 in *Conquer Your Critical Inner Voice* (Firestone et al., 2002) for suggestions related to giving up addictions, recording goals, and tracking progress toward those goals.

5

A FEELING VERSUS
NONFEELING EXISTENCE

I consider many adults (including myself) are or have been, more or less, in a hypnotic trance, induced in early infancy: we remain in this state until—when we dead awaken, as Ibsen makes one of his characters say—we shall find that we have never lived.

—R. D. Laing (1969/1972, p. 82)

In exploring obstacles to living a better life, it is worthwhile to consider factors that diminish one of the most important human potentialities: the capacity for deep feeling. As noted, there are many impediments to living a feelingful existence that are based on defenses people form early in life as they attempt to protect themselves against interpersonal pain and the fear of death. These defenses persist into adulthood and interfere with the ability to feel compassion for oneself and empathy for others.[1]

By identifying internalized voices that predispose defensive living and by regaining feeling for themselves, individuals can develop counter-measures—ways of living and being that challenge their tendencies to relive the past. Living a less defended, more vulnerable lifestyle enables people to preserve rather than distort or block out experience, remain connected to their feelings, and fully appreciate the richness of life.

THE NATURE OF FEELING

Feelings arise involuntarily and are experienced as sensations in the body.[2] Individuals who are close to their feelings experience a sense of inner harmony, respond appropriately to positive and negative events in their lives, and are generally more capable of coping with life than people who have less access to their feelings. Being in contact with one's emotions —sadness, anger, fear, disgust, envy, shame, joy, happiness, amusement, exhilaration—is essential to maintaining one's sense of identity, leading a life of integrity, and finding meaning in one's life. Indeed, there is no hidden significance to life that may be discovered; rather it is only an individual's investment of his or her feelings in other people, in objects, in activities, and in transcending causes that gives life its special meaning.

Emotional processes are inextricably tied to the motivational system— that is, to one's wants, needs, and desires; therefore remaining connected to one's feelings is crucial to pursuing one's goals in life. Oatley (1996) has stressed the central role that feelings play in motivating human behavior: "Sadness organizes the cognitive system to relinquish a goal, anger prompts new plans to surmount a frustration or remedy a wrong so that a goal may be reinstated, fear prompts escape, attention to safety, and deference" (p. 313), and "happiness tends to induce cooperation" (p. 315).

Feelings can be conceptualized as flowing through the individual, freely, without purpose or intent. When that natural flow is interfered with—for example, when painful or sad feelings are blocked—people tend to become suspended in a cut-off, defended state. They disengage from themselves as a center of feeling, perception, cognition, and behavior. In an effort to disown their "unacceptable" feelings they may try to cover them up, project them onto others, or substitute role-determined responses.

By *not* experiencing painful feelings that inevitably arise in the course of life, people cause themselves considerable harm. When they are in a cut-off state, they tend to act out behavior that is profoundly detrimental to their well-being. Referring to one of the many psychological costs of suppressing feelings, Parrott and Harre (1996) emphasized the part that feelings play in self-control:

> Feelings inform our reflective selves about our current automatic tenden-cies. Only if we are aware of these tendencies can we exercise self-control over them. Therefore, if we are to have more control over our emotions we must become more aware of their existence. (p. 18)

LOSS OF FEELING AND "INWARDNESS"

The term *inwardness* refers to a state of mind and a corresponding way of living that has drawn our attention for many years. A disturbing number of people appear to exist in a dazed, emotionally deadened state, with little comprehension of the essential reality of their lives. For the most part, they are unaware that the defenses they developed early in life to avoid experiencing painful emotions predispose their living out a destiny that is not truly their own.

Inwardness represents a retreat into oneself, resulting in varying degrees of a depersonalized state of mind and a lifestyle characterized by a decrease in feeling for oneself and others, a reliance on painkilling habit patterns and substances, and a defensive, self-nurturing orientation toward life. When this syndrome of traits and behaviors dominates the personality, it plays a key role in all forms of psychopathology and is detrimental to relationships. Satisfaction of wants and needs is sought internally; inward people are ministered to and punished by their internalized voices. They relate to these negative parental introjects instead of real objects (or people), which leads to a reduction of both giving and taking operations, thereby significantly diminishing transactions with others. *It is this withdrawal of personal feelings in important relationships that most characterizes an inward state* (Firestone, 1985).

It is important to distinguish inwardness from self-reflection, introspection, time spent alone for creative work or planning, contemplation of nature, meditation, and other forms of spiritual or intellectual pursuits. Living in an inward, unfeeling manner entails being generally insensitive to one's personal feelings and viewing oneself (and others) more as objects than persons. From this detached vantage point, one is observing oneself rather than experiencing one's life. The person's gaze is focused inward, on him- or herself, rather than outward toward others. Events in the interpersonal environment are filtered through this distorted lens of self-absorption, transformed (given a negative loading) by the voice process, and responded to inappropriately in a self-defeating manner. Moreover, in relating to themselves as an object, individuals give little or no value to their experiences and are often indifferent to their physical health and emotional well-being.

An inward, unfeeling state and a feelingful state can be conceptualized as points on a continuum, as depicted in Table 3.1 in chapter 3. Between these extremes is a gray area in which most people live and where they continually contend with internalized voices. This type of existence effectively diminishes their ability to experience their feelings and leaves their sensitivity and spirit considerably blunted. All people tend to move in and out of this self-protective, inward state; some individuals spend their entire lives caught in this unfeeling mode, experiencing little compassion or love or any genuine emotion for long periods of time. The occasions when they are sensitive, empathic, loving, and close to their feelings are notable exceptions.

One cannot selectively suppress one's feelings. In blocking out painful emotions, one limits feelings of joy and exhilaration as well. The unconscious aspect of becoming inward and recapitulating one's past in one's adult relationships has other pervasive and far-reaching destructive consequences. The very process of repressing painful episodes causes their inevitable repetition through succeeding generations (Fraiberg et al., 1980). This outcome is predictable despite the best intentions of people who originally were victims themselves but who now act as agents or perpetrators.

Schizoid personality disorders, dissociative disorders, as well as narcissistic and antisocial personality disorders may develop in individuals for whom the cluster of symptoms reflecting an inward state has become the dominant mode of existence (Fairbairn, 1952; Guntrip, 1969; Kernberg, 1984; Laing, 1960/1969). The presence of flat affect, a sense of being removed from the mainstream of life, the absence of appropriate emotional reactions, obsessive ruminations about the past, the lack of a sense of direction or interest in concrete goals, all point to the fact that a client has become seriously withdrawn and inward in his or her lifestyle.

ORIGINS OF THE INWARD STATE: SUPPRESSION OF FEELINGS IN CHILDHOOD

The process of blocking out feelings and emotional responses begins early in life. In response to emotional pain, the infant or child depersonalizes to some extent, renounces his or her true self, and retreats to an emotionally deadened existence. These self-protective measures help an individual survive an unhappy childhood at the expense of a richer, fuller life as an adult.

The Infant's Assimilation of Parents' Feeling States

It is virtually impossible for a fearful, nervous parent to not communicate his or her anxiety to the baby. Infants sense their parent's emotional state and automatically take it on as their own, eventually experiencing the sensation of fear or anxiety as if it had originated within them.

Research studies have focused on parents' physical touch, facial expression, and other behavioral cues that transmit their varying emotional states to their babies beginning at birth. Joseph Rheingold (1964) noted that "perhaps on the basis of observations we must accept the existence of direct communication between the mother's unconscious mind and the child's organism and await elucidation of the phenomenon" (p. 31). In fact, more recent studies have demonstrated some of the ways that the mother's feeling state is transmitted to her infant (LeDoux, 1996; Schore, 1994; D. Siegel 1999; Stern, 1985, 1995).

Stern (1985) provided numerous examples of the infant's remarkable ability to respond to his or her mother's feeling state. His writings include detailed accounts of mothers' efforts to match their responses to their infants' level of excitement or activity ("affect attunement").[3] Stern has spent the past 30 years investigating through a form of microanalysis of parents' interactions with their infants. More recently, in his book *The Motherhood Constellation*, Stern (1995) delineated specific elements in mother's and father's behavioral repertoire that he proposed were enactments of their representational system or internal working model.

In closely examining and coding an infant's behavioral and feeling reactions during selected close interactions with his or her mother, Stern noted that the mother's internal emotional state (and internal representations) powerfully influenced her baby's state of arousal and emotional responses. Misattunements on the part of the mother—intrusive overstimulation; understimulation from a depressed mother; or chaotic, inconsistent stimulation—tended to disrupt the relaxed, alert state in the infant (the optimal state for early learning), referred to as a state of "going on being" by Winnicott (1958) in his work on child development.

Margot Waddell (1998) described the origins of both healthy and pathological developmental pathways. She asserted that:

> Where an infant's cry or smile goes without any answering echo in the mother, there will be no opportunity for the baby to take back in, or to introject an experience of having painful feelings understood and held by a mind, or by an emotional presence, that is felt to have the care and capacity to make things bearable for him. The bad "something" that is felt will be taken back in; it will be a "something" which is experienced as not fitting, or as a "foreign body," or as a persecutory feeling inside. (p. 215)

Waddell's analysis is congenial in many respects to the first author's formulations regarding the sources of negative parental introjects or internalized voices; these somethings cannot be fully integrated into the personality because they are antithetical to a child's continued growth and development.

The Threat to Parents' Defenses Posed by the Child

Many well-meaning parents inadvertently damage their children's capacity to feel and care deeply for themselves and other human beings because, as noted in chapter 2, their own defenses are threatened by the activity, aliveness, and spontaneity of their children. The innocence of a child reminds parents of the hurts they suffered in growing up and reactivates the pain that they have successfully suppressed for years. Furthermore, children's direct and candid way of speaking and their open expression of feeling often intrude on the defensive equilibrium the parents have established in the household. Loving responses from an infant must be suppressed in many instances as well because they disrupt their parents' defenses and emotional equilibrium. Spontaneous actions, freedom of movement, and the lack of shame typical of young children arouse feelings of tension, embarrassment, and guilt in many mothers and fathers. In general, a child's helplessness and vulnerability remind everyone of their own weaknesses and insecurity.

Parents react to their own reemerging pain and anxiety in a number of ways. They may become angry, hostile, or indifferent to their offspring, or they may become defensively overprotective and nervously focused on their child. Parents often find themselves treating their offspring in the same destructive ways they were dealt with during their formative years. (See chapters 12 and 13.) There is evidence that parents experience discomfort when their child passes through stages of development that were particularly painful or traumatic for the parents themselves. During this transition, they can become unusually insensitive or punishing to the youngster (Gerson, 1995). These types of responses cause their children pain, which they in turn attempt to suppress. Children also learn to suppress their perceptions of, and feeling responses to, family members to protect their parents' illusions of goodness and adequacy.

To some extent, all parents are inward and defended because of the frustrations they encountered in their own early lives. When they sense that their defenses and self-defeating behaviors are damaging to their children, they tend to feel guilt and remorse, but these guilt reactions only serve to compound the problem. In his Foreword to *Compassionate Child-Rearing*, the late British psychiatrist R. D. Laing (1990) described these parental reactions as manifestations of *diaphobia*—that is, *"The fear of being affected, of being directly influenced by the other"* (p. ix).

> Babies, and infants, before they have become normalized (dulled and deadened, etc.) have to be defended against. They are tiny foci who emit signals genetically programmed to elicit reciprocity from adults. The schizoid narcissistic, autistic, paranoid adult who is diaphobic is terrified of spontaneous reciprocity. The baby's genetic programmed devices to evoke responses which are cultured out of the normal adult pose a paranoid danger therefore to the normal adult. . . .
>
> Those outstretched arms open up a well of loneliness. The resistance to being drawn into the sphere of . . . reciprocal influence out of the stable isolation . . . brings up *gushes* of "bad" feelings—physical feelings, horrible feelings, feelings one has never felt before. But in these feelings, mixed up in them at once physical smells new and stale of ghosts of awakened sensations in oneself, are evoked, by that dead *me*, that me that was me, I see in the baby. . . .
>
> The baby is still appealing to me with the language of the heart, the language I have learned to forget, and to mistrust with all my "heart." I can go in different directions. I can hate the baby for making me feel bad. I can envy the baby for still being human. I can feel bad/guilty/ for feeling bad. I can feel a terrible burden of responsibility because I feel incapable to respond spontaneously.
>
> I feel I *ought* to respond, but I feel I ought *not* to respond. Two feelings demand, forbid, and cancel, each other. I forget. I feel nothing. I *feel*—nothing. Finally I do *not* feel—anything. (pp. ix–xi)

Parents' Rejection of the Child's Loving Feelings

Many parents find it difficult to accept expressions of love from their offspring and tend to react negatively in overt or covert ways when their children are loving or affectionate. Gradually, children learn to disengage from themselves and suppress their positive feelings. Many come to believe that there is something wrong with their loving feelings and believe that their affection or their physical nature is somehow unacceptable. They often defensively resolve to hold back their warmth and tenderness in future interactions.

In a therapy group, Angela recalled her parents' reactions to her demonstrations of affection:

> I remember that a few times when I was really young, I would run up to my father or mother, just spontaneously run up to them, wanting to jump in their arms, or jump in their lap. And I remember each one of them having such a negative reaction. I remember my father just kind of pulling away, and my mother also pulling away from me. I felt so angry and I said to myself: "Forget it, I'm never going to do that again."

Children are injured psychologically as their parents vacillate between being self-protective or inward and being in a more emotionally responsive state. At the times parents are in a feeling state, they are more sensitive to their offspring; they may be able to feel and express the love they characteristically withhold. The child, in turn, naturally responds to his or her parents with love and affection. However, when parents revert to a more defended state and a more impersonal mode of relating, they are blocked in their sensitivity and concern for their child. Their withdrawal causes considerable hurt particularly when it occurs following unusually close experiences with their offspring.

The Child's Reaction to Overwhelming Anxiety and Pain

When early interactions within the family are painful, conflicted, or toxic, children suppress these experiences and detach from themselves emotionally. Gordon (1998) has explained how the hurt or traumatized child necessarily develops two "impossibly different representational schemas" (p. 44) that cannot be integrated.

> One system involves organizing instances of an evil, toxic, abused child self with an infantile or sadistic, out-of-control parent abuser. . . . The other system incorporates instances of self with other in which nurturance, caretaking, protection, and warm affection predominate along with moments of relative safety, bodily sensations of quiescence and soothing. These representations of self and other are dramatically

incompatible as are the intense affective linkages and organizing fantasies that unite them. (p. 44)

Perhaps the most powerful manifestation of this depersonalization or
split can be seen in the defense of identifying with the aggressor, as described
in chapter 2, in which children identify with the person who is the source
of their suffering in an effort to possess that person's strength or power. In
so doing, they take on the very characteristics manifested by the person
who hurt them—that is, the anger and hostility expressed by the parent
during times of punishment and stress. Later as adults, when experiencing
anxiety and stress, they essentially become duplicates of their parents
(Ferenczi, 1933/1955; A. Freud, 1966).

Moreover, in identifying with the punitive parent, one gives up identifying with oneself as the hurt, helpless child and develops a protective
facade. This false front is symptomatic of the withdrawal of affect and
genuine investment in other people and in oneself. One no longer stands
behind one's own point of view, but conforms instead to other people's
opinions. The individual loses or fails to develop a sense of identity and
personal values and instead seeks approval or criticism from significant
people in his or her life.

Children necessarily imitate their parents' methods for coping with
tension, anxiety, and painful feelings (Bandura, 1975). In addition, parents
feel an obligation to instruct their children in the basic ways they have
learned to cope with stress and pain. For example, many parents offer their
child food—candy, a cookie—any time he or she cries rather than try to
discover the source of his or her distress. At the same time, in the name
of encouraging children to be "tough and strong," parents often teach them
to not be vulnerable, whereas being vulnerable is a basic human quality.
Similarly, parents who are suspicious and paranoid will pass on to their
children a paranoid orientation to life. Parental prejudices and stereotypical
attitudes toward women or men and other ideas that predispose alienation are
also taken on by children as part of their belief system (Kerr & Bowen, 1988).

THE EFFECTS OF SUPPRESSING FEELINGS

The vulnerability of the human infant and its capacity for experiencing
pain in its undefended state is great. It appears that no one comes through
childhood without being emotionally scarred to some extent. The suppression of feelings and the subsequent formation of symptoms act as a powerful
limitation throughout life. The process of forming defenses against pain
dehumanizes the individual and predisposes a gradual loss of personal identity
and feeling. When one defends oneself and retreats from life into an inward,
self-protective state, there are a number of consequences.

First, there is a significant loss of freedom and meaningful experience, a shrinking of life space. The process of disengaging leads to a fundamental existential guilt about retreating from and denying life. Second, the repression of thoughts and feelings leads to increased anxiety and tension. The price for obscuring the truth is a build-up of internal pressure. Not only are there the loss of initiative and the development of symptoms of distress, but the causes of this distress are obscured. Third, human beings cannot be "innocently" defended. Because defenses have the same properties as an addiction, there is a progressive debilitation in broad areas and a depletion of energy required for optimal functioning. The crippling effects are felt throughout the whole spectrum of one's life and have particularly adverse effects on one's closest relationships.

Much of human behavior is directed toward the avoidance of feeling— painful primal feelings from childhood as well as sad and hurtful feelings in the present (Fosha, 2000; Janov, 1970). People who take refuge in an unfeeling state are likely to have varying degrees of self-hatred and cynicism toward others and yet may feel little emotional pain. Indeed, some patients reported that, before therapy, they had succeeded in repressing much of their emotional distress and had actually felt somewhat content in their lives. They sought professional help only after an unusual negative event had caused them enough distress that it broke through their defenses.

People who are cut off from their feelings often experience inappropriate emotional reactions. They may mistake dramatic expressions of emotions for real feeling without realizing that these strong emotions are generally based on deep feelings from the past rather than being genuine feeling reactions to present-day circumstances. They may respond in an indifferent manner to important events in their lives and have strong emotional reactions to what would seem to be relatively unimportant, or "pseudo," events to the objective observer.

When people are defended in this manner they are usually not spontaneous or flexible. Their lives and their everyday activities become routinized and are determined more by role-playing than by their genuine inclination. Birthdays, anniversaries, weddings, and funerals are typical examples of occasions in which people feel compelled to offer socially determined responses. People believe that they are *supposed* to feel something at these events, but they often stifle their spontaneous emotions to be able to show the "right" (socially accepted) feelings.

Finally, it is the nature of emotional pain that if it is suppressed instead of experienced, it does not dissipate, but retains a bodily component, whereas a conscious awareness of the pain is repressed or forgotten (Fosha, 2000; Janov, 1970; A. Miller, 1980/1984a). Primitive pains and longings that are suppressed cause tension and psychosomatic illnesses as well as depression and anxiety (Mrazek, 1993; Paykel, 1974). Emotions that are not fully experienced at the time also find symbolic expression through patterns of self-defeating and self-destructive behavior. The avoidance of pain leads to repetition of behaviors appropriate to the past. The defended person continually manipulates his or her environment so that this repressed pain will not surface. However, if one enters a psychotherapy where the atmosphere is conducive to the expression of these feelings, one can retrieve this pain and experience it, which results in a reduction of rigidity and bodily tension.

Evidence From Intense Feeling-Release Therapy

As described in the Introduction, participants in the marathons began to have emotional reactions that were primal in nature—that is, deep expressions of intense childhood trauma. Similarly, in working in an intense feeling-release therapy over a four-year period, we found that, without exception, every individual expressed deep, primitive feelings of sadness, desperation, and rage associated with painful or traumatic events in childhood. Before this experience, they had been attempting, on an unconscious level, to avoid experiences that might remind them of the emptiness and fears they suffered as children.

In feeling-release therapy, people reexperienced suppressed feelings from the past that they had found too threatening to allow themselves to fully experience at the time.[4] At critical times in therapy when people were close to important feelings, our method was to ask them to breathe deeply, to release sounds as they exhaled, and to freely verbalize any thoughts that came to mind. As they expressed powerful feelings, they were able to form their own insights and spontaneously interpreted their primal experiences. In analyzing the content of their thoughts, feelings, and memories, they generally gained a new perspective on their early childhood, current behavior, and way of living.

Jane, 48, a school teacher and mother of three, continually deferred to her husband in spite of being a highly intelligent and capable woman. In her first sessions, she became aware that the difficulties in her marriage were largely determined by feelings and memories about her father that she had successfully repressed. After the sessions, Jane recorded her experiences:

> Session #5: I felt unloved and unlovable. I cried and cried. I could feel it really hurt. I felt that my father was always angry at me. I struggled to get the words out—as if I couldn't yet talk. With great effort, I said "You, you, you—you don't, you don't, you don't—you don't let me talk." I screamed with anger. I had the feeling—"you don't love me as much as"—Who? My sister? I felt really sad. I felt it very deep all the way to the bottom.

Near the end of the session, I thought about these experiences and realized that a lot of this applies to the way I react with my husband. In the past especially I have been afraid to talk around him ("you don't let me talk"). I take second place to him. I have felt that my husband likes any other woman more than me. After the session I felt very good from making a distinction between the past and my life today.

The knowledge of self and personal understanding gained through feeling-release sessions are unusually direct and pure. It is as if people are able to envision their childhood situations and "see through" their present-day problems rather than intellectually analyzing them.

The results of our involvement with feeling-release therapy tended to confirm the findings of Janov (1970) and Stettbacher (1990/1991) as well as our views that defenses are basically a protection against feeling primal pain. In contrast to Janov, however, who felt that repeated expression and release could empty the reservoir or "pool of primal pain" and lead to a "cure," our investigations demonstrated that this "pool" cannot be emptied as such. If defenses formed early in relation to interpersonal pain stood alone and were not reinforced by reactions to death anxiety, Janov's assumptions and hopes might have been realized. As noted earlier, the dread of vulnerability and the fear of being overwhelmed by irrational feeling, characteristic of early childhood, are reactivated later on when the child comes to the realization of his or her mortality. Once again, the child is vulnerable and at the mercy of forces beyond his or her control. This existential reality affects individuals throughout the life span.

Furthermore, we found that feeling-release techniques were not sufficient to change an individual's basic negative beliefs or character defenses.[5] As important as it is for clients to understand the connection between their current behavior and painful events of the past and to have access to their deepest emotions, this methodology in and of itself does not necessarily alter their tendencies to compulsively reenact destructive patterns or to live a restricted, inward lifestyle, nor does it appear to modify their preference for fantasy gratification and self-parenting defenses.

During the years that we were studying feeling-release therapy, we spent considerable time evaluating the results, recording and transcribing the material from individual and group sessions, and appraising people's progress. We concluded that this therapy represented a significant advance over free association as a technique for recovering memories and experiences from one's childhood. The participants interpreted their own material and integrated it without assistance or intervention from the facilitator. An added advantage was the fact that the uncovered material validated many of the first author's theoretical formulations regarding the neurotic process.

To summarize, feeling-release sessions offer a heightened awareness of those childhood experiences that affect current behavior. They help people become less defensive, and there is often a significant reduction in the tension and anxiety that are associated with repressed feeling. In addition, feeling-release sessions assist people in coping with the intense emotional reactions linked to the verbalization of negative thoughts in voice therapy.

The Role of the Voice in Suppressing Feelings

The voice process acts as a defense mechanism that represses spontaneous emotions that, in turn, keeps people from feeling fully alive to present-day events. Internalized voices promote a state of chronic passivity and feelings of self-hatred. Moreover, the obsessive quality of voice attacks is antithetical to maintaining an ongoing state of feeling. Genuine emotional responses are significantly diminished or obliterated in the process of listening to the voice and acting according to its dictates. Ideation gradually replaces feeling as people become more withdrawn and isolated, and their reactions become more automatic and cerebral.

Negative thoughts and attitudes function to stifle spontaneous emotional expressions, especially feelings of enthusiasm and joy. Warnings and injunctions such as: "Don't get so excited! Why are you feeling so good? What's the big deal? Don't make a fool of yourself," are accompanied by the same derisive tone that parents often use and effectively subdue children's excitement, fun, and passion. Internalized voices also caution individuals, in seemingly self-protective terms, that good times and happiness are invariably followed by trouble and misfortune. "You're getting too happy for your own good. Watch out, the ax is bound to fall! Don't expect this relationship to last. If you do, you're going to be really disappointed." On formal occasions or in social settings, people frequently tell themselves that being deeply touched or moved to tears is embarrassing and shameful on the one hand: "You're overly sensitive. You're embarrassing yourself and everybody else by being emotional. Pull yourself together," or phony and sentimental on the other hand: "You're just a stupid, sentimental jerk. Who are you trying to fool? You don't really feel much of anything. You've always been a cold fish."

When people believe these voices—that is, when they fail to subject them to reality testing, their enthusiasm, vitality, and spontaneity are dampened. They tend to become subdued or passive and increasingly removed from their bodily sensations and deepest feelings. If their self-attacks and distorted views remain beneath the level of conscious awareness, they may spend most of their lives suppressing their feeling responses, in effect trying to keep one step ahead of their pain and fear. In retreating into an inward state, they are no longer able to experience the richness of their inner life nor are they open to experiencing love from other people.

Internalized voices also play an important role in maintaining the view that most people have of themselves as being unworthy and undeserving of love, beliefs that interfere with their maintaining an ongoing feeling state. We have observed an interesting phenomenon that clearly illustrates the pervasiveness and persistence of this negative view of self, even in so-called normal individuals. In working with children and participants in feeling-release therapy, we were impressed by the fact that most of these individuals held deep-seated beliefs that they were bad. When asked to make positive statements about themselves and to take these statements seriously, they often broke down and cried. Simple statements such as "I'm not bad," "I'm a good kid," "I'm a decent person," or "I'm lovable" were accompanied by extreme sadness and sobbing. Making positive statements about themselves interrupted a negative self-image formed early in life. This separation from a negative identity appeared to be related symbolically to a disruption of the fantasy bond with their parents and aroused separation anxiety as well as feelings of grief and sadness. Even those adults who were geographically distant from or independent of their parents were initially afraid to make positive statements about themselves, as though a basic change in self-concept would break the imagined connection with their parents. It appears that most people may accept positive recognition on an intellectual level but cannot experience it on a feeling level.

The Distinction Between Sadness and Depression

Some psychologists as well as lay persons mistake the experience of sad feelings for depression. There are significant differences between the two states. Experiencing feelings of sadness tends to put people in touch with themselves, makes them feel more whole and more integrated. Depression is primarily anger turned against the self but also has other components, including unresolved grief and guilt.[6]

Many individuals are reluctant to experience or express deep feelings of sadness. Anticipating these feelings appears to arouse primitive fears and often extreme tension, whereas the actual experience of sadness frequently brings relief. After expressing emotional pain or deep feelings of sadness, people usually feel more unified or integrated and report a stronger sense of identity. For example, in a discussion group with adolescents, we observed that when the youngsters expressed previously suppressed feelings of sadness, their perspective on their problems shifted considerably in a positive direction. Before the group meetings, many of the young people had been involved in acting out negative, hostile behaviors. It appeared that they engaged in these actions in an attempt to avoid underlying feelings of sadness that they perceived as being embarrassing or unacceptable.

Similarly, in feeling-release therapy, many people feared that allowing themselves to "get into sad feelings" would lead to a depressed mood from which they would be unable to extricate themselves. Contrary to their expectations, experiencing the full range of their feelings, especially sadness, often left them happier and more alive than they had been in years.

HELPING CLIENTS EXPAND THEIR CAPACITY FOR FEELING

Over the past two decades, psychotherapists have increasingly focused attention on theories of emotional processes, using them to expand their understanding of mental disorders and as a basis for clinical interventions (Harre & Parrott, 1996).[7] For example, S. Epstein (1994) hypothesized that human beings possess two information processing systems: one based on emotions, the "experiential system," and one based on cognitive processes, the "rational system." According to Epstein, people develop basic *schemata* or *implicit beliefs* in the experiential system rather than the rational system. These beliefs "consist primarily of generalizations derived from emotionally significant past experience" (p. 715).

Perhaps partly in response to the expanding theoretical interest in emotions, a number of psychodynamic and cognitive therapies, including short-term psychodynamic therapy as described by M. Solomon et al. (2001) and emotionally focused therapy (S. Johnson, 1999) use deep emotional expression as an integral part of their treatment. Cognitive therapist Judith Beck (1995) asserted that the release of suppressed feelings helps clients identify "hot cognitions" that are made up of core schema or previously unconscious beliefs about self, others, and the world. She stated that "eliciting the hot cognitions are important because they often are of critical importance in conceptualization. Generally, these affect-laden thoughts are the most important to work with" (p. 80).

In any form of psychotherapy, it is important that therapists be comfortable with the release of intense emotions and encourage their full expression, as opposed to making interpretations that cause the client to withdraw from such expression. As mentioned, many clients are particularly reluctant to experience or express deep feelings of sadness. The anticipation of these feelings appears to arouse primitive fears and considerable tension, whereas the actual experience of sadness often brings relief. It is important to note that therapists who are threatened by the expression of strong emotions may, in subtle or not-so-subtle ways, discourage clients from experiencing or expressing these feelings in an attempt to avoid experiencing the feelings themselves.

It is crucial that clients learn to consider and accept uncritically any feeling or thought they have, no matter how seemingly unacceptable. They need to become familiar with negative thoughts or internalized voices they may be experiencing, especially those they use as rationalizations for suppressing a specific feeling or thought.

People also need to become aware of the times they become involved in a self-attacking process. By noticing when their emotional state has shifted to a more depressed mood, they can recognize that they may be experiencing self-critical thoughts. Negative attitudes toward self interfere with an individual's sense of well-being and detract from a vulnerable, feelingful state. Simply recognizing that one is involved in a process of self-attack is beneficial in itself. It is the first step in changing destructive, defensive thinking and regaining feelings of compassion for oneself.

It is important for the therapist to educate clients regarding the distinction between melodramatic emotional states and genuine feeling responses. He or she can recommend that clients record any exaggerated feeling reaction in a journal and reappraise whether the client's emotional response was appropriate to the incident or indicated a lack of concern or sensitivity toward him- or herself or another person. It is valuable for the client to identify the events or the thoughts that triggered the intense emotional reaction and understand its source. This form of self-analysis can be effective in avoiding feelings of depression and minimizing self-defeating, acting-out behaviors.

The therapeutic process challenges people's resentful, suspicious views of others. As patients progress in therapy, they increase their awareness of the times they become irritated or angry with other people. They come to realize that even when their negative thoughts about another person have some basis in reality, obsessively focusing on these thoughts damages *them*. It is important for clients to realize that holding a grudge based on internalized voices increases their indifference toward life in general and cuts them off from their natural feelings of compassion and empathy.

Finally, it is of the utmost importance for clients to learn how to "be themselves" in an ongoing motivational state, experiencing their emotions rather than observing or attending to themselves or treating themselves as objects. Living a more outward life, while at times anxiety-provoking, eventually diminishes internalized voices to a considerable degree, freeing energy for active pursuits.

Clients who try to avoid the direct experience of emotional pain by becoming removed from themselves tend to think of themselves as the "poor, misunderstood child," bravely contending with a hostile world. Operating from this perspective, they give themselves approval or praise or reward themselves for success, while denigrating and castigating themselves for errors or failures. In a sense, they pat themselves on the head when they are "good" and lash out at themselves when they are "bad."

Unfortunately, a number of counseling techniques used with recovering addicts and codependent individuals have supported this particular dimension of inwardness—that is, the tendency to treat oneself as an object. Any manner of self-parenting, reparenting oneself, or repeating self-affirmations that involve addressing oneself as an object is detrimental, no matter how benevolent or optimistic. The process of viewing oneself as the forlorn, rejected child in the sense of trying to minister to one's "inner child" and offering oneself the loving care one was deprived of in childhood fosters regressive trends.

METHODS USED BY PARTICIPANTS IN THE FRIENDSHIP CIRCLE TO EXPAND THEIR CAPACITY FOR FEELING

People in the group of friends have been able to expand their capacity for feeling by (a) placing a high value on the experience and honest expression of feeling; (b) learning that irrational feelings are acceptable and that only actions need to come under moral scrutiny; and (c) understanding the wide range of emotions that they experience in their interactions with one another. They came to recognize that frustration almost always leads to anger, that anger does not need to be justified or rationalized, and that when it is, it generally develops into feelings of victimization. People found that when they judged their anger on moral grounds, it tended to become internalized as hostility toward themselves or developed into attitudes of cynicism toward other people. In their group discussions, they applied this knowledge and have progressed in understanding their feeling reactions to events in their lives.

Personal Examples

During the years that the people in the friendship circle explored ways to have access to their feelings on a deep level, they underwent a number of basic changes. They became more vulnerable and emotionally responsive; they were closer to their feelings, especially those of sadness. For example, one couple was somewhat removed from their feelings and tended to relate to each other and to their children on an impersonal level. Both partners focused on appearance and performance more than on feeling responses or simple personal interactions. Most significantly, their children had learned, through imitation, their parents' methods for cutting off feelings. In the case of Ryan (35), their son, the pattern was one of compulsive work, which had helped alleviate his father's emotional pain in relation to the distress and unhappiness in his marriage and was a compensation for how his own father had perceived him. As he investigated his feelings, Ryan gained insight into the ways he had detached himself from painful childhood experiences, and he recorded his perceptions in a journal:

> In my family, fathers invariably raise their sons the way they were raised. They have found a way to numb themselves by somehow packaging their negative experiences and delivering them to the next generation. I know this from watching my father and grandfather relate on our visits to the family home in Ohio. In their tense conversations, I could see my grandfather's disrespect for my father. My grandfather maintained an indisputable image of my father as a person who would find every possible opportunity to get out of work. In response to that notion, he worked my father as if he were a run-down tractor that was not worth the cost of maintaining.
>
> When I was seven, my father bought a new house in a small subdivision in West Covina. It resembled every other house on the block, but it became an empty canvas to him and he set to work on elaborate patios, small gardens, attractive fences, and fine paths over well-manicured grass. He pictured a family living there in harmony, and that dream fueled his enthusiasm.
>
> But in his youth my father had been robbed of the ability to feel the satisfaction of accomplishment; now he worked as if my grandfather were still critically supervising his labor. He'd work endlessly into the night until a neighbor would call and ask him to please quit sawing or hammering so their children could sleep. He'd work in downpours and the blazing sun for hours as if he were immune to the elements and to his own fatigue.
>
> He worked as if his problems would cease with the completion of that house. It would close the remaining windows to his past and open the door to his new life. And when there was finally nothing left to do, when his beautiful home had been completed, its perfection dragged the miserable reality of his marriage into foreground. His home had been tailored for a family that did not exist. I think it was a bad awakening which he never recovered from.

The most significant changes in Ryan's parents and their adult children were the openness they developed in revealing the thoughts and feelings they had kept hidden from one another and the compassion they began to feel and express. The exploration of their deeper feelings expanded each family member's ability to relate to and trust other people.

This couple, as well as their children, participated in discussion groups in which people openly shared their knowledge and insights and revealed important aspects of their personal lives. In these meetings where expression of feelings was encouraged, the family members became aware of the pain and sadness they had been suppressing in everyday life and the strategies they had used to avoid feeling. The honest dialogue in the discussions also broke into their tendencies to be impersonal in their communications and style of relating.

The Process of Regaining Feelings in Discussion Groups With Parents

Since 1978, 30 children have been born to participants in the friendship circle. Because these parents had learned about the kinds of interactions that had hurt them in their formative years, they wanted to avoid treating their children in a similar manner. They began to meet on a regular basis to apply the insights and understanding they had achieved over the years to the problems they encountered in childrearing. In their discussions, they continually shifted from a retrospective exploration of themselves as children and the sources of their limitations and negative attitudes toward self to an investigation of themselves as parents and ways in which they extended these hostile views of themselves to their offspring.

The parents in these talks came to many interesting conclusions relevant to child development. A number of them realized that they generally averted painful primitive emotions by remaining distant and unconsciously avoiding genuine contact on a feeling level with their children. They became aware that especially close personal interactions tended to reawaken repressed feelings of sadness and pain. For example, in a discussion group, one father revealed that it caused him sadness to feel his 2-year-old son's affection. (As described in the preface, in the following excerpt, the first author is referred to as "Robert Firestone" to indicate his role as a participant/observer in this group discussion.)

> *Jerry (29):* I was watching a movie with Sean sitting in my lap, and about three times during the movie, he would look up at me, and he would touch me on the neck and smile. He would look at me for a long time, and it just felt painful. I didn't feel like stopping it or anything. I just looked back. It felt really nice to look at him, but it caused me pain.

In the same discussion, a number of other parents reported that having eye contact with their child caused them pain and sadness:

> *Robert Firestone (57):* If you picture yourself looking at your children, what do you see? What do you feel?

> *Rachel (41):* I don't know, but I know it makes me so pained. I don't know what I see because I don't look most of the time.

Robert Firestone: What do you imagine you are going to see if you picture looking at them now?

Rachel: The first thing I thought of, if I pictured my little girl, I thought I would see myself. I don't know why that was so hard.

Robert Firestone: Somehow you see yourself.

Rachel: But not happy, not a happy self.

Malina (56): I feel mostly sad, because the child is so vulnerable. You can't avoid seeing it. You might see it in yourself, and you don't want to.

Andrea (38): When I thought about looking at my children, I thought that I would see something so precious that it would break my heart. When you talked about being vulnerable, I pictured them being so open, and I thought that it would just make me feel so sad.

Robert Firestone: A lot of damage that we do to children is to keep them from being vulnerable. We pass on our own defenses. In other words, a lot of what we teach them is to *not* be vulnerable, *not* to feel, *not* to be open to hurt; but what we're really teaching them is to close off their feelings, to not invest in life, to go to sleep, to not feel, to move away from trust and closeness and intimacy, which they never recover from. That becomes a big part of their defense system, and it limits their life.

There is also a painful kind of poignant sadness when you notice yourself being compassionate or unusually tender in a personal interaction. I think people shy away from that in general and in close contact they become hardened to one another.

Andrea: I also pictured my children looking back at me, too, and I thought that I would feel so sad, because I knew that they were going to die. I'd feel so sad to see such openness. I'd be afraid they'd look at me and see me feeling sad, and then they'd figure out why I was feeling sad, and it would make them feel terrible. It's like I had a secret about them or I would feel like I had some kind of information about them that they didn't have.

What it reminded me of is this recurring nightmare where I'm in a group of people, which I always think represents my family, and I know something that they don't want to know or they don't want me to know. It's bad information in relation to them, and they're chasing me to try to get me, to try to kill me because I know this. That was the feeling I had about death and dying when I was a kid. I knew they didn't want to know. I didn't know where to go with the feelings either, because I knew that they were unacceptable there.

I was a really, really dazed child, and I think it's because I didn't know where to go with those feelings. I think that I wouldn't have been so dazed, that I would have had an awareness about my life, and I would have had a poignant feeling about things that I experienced, but I wasn't allowed to have those feelings. But I think that's what I'm afraid of when I look at a child—to have those feelings in relation to them.

Russell (29): When I'm feeling this at all in relation to myself, it's really painful to look at my son, David, because I feel what it would mean to him to lose me. It's a really painful feeling. I feel that with my daughter Amelia, too, especially when I feel close to her—it's almost like that brings that feeling out. When I really feel like I love them or I make them feel good, I feel like I can't stand the thought of them losing me.

Robert Firestone: We tend to teach children the wrong thing because we want to protect them and ourselves from the true pain of existence. We teach them to deny their aloneness, their separateness, their individual identity. We teach them to form destructive fantasy bonds rather than real relationships. We teach them to rely on imagination and to deny reality, in a sense.

But we could do the opposite. We could suffer through this pain along with our children, have a true sense of empathy, and go through life in a nonalienated posture toward our children, which would allow them to live and feel for themselves. So there is hope in understanding the dynamics that cause pain emotionally and in facing up to these issues.

After talking about their experiences in the discussion group, many of these men and women found themselves relating on a deeper, more personal level with their offspring. Regaining feeling for themselves appeared to be the crucial factor that allowed them to alter their child-rearing practices in a positive direction.

CONCLUSION

The choice to live an inward, self-protective life limits people's capability for feeling and affiliating closely with others, causing corresponding damage to loved ones, especially their children. In contrast, leading a relatively undefended life leads to an increased potential for feeling and experiencing all of one's emotions. Emotionally healthy individuals are more open to their feelings and can tolerate irrational, angry, competitive, or other "unacceptable" emotions. Therefore, they are not compelled to act out these feelings on family members and friends.

This particular understanding of mental health principles has broad psychological implications. For example, in cases of both emotional and physical child abuse, we found that the *inability* to accept feelings of anger, hostility, and resentment caused many parents to extend these feelings to their children. Later, when parents were able to recognize and accept destructive feelings in themselves toward their offspring, tension was reduced and damaging responses were minimized.

People who remain connected to their emotions retain their vitality and excitement in living. The capacity for feeling contributes to their spontaneity and creativity and adds dimensions to their personality. Psychologically healthy individuals have a strong emotional investment in living and respond with appropriate affect to both positive and negative experiences in life. However, basing one's emotional reactions on real events and circumstances rather than maintaining a self-protective stance does leave one more open to painful feelings.

A prevailing view of emotional suffering has been that it is unacceptable and that people who are in psychological pain are sick or abnormal. To the contrary, only by experiencing the painful emotions that arise in life can people feel joy or experience genuine happiness. Furthermore, when disturbing feelings are accepted or allowed full expression, there is a corresponding reduction in compulsive reliving, maladaptive uses of affect, and attempts to manipulate or control others in the interpersonal environment (Valliant, 1997).

Although one can appreciate the need to defend oneself against pain, one must recognize the destructiveness it implies to oneself and to other people, especially one's children. Regardless of other considerations, if an individual's capacity for feeling is damaged by either familial or societal processes, we must consider that socialization process to be oppressive and abusive and therefore immoral.

An effective psychotherapy would help clients recognize and gradually give up the authority of the voice as an antifeeling, antilife, regulatory mechanism, which would allow them to feel far less victimized and blaming and far more compassionate toward themselves and others. They would regain the capacity to feel the joy and happiness of life and would be able to tolerate intimacy; at the same time they would have a heightened awareness of future loss in death. In general, people who do not defend themselves against painful emotions feel more integrated, experience more fulfillment and tend to be more humane toward others.

NOTES

1. See Schore (1994), where he noted that:

   > The mother of an insecurely attached infant does not instigate interactive repair nor does she initiate distress relief sequences. As a result the infant remains stuck fast in stressful unregulated disorganized states of unmodulated negative affect. In the critical period of the imprinting of orbitofrontal circuits, this may be associated with the competitive elimination of mesocortical dopaminergic circuitry. . . . This neurochemical system . . . is critically involved in emotionality, regulation of affective responses, movements to motivational stimuli, and cognitive representational processes. (p. 402)

2. Many different components involved in the experience of emotions have been considered in the psychological literature, including the bodily component (Fosha, 2000; Valliant, 1997) and elements of evaluation, perception, sensation, and feeling (L. Greenberg & Safran, 1987). Also see Chodorow's (1999) *The Power of Feelings* for wide-ranging scholarly essays on subjectivity and intersubjectivity in psychoanalysis, cultural relativism, the anthropology of self and feeling, and the creation of personal meaning.

3. According to Stern, "affect attunement" refers to a true sharing of feelings and is different from simple imitation.

4. Before the sessions, individuals followed a routine suggested by Arthur Janov (1970) and were asked to avoid painkillers—cigarettes, alcohol, and other self-feeding habits—and encouraged to spend time in isolation and self-contemplation while developing a written history or journal of their life. The

prohibition against the use of substances and the interruption of routines had the effect of creating an immediate state of heightened tension, and anxiety and feelings that had previously been suppressed tended to surface.

5. A detailed account of intense feeling-release therapy can be found in *The Fantasy Bond* (Firestone, 1985) and in *Voice Therapy* (Firestone, 1988).

6. Valliant (1997) delineated aspects of adaptive sadness or sorrow as including, "Compassion for self; relief follows; good memories integrated with bad; hopeful about future; feels close to others; listener feels deep compassion." She also listed aspects of defensive sadness or sorrow, which include, "Self-blame, self-pity, self-attack; frustration follows—hopelessness; bad memories predominate; bleak, hopeless about future; feels more distant; listener feels attacked or helpless" (p. 238).

7. See *Emotions in the Practice of Psychotherapy* (Plutchik, 2000), *Emotion in Psychotherapy* (L. Greenberg & Safran, 1987), and *Expressing Emotion* (Kennedy-Moore & Watson, 1999). Safran (1999) has noted that "the prevailing view is shifting away from one in which emotions are seen as operating in opposition to reason to one in which they contribute to reason and to adaptive functioning" (p. xi).

6

COPING WITH ANGER, PASSIVITY, AND A VICTIMIZED POINT OF VIEW

Reject your sense of injury and the injury itself disappears.
—Marcus Aurelius, *Meditations*

In trying to live a feelingful existence, people often experience considerable difficulty in relation to their feelings of anger. Learning to deal effectively with angry emotions as they arise in the course of everyday life is crucial to achieving harmony in one's closest associations. Accepting anger as a natural emotion and learning to use aggression constructively are vital to mental health and a sense of well-being. In addition, coping successfully with hostile feelings plays a significant part in the fulfillment or lack of fulfillment in the pursuit of personal and vocational goals. Ineffective anger management seriously impairs an individual's potential to gratify the fundamental human need for social affiliation.

Contrary to the suppositions of some theorists (S. Freud, 1925/1959; Klein, 1948/1964) who argue that the infant possesses innate aggression and projects his or her own rage onto the parents, we contend that human beings are not born aggressive, destructive, or self-destructive.[1] They become angry or hostile and act out aggressive or self-destructive behavior because of the pain or frustration they experience first in relation to deprivation of their basic needs and later in relation to death anxiety. Angry feelings that are aroused in early interpersonal relationships are reinforced by frustration and anguish brought about by the child's growing awareness of the concept of his or her personal death.

131

ANGER VERSUS PSEUDOAGGRESSION

When people are frustrated in fulfilling their wants or needs, they experience feelings of anger, which is a normal and healthy phenomenon. Even if they are in denial in relation to their ongoing wants and desires, they still feel the resultant anger when they are frustrated. However, in that case, they cannot clearly identify the source. This lack of recognition of the reason for aggressive feelings, and the subsequent failure to experience anger directly, contribute to inappropriate acting out behavior, feelings of disorientation, a sense of weakness, outbursts of irritability, internalized self-attacks, or the development of psychosomatic symptoms.

Children are taught to be reasonable and rational and learn to deny or negate their anger when it seems unreasonable or irrational. In actuality, people feel angry in proportion to the degree of frustration they suffer regardless of whether their wants are acceptable or unreasonable. Ideally, rather than repress the emotion, it is functional to accept angry responses to frustration while clearly distinguishing between feelings and actions.

Pseudoaggression is different from genuine anger because it is not necessarily a response to what most people would generally equate with frustration; in fact, it is often a reaction to positive gratification or acknowledgment. When people experience uniquely positive responses in a manner that conflicts with their original identity in their family of origin or challenges their negative self-concept, their psychological equilibrium is disturbed. This fosters a state of anxiety. Paradoxically, unusually positive experiences often give rise to painful feelings of deep sadness as well as anger. When a person experiences this discomfort, he or she attempts to shut off the pain by manipulating, pushing away, or otherwise controlling the person offering the positive response of approval, affection, or love.

The term pseudoaggression refers to anger that is used to provoke rejection, create distance, and restore psychological equilibrium. This is accomplished through acts of defiance and hostility, verbal aggression, and the acting out of withholding behavior patterns that provoke others and create emotional distance. In this way, individuals control the psychosocial world around them and maintain their psychological defenses formed early in life at the expense of a richer, more fulfilling existence.

A VICTIMIZED POINT OF VIEW

The tendency to develop a victimized orientation represents a conversion of normal anger into feelings of being hurt or victimized, a chronic maladaptation that is not suitable for coping with events in one's life. The victimized feelings of a child may be a fitting response to his or her state of helplessness but are not appropriate for adults. Children lack power and are at the mercy of their parents, and events often do happen to them that are beyond their control and understanding. The adult who maintains the victimized posture of a child will fail to make adaptive responses to events in his or her life. Rather than contending with challenging situations, individuals in a victimized state complain, feel overwhelmed by external circumstances, and focus on the unfairness of events.

A preoccupation with rights and fairness, even when justified, is not helpful in problem-solving. In situations in which events are realistically overpowering, it still serves no purpose to dwell on the fact that one is the helpless victim. In the worst of circumstances imaginable, such as confinement in a concentration camp, it is not functional to feel victimized, although an obvious case could be made for feeling this way. One would be better off actively planning tactics of survival or escape rather than focusing on injustice and wrongdoing. Frankl (1954/1967), when writing of his personal experiences in a German concentration camp, emphasized the importance of an attitude diametrically opposed to the posture of victimization:

> Though on entering the camp everything might be taken away from the prisoner . . . this freedom remained to him; and it remained to him literally to the last moment, to the last breath. It was the freedom to bear oneself "this way or that way," and there *was* a "this or that." (p. 98)

People who play out the victim role feel that they have an inherent right to have their needs met. They believe they are entitled to good treatment from families, friends, and from their mates. For example, a woman patient once complained that every evening she prepared dinner for her husband but he typically arrived home one or two hours late without phoning ahead to let her know. She wondered if this was "right?" In reality, the core issue in this case was not whether her husband was right or wrong but how she faced the frustration and resultant anger stimulated by her husband's lateness. She had every right to feel her anger and to appraise her options in terms of response, but reacting as a helpless victim was maladaptive and ultimately meaningless.

A person has the right to *feel* angry and to consider constructive action directed toward changing circumstances, including acting out angry responses when the person considers it to have an adaptive function. In contrast, a person who assumes a victimized posture becomes preoccupied with "rights" and "shoulds," which leads to inward brooding and an obsessional buildup of feelings of revenge (Dutton, 1995b; Motz, 2001; Pearson, 1997).[2] When people internalize anger in this way, it intensifies until it becomes so inappropriate that there is no reasonable outlet.

People who assume a self-righteous stance are merely acting out a sophisticated form of this victimized role. They are angry because the world is not the way they think it should be. They tend to disguise their feelings of childish rage by issuing judgments and evaluations of others and by insisting on authoritarian methods of punishment for those who make mistakes. Usually they disclaim any personal responsibility for events that have gone wrong.

Passive–Aggression: Manipulations of "Negative Power"

Blackmailing another person through weakness, sickness, incompetence, or even mental illness are all expressions of negative power that may be used when one feels too guilty or fearful to be directly angry. Manipulations that precipitate guilt or fear reactions exert a powerful influence on others. Most children are taught that they are "selfish" for expressing their wants and needs and learn to be indirect and fundamentally dishonest about their desires. As a result, in their adult lives, they continue to rely on manipulative rather than forthright means of attaining their goals and also remain vulnerable to manipulation by others. These controlling behaviors are often subtle but nonetheless intimidating.

Although both men and women tend to manipulate through negative power plays, the traditional roles that women have historically been forced to accept have led them to adopt a more passive posture. Despite the fact that there have been indications of change in recent years, in the past cultural prejudices and a patriarchal society largely prevented women's full participation in social, economic, and political arenas (C. Gilligan, 1982). The lack of access to real power caused women to exercise indirect or passive–aggressive means in attempting to fulfill their human potentiality. Although the stereotypical view of men is that they are strong and assertive, they too can use passive methods to express their anger, such as sulking, using the "silent treatment," becoming depressed, or withdrawing.

The Paranoid Process

Paranoid thinking is a serious disorder of focus and perspective whereby the subjective world of the individual—sensations, feelings, perceptions— is experienced as happening to him or her rather than originating in or being caused by him or her. According to R. Siegel (1994), "In the paranoid mode of thinking, something is always happening to the person" (pp. 9–10). Ogden (1989) conceptualized the paranoid schizoid mode as "a mode of generating experience characterized by . . . a very limited capacity to experience oneself as the author and interpreter of one's thoughts and feelings" (p. 149).

When feelings of victimization have become a characteristic pattern for an individual, the anger that would be felt in reaction to the frustration of not getting what he or she wants is continually distorted into feelings of having been wounded, oppressed, or exploited. The primary cause of this process of distortion is the inability to accept aggressive or competitive feelings in oneself. The paranoid client characteristically denies his or her angry, aggressive feelings and tends to project them onto the external world and other people. This leads to a kind of chronic passivity in relation to events and to an expectation of harm from the outside.

The paranoid individual is hypervigilant and constantly scans the environment to determine if someone is disapproving, angry, critical, indifferent, or threatening.[3] With this expectation and an abnormally high sensitivity to aggression in others, there is a tendency to distort and even to invent malice in other people, as noted previously. People who have tendencies toward paranoia anticipate from others the anger and competitiveness, in a magnified version, that they deny in themselves. Our research (Doucette-Gates et al., 1999) and other studies (J. Gilligan, 1996, 2001; Skodol, 1998; Toch, 1992) demonstrate that a paranoid, victimized orientation and attitude increase an individual's propensity to act violently and to feel justified in doing so. In terms of the voice, the person is telling him- or herself, "It's the other person's fault."

In his work with violent men, James Gilligan (1996) has suggested that:

> Violence toward others may be thought of as the behavioral equivalent of paranoia. . . . But paranoia itself is the form of psychopathology that results when a person's ability to differentiate between feelings and facts is overwhelmed by feelings of shame, so that even ordinary experiences may be perceived mistakenly as shameful, culminating in the increasing delusion that one is actually being shamed or exposed, spied on and observed, held up to ridicule and scorn, criticism, and scurrilous gossip. (pp. 75–76)

In analyzing how the projection process and the tendency to attribute blame to others contributes to paranoia, Meissner (1986) emphasized that the process of projection could even be a relatively normal process. He proposed that "Whenever we attribute the causes of internal sensations to external events rather than looking for internal causes, we are experiencing a form of projection" (p. 84).

In general, therapists treating clients who have paranoid thought disturbances or who externalize their inner conflicts will be included in the clients' paranoid ideology, especially when the therapist encourages the client to directly confront the belief that outside sources are wholly responsible for their suffering.[4] Attempts to correct distortions or to point out reality are usually met with anger or rage or an abrupt termination of therapy. In part, this anger is related to underlying feelings of vanity or narcissism. Both Kernberg and Meissner have described the role played by narcissism in paranoid pathology. Meissner (1986) focused on understanding why patients are so resistant to giving up paranoid ideation and the victimized position, explaining that this resistance is a result of the inherent narcissistic dynamics of the introjects themselves. According to Meissner, surrendering these introjects:

> Requires some form of confrontation or working through of the infantile dependence and the narcissistic investment in the introjects. Not infrequently, as the narcissistic defenses are diminished, one begins to meet the intense rage against and envy of the significant objects. . . . This rage and envy often play themselves out in the relationship to the therapist. (p. 60)

In intimate relationships, one partner may become paranoid, suspicious, or accusatory, for example, expecting infidelity and deception on the part of his or her loved one, even in the face of strong evidence to the contrary. The paranoid process may begin at a point where the partner's focus shifts from feeling and experiencing his or her own love for the other to a preoccupation with and questioning of the other's love (McCormack, 2000; M. Solomon, 1989).[5] Relating to another person in terms of obligations rather than free choice can also set the stage for paranoid, victimized thinking. The process of punishing, accusing, and feeling exploited or unfairly treated is debilitating; it often leads to a low-grade anger, which is expressed through passive–aggressive withholding behaviors and can at times lead to violent behavior.

Origins of Passivity and the Victimized Stance

A victimized orientation to life is determined by a number of factors: (a) by the child's denial and displacement of the negative characteristics of the parental environment onto other people, as described in chapter 3. In an attempt to partially relieve the pain and anxiety of emotional deprivation in a climate where one's needs are not met, the child tends to negate unpleasant realities and fantasize an image of the parent or parents as good and loving, as has been discussed earlier (Arieti, 1974; Firestone, 1985). The child consciously retains an idealized image of the parents while unconsciously retaining the negative image of the parents, which is projected onto others in the interpersonal milieu. (b) When the general atmosphere in the home is inadequate, rejecting, or hostile, the child's feeling reactions to these conditions are later transferred to new relationships and to the world at large. For this reason, some people live in a threatening and dangerous world of their own making. When children's angry reactions are met with disapproval and counterhostility, they have no outlet for their anger. They become passive and inward, either internalizing their hostility or projecting it onto others. When they project it outward, they distort other people by perceiving them as being more angry or hostile than they really are. Even when they experience a minimal amount of hostility directed toward them, they will most likely exaggerate its intensity. In addition, by acting on expectations of anger from others, the victimized or passive person actually elicits angry reactions and rejection in new associations (Firestone, 1985; M. Solomon, 1989). The process acts as a self-fulfilling prophecy that seriously affects personal relationships and career opportunities. (c) People who are passive and feel victimized often view themselves as objects (Laing, 1960/1969; Lasch 1984). Their eyes are turned inward on themselves rather than outward toward the world, and as a result, they tend to become excessively self-conscious and often distort reality. Lasch (1984) asserted that many people in our modern "narcissistic culture" "have to learn the trick of observing themselves as if the events of their lives were happening to someone else . . . a withdrawal from the beleaguered self into the person of a detached, bemused, ironic observer" (p. 96).

When children are treated as objects or possessions by parents, they depersonalize to a certain extent and cut off feeling for themselves. As noted, people who are detached from themselves in this way often view themselves as the poor, misunderstood child, valiantly contending with a hostile world—in effect, a noble child syndrome. This attitude is particularly maladaptive in close personal relationships.

In describing the psychodynamics underlying more severe forms of paranoia, Meissner (1986) conceptualized the patient's "self-organization" as including an amalgamation of "introjections of the sadistic, harsh, punitive, hostilely destructive, and rigidly demanding father on the one hand, and of the depressive, masochistic, and victimized image of the mother on the other" (p. 256). Meissner went on to argue, "Consequently, the interlocking of the parental projection with the child's internalization provides the matrix out of which the paranoid process derives" (pp. 256–257), and added, "the child's interaction with the mother carries the mother's implicit conviction that the child is somehow defective, weak, and inadequate" (p. 257).

Basic Paranoia in Relation to the Knowledge of Death

When children first learn about their personal death, this knowledge contributes to a basic distrust or paranoia that later may be projected onto real-life situations that have nothing to do with the original cause. In some sense, paranoia is an understandable response to the existential truth that powerful forces beyond our control are acting on us; they are alien to our physical and mental well-being and eliminate any possibility of ultimate survival. As adults, many individuals overreact with rage, fear, and panic to events that do not justify an intense reaction of helplessness or powerlessness.

For example, Meyer (1975) drew attention to the fact that the displacement of problems connected with the fear of death is apparent in agoraphobia, fear of cardiac arrest, animal phobias, and claustrophobia. People often create adversity and trouble in their lives or become preoccupied with pseudo problems to avoid anxiety regarding the core issues of life and death.

The origins of passivity and a victimized point of view have been studied in the laboratory with both animals and humans. Martin Seligman (1975) developed his "learned helplessness" model of human motivation, which he defined in a later work as "the state of affairs in which nothing you choose to do affects what happens to you" (Seligman, 1990, p. 5). Through a series of experiments, he found that when aversive events were unpredictable, uncontrollable, and inescapable, an individual's emotional, cognitive, and behavioral responses were disrupted, which led to extreme passivity or paralysis.

Seligman (1975) noted that "a child's or an adult's attitude toward his own helplessness or mastery has its roots in infant development" (p. 150). Linking learned helplessness, passivity, depression, and a pessimistic world view to early stimulus deprivation, he suggested that maternal deprivation "results in a particularly crucial lack of control" (p. 146); "an infant deprived of stimulation is an infant thereby deprived of *control* over stimulation" (p. 144). His analyses included experimental and natural settings where the infant or child was deprived of opportunities to learn how to deal with frustrating, but resolvable, conflicts: "When the child, by his own actions, copes with anxiety and frustration, his sense of effectiveness increases. If either the frustrations remain unresolved or the parents resolve them for the child, helplessness tends to build" (p. 147). "When an infant has a rich supply of powerful synchronies between his actions and outcomes, a sense of mastery develops. Responsive mothering is fundamental to the learning of mastery" (p. 150).

In later studies, Seligman (1990) found that a pessimistic explanatory style (the reasons people give for failure or for aversive events) "changes learned helplessness from brief and local to long-lasting and general. Learned helplessness becomes full-blown depression when the person who fails is a pessimist" (p. 76) In other words, according to Seligman, an individual's explanatory style or attitude of victimization or nonvictimization is crucial: "Changing the destructive things you say to yourself when you experience the setbacks that life deals all of us is the central skill of optimism" (p. 15).

HELPING CLIENTS LEARN TO COPE WITH ANGER

Many people have considerable difficulty accepting feelings of anger and aggression in themselves. Individuals who tend to externalize their internal conflicts or blame others for their problems have a self-righteous approach to anger. They often manifest a sense of entitlement; they believe that they deserve to get what they want and that they are supposed to be loved. These attitudes and beliefs pervert their normal feelings of anger, transforming them into feelings of being a victim, and contribute to a passive, paranoid orientation toward life.

Clients who handle their anger by expressing it through passive–aggressive behavior, righteous indignation, or victimized brooding need to relinquish the basic assumption that they are innocent victims of fate. It goes without saying that this presents a challenge for many people both in and out of therapy. It is understandable that people who are afraid of their anger would prefer to believe that they have no recourse except to use indirect means of expressing it when resolving their conflicts. Nevertheless, during sessions, they need to challenge attitudes that perpetuate a victimized mode of thinking.

We have found that if borderline, paranoid clients, who tend to externalize their problems, are allowed to vent their feelings of being used, exploited, or slighted for even a brief period of time without being responded to, they often mistake attentive listening for agreement with their victimized point of view. Unless these feelings are dealt with, clients often become worse. In a therapy where rapport has been established, the victimized or paranoid client's recounting of grievances can be interrupted through direct confrontation. Exposure of paranoid attitudes combined with good humor, along with the therapist's genuine caring, empathy, and concern, is most effective.

Common Misconceptions About Anger

In educating clients about anger, it is worthwhile to challenge some of the false assumptions about aggression. A common misconception is that anger is invariably "bad" and the person who feels angry is a bad person. Another inaccurate belief is that being angry at another person implies accusing him or her of wrongdoing.

Many people believe that anger is the opposite of love and that manifestations of anger have no place in a close and enduring relationship. They find it difficult to deal with the essential ambivalence of real-life situations. In a close relationship, partners must be able to manifest both anger and love appropriate to the vagaries of their partner's responses to them.

People who were physically abused as children or who witnessed incidents of domestic violence learn early in life that anger is always dangerous, and later find it difficult to counter this overgeneralization. According to Garbarino (1999), "maltreated children and those who witness violence *"become hypersensitive to negative social cues . . .* [and] *oblivious to positive social* cues" (p. 81).[6] Many individuals from abusive or violent families react as though the person who provokes or frustrates them is responsible for their angry reactions. They mistake the stimulus for the cause. "You *make* me angry" is a statement that reflects the assumption that they conceptualize anger as a passive process in which someone else is always to blame for their aggressive feelings. They refuse to accept active responsibility for their own emotions.

As individuals progress in psychotherapy, they generally develop a new perspective on their anger and tend to view it more realistically, as a natural and automatic response to frustration. This change in perspective enables them to gain control over their lives in ways they never thought possible. It is vital that people develop personal power, responsibility, and strength even in situations that cause them suffering rather than complain that life is unfair.

Constructive Uses of Anger

Despite the negative connotations assigned to anger, it is obvious that it has a number of constructive and adaptive functions. Throughout evolutionary history, the experience of anger was clearly necessary for the survival of Homo sapiens. Threats from dangerous predators and other menacing situations aroused fear in our ancestors, and they responded with "fight or flight" reactions. Feelings of anger provided the energy and motivation required for aggressive "fight" behaviors used in self-defense or in defense of the tribe, which often resulted in the survival of the defenders.[7] In addition, in contemporary society, anger and outrage at social injustices and inequities provide the passion and drive necessary for making important positive changes in the political and social sphere.

There is an analogy in personal relationships where anger, when manifested appropriately, can serve to alter destructive behavior and eliminate barriers to maintaining an intimate relationship. On the other hand, when angry attitudes are not effectively communicated, there is a concomitant buildup of hostile feelings and cynicism that damages each person and leads to serious distancing behaviors. In addition, when these feelings are acted out in passive–aggressive behavior rather than dealt with directly, they predispose distance and alienation in the relationship.

Helping Clients Accept Anger in Themselves

Clients can learn that in dealing with angry feelings as with any other emotion, their feelings are involuntary, yet they must be felt. On the other hand, they need to consciously decide how to respond in situations that arouse anger or aggression. It is important that clients develop a basic understanding that their actions, unlike feelings, are a moral issue as well as a survival issue, whereas how they feel should come under no such restrictions. Feelings are automatic responses to favorable and unfavorable events, and no one can be judged for what he or she feels. People who have learned this principle are able to live their lives more fully and honestly. They are in control of their lives as far as their actions are concerned. They tend to act in their own interests and manifest fewer destructive behaviors toward others. They may even learn to treat these thoughts with some humor because they are harmless.

Individuals who have problems with anger need to learn to give themselves time to reflect on what they are feeling or thinking without automatically acting on their anger. Through the technique of free association, clients can learn to accept a wide range of emotional reactions, including anger and hostility within themselves. This acceptance in turn enables them to gain more perspective on a hostile exchange with another person—for example, by allowing themselves sufficient time to reflect on their reactions and develop insight into the dynamics operating in the interaction.

To accept anger and manage it effectively, it is essential that clients recognize that when they are having a dramatic reaction to a current event, their response is most often infused with elements from the past that caused them considerable psychological pain. One technique or corrective suggestion is to have clients ask themselves how much their angry reaction has to do with the current situation and how much it has to do with past experiences.

Modifying the Victimized Orientation to Life

Maintaining a victimized point of view precludes further emotional growth and causes untold damage to other people and to oneself. Giving up a victimized point of view is therefore vital to an individual's personal development. Therapists can help clients learn to control the destructive urge to adopt a victimized role. They can counter the client's desire to blame others by acknowledging that the world does in fact contain many inequities; there are innumerable injustices that are discriminatory and unfair to individuals or to groups of people. They should be encouraged to accept the fact that the world does not owe them anything—neither a living nor happiness nor pleasant surroundings.

In reality, individuals may be unable to find remedial solutions for many of the conditions of society, but they can change themselves. Clients who progress in therapy are often able to envision solutions they previously ignored because they preferred to feel victimized. It is important that they come to realize how much more productive it is to view life from this more optimistic perspective than to remain mired in blaming failures on others or outside circumstances. In reacting to injustices in a powerful, nonvictim-ized style, one can actually facilitate changes in society as well.

In dealing with personal relationships, psychotherapists should make clear to clients that they do not inherently deserve, or not deserve, to receive anything in the way of good treatment from others, and therefore it is not meaningful for them to speak of someone being unfair to them in that sense. When clients continue to believe that they deserve to be loved, or that they are entitled to something better than they have now, they tend to become increasingly futile and hopeless in their outlook, and what is worse, this orientation solicits sympathy from others.

In working with clients, it is important to help them to make the distinction between sympathy and empathy. The therapist can point out that both giving or arousing sympathy in another person is damaging to self and others in that it reinforces victimized thinking. Commiserating with others as contrasted with having empathy for other people's misfortunes can be counterproductive and unhealthy for all concerned. Clients can learn to be sensitive and compassionate toward friends and family members without being overprotective, sentimental, or falsely supportive. When at-tempting to give up a victimized role, clients often discover that their choice of friends is crucial during this transition, in terms of avoiding destructive "sympathetic" responses from well-meaning family members or friends.

Helping Clients Assume Responsibility for Their Lives

On a behavioral level, clients can become active agents in determining the direction of their lives. If they feel stuck in an unsatisfactory relationship or barred from getting ahead in a career or job, or if the same negative events seem to keep happening, they can explore the possibility that passive attitudes or feelings of victimization had more to do with these events than they realized. It is also important that clients learn to avoid complaining about their problems to others in a style that "dumps" the problem on them. In fact, complaining and discounting one's own role in maintaining negative circumstances are dysfunctional approaches that should be eliminated en-tirely. This process injures personal relationships and can lead to failure in the workplace.

When clients change their victimized manner of speaking about events they have experienced and the crises that resulted, it is possible for them to develop a different and more effective form of communication, one that involves taking full responsibility for their own feelings and actions. The problem-solving perspective that they eventually develop in therapy con-trasts with fault-finding and registering dissatisfaction and leaves them free to explore alternatives. In close relationships, a responsible, positive approach helps clients to arrive at constructive solutions and takes the burden off other people.

Giving Up Victimized Language and Thinking

It is beneficial for clients to drop certain words from their vocabulary, such as "fair," "should or shouldn't," "right," and "wrong" because these words support a passive judgmental orientation to life. These words and phrases are generally used by people to coerce or otherwise manipulate those they feel victimized by. In addition, this type of vocabulary supports attitudes of condemnation toward people and circumstances and is destructive when applied to oneself. It interferes with coping behaviors and distracts a person from the real issues involved in life.

Relating to another person in terms of shoulds and obligations is another method whereby people set themselves up for paranoid thoughts: "If you really loved me, you wouldn't want to go off with your friends on the weekend." "You should spend more time with me and the kids." "You owe us, after all we are your parents." "It's not fair the way you treat me."

In a relationship, a person has every right to ask for what he or she wants, and the other has every right to refuse. If people attach the frustration at not getting what they want to an expectation that someone is obliged to satisfy them, paranoid feelings are inevitable. It is functional to react to problems with appropriate feeling and action rather than to evaluate the fairness of the situation. When the client's focus is shifted back to a clear knowledge of what he or she wants and feels and away from judging the responses of others, then he or she will have a more realistic perspective on the world.

Helping Clients Avoid the Use of Pseudoaggression to Maintain Emotional Distance

Real closeness and intimacy threaten people's defenses. It is frightening and often emotionally painful to be vulnerable and close to another person, to experience real wanting and real desires, to feel love, and to feel worthwhile. When clients have become anxious because their psychological equilibrium has been disrupted, they often resort to pseudoaggressive responses that push others away. To develop personally, they need to learn how to sweat through this anxiety rather than acting out distancing behaviors. For this reason, it is important to have clients carefully explore their feelings and actions. They can be alerted to the fact that positive responses from people they love and respect may be threatening and could precipitate negative thoughts and attitudes toward themselves and their partner.

Therapists can help their clients become more objective and noncritical in their attitudes toward their loved ones and especially to avoid cynicism. Hostile, cynical, and condescending attitudes usually reflect an alien point of view that is in conflict with one's real feelings. In this regard, it is important to teach clients how to give away their angry thoughts rather than act them out with their partner. This process involves talking about anger in a nondramatic tone and admitting any irrationality or feelings of being victimized. This type of communication is less likely to arouse counterhostility and enables people to deal with their anger in a way that causes the least amount of pain to one another.

In addition, clients need to relinquish indirect ways of expressing their anger to their mates. For example, passive brooding and sulking serve to alienate the other person. Sarcasm, humorous ridicule, or gossiping to a friend about one's mate generate hurt feelings, resentment, and anger in one's partner.[8] Therefore, clients need to let go of personal grudges and deal with negative feelings directly as they make efforts to regain closeness in their relationships.

It is clear that absolutism, feelings of superiority, rigidity, and defensiveness are barriers to good relationships. Therefore, it is advantageous for partners in close relationships to relinquish their stubbornness about being "right" and to adopt a more flexible posture. Indeed, nothing has more power in changing a relationship for the better than "unilateral disarmament" (see chapter 10). This occurs when one or another partner puts the goal of maintaining loving feelings ahead of proving he or she is "right" and becomes more open and vulnerable in the heat of an argument. Honestly exposing cynical, hostile thoughts toward others as well as toward oneself often has the positive effect of ending this need to be right.

OVERCOMING THE VICTIMIZED POINT OF VIEW IN THE FRIENDSHIP CIRCLE

Individuals in the group of friends have made important strides toward giving up aspects of a victimized posture. Their efforts include (a) learning to accept and appropriately express angry feelings, (b) learning to be nondefensive and open to feedback, and (c) becoming active participants in a variety of shared endeavors and projects.

Dealing With Angry Feelings

Over the years, people in the group of friends have learned how to talk about and express their anger rather than acting out aggression indirectly through sarcasm or directly through verbal attacks. Many individuals who always "edited" their negative or angry thoughts have found that they could disclose angry, critical thoughts to a friend or a partner and not be punished for their perceptions. For example, one woman, Beverly (41), who was afraid of her own anger, had been instructed as a child to say nothing unless she had something "nice" to say. After taking a chance on disclosing her angry feelings to her partner in a discussion group, she said she felt "freed":

> I felt totally "there" in the conversation. I felt like I was in my own skin, that I wasn't hiding or censoring anything. I felt trusting of the other people in the room and it made such a difference. Now I feel that though there may be issues between us, I can talk about my anger, I'm not afraid that what I'm thinking is so terrible or devastating.

People have also become familiar with the process of investigating the origins of their anger, cynicism, and hurt feelings. They have come to understand that cynicism, in particular, is a protection against early painful feelings of rejection and abandonment and is devastating to a relationship. Brad (52), who has had a close relationship with Beverly for a number of years, describes how he felt after responding to her expression of anger in the discussion group:

> I feel like the only thing that is important is to let my feelings come out and not to withhold anything, to not be cynical, to not say anything cynical at all. And it really has had an effect on me. Of course, I wish our relationship were better, but on one level, it doesn't matter as long as I don't feel cynical. As long as I don't say anything cynical then I'm in good shape.
>
> It seems like the damage that I've done from being cynical was mostly to myself; it wasn't the external events or the way the relationship was going. It was the way I was reacting with cynicism, the kind of seething anger I was into, that was hurting me. This issue has ruined my life for so many years. I realize that the cynicism and withholding go hand in hand.

People have learned to be nondefensive when listening to negative feedback—that is, they do not respond with counterattacks, exaggerate the negativity of the information they receive, or intimidate other people by threatening to fall apart. Instead, they try to examine the information and explore its truth or falsity in a rational manner. At the same time, they have learned that giving negative feedback to someone in a judgmental or evaluative tone, or trying to fulfill a need to always be right, is nonproductive and harmful to them as well as to the recipient.

Nondefensiveness does not imply that one person has to compromise or give up his or her point of view to resolve an issue. People approach feedback with a view of using it as constructive information regarding important changes that they are attempting to make in their lives. In their disagreements, they are interested in finding out what is real and in exploring the possibility of finding the common reality between themselves and another person. As one participant put it, "The main thing in a lot of these exchanges is not to agree on what happened, but to see how ridiculously unimportant and trivial the argument really is."

Active Participation in Life as an Antidote to a Passive, Victimized Posture

People in the friendship circle have found that active participation in life, besides its definite appeal, is valuable in counteracting a passive acceptance of the status quo and in challenging victimized attitudes. In particular, sailing as an activity has provided a real-life laboratory that facilitated insights and important changes in self-limiting behaviors that were based on a victimized approach to life.

In their travels, the friends have never considered themselves as simply passengers. On voyages, everyone participates as a member of the crew, standing watches, learning navigation and helmsmanship. All the crew members, including the children, feel that they have contributed something to getting their ship across oceans. For them, the voyages represent a life of calculated risk-taking, a life that heightens their appreciation of being alive and reflects a balance between living life fully and spontaneously while taking safety precautions seriously. The friends have also learned to calmly accept circumstances they cannot change. For example, there are few complaints about the weather, physical ailments, seasickness, or tiredness among this group of people. Witnessing wind and water conditions change from a dead calm to a full gale within a few hours has impressed them with the ludicrous aspects of complaining about something completely beyond their control.

The opportunities afforded the young people from the sailing adventures cannot be overstated. Several took part in the circumnavigation, and on their return home, they gradually assumed positions of leadership in the fledgling businesses of the group. For example, Alex (42), who had been an angry, passive, sullen teenager, became a watch captain on the ocean voyage. Before the trip, Alex's mother had literally been unable to get him out of bed to attend school; his low grades did not reflect his innate intelligence but represented an acting out of defiant, passive–aggressive attitudes. In fact, on some level, Alex was proud of the fact that he was a failure, depreciated anyone over the age of 30, and strongly resented authority.

In the adolescents' discussion group, where he was able to talk about his anger and express it directly, Alex felt supported in many of his views and the hostile feelings he had toward his parents and other adults who exhibited similar negative characteristics. Moreover, the chance to relate on an equal basis with the group leader, one of the parents, and other adults who occasionally visited the group, helped him overcome his passive–aggressive tendencies and feelings of being victimized. Later, because of his skills in boat-handling and navigation, he was elected watch captain on the voyage around the world and became active in assuming responsibility for the people on board. In a recent interview, Alex described the changes he had made as a result of taking part in the discussion group and sharing the sailing adventures with his friends:

> The example that I had from my family was that you grew up. You got in a dead-end job. You came home. You were unhappy to see your wife. The kids were trouble. You had some drinks and you tried to ignore things. That's what I learned from my father.
>
> So, the teenage talk, and sailing, the opportunity to get to know adults, trying to treat adults as other people rather than as people who are just there to tell you what you can't do, opening up like that, made a big change in my life. In fact, I wouldn't have thought possible some of the things that came into my life. I had always thought that I was going to be angry and sullen and alone through my whole life.

Overall, the group meetings provided a social pressure against passive–aggressive behaviors on the part of both adolescents and adults. The participants exerted a powerful influence on one another not to complain, act out passive–aggressive responses, or feel victimized. People who spoke from the victimized position often received feedback about this style of communication. Although the participants were empathic and understanding in offering this feedback, they were also direct and straightforward in their challenges.

CONCLUSION

Anger is an appropriate response to frustration and stress. When people can accept angry emotions they are less likely to act them out destructively. In a healthy response to anger, one does not attempt to justify angry emotions by becoming self-righteous. Relinquishing the child–victim role leaves people free to pursue career and personal goals without using nonproductive techniques of sulking, complaining, pretending to be helpless, or other manifestations of negative power. Unfortunately, the role of the victim, with its associated manipulations of negative power, has become a standard in many families and has a myriad of destructive effects on all of the members. Freeing oneself from the guilt and misery of maintaining a passive, victimized posture in life is energizing and lends itself to more effective coping responses. In taking a stand against negative power plays and leading a more feelingful, honest, and open life, a person will experience more self-respect, integrity, and personal satisfaction.

NOTES

1. A number of theorists, among them Lore and Schultz (1993), have asserted that prevailing theories of aggression (the instinct theory, the aggression–frustration model, and social learning theories) are contradictory and should be reexamined to clarify the specific environmental conditions that arouse aggressive impulses and violent acts in individuals.
2. See Pearson's (1997) discussion of the "culture of victimhood," whereby homicidal acts committed by women are often rationalized or excused, and *The Psychology of Female Violence* (Motz, 2001).
3. In *Cognitive Therapy for Delusions, Voices and Paranoia*, Chadwick, Birchwood, and Trower (1996) described two distinctive types of paranoia: the "poor-me" and the "bad me" orientation:

   > The poor me paranoid is other-focused rather than self-focused . . . [and] attributes causality to the other as object, and finally blames the other as the cause of his demise—a form of the self-serving bias seen in ordinary people except more so. The outcome will be a set of other-blaming beliefs and demands—he should not treat me this way! He is a worthless rat! He should be condemned! etc. So long as the poor me paranoid can maintain his strategy, he will retain a *high* self-esteem. (pp. 159–160)

   These beliefs are similar in content to a number of items on the *Firestone Assessment of Violent Thoughts* (FAVT)—for example, "They're just trying to humiliate you." "They're the ones who are crazy, not you." "Just look at what he(she) did to you!" (Doucette-Gates et al., 1999). We conjecture that the poor-me individual may be more likely to manifest outward aggression or violent tendencies than the bad-me individual.
4. Kernberg (1984) has described paranoid developments in the transference, "characterized by the appearance in the patient of intense suspiciousness of the analyst, which may take on delusional qualities and characteristics and may last for a segment of a single hour to several weeks or (rarely) months" (p. 290).
5. See M. Solomon's (1989) discussion of relationships in which the defense of projective identification has allowed partners to avoid "some nameless dread, such as the terror of abandonment or destructive fantasies" (p. 92). When these dreaded feelings do emerge, "There is often an entitled, demanding, rageful insistence on justice that goes beyond specific issues. Each spouse, of course, sees the difficulties as emanating from the other" (p. 92).
6. For a summary of research on which Garbarino's statements are based, see Dodge, Pettit, and Bates (1997).
7. In discussing the evolution of the human brain, Kotulak (1996) has noted that hormones such as adrenaline and cortisol are "designed to respond to psychological or physical danger" and "prepare the body for fight or flight" (p. 38).
8. See pp. 200–221 in Lerner's (1985) book *The Dance of Anger* for suggestions about ways clients can learn how to handle anger. Also see *Angry All the Time: An Emergency Guide to Anger Control* (Potter-Efron, 1994); and *The Anger Workbook* (Bilodeau, 1992).

7

GENEROSITY VERSUS WITHHOLDING

> You can hold yourself back from the sufferings of the world, this is
> something you are free to do and is in accord with your nature, but
> perhaps precisely this holding back is the only suffering that you might
> be able to avoid.
> —Franz Kafka (quoted in Laing, 1960/1969, p. 82)

Each dimension of a life-affirming existence challenges the ways that individuals impose unnecessary limitations, restrictions, and suffering on themselves. Nowhere is this more evident than when people have the opportunity to extend themselves to others through sensitive acts of kindness and generosity. Giving freely of oneself and of one's time and energy counteracts self-protective defenses, increases feelings of self-esteem, and makes one feel worthwhile. The process is circular: As people give themselves more value and come to cherish their experience, they naturally feel motivated to extend this same valuing and appreciation to others through altruistic, generous behaviors. Being able to act on the desire to contribute to the well-being of others brings one pleasure and imbues life with meaning. Indeed, the goal of becoming more generous and giving is based on sound mental health principles rather than on moral imperatives.

Generosity refers to behaviors that are outward expressions of subjective feelings of empathy and compassion toward one's fellow human beings. Generous actions ideally involve an equal exchange between people, a mutual give-and-take, accompanied by benevolence on the giver's side, and an openness to accepting the offering on the part of the recipient.

Withholding, in contrast, refers to a withdrawal of positive feelings and behaviors from others and includes a holding back of pleasure or fulfillment from oneself (self-denial) as well. People who are withholding resist involvement in emotional transactions; they are reluctant to offer love and affection outwardly or to take love in from the outside.

Withholding in the broader sense is not limited to the holding back of affection and sexual responses but relates to restricting one's capabilities and a tendency to retreat from leading a productive, fulfilling life. Whenever people inhibit behaviors or qualities that were once an important expression of their personal wants, motivation, or identity, they are no longer goal-directed and are therefore prone to failure in their personal or vocational pursuits. Examples of withholding can be observed both in relationships and in the workplace: Children are damaged unintentionally by withholding parents, adults waste hundreds of hours resisting accomplishment while believing that they are working hard (McClure, 2000), and much of the distress in relationships is caused by one or both partners taking back the love they once expressed.

WITHHOLDING AND PASSIVE–AGGRESSION

Passive–aggression as a result of suppressed anger, as described in the previous chapter, is one form of withholding. It is characterized by the presence of oppositional, negativistic traits and behaviors and expressions of indirect hostility. Passive–aggressive withholding is prevalent in the workplace, in which one can observe patterns of procrastination, fatigue, incompetence, insolence, and other nonproductive work styles.

Similarly, children may develop a passive–aggressive orientation and learn to control their parents through regressive, withholding behaviors of noncompliance, incompetence, dawdling, and procrastination (Karen, 1994; Roberts, 1995).[1] They discover that by *not* performing, by not doing what their parents want, they are able to exert a considerable influence. In some cases, withholding takes the form of a more active rebelliousness or stubbornness. These children actually develop a sense of identity from being defiant, from going against parental wishes and directives. This type of defiance may be manifested early in life. Although rebellious or defiant behavior can reflect a child's desire to express independence and separation from parenting figures, continued defiance is symptomatic of a more general withholding.

Children who restrict or give up their special talents and abilities in this manner—for example, youngsters who refuse to function or perform at their level of capability in school, later have difficulty living up to their potential in their chosen careers. Eventually they adopt an overall style of holding back that operates even in areas where they themselves want to excel. These individuals have learned to say "no" to everything, including their own wants and aspirations (Brooks & Goldstein, 2001; Gootnick, 1997).

Passive–aggressive withholding occurs between employers and employees on a routine basis. Both men and women characteristically restrict their own effectiveness to provoke authority figures, whose superior positions they resent. In business meetings, in industry, at school, and in other formal situations, direct expressions of anger are not usually tolerated; therefore angry feelings emerge in passive ways, through lack of concentration, disorganized or nonproductive working styles, complaining and acting overwhelmed, forgetfulness, and errors that could otherwise easily be avoided (Gallwey, 2000; McClure, 2000).

WITHHOLDING PRECIPITATED BY POSITIVE EVENTS

In their personal lives and in the work arena, many people tend to hold back desirable qualities that receive unusual recognition. In fact, serious, long-term regression can occur in reasonably well-adjusted individuals when they experience an atypical success or achievement. Many examples of incompetency, inadequate performance, and the onset of other withholding behaviors following the achievement of public acknowledgment or an important promotion have been well-documented in the psychological literature (Clance & Imes, 1978; Holmes & Rahe, 1967).

In one case, Dillon, a high-level executive, encountered difficulties in managing his company after becoming self-conscious about his outstanding success. In an interview, he related the story of his rise, fall, and subsequent recovery in business:

> I had an opportunity to participate in a business with two people, one who was a man I respected a great deal and another a man who I had worked with in another business. This particular business felt like the opportunity of a lifetime because it was exactly what I wanted to do, which was to try my skills that I learned in other businesses at running a business with these two other people. Over the first couple of years, the business was an enormous success, and I felt like I was emerging as a person, as a man.
>
> Another dynamic in that situation was that there were a couple of other friends who had invested in the business. They were also enjoying sharing the excitement and the benefits of the company's success. I found myself in a completely different position than I ever intended to be in, in that I was high profile, whereas always before my stake was in maintaining a very low profile and just sort of remaining in the background, participating in events but not drawing attention to myself. But I was loving it. I was absolutely loving it. I felt like I was getting to know myself in a completely different way, and I was a different person than I thought I had been.
>
> Then it really hit me that I was touching other people's lives, and I felt fear at that point and self-conscious. I started to feel the same kinds of feelings I felt as a kid—sort of being unappreciated, like I

wasn't acknowledged in some way. So my attention shifted from the simple practicalities of the day-to-day business to trying to get that acknowledgment, but more importantly being angry at not getting it.

I began rejecting my friends' appreciation, their genuine feelings toward me. Their feelings had shifted from practical acknowledgment to just genuine warmth, and that's what I felt uncomfortable with, the warmth being directed toward me, to the point where I just felt like giving up.

I felt like "I can't do this. I'm in over my head. I don't deserve this position. I just can't do it. They ought to replace me." That was sort of the feeling, and then at some point I just told myself: "This is insane. I feel absolutely terrible in the situation, and I've got to just put all the thoughts aside and go on." So I just tried to fight with each little issue. And I gradually got back on track.

But looking back to that time, where I felt the best, I think that at the peak of that feeling of running free, there was a role reversal where the people that I had always counted on taking care of me had become equals and were counting on me. It's interesting, too, that one of the people benefiting from the company's success was my father. I never understood it entirely before, even though I've understood it sort of intellectually. But I feel that recently I have much more of a feeling for myself. And it's the core issue of my life.

Positive events may be even more important than negative ones in triggering withholding behavior. (See S. Freud, 1915/1957a; Holmes & Rahe, 1967; Rank 1936/1972.) In general, we propose that any positive event that indicates a change in a person's identity, that disturbs his or her psychological equilibrium, that emphasizes his or her difference from the family, especially from the parent of the same sex, or that fulfills an important personal goal has the potential for precipitating a long-term regression and self-limiting, self-defeating behavior (Clance & Imes, 1978; Firestone, 1990a).

Often, when people achieve an important success or fulfill their dreams, either vocationally or personally, they do have a positive reaction initially that fits the logic of the real situation. However, this sense of accomplishment is frequently short-lived. After becoming aware of their successes, people often go through behavioral changes that are apparent, but rarely understood, in relation to the fact that it was a positive circumstance or unusual achievement that triggered the regression. Many times individuals withdraw and withhold the very behaviors that led to the success.

THE EFFECTS OF WITHHOLDING ON RELATIONSHIPS

Withholding is a major dimension of the defensive process that profoundly affects an individual's ability to sustain closeness in his or her intimate relationships. Defensive behaviors in relationships are based on the need to maintain psychological equilibrium. People push away positive experiences that do not correspond to their image that was formed in the family of origin. In couple relationships, both members attempt to regulate the flow of love and affection—that is, the amount of gratification they will accept. By holding back qualities that are most admired or valued by one's mate, one can turn a partner's love into anger or even hatred, thereby maintaining a more comfortable distance while keeping one's defenses intact (Firestone & Catlett, 1999). For example, a man who told his bride that he admired her slim figure was hurt and disappointed when she put on weight in the months following the wedding. A woman felt confused and angry when her boyfriend gradually gave up skiing and interest in other sports after she indicated that she especially enjoyed sharing these activities with him.[2] These self-protective, restrictive responses, which are often subtle and difficult to identify, damage relationships, sometimes irrevocably. Both parties become more inward and defended against each other as the withholding patterns become well-established.

Men, women, and children inhibit their positive responses in a wide variety of situations in everyday life. Both men and women may be habitually late, fail to manage the family budget, or refuse to share the responsibilities of child-rearing. Adolescents may promise to do their share of the chores while procrastinating in performing these tasks. These manifestations of withholding are so prevalent that they tend to be accepted by many people as "normal"; nevertheless, they have an insidious, undermining effect on marriages and family life.

Unusual success or personal recognition in a love relationship triggers anxiety states, which in turn may lead to withholding behavior. People retreat to a defended posture *before* they are consciously aware of feeling anxious, and only in retrospect are they able to recognize the events that precipitated their inappropriate responses. For example, Nancy, an energetic, attractive woman of 48, was interviewed several years after separating from her boyfriend.

> *Nancy:* I started going out with a man who I really liked, and we soon became close friends. I liked being with him sexually and I really became happy. I had something I felt I'd never had before in my life, and I felt very different from my mother, who taught me how much she hated men. I think that was always her thinking. I never felt that was really my point of view, but it had always come out anyway in my relationships.
>
> But this time, for a period of my life, it didn't come out that way. I was really liking him, seeing him as a nice person. I used to go to his office every day and at

the end of the day we would talk about our day. I would bring him a flower or I'd bring him fruit; it was like a daily thing, about four or five o'clock.

But then one day I was with some friends, and one of my friends who I respect a lot said, "You're romantic, you're very generous." He is a person I really admire, and he said "You're in love." There were other friends listening, and I kind of stood out. It's like I was being recognized as being different.

And what happened the next day is that I forgot to go to visit my boyfriend. When he saw me later, he said, "Where were you?" I said, "Oh, I didn't think it mattered that much." It was the first time I had not gone to visit him. My thoughts started changing. I didn't even think he'd miss me. I just didn't show up and I didn't even know why. Then after that it was like he was demanding it almost, this is what I thought. It was almost like he expected me to be there. I thought "He's really being mean to me, like he wants me to be there." And then anything he would say pretty soon was turned into something mean. He really became mean in my mind.

Dr. Firestone: What was just a simple pleasure was turned into a obligation in your own mind.

Nancy: Yes, and I used to love doing anything for him. Anything. I loved going to the laundry for him. I loved doing anything. Then it became like, "Why am I doing this?" It was almost like he was making me go to the laundry. That was the feeling. I was turning him into being this mean person, making me do all these things for him, and it wasn't really like that. But my thoughts started deteriorating and getting worse and worse until the relationship broke up. And in a way I've never been quite the same since I turned on that relationship. I've never quite gotten over it. It was a turning point in my life. I felt very different.

Dr. Firestone: And it dated from your becoming self-conscious, from being acknowledged as a loving person, as a romantic person.

Nancy: Yes. I remember the word "sweet," because it's something I always wanted to be seen as, all my life, is sweet. I remember the way I was. I was sweet, and it's a word that even if anyone says that to me today, I squirm. As

	a little girl, I remember seeing these little girls and thinking, God, she seems so sweet. I wish I was like that. I always felt I wasn't a sweet girl. I wasn't a sweet woman.
Dr. Firestone:	So when they acknowledged you, it was a shocking change of identity from how you would have conceptualized yourself. That stood out enough to make you self-conscious and then it actually switched, dramatically. Before you were conscious of it, a process of withholding had started to take place, because you didn't consciously plan not to go.
Nancy:	Yes.
Dr. Firestone:	So it must have caused you anxiety to see yourself as different and to see yourself in such a favorable light. And then you turned it all around and proved that he was mean.
Nancy:	I can't believe how mean I thought he was, mean and demanding, and I felt obligated.
Dr. Firestone:	And that relationship deteriorated totally.
Nancy:	Totally.
Dr. Firestone:	And you lost something precious in your life that was really valuable to you.

Once withholding patterns become established, a sense of obligation takes the place of real desire or initiative. To substitute obligation for free choice is to give up a vital aspect of freedom, a function that is uniquely human, and it symbolizes living more on a herd or imitative level. Surrendering one's own wants and desires to another may represent a desperate attempt on the part of an individual to avoid the awareness of existential issues of separation, aloneness, and death.

WITHHOLDING AND SELF-DENIAL

Withholding behaviors encompass more than passive–aggressive inhibitions of performance or those that provoke rejection in one's relationships. They also include a holding back that is largely directed against *oneself* in the form of self-denial that is only incidentally damaging to others. Withholding and self-denial are defense mechanisms that serve to maintain the illusion of total self-sufficiency—that is, the fantasy bond.

IDENTIFYING INTERNALIZED VOICES THAT FOSTER WITHHOLDING

The process of altering withholding patterns begins with an identification of specific destructive thought processes that control them. Withholding from oneself and others is regulated by these thoughts and attitudes. Positive responses that would otherwise be expressed are held back because of an individual's critical self-attacks. Work performance is often inhibited by destructive thoughts such as: "Why should you always be the one?" "Nobody appreciates how much you contribute." "Why bother to finish the job? Everyone else is slacking off." In holding back their spontaneous expressions of affection in a relationship, people may tell themselves: "Don't show him (her) you like him (her)." "Don't be enthusiastic to see him (her), just sit there." "Why should you go out of your way for him (her)?"

These patterns of negative thinking are incorporated early in life. When parents are unable to meet a child's needs, the child tends to turn against his or her wants and perceives them as bad.[3] Children are often told: "You don't deserve the things you get," or "You only think of yourself; you're so selfish." By distorting and attacking children's desires in this way, parents (and later the incorporated parental "voices") effectively stop their children from expressing genuine responses that would otherwise be a natural part of their personal interactions. Sometimes emotionally hungry or intrusive parents contribute to their child's becoming withholding. In these cases, the child may believe that holding back his or her talents or positive responses is the only way to survive, that otherwise, he or she would be drained or depleted of his or her emotional resources.

Individuals whose love and affection were rejected by their parents become hesitant whenever they feel like being generous and may tell themselves: *"They don't want anything from you!" "Nobody wants your love."* If their generous impulse takes the form of wanting to give a gift to a loved one, they may think: *"He (she) won't like it." "It's not good enough."* Sometimes their voice may take the form of a cynical, hostile view of the other person: *"What did he (she) ever do for you?"* In listening to the voice, people deny themselves the pleasure and happiness of being generous toward others.

Some people make a virtue of self-denial and see it as constructive. Their self-righteous attitudes and self-denial hurt other people, especially their children. A withholding posture is obvious in people who have learned to be stingy and ungenerous. They have stopped questioning why they routinely say "no" to their own wants and to the needs and wants of others. Their tightness, rigid styles of relating, and sullen facial expressions reflect the constriction that has become an integral part of their character structure.

OVERCOMING WITHHOLDING THROUGH
CORRECTIVE SUGGESTIONS

People have strong resistance to altering withholding behaviors because these habit patterns are closely related to the primary fantasy or illusion of self-sufficiency. They have become accustomed to restricting their emotional transactions with others to maintain their pseudoindependent posture and psychological equilibrium. Corrective suggestions that break into well-established patterns of inhibition, withholding, and self-denial often precipitate anxiety states because they disrupt core defenses and threaten this equilibrium.

We have found that suggestions about being generous, both with oneself as well as with other people, can be effective in dealing with this type of resistance. In one case, a woman tended to be self-sacrificing and spent large amounts of money on her children, but never on herself. It was suggested that she spend some money routinely on herself each week. In another case, a wealthy businessman who was self-centered and ungenerous was given the suggestion to buy dinner for his friends. Later, realizing that most of his employees were enthusiastic baseball fans, he came up with the idea of surprising them with tickets to a major league game. Although he enjoyed the game himself, he reported that his greatest satisfaction came from offering his employees an experience that he knew they really appreciated.

An act of generosity, when performed to elevate one's status or to maintain a superior position, is not representative of a genuine giving attitude and can be destructive to both the giver and the receiver. Generosity is a sensitive, feeling response to another person's ongoing motivational system. Empathy and understanding are fundamental to being truly generous. Empathy has been defined as "seeing the other person in his or her own terms. . . . [It] consists not in seeing how I would feel if your experience, X, were to happen to me but in seeing how you feel when X happens to you" (Duck, 1994b, p. 90).

Empathy is based on an understanding of the commonalities that exist between two people as well as a recognition of their differences. When two people honestly reveal their commonalities and differences, this disclosure has the positive effect of making each feel seen and unique. Acts of altruism and generosity that are an outgrowth of one's understanding of the other's uniqueness are the most appreciated by the recipient and bring the most joy to the giver. It is important for the recipient to be open and gracious in accepting gifts and acts of kindness from others. There are three steps involved in what might be described as a healthy or appropriate response to a generous act on the part of another person. The first includes being open to accepting help, allowing someone else to meet one's need; the second involves expressing genuine appreciation; and the third entails trying to "pay back."

Paying back is an important concept. The term implies that the recipient attempts to return the act of generosity by offering something back that is sensitive to the giver's unique needs or wants. It is not necessary to repay exactly in kind; however, it is worthwhile to try to pay back in full—that is, to the extent that one is capable of giving. The give-and-take transactions that take place between two people in a close relationship are constantly in flux in terms of which partner is currently giving and which one is receiving. In some cases, however, one partner may give more than the other in general, which creates an imbalance or inequity within the relationship. The partner who is more often on the receiving end gradually becomes "indebted" to the giver and may begin to experience feelings of guilt and a sense of obligation. Efforts on the part of the recipient to pay back can reduce or erase this deficit, thereby enhancing the recipient's self-esteem. Being committed to the principle of giving as much as one receives in one's friendships and close relationships does not necessarily lead to feelings of being depleted or to becoming self-sacrificing. To the contrary, efforts directed toward paying back contribute to feelings of fulfillment and a sense of well-being.

The process of being open to generosity, expressing gratitude, and paying back is the opposite of the inward state described in chapter 5. People who are inward and self-protective have drastically reduced quantity and quality of their emotional transactions with others; they are generally tight and self-centered; lack self-esteem; and avoid close, meaningful relationships. Being generous challenges each dimension of inwardness and disrupts patterns of withholding; being genuinely grateful for what one has been given effectively neutralizes feelings of being victimized; and paying back increases feelings of self-esteem and well-being. Enthusiastically immersing oneself in each step of this cyclical process of giving and receiving leaves little time for one to engage in negative ruminations of the voice that can lead to feelings of cynicism and depression.

The concept of generosity is not only a mental health principle; it may be beneficial to an individual's physical health as well. For example, it has been found that generosity may actually increase people's life expectancy. A five-year study of older married adults showed that "death was significantly less likely for individuals who reported providing instrumental support to friends, relatives, and neighbors, and individuals who reported providing emotional support to their spouse [whereas] receiving support had no effect on mortality" (Brown, Nesse, Vinokur, & Smith, in press).

In essence, generosity is the most effective antidote to withholding. Consideration and kindnesses extended to others without an expectation of reciprocal treatment have a powerful influence in countering attitudes of tightness and habitual patterns of withholding. Being generous and sharing one's resources help overcome a negative self-image as well as cynical, distrustful attitudes toward others. When giving to others, people tend to feel liberated in terms of having more energy for productive work, and they feel both more vulnerable and satisfied in their relationships.

COPING WITH DESTRUCTIVE VOICES THAT UNDERLIE WITHHOLDING

In general, by talking honestly about their withholding and self-denial, people can become more aware of and then change these self-defeating patterns. The process of changing behaviors that alienate others significantly affects an individual's emotional life and social experiences. The gratification and positive reinforcement that result act to support the learning of new responses. Clients in psychotherapy need to become familiar with the specific negative thoughts that are regulating their self-denying and withholding behavior patterns, internalized voices that instruct them to be wary about extending themselves in acts of generosity to their loved ones. As noted, these self-critical attitudes and cynical views of others can be counteracted through positive action, including acts of kindness and generosity. As individuals become more sensitive to others over the course of therapy, they begin to consider the well-being of others and put those feelings above their own impulse to hold back or withdraw.

As noted, it is equally important to learn how to accept generosity from others. However, many people experience voice attacks when kindness is directed toward them, for instance, *"What are you? A charity case? They're humiliating you."* To counteract such distortions, clients need to understand how important it is to allow others to be kind to them; they must come to recognize that positive responses and expressions of appreciation are generous acts in themselves. The act of accepting kindness and help rather than remaining self-sufficient or pseudoindependent brings pleasure to the giver and is a key element in an interaction that is mutually rewarding.

Many individuals seeking professional help have learned to take pride in being self-denying. Very few clients realize that their tendencies to be self-sacrificing and selfless cause hurt to others who are honestly striving toward self-fulfillment. As they learn to give more value to themselves and stop denying themselves pleasure and enjoyment in life, they come to understand that it is highly moral and ethical to be "selfish"—that is, to pursue their own goals while being sensitive to others.

OVERCOMING WITHHOLDING BEHAVIORS IN RELATIONSHIPS WITHIN THE FRIENDSHIP CIRCLE

There are a number of actions that participants in the friendship circle have taken as they challenged withholding behavior patterns in their interpersonal associations. In their discussions, they became aware of specific areas in their relationships where they were inhibiting their affectionate or sexual responses, identified the specific patterns, understood their sources, and took steps to alter these responses. The crucial element in altering their tendencies to inhibit positive responses appeared to be related to their regaining feelings of compassion for themselves regarding early experiences in which they had been damaged.

In their intimate relationships, partners learned to maintain closeness rather than acting out behaviors that would push the other person away. This was accomplished by partners communicating honestly about the thoughts underlying these behaviors, giving these thoughts away, and making efforts to respond positively in situations where they typically had reacted in a negative manner.

For example, throughout her life, Samantha (56) had a pattern of becoming involved in a relationship, then withdrawing while rationalizing the rejecting behavior that ultimately resulted in the breakup of the relationship. In the beginning, Samantha was happy with her relationship with Malcolm (62), especially with the affection and sexuality. Gradually, however, she began to perceive Malcolm as being needy and demanding. Her primary complaint was that Malcolm invariably asked her for another date immediately after they had had a close time together. Her usual response was a categorical "no," followed by a variety of reasons for not committing to another date. Ultimately, she broke off the relationship. Confused and angry, Malcolm brought the subject up in a discussion group, which gave Samantha an opportunity to rethink her decision. In a recent interview, Samantha described that conversation:

> As Malcolm spoke, I felt something shift in the way I was seeing things. Then someone pointed out that this had happened at least twice before, first with my former husband, and then with a boyfriend. Someone else jokingly said "Yeah, three strikes and you're out!" But these comments were said in friendly humor. It was so friendly that I had to laugh. I didn't feel defensive. Whatever was going on in the conversation was so much on my side. And then someone asked "If this could be strike three, why give up a chance for companionship? Why be alone? How long are you going to wait to be close to someone? It could be your last chance." So it was a combination of everything my friends were saying, the whole sequence, starting with the humor, that made me start thinking.

I found that I was saying "yes" myself in the conversation. It wasn't any more complicated than that. It was something that I wanted myself anyway, and I felt I was given permission to say it. There was no other voice in that room saying "no," something opposed to that. I had a strong feeling, "That's what I want!"

Changing my mind wasn't like thinking: "Oh, my God, I'm changing my life." It wasn't dramatic. It was simply the right thing to do for me. It was right for me. I felt that it was what I wanted. I *do* want companionship. I *do* want sex. I *do* want to be generous. I *do* want to be able to give to someone. I felt that it was just me.

Samantha recognized that although she had recovered her own point of view in relation to Malcolm, she still possessed deeply ingrained tendencies to be self-denying and inhibited in her responses. In attempting to challenge her withholding, she first identified the thoughts that had been driving her to respond in a negative way to Malcolm's expressed desire to be with her. She revealed that whenever Malcolm asked her for a date, she had thoughts like: "*What? Is he crazy? Who does he think he is? You don't have time for him. You don't need him.*" After verbalizing these internalized voices, she realized that her parents had led isolated, reclusive lives. They had also restricted her activities and friendships, telling her that she didn't need anyone but them.

I served as a caretaker for my mother from the time I was about 10 until her death when I was 13. That left no time for any outside activities or any fun. I felt that my parents needed me there, in that role, 100 percent of the time, and so here I was, telling Malcolm that I had no time for him. When I was a child, I really felt used, exploited by my parents. I remember when I saw the movie *Amadeus*, I identified a lot with Mozart and how he was exploited, actually drained of life, by Saliere. I had definite thoughts warning me that Malcolm was going to exploit me the way my parents did.

"*You have to avoid him. Be nasty. He's a pathetic little man. You're bigger, stronger, more of a real person than he is.*"

I knew that I was seeing Malcolm the way I had seen my mother when I was taking care of her. She was obese and crippled and I was embarrassed by her condition. I remember thinking to myself: "*Your friends will laugh at you being with her.*" Then I realized I was thinking the same kinds of things about Malcolm. "*Don't be seen with him. Don't associate with him.*"

But it could have been any man that my voice was attacking. I also had vicious attacks on myself, like: "*You're a freak. Don't let anybody know you. Don't let anyone get near you. You're disgusting! Despicable! You'd better hide, then they'll never know. Maybe you can get away with this for your whole life. I'll help you do it. You'd better hide.*"

I recognized that as my father's voice. Actually, both of my parents hid from people. My mother was always sick, so fat that it was humiliating to imagine being seen with her. And my father was basically a loner—he would never join any of those men's clubs or lodges because he stuttered. He was afraid they would ask him to give a speech or something like that.

In the interview, Samantha also stressed how important it was for her to think of actions to take that would lead to a different outcome in her interactions, not only with Malcolm but also with other significant people in her life.

Several months later, someone asked me, "What are some of the actions you took to make things different?" I believe that one of the major things was very simple. I began to say "yes" to everything, instead of "no." It was just that simple. "Would you like to go to lunch?" I would usually say "Oh, no, I can't" but now I say "Yes" to whatever it is. "Would you like to help out with such and such?" "Yes." Just to take the chance. At the point where I was starting to change, I felt I needed to say "yes." It was almost like a physical change of direction in my life to say "yes." I found out that my positive response would take me into entirely different situations than when I had said "no."

In a way it wasn't hard to change. Malcolm still says some of the things that used to irritate me, but now I don't have a negative reaction to what he's saying. Basically, when I started feeling nice toward him again, and didn't respond in the old way, I realized that he is no different from me, that we are both two vulnerable human beings. Today, I'm very happy. For the first time in my life I feel fulfilled in a relationship with a man. And I really want to continue to share life with him.

ACTS OF KINDNESS AND GENEROSITY IN THE FRIENDSHIP CIRCLE

Casual observers are often struck by the generosity and acts of kindness that the people in the friendship circle typically extend to each other. In an important sense, the people in this group of friends have created a blueprint for a democratic society where people look after each other. Through their experiences with giving and sharing their resources, the friends have found that it is healthier, more functional, and far more rewarding to be generous and kind than to be withholding.

Being generous frees up energy; people who have worked through their attitudes of tightness have become more dynamic and productive in other areas of their lives. The spirit of altruism is contagious; it spreads to other people, who then discover for themselves that giving generates a sense of well-being and happiness unlike anything they anticipated. When generosity is an expression of a feeling of compassion for other people and part of an empathic response to meeting needs, there is a profound sense of pleasure associated with the process of giving.

Acts of altruism and kindness can take any form. Within the friendship circle, people who are wealthier routinely share their wealth with friends with lesser incomes. Although monetary gifts are the most measurable, they may be of less psychological significance than other forms of generosity in this community. For example, people in this group will drop anything to do a favor or run an errand for somebody else. They look forward to opportunities to respond to a need in their friends. This spirit of generosity and benevolence had a profound impact on Chris (22) when he first met some of the people in the friendship circle.

Chris's father and mother were divorced when he was 2 years old, and Chris lived with his mother. When he was 8, he spent the summer with his father and traveled to Hawaii with him and several of his friends, participants in the friendship circle. He made friends with some of the children and got to know several of the adults. Chris recalls one event during the summer that touched him.

> On the trip to Hawaii, I got to know Bob and Brad. Before that, I had always seen them from a distance. As a kid, I was used to being on my own and just running around, playing a lot, but on that trip they both noticed me and expressed a generosity toward me that I had never really had expressed toward me before. It had a huge impact on me.
>
> I was hanging around outside the tennis court with another kid, watching Bob and Brad play, and they yelled over to me, "C'mon in, Chris, and watch the game." So I did. They must have noticed I was interested in the game because after their game was over, they offered to get lessons for my friend and me for that week. They were very friendly about it and very personal about it. And it shocked me. It shocked me that people could be generous toward one another without having some kind of blood line. Without it being family. Even my family wasn't that generous. It really impressed me as a kid.

People have extended their generosity to individuals outside of their immediate families, friends, and acquaintances. Brad (56) recalls a time when he and his friends helped someone who was facing a crisis in his life:

> I personally think that generosity is more than people helping each other out financially. It's been a fundamental issue in changing people's lives here and maintaining the way we live. Years ago, I had a friend who was a minister in New York City, and he got into a situation where he desperately needed some money for personal reasons. He had been a very good friend of mine all the way through college and law school. When I told my friends of his plight, they immediately contributed the money he needed, which was a substantial amount. And that was during a time that we didn't have a lot of money either.

In essence, the friendship circle represents an ideal extended family situation with a sharing of wisdom and resources. The people in this circle of friends have achieved far more as a group by being generous, pooling their resources, and sharing life together than they would have as individuals.

CONCLUSION

Patterns of withholding are generally unconsciously determined and are closely tied to the core defense or illusion of self-sufficiency; therefore, they are resistant to change. They are also a manifestation of passive–aggression and self-denial. The withdrawal of affection, sexual responses, performances, and positive personal qualities especially valued by others actually relieves the anxiety and fear associated with contemplating the possibility of rejection, separation, and death. However, the process of systematically being generous, in situations where one would normally withhold, is a powerful antidote to inward, self-limiting states established early in childhood. Learning how to be generous to others as well as how to accept love, friendship, and kindness counters self-denying tendencies, shifting the balance toward the pursuit of more pleasure and satisfaction in life. Breaking patterns of withholding leads almost immediately to a freer, more energetic feeling and a happier state. Changing these habitual responses that have functioned to alienate others significantly expands one's emotional life and social experience.

NOTES

1. In *Becoming Attached*, Karen (1994) reported a conversation with social psychologist Cindy Hazan in which she described ambivalent/anxiously attached adults who tended to procrastinate:

   They had difficulty concentrating, and were most distracted by interpersonal concerns. They also had the lowest average income. "It's very parallel to infants in the Strange Situation," Hazan says, "where the ambivalent kids are not able to engage in exploratory behavior because they're so preoccupied with where their mother is and what she's doing" (p. 387).

2. Descriptive examples of withholding and double messages in a wide range of everyday situations, friendships, and relationships can be found in *Stop! You're Driving Me Crazy* (Bach & Deutsch, 1979).

3. In *Handbook for Treatment of Attachment-Trauma Problems in Children*, James (1994) stressed that:

   Children of all ages—infants to adolescents—alter their behavior in service of preserving attachment relationships when their parenting needs are not met. . . . Thus we see children suppressing spontaneous thoughts, feelings, and wishes and instead playing adaptive [yet unhealthy] roles in order to stimulate caregiving behavior in their parents. (p. 6)

8

CHALLENGING SELF-DESTRUCTIVE, MICROSUICIDAL, AND SUICIDAL TENDENCIES

In the end each man kills himself in his own selected way, fast or slow, soon or late.

—Karl Menninger (1938, p. vii)

Our discussion of a life-affirming existence can be further illuminated by comparing its dimensions with those of its antithesis—a self-destructive existence. Sustained use of the methods developed early in life to ward off anxiety, emotional pain, and the dread of death can eventually lead to what could rightfully be called a "death of the spirit," and in certain circumstances, to actual physical destruction of the individual.

The difficulty with identifying the means by which people "kill themselves" on an emotional or psychological level is that the methods are often so subtle and commonplace that most people are unaware of their potential destructiveness. Although only a small percentage of self-destructive behaviors and lifestyles actually culminate in suicide, they nonetheless contribute to the gradual deterioration of the personality. An overreliance on the defenses described in previous chapters, particularly those that characterize an inward lifestyle, can predispose a serious suicidal state in individuals who are experiencing trauma, rejection, loss, or a significant failure.

In this chapter, we focus on behaviors that may not be immediately life-threatening but are so prevalent in the general population that we have described them as the microsuicides of everyday life. Microsuicide refers to those behaviors, communications, attitudes, or lifestyles that are antithetical to, limit, or endanger an individual's physical health, emotional well-being, or personal and vocational goals. Examples of microsuicidal behavior include patterns of progressive self-denial, inwardness (chapter 5), isolation, withholding (chapter 6), and addictions and the formation of addictive fantasy bonds (chapter 4). These behaviors, as well as the destructive thought patterns and attitudes that control them, function as a basic defense, first against separation anxiety and abandonment issues and later against the fear of death (Firestone, 2000).

All self-destructive behaviors are related—that is, they differ only in quantity, nature, and degree (Farberow, 1980). These self-damaging lifestyles and behavior patterns have been labeled indirect suicide, partial suicide, parasuicide, embryonic suicide, and chronic suicide (Durkheim, 1897/1951; Menninger, 1938; Shneidman, 1966). Although there are minor distinctions between these terms, they all describe lifestyles of gradual self-destruction. Suicidologist Edwin Shneidman (1966) identified what he refers to as "inimical patterns of living"—in other words, the "multitudinous ways in which an individual can reduce, truncate, demean, narrow or shorten his own life" (p. 199). In *The Many Faces of Suicide*, Farberow (1980) delineated specific self-destructive behaviors which:

> by their very familiarity and frequency of occurrence . . . must merge into the normal, acceptable end of the continuum of behavior. On the other hand, if they can be so self-destructive or self-injurious, they must merge into the pathological end of the continuum represented by overt suicidal activity (p. 2).

Statistics show that suicide intent is high in prisoners awaiting execution on death row, necessitating strict preventive measures such as suicide watch (Death Row, 2001). In considering this paradox, one is led to other conclusions about human self-destructiveness. The circumstances facing a convicted killer are analogous to the predicament facing all human beings: like the prisoner, all individuals are conscious of an inescapable sentence of death as a function of life itself. The convict, faced with the knowledge of the exact hour of execution, attempts suicide to take life and death into his or her own hands, while the "normal" individual commits microsuicide in an effort to accommodate to death anxiety. From this perspective, we can say that all people have the potential for suicide; it is only the idiosyncratic style and strength of the movement toward self-obliteration that varies (Firestone & Seiden, 1987).

In the following pages, we first examine the myriad self-destructive behaviors that are so ubiquitous that the clinician may fail to appreciate their diagnostic importance or the profound effect they exert on clients. Second, we analyze the underlying thought processes that regulate these actions and lifestyles.

PSYCHODYNAMICS OF MICROSUICIDE

Microsuicidal behaviors and the destructive thought processes that govern them can be understood in terms of their role as a basic defense against painful feelings. Self-denying and self-destructive behaviors derive from internalized feelings of self-hatred and negative attitudes toward self, incorporated by children to protect themselves from the full realization of parents' inadequacies or actual hostility.

The primary influences that predispose the destructive thought processes that regulate microsuicidal behaviors are related to: (a) the projection of negative parental traits onto the child; (b) the child's imitation of one or both parents' maladaptive defenses and addictions; and (c) the internalization and incorporation of parental attitudes of covert and overt aggression toward the child.

As described in chapter 2, children make a strong identification with the same forces that produce the torment they are trying to escape. As the degree of trauma experienced in childhood increases, so does the intensity level of voice attacks, resulting in increasingly angry, vicious attacks on the self. These internalized thoughts and attitudes are manifested in an individual's retreat into an inward unfeeling state, malicious self-recriminations, and eventually impulses toward self-destructive action. Internalized voices reach their most dangerous and life-threatening expression in suicidal behavior, while on a microsuicidal level they effectively limit one's independence and growth potential.

MICROSUICIDE AS AN ACCOMMODATION TO DEATH ANXIETY

On an intellectual level, all people are aware of their limitation in time and are faced with a basic existential conflict or dilemma. They want to live their lives, act on their wants and priorities, individuate, and find personal satisfaction, yet these goals are compromised by a fundamental ambivalence toward self. As a result, people vacillate between motives to actualize, on the one hand, and to destroy themselves, on the other. Most tend to give up their lives to varying degrees through self-denial and self-destructive habit patterns. In this way they are able to maintain a false sense of omnipotence, as if they retained some power over life and death. In withdrawing feeling or affect from personal pursuits and goal-directed activity, they reduce their vulnerability to hurt, rejection, loss, or death.

We believe that this universal tendency for self-destruction is not a result of a death instinct but in fact represents a powerful defense against death anxiety. People do not want to die; therefore they want to protect themselves when faced with the specter of death. Through a process of self-denial, the terror of death is transformed into a fear of living or of becoming too attached to life. In other words, people are self-destructive *because* they achieve an illusion of mastery over life and death by committing small suicides on a daily basis.

THE CONTINUUM OF MICROSUICIDAL BEHAVIORS AND DESTRUCTIVE THOUGHT PATTERNS

We propose the following hypotheses regarding the relationship between destructive thought processes and microsuicidal behavior: (a) thoughts antithetical to the self vary along a continuum of intensity from mild self-reproach to strong self-attack and actual suicidal thoughts; (b) microsuicidal behavior exists on a continuum from self-denial and self-limitation to isolation, drug abuse, medical noncompliance, and other self-defeating behaviors, culminating in actual bodily harm; and (c) both processes, behavioral and cognitive, parallel each other, and suicide represents the acting out of the extreme end of the continuum (Firestone, 1997b).

Any combination of the voice attacks listed on the Continuum of Negative Thought Patterns (Exhibit 8.1) can lead to serious suicide intent, especially those that characterize an inward, self-protective state. Thoughts leading to isolation, ideation about removing oneself from people's lives, beliefs that one is a burden to others or has a destructive effect on others, voices urging one to give up special activities, thoughts urging self-injury and planning suicide, and having previously succumbed to these thoughts are all indications of high suicide potential.

In normal situations, only fragments of this destructive thought process reach consciousness. They are isolated phrases from a well-integrated system of hostile thoughts directed toward the self. Under certain circumstances, the voice can become progressively ascendant and take precedence over thoughts of rational self-interest. When these voice attacks are not challenged, people tend to manifest objectionable traits and self-defeating, self-destructive actions that generally cause them to be ashamed. Thus, the process of "listening" to the voice predisposes one toward microsuicidal behavior and lifestyles.

DEVELOPMENT OF A SCALE TO ASSESS SELF-DESTRUCTIVE AND SUICIDAL POTENTIAL

The Firestone Assessment of Self-Destructive Thoughts (FAST; Firestone & Firestone, 1996) was developed to assess the content and frequency

EXHIBIT 8.1
Continuum of Negative Thought Patterns

Levels of increasing suicidal intention	Content of voice statements
Thoughts that lead to low self-esteem or inwardness (self-defeating thoughts):	
1. Self-deprecating thoughts of everyday life	*You're incompetent, stupid. You're not very attractive. You're going to make a fool of yourself.*
2. Thoughts rationalizing self-denial; thoughts discouraging the person from engaging in pleasurable activities.	*You're too young (old) and inexperienced to apply for this job. You're too shy to make any new friends. Why go on this trip? It'll be such a hassle. You'll save money by staying home.*
3. Cynical attitudes toward others, leading to alienation and distancing.	*Why go out with her (him)? She's cold, unreliable; she'll reject you. You can't trust men (women).*
4. Thoughts influencing isolation; rationalizations for time alone, but using time to become more negative toward oneself	*Just be by yourself. You're miserable company anyway; who'd want to be with you? Just stay in the background, out of view.*
5. Self-contempt; vicious self-abusive thoughts and accusations (accompanied by intense angry affect)	*You idiot! You bitch! You creep! You don't deserve anything; you're worthless.*
Thoughts that support the cycle of addiction (addictions):	
6. Thoughts urging use of substances or food followed by self-criticisms (weakens inhibitions against self-destructive actions, while increasing guilt and self-recrimination following acting out)	*It's okay to do drugs, you'll be more relaxed. Go ahead and have a drink, you deserve it. (Later) You weak-willed jerk! You're nothing but a drugged-out drunken freak.*
Thoughts that lead to suicide (self-annihilating thoughts):	
7. Thoughts contributing to a sense of hopelessness, urging withdrawal or removal of oneself completely from the lives of people closest	*See how bad you make you family (friends) feel. They'd be better off without you. It's the only decent thing to do—just stay away and stop bothering them.*
8. Thoughts influencing a person to give up priorities and favored activities (points of identity)	*What's the use? Your work doesn't matter any more. Why bother even trying? Nothing matters anyway.*
9. Injunctions to inflict self-harm at an action level; intense rage against self	*Why don't you just drive across the center divider? Just shove your hand under that power saw!*
10. Thoughts planning details of suicide (calm, rational, often obsessive, indicating complete loss of feeling for the self)	*You have to get hold of some pills, then go to a hotel, etc.*
11. Injunctions to carry out suicide plans; thoughts baiting the person to commit suicide (extreme thought construction)	*You've thought about this long enough. Just get it over with. It's the only way out!*

Note. Any combination of the voice attacks listed can lead to serious suicidal intent. Thoughts leading to isolation, ideation about removing oneself from people's lives, beliefs that one is a bad influence or has a destructive effect on others, voices urging one to give up special activities, vicious self-abusive thoughts accompanied by strong anger, voices urging self-injury and a suicide attempt are all indications of high suicide potential or risk. Copyright © 1996 by The Glendon Association.

of self-destructive thinking as well as a client's suicide potential. The FAST is a self-report questionnaire consisting of 84 items drawn from the 11 levels of progressively self-destructive thoughts listed in Exhibit 8.1. A number of other clinicians and researchers have developed instruments to assess aspects of a client's beliefs and current thinking about depression and suicide, including the Beck Depression Inventory (A. Beck, 1978a), the Beck Suicide Inventory (A. Beck, 1991) and the Beck Hopelessness Scale (A. Beck, 1978b). The majority of these scales focus on descriptive information regarding behaviors known to be correlated with suicide,[1] whereas the FAST is based on accessing and measuring a partially *unconscious* process hypothesized to underlie self-destructive and suicidal actions.

The items on the FAST were derived from the actual statements of clinical outpatients using the techniques of voice therapy. The most actively suicidal thoughts were gathered from individuals who had made serious suicide attempts or those who were currently suicidal. Combined with the theory underlying voice therapy, the FAST provides clinicians with a comprehensive framework for understanding the dynamics of alienation, self-attack, microsuicide, and suicide.[2]

MANIFESTATIONS OF MICROSUICIDE

Two basic divisions of microsuicidal behavior can be delineated: first, behaviors that adversely affect physical health, and second, increased involvement in an inward lifestyle, including (a) the use of the fantasy bond to support an isolated lifestyle; (b) withholding—renunciation of personal and vocational goals; and (c) progressive self-denial—giving up interest in life-affirming activities.

Behaviors That Adversely Affect Physical Health

Working compulsively to the point of exhaustion, medical noncompliance, certain psychosomatic illnesses, and at times accident-proneness are among the manifestations of self-destructive tendencies that have long been recognized (Nelson & Farberow, 1982; Szanto, Prigerson, Houck, Ehrenpreis, & Reynolds, 1997). In addition, many other behaviors, including drinking to excess, drug abuse, overeating to the point of obesity, anorexia, and bulimia represent direct assaults against the individual's physical health and emotional well-being. As noted in chapter 4, destructive thought processes encourage and perpetuate an insidious cycle of addiction that can become well-established before an individual is aware of its self-destructive potential.

Increased Involvement in an Inward Lifestyle and Withdrawal From Relationships

A gradual withdrawal into isolation and fantasy, loss of feeling for the self, obsessional ruminations, unusual reserve and quietness, withdrawal of affect, and a shirking of responsibilities are all examples of microsuicidal behaviors and a retreat to an inward posture. Many people "listen" to a voice telling them that privacy and isolation are necessary. During the early stages of withdrawal, movement toward isolation is difficult to distinguish from constructive time spent alone for concentration or creative work. However, following the dictates of apparently self-protective voices that encourage isolation is a form of microsuicide. Thoughts such as "*Your life has been too hectic lately,*" or "*You need some time alone,*" or "*You need your own space*" often mask self-destructive motives in people who are actually seeking isolation from others and are gradually retreating from gratification in the interpersonal environment (Firestone, 1997b).

Extended periods of time away from social contact can be conducive to depressive reactions and progressive withdrawal.[3] A woman who came close to dying from a serious suicide attempt reported that before her self-destructive act, her voice advised her, "*You've got to make time for yourself, to do what you want to do. You need to get away so you can have more time to just relax and think.*" Once she was alone, she began planning the details of her suicide. In retrospect, she realized that suicidal thoughts had not occurred to her when she was among friends, yet she had felt compelled by her voice to seek isolation, where she was at the mercy of vicious self-attacks and suicidal urges (Firestone, 1986).

People who seek isolation often do so in an attempt to maintain an inward posture that allows them to more freely act out self-destructive habit patterns. Other manifestations of the tendency toward isolation can be observed in the breakup of a relationship for no apparent reason. Self-critical attitudes and cynicism toward others are generally responsible for the person's retreat.

Use of the Fantasy Bond to Support an Isolated Lifestyle

Most people are terrified of being alone while at the same time they have a fear of intimacy. Their solution is to form a fantasy bond, which allows them to maintain emotional distance while relieving loneliness and, in the process, meeting society's expectations regarding marriage and family. People who use the fantasy bond to maintain their isolated, inward posture usually resist recognizing that they have lost much of their original feeling for their partners and have become alienated. They attempt to cover up this reality with a fantasy of enduring love and substitute form for the substance of the relationship. Often marital partners come to share negative attitudes and cynical views of other people. In more serious cases, they develop distrustful paranoid attitudes about the world at large that reinforce their tendency to isolate themselves (Firestone & Firestone, 2002b).

Withholding—A Renunciation of Personal and Vocational Goals

The patterns of withholding described in the previous chapter represent a form of microsuicide, a systematic retreat from living that many people fail to recognize as harmful or potentially dangerous. The process of inhibiting actions motivated by one's basic wants has serious consequences. It is an indication that one has withdrawn affect and psychic energy from external objects, which represents a movement toward stagnation and psychological death. The end result of withholding is a shutting down, a paralysis of that part of the person that strives for emotional health and growth and involves a progressive elimination of the self as a feeling being. Indeed, withholding, as an ongoing defensive posture, is symptomatic of a pervasive tendency to renounce life.

Progressive Self-Denial—Giving Up Interest in Life-Affirming Activities

Self-denial is a holding back of pleasure and happiness from oneself on a behavioral level. Attitudes and thoughts that govern self-denial and asceticism are widespread in the general population. Rationalizations promoted by the voice allow individuals to casually give up activities and friendships they especially enjoy. For example, many people use rationalizations to postpone vacations and recreation until they retire, only to find themselves plagued by ill health and serious monetary concerns when they have the freedom to travel.

Early in life, most people learn to disregard themselves and their wants. They restrict and limit themselves and fail to notice that they are giving up broad areas of functioning in their lives. Seemingly innocuous patterns of self-denial often lead to more serious regressive behavior. As people begin to retreat from activities that are important and exciting to them, they become increasingly indifferent to life and thereafter find it easier to renounce still other activities they once found pleasurable and meaningful.

As people approach middle age, they naturally anticipate the next stage of life, old age, with its prospect of illness, physical deterioration, infirmity, and death, and often become fearful and apprehensive. Harmful patterns of behavior regulated by the destructive thought process that have gone unchallenged throughout life have had a profound effect on an individual's functioning by the time he or she reaches the middle years. As individuals follow the dictates of the voice and reduce their activity levels, they generally remain unaware that they are acting against their own best interests. People rarely question their loss of enthusiasm or excitement for the lively pursuits they enjoyed when they were younger. During the final stages in the developmental sequence, the defended individual is plagued by painful existential guilt about a life unfulfilled, a life not really lived. When people can no longer deny the emptiness of their lives, these feelings of existential guilt erupt into consciousness and often take the form of self-recriminations. The cycle of despair and hopelessness that follows can lead to the development of addictions and other forms of microsuicide or indirect self-destructive behavior.

Progression Toward Suicidal Behavior

At a certain point in the continuum, the insidious results of progressive self-denial and increased involvement in isolated activities are evident. Self-harm is more likely to be acted out when people withdraw their interest and emotional investment in themselves and avoid pursuing important personal goals. Angry self-attacks and obsessive ruminations further deplete the vitality of people who have denied their wants and desires over a prolonged period of time and now feel they have nothing left to live for. They may tell themselves: "*Nothing matters any more. There's nothing to look forward to.*" In many cases, the internalized voices underlying the tendency toward isolation have succeeded in convincing the individual that his or her family and friends would be better off without him or her. The sense of hopelessness engendered by this way of thinking has been found to be the strongest predictor of suicide (A. Beck, Steer, Beck, & Newman, 1993).

As the voice gains in ascendance over rational thought processes, the individual becomes increasingly cut off from feeling and dissociated from him- or herself. Malicious thoughts about the self, others,[4] and the future are completely accepted by the person as factual or realistic, and suicidal ideation can drastically increase. In these circumstances, microsuicidal behavior has a lethal potential as one approaches the extreme end of the continuum.

To summarize, destructive thought processes underlying progressive self-denial appear to be directed toward limiting life experience by persuading the individual to gradually eliminate exciting and spontaneous pursuits. In following the injunctions and in believing the rationalizations of the voice process, people still can maintain their physical life, yet commit emotional suicide on an everyday basis by gradually narrowing their world and trivializing their experience. When these self-castigating thought processes become paramount, actual suicide may occur.

Societal Influences on Self-Denial: Conformity to Misleading Age-Appropriate Standards

Progressive self-denial is reinforced by social mores that define (and misinterpret) age-appropriate roles and behaviors in a severely restrictive manner (Firestone, 2000; Richman, 1993). In spite of society's professed beliefs in the value of staying vital and lively and remaining youthful, prevailing concepts of "maturity" tend to be misleading and often imply a retreat from energetic activities as people grow older. At times, remaining involved, lively, and vital elicits disparaging remarks from relatives or friends, comments that reinforce the voice: *"Still playing baseball at your age? That's ridiculous!" "It's time to settle down and act your age." "You're too old for romance." "There's no fool like an old fool."*

In general, microsuicidal attitudes and behaviors as well as self-destructive lifestyles are indicative of a broader pattern in the larger society and are supported by its institutions and mores. Many cultural tenets and social mores represent a form of adaptation to the fear of death. It may well be that defended individuals and families do not want to be around those who remind them of their own mortality. The resultant attitudes of ageism and depreciation the elderly individuals can be observed on a societal level. For example, when describing the devaluation of older people in advertisements, television, and other media that glamorize youth, perfection, and physical beauty, McIntosh (1995) commented that "the old tend to be viewed as expendable, as having lived long enough and, perhaps, as having outlived their usefulness" (p. 190). Joseph Richman (1993), in *Preventing Elderly Suicide*, also noted the prevalence of social beliefs that perceive old age "purely as a time of decline, illness, sexual impotence, physical weakness, mental senility, and approaching death" (p. 81). Early retirement, a premature giving up of participation in sports and physical activities, a waning interest in sex and reduction in sexual activity, a loss of contact with old friends, and a decline in social life in general are all indicative of a conformity to the dictates of internalized voices, which are supported by certain cultural patterns and societal attitudes.

IDENTIFYING AND CHALLENGING MICROSUICIDAL BEHAVIOR IN PSYCHOTHERAPY

In treating individuals who act out self-defeating, self-destructive behaviors, therapeutic interventions should elicit and counter the underlying thought patterns delineated in Exhibit 8.1. During assessment and the intake interview, the FAST (Firestone & Firestone, 1996) can be used to pinpoint specific microsuicidal behaviors that are core issues in a client's life and to identify the underlying thoughts and attitudes. Subsequently, voice therapy, the cognitive–affective–behavioral methodology described briefly in chapter 3, can be used to separate and bring into consciousness the destructive thoughts that regulate these behaviors.

Step 1: Eliciting and Identifying Destructive Thoughts and Releasing the Accompanying Affect

Clients articulate their self-critical thoughts in the second person— that is, *"You're no good;" "You're stupid,"* as though they are being spoken to by an outside person. The process of identifying the contents of self-critical or hostile thought patterns can be approached intellectually as a cognitive technique or more dramatically using cathartic methods. In the latter technique, there is an emphasis on the release of affect accompanying the expression of self-destructive thoughts. In the more abreactive method, clients are asked to express their negative thoughts more emotionally, with instructions to "say it louder" or "let go and say anything that comes to mind."

In early investigations using voice therapy procedures, the participants frequently adopted this style of expression of their own volition. When asked to formulate their negative thoughts in the second person, they spontaneously began to speak louder and with more intensity of feeling. As they revealed patterns of derisive self-accusations that held special meaning for them, much information spilled out, including deep-seated beliefs or core schema of which they had previously been unaware.

Step 2: Developing Insight

In the second step, clients discuss their spontaneous insights regarding the sources of their self-attacks and analyze their reactions to verbalizing the voice. Next they attempt to understand the relationship between their voice attacks and their self-destructive behavior patterns. Subsequently they develop insight into the limitations that they impose on themselves in their everyday life functions.

Frequently, clients feel motivated to "answer back" to the voice from their own point of view and with a more realistic objective self-appraisal. Many individuals who identify the voice in relation to parental figures end up "talking back" to these figures directly in a form of psychodrama. However, because voicing angry, hostile feelings toward parental introjects in a session tends to disconnect the client from imagined or symbolic sources of security, which in turn can precipitate regressive trends, we tend to discourage dramatic answers to voice attacks for clients who appear to lack sufficient ego strength to cope with the resultant guilt and anxiety.

CHALLENGING SELF-DESTRUCTIVE TENDENCIES   *175*

Often, therapist and client discuss and evaluate the reality of the client's self-criticisms. They collaborate in subjecting the content of the client's voice attacks to a process of reality-testing, which is an important part of the therapeutic procedure. Even when people's destructive thoughts toward themselves are made up of real elements regarding undesirable behaviors or personality traits, malicious attacks on the self are always unjustified. Self-appraisals that are realistically negative, yet objective, based on the premise that a person can change, are very different from voices that categorize him or her as inherently defective. During this stage of psychotherapy, clients learn that it is not appropriate to attack themselves for shortcomings or weaknesses; rather it is more productive to work on modifying behaviors they dislike.

Step 3: Suggestions for Modifying Self-Destructive Behavior and Alleviating Depression

In the third step, client and therapist identify the specific behaviors regulated by the voice that are self-destructive and constricting, and, as discussed in chapter 3, both participate in formulating ideas about altering routine responses and habitual patterns of behavior. These suggestions act as a catalyst to help clients approach new, unfamiliar, or open-ended situations in which they will be more vulnerable and less defended.

A number of corrective suggestions, including plans for interrupting addictive habit patterns, have been described in previous chapters. One of the most powerful interventions is to encourage clients to develop an awareness of the times when they start to experience self-critical thoughts or injunctions to engage in a self-destructive behavior. It is important that they identify situations and interactions that trigger painful mood swings, emotional distress, or a depressed state. As noted, the fact that an individual's mood has shifted in a negative direction probably indicates that he or she is interpreting the event or interaction through the filter of the voice process. It is not necessary for clients to either agree or disagree with these negative thoughts; it is sufficient to simply recognize them as attacks when they occur, rather than accept them as accurate self-appraisals. Merely realizing that they are involved in a process of self-attack is often effective in neutralizing the control that destructive thinking has exerted on their feelings, overall mood, and self-defeating behaviors.

Clients can also attempt to identify the specific contents of their self-attacks. After thinking about the details of an event or interaction that affected their mood in a negative manner, they can attempt to recall what they were telling themselves at the time. Although many situations and encounters can be distressing or anxiety-producing, the way people interpret these events is the primary issue. The distinctive negative thoughts and beliefs that people have in relation to the event, about themselves and others, exerts far more influence over their ongoing emotional state than the event itself.

Another recommendation is that of encouraging clients to fully express their feelings of depression in the session. The therapist can suggest that clients "go ahead and feel" or "let out" their feelings of anger, despair, or sadness and experience the full extent of their depressed feelings; the resultant catharsis helps alleviate emotions associated with depression and dysphoria. Clients can be encouraged to fully express the negative parental introjects or voices during the session. The process of verbalizing their voice attacks and expressing the accompanying affect gives clients a new perspective on their cognitive distortions and hostile attitudes. They can see that these destructive cognitions originate from an external source and can begin to question their validity.

These two suggestions help break through the resistance with which depressed clients tend to hold on to self-depreciating attitudes and core negative beliefs about themselves. In addition, to help clients separate a negative point of view represented by internalized voices from a more rational or positive point of view, it is sometimes recommended that they keep a journal in which they record self-depreciating or self-critical thoughts they experience on one side of a page and a more realistic or positive self-appraisal on the other.

It is important that clients understand that even though a self-destructive habit pattern or behavior may temporarily eliminate or reduce pain and anxiety, these behaviors invariably have a detrimental effect on their lives. It is also crucial that they come to realize that the thoughts underlying their self-destructive actions are opposed to their best interests and ongoing development as unique individuals. As clients examine, with their therapist, the items they endorsed on the FAST, they become more aware of the behaviors they use to cut off feeling, to minimize social contact, or to avoid actively pursuing their priorities in life. At this point, as an adjunct to the session, the therapist can recommend that clients record in a journal any negative thoughts that continue to influence them to engage in the self-destructive behavior they have identified. Clients are also asked to record the plans they have made for changing these behaviors and, in the next session, to discuss the progress they have made in moving toward this goal.

Clients need to be able to identify the rationalizations they use to justify their self-defeating actions. As noted earlier, many of the reasons for denying themselves are seemingly rational or appear to be positive, and others are based on restrictive moral imperatives or "shoulds." *"It's too much of a hassle to go on vacation this year." "You shouldn't go the movies tonight with your friends, you've got too much work to do." "You shouldn't be so generous with your time, you'll be taken advantage of and exploited." "You shouldn't start building that new house, you probably won't be around to enjoy it."*

Finally, the therapist needs to educate clients regarding the temporary increase in anxiety and voice attacks that invariably accompany any positive change or progress. Many people believe that anxiety is something to be avoided at all costs, through self-medication or other forms of escape. However, people cannot achieve basic changes in their defenses without experiencing a certain degree of discomfort or anxiety. Clients need to understand that it takes courage to alter well-established behaviors, but if they persist in engaging in a new, constructive action or refuse to indulge in a self-destructive behavior pattern, their anxiety will gradually diminish in intensity and their self-attacks will fade into the background.

Seeking Goals That Go Beyond Concern With Oneself

The process of valuing someone or something outside of oneself gives one's life meaning. This altruistic focus can help interrupt an inward state and sometimes it may be the only way to avert a negative spiral into a serious self-destructive state for some individuals. In the following excerpt, the first author (R. Firestone) describes how one father's concern for his daughter may have averted his suicide:

A 42-year-old male patient, Timothy, appeared to be seriously depressed and reported that he had suicidal thoughts. In talking with him, I was impressed by the degree of his demoralization and the lack of affect as he described his situation. I was heartened, however, to see that when he spoke about his 10-year-old daughter, a spark of life came into his eyes. As he described his efforts to spare his little girl the distress of the divorce proceedings with his wife, I was struck by the fact that this man's love for his daughter and his concern for her happiness and well-being were the only meaningful things in his life. It appeared that this concern and his thoughts about what he could do to make his daughter feel better and improve her situation were the only reasons this man was still alive. His daughter was heartbroken because she was moving with her mother to a distant city after the divorce and would be forced to leave her friends. Timothy also was seeking employment in another town following the divorce.

I helped Timothy to reveal and cope with the negative cognitions and feelings underlying his depression. Later, as we discussed plans for his daughter, he came up with an idea that he believed might help solve his daughter's dilemma. He decided to talk with his wife about the possibility of their little girl spending summers with mutual friends whose children were her close friends. Timothy's wife agreed with his plan because she was also concerned about her daughter's emotional well-being. The actions that he took on behalf of his daughter helped this father overcome his depression and probably helped save his life as well.

This example can be generalized to other situations. The process of planning and carrying out acts of generosity and kindness for others beyond one's narrow self-interest help to build up self-esteem in many people who may otherwise be demoralized or feel hopeless. As people reach out to others, they begin to feel that "things *do* matter" in contrast to their previous attitudes of indifference and cynicism. Regaining feeling for what matters to them in life and rediscovering their own wants, goals, and priorities helps disrupt stubbornly held patterns of self-denial and other microsuicidal machinations.

Resistance to Identifying Microsuicidal Behaviors and the Underlying Thoughts

Most people are resistant to identifying and modifying specific self-destructive activities and behaviors despite the fact that they recognize the limitations these actions impose on their lives. Each aspect of a client's resistance can be understood in terms of how it functions to protect the primary defense or self-parenting process. Therapists can generally determine the link between the types of voice attacks identified by the client, the self-defeating behaviors he or she elects to change, and the specific dimension of the defensive process being challenged. This in turn is helpful in predicting the points at which resistance and subsequent regressions may occur.

For example, one woman in psychotherapy identified voices she used to rationalize her self-denial, a core issue in her life. After identifying this process, she felt a renewed sense of energy and was motivated to take steps to counteract these voices. She started to pursue activities that had been interesting and exciting to her when she attended college. For instance, she enrolled in a modern dance class and later performed with her dance troupe at concerts in her community. This activity and others gave her a newfound sense of pleasure and happiness. In her sessions, she realized that one of the reasons she had denied herself fun and excitement was because her parents had consistently denied her anything for which she expressed a desire. Facing this truth threatened her idealized image of her parents as loving, generous people and aroused anxiety and primitive fears of abandonment. At this point, she had a negative therapeutic reaction, missed several sessions, and for a period of time resumed her habitual pattern of denying herself the things she found most pleasurable in life. After months of vacillation, she was gradually able to regain the territory she had lost and thereafter continued to progress in therapy.

Feelings of anxiety caused by disrupting strong dependency ties and imagined connections with other people arise in all therapies and may well be a crucial factor underlying therapeutic failure. In some sense, individuals are always in flux, moving either toward defensive security measures or toward independence, self-assertion, and freedom.[5] Moving away from the parts of relationships that are characterized by a fantasy bond and toward increased individuation arouses strong feeling of guilt and anxiety. This in turn may have a significant impact on clients' resistance to continued progress.

REGRESSION

Before finalizing our discussion of microsuicidal behaviors, it is important to emphasize that positive events often trigger regressive trends in which self-destructive manifestations are predominant. On the other hand, negative events that demoralize and set one back fit in with the usual understanding of regression. Clinicians have long recognized the importance of negative events as factors in regression, whereas they often have overlooked negative reactions to positive events because they do not fit conventional logic. Successes, unusual accomplishments, happiness in a close relationship, or achieving a victory over real or symbolic competitors often precipitate a regression and subsequent microsuicidal behavior. As people progress in their personal lives, they reach a point where they experience a strong sense of self, of being a separate individual, of being a valuable person, of being lovable. At this point, they often become anxious and turn against themselves, renounce the gratification, sabotage the successes they have achieved, or give up a relationship that they especially valued and loved. We are familiar with many cases in which adverse reactions to positive events were precipitating factors in depressive reactions, self-destructive acting out, and suicidal crises.

The process of relinquishing microsuicidal machinations such as withholding, isolation, self-denial, and objectionable behaviors that alienate others can lead to anxiety states that have the paradoxical effect of increasing resistance to positive change. In general, progress in therapy tends to generate positive emotional responses or acknowledgment from people in one's interpersonal environment as well as an increase in one's own feelings of well-being. The change in one's identity, the newfound strength, the unusual feeling of joy and happiness, and the new interest in life all function to increase one's sense of vulnerability. This may cause considerable discomfort at some point. Clients find themselves in a high-risk situation; they now have something to lose and have a heightened sensitivity to any experience that contradicts the new reality. The result is frequently an emotional overreaction to even small challenges to this new, more positive identity.

Such regression, following positive life events, becomes more understandable when we view regression as a reaction to the trauma of separation—both the original separation from the parent and the later anticipation of death as the final separation from the self. Positive or especially fortunate circumstances make people acutely aware of how they value their lives. Good feelings and happy times are often accompanied by moments of clarity and an unusual awareness of separateness and limitation in time. Positive experiences and real satisfaction in an intimate relationship as compared with fantasy gratification somehow threaten people's illusions of immortality.

Therefore, in treating clients who manifest self-destructive tendencies, therapists need to be familiar with the specific conditions in each client's life that have symbolic meaning relevant to the trauma of separation and death anxiety. In that way, they can begin to sort out the complex causality underlying their clients' regressive and self-destructive responses to these events and plan appropriate interventions to counteract their microsuicidal behaviors and self-destructive ways of living.

INSIGHTS ABOUT MICROSUICIDAL BEHAVIOR GAINED BY INDIVIDUALS IN THE FRIENDSHIP CIRCLE

How can people who have been damaged by their early programming challenge the suicidal process that exists, to varying degrees, within each person? We have briefly described how the techniques of voice therapy are applied to help counteract self-destructive trends in clients. By emancipating themselves from these negative parental prescriptions, people can often develop the courage necessary to individuate and gradually develop their own ideals, values, and sense of identity. In learning to deal with intensified voice attacks aroused by moving toward individuation and by holding on to the progress made, they can ultimately liberate themselves from self-destructive propensities that once overpowered them.

Similarly, in the friendship circle, people found that by exploring the sources of internalized voices and understanding their destructive effects in their present-day lives, they could begin to separate the dictates of this negative thought process from a more realistic or compassionate point of view. Historically, when the individuals in this group first began to investigate negative thought processes in their discussions, they were shocked at the intensity of the anger and hostility underlying their self-critical thoughts and disconcerted at the degree to which they were divided within themselves.

Many of the participants identified their hostile thoughts as statements they heard one or both parents make to them during their developing years.

Others recalled harmful attitudes they had picked up in their parents' tone of voice, body language, or other behavioral cues—attitudes that appeared to be directly related to the individual's specific self-attack. They found that externalizing negative thoughts and attitudes helped separate out an alien, destructive point of view represented by the voice from a more realistic, congenial self-appraisal. Subsequently, they were able to cope more effectively with self-defeating, self-limiting, and self-destructive tendencies.

Over the past 25 years, through the process of identifying the dictates of the voice and regaining feeling for themselves, people in the friendship circle have developed countermeasures—ways of living and being that challenge their tendencies to relive the past rather than live their current lives. The methods of voice therapy have proven valuable in pointing the way toward a style of living that breaks with inimical forces in the personality that distort people's perceptions and emotions, limit their personal and vocational successes, and prevent them from fulfilling their natural evolution.

In addition to communicating their deepest personal feelings and internalized voices in a group setting, talking to a trusted friend about their self-critical thoughts and attitudes has been beneficial for people in the friendship circle. Revealing feelings of irritation, anger, fear, anxiety, and sadness to another person involves a process of reality-testing. When people externalize their thoughts and feelings in a meaningful conversation with a congenial friend, they often develop a fresh perspective that allows them to explore other options in dealing with unpleasant feelings. Conversely, when people keep these types of thoughts and feelings to themselves, these painful emotions and destructive ways of thinking tend to increase in intensity.

This practice clearly has ramifications for enhancing one's physical health as well as one's sense of well-being. For example, recent research with cancer patients has demonstrated the benefits of their articulating negative feelings and thoughts about their illness. One longitudinal study with 92 breast cancer patients (Stanton et al., 2000) showed that "coping through actively processing and expressing emotion" (p. 875) was "associated with decreased distress, increased vigor, improved self-perceived health status, and fewer medical appointments" (p. 879). These researchers conjectured that "repeated expression may decrease the attendant negative emotion and psychological arousal" (p. 881).

Disclosing the contents of voice attacks to a friend who understands the dynamics of the voice process and who knows one's priorities and special interests also increases an awareness of the rationalizations typically used to explain away self-defeating actions and lifestyles. Overall, meaningful communication with a close friend on an everyday basis diminishes the frequency of self-attacks, breaks into self-denying habit patterns, and challenges tendencies toward living an inward, self-protective lifestyle.[6]

NOTES

1. These methods of suicide risk assessment are described in *Suicide Risk: The Formulation of Clinical Judgment* (Maltsberger, 1986) and *Assessment and Prediction of Suicide* edited by Maris, Berman, Maltsberger, and Yufit (1992).

2. Another study has been initiated to develop a new instrument, the *Firestone Assessment of Violent Thoughts* (FAVT), for assessing violence potential for both criminal and family violence.

3. A study conducted by Gove and Hughes (1980) indicated that inwardness and isolation are related to self-destructive and suicidal behavior. Their findings showed that alcoholism and suicide are two forms of social pathology that relate to social isolation and were much more prevalent in those people living alone than in those who lived with others. Their study agreed with the results found in research relating high suicide rates to areas of low population density with its resultant physical and social isolation (Seiden, 1984).

4. In some people, the tendency to distort others or to view them with suspicion is more prominent than attitudes of inferiority or low self-esteem. In these instances, the voice fosters feelings of victimization and paranoia by promoting a state of passivity, as noted in chapter 6. Reacting to events as a victim contributes to a buildup of hostility. Extremely hostile voices toward and about others are at the core of all forms of criminal and explosive behavior. A mode of thinking that rationalizes revengeful action is also characteristic of perpetrators of domestic violence: *"She had it coming to her. She knew which buttons to push."* Or *"He thought he could get away with it. Next time he'll think twice before he fools around with another woman."*

5. See *Constructive Thinking* (S. Epstein, 1998), especially chapter 7, "Why We Do What We Do: A New Understanding of Human Behavior," and chapter 16, "Evaluating Your Automatic Thinking," and "Suppression of Continuity-Benevolence Assumptions (CBA) Voices: A Theoretical Note on the Psychology and Psychotherapy of Depression" (Stiles, 1999) for other perspectives on destructive thought processes that have some commonality with descriptions of the "voice" depicted in this chapter.

6. The dynamics of this type of communication in the context of a close friendship is discussed in more detail in chapter 17.

9

DEFENSES AGAINST DEATH ANXIETY

The irony of man's condition is that the deepest need is to be free of
the anxiety of death and annihilation; but it is life itself which awakens
it, and so we must shrink from being fully alive.
                                          —Ernest Becker (1973/1997, p. 66)

Human beings are very frightened animals. We are able to deal with
abstract symbols, view ourselves as objects, and are therefore cursed with
the conscious awareness of our own mortality. On the other hand, our
remarkable propensity to experience life on a feeling level combined with
our ability to use symbolic logic adds a multitude of dimensions to the life
process. In addition to these endowments, we have the exquisite sensitivity
to feel deep emotion; we can feel for ourselves and our own life and have
the extraordinary capacity for empathy toward other people as well.

This curse of consciousness leads to an acute awareness of death's
inevitability, which in turn gives rise to a fear reaction of serious proportions.
Indeed, the manner in which an individual handles death anxiety as an
evolving being, faced with a growing awareness of existential issues, acts as
one of the primary determinants of the course of his or her psychological
life. Children go through a series of stages in their development as they
learn about their finite span of life. Faced with this tragic awareness, the
child must choose between a life of denial or self-affirmation—in other
words, whether to regress to an infantile state of nonawareness or embrace
life, in spite of death.

The extent and mode of defenses that the child develops bear directly
on the resolution of this core conflict: whether to feel his or her emotions

or to disconnect and cut off emotional investment in life, whether to develop compassion for him- or herself and others or resort to a soothing but numbing and addictive lifestyle in which people remain in the background. The greater the pain in the early years before the realization of death's inevitability, the more likely the child will choose the latter alternatives, albeit on an unconscious level (Firestone, 1994; Yalom, 1980). In this context, it is interesting to note the findings of Mikulincer, Florian, Birnbaum, and Malishkevich (2002), showing that individuals classified as having an anxious attachment style expressed more death fears than those who were classified as having a secure attachment style.

If an individual chooses to cultivate life and lead an honest undefended lifestyle, he or she will experience both the joy and pain of existence, whereas the defended person's attempt to block out pain neutralizes the life experience and deprives him or her of life's enrichment. A damaging psychological environment condemns the child to a substandard existence, and the situation is difficult to reverse.[1]

Understanding people in relation to death anxiety helps to explain many strange and puzzling phenomena about human behavior, not the least of which are people's propensities for self-destructive responses. Many people relinquish their freedom, give up their point of view, choose conformity over personal expression, and find innumerable ways to sacrifice their autonomy and humanness. They avoid personal gratification and prefer not to be loved and valued by others because it makes them more vulnerable and cognizant of their own death. Their philosophy seems to be, "*Why care, when your destiny is so futile? Who needs people, anyway? You'll just get hurt if you invest emotionally, you can't trust anyone. Even if you do find someone to love, relationships don't last forever. If you don't want anything, you won't be disappointed.*"

DEFINITION OF DEATH ANXIETY

Death anxiety is a complex phenomenon that represents the blend of many different thought processes and emotions: the dread of death, the horror of physical and mental deterioration, the essential feeling of aloneness, the ultimate experience of separation anxiety, sadness about the eventual loss of self, and extremes of anger and despair about a situation over which one has no control (Choron, 1963; Tomer, 1995; Tomer & Eliason, 1996).[2] In some ways, the death issue reflects a core paranoia, because human beings *are* at the mercy of outside forces beyond their power or control, forces that threaten their very existence. It is especially tragic when this basic feeling of paranoia is generalized and frames one's perception of his or her interpersonal world. Although death anxiety includes a broader spectrum of painful emotions, as noted previously, our essential definition refers to the full realization that life is terminal, an unbearable imagination of infinite noth-ingness or nonexperience, a mental state that when faced directly can be truly intolerable.

Death anxiety can be distinguished from the poignant feelings of sadness that emerge when we contemplate the inescapable end of our exis-tence. We can never overcome the sadness associated with the obliteration of the self as we know and experience it in our everyday lives. In a sense, people must mourn the anticipated loss to retain their capacity for genuine feeling. Sadness is therefore an inescapable part of a feelingful existence.

Although there are a myriad of defenses against death anxiety and numerous approaches to the subject, these are never fully comforting because people are generally fearful of change or any alteration of habitual modes of experience. Changing jobs, moving, getting married or divorced, and retiring are all disturbing transitions for the average person. Patients' fear of change in psychotherapy, even in a positive direction, makes up the fundamental resistance to the therapeutic process (Firestone, 1985). Indeed, any change of major proportions in one's life circumstances can disrupt psychological equilibrium and predispose an unpleasant anxiety state. The essential ambiguity about life and fears about the unknown exaggerate this reaction and are especially threatening. Death clearly represents a change of major proportions. The anticipation of this ultimate change, the final cessation of consciousness as we know it, is extremely distressing for most people despite their defensive structure.[3]

INDIVIDUAL REACTIONS TO DEATH ANXIETY

Most people react to death anxiety by regressing, becoming cut off emotionally, and to varying degrees choosing to depersonalize. Heavy reli-ance on a defensive posture in life tends to limit their capacity to relate to others (particularly their children), restricts their capacity to make choices, and shrinks their life space. Rigid belief systems that offer some respite from death fears often inspire distrust and hatred toward people who have different beliefs. Many religious wars have been fought over sectarian systems of thought (Firestone, 1996).

Positive Reactions

Some people who show unusual courage manage to turn the core issue of death's inevitability to their advantage, giving greater meaning to their lives and behaving in a manner that is truly respectful of others. Over the past 40 years, we have talked personally with a number of individuals who appeared to be less defended than most in relation to the subject of death. These individuals had greater access to their feelings in general and had integrated the emotions associated with their personal mortality. In one conversation, a 54-year-old political analyst and journalist related a dramatic encounter with death that had a powerful impact on his life:

In August 1989, I had an experience which was to change my life forever. I was in Florida and spending time with my mother who had recently suffered a stroke. The experience had shaken the foundations of my psyche, loosening rigid structures that only those who have participated in the slow deterioration of a parent can fully understand. Also, I was doing a lot of meditating during this period, focusing on observing my thoughts, feelings, and body sensations as they arose. It was thus perhaps no coincidence that I had this particular experience at this particular time.

It was early in the morning, 3 or 4 AM, and I awakened from a deep sleep. My defenses were down. As I lay there, half asleep, half awake, I noticed a fear of death beginning to arise. For the first time in my life, I noticed the fear as it emerged and noticed myself automatically start to push it away as well. And, suddenly, I found myself saying, *"No! I won't push it away this time. Let it come!"* And I did. I let it come.

The next few minutes were the most excruciating I had ever experienced. My whole body went into shock. I felt paralyzed, as if I could not move. I had difficulty breathing; at times I felt as if I were suffocating. At other times, I felt like I was burning alive, like I would not survive this. I was out of my head, in some kind of unexpected hell that I had never before known existed.

What I remember most was screaming at the top of my lungs. Only I was so in shock, so paralyzed, that no sound would come out. Over and over again I would scream. And over and over again no sound would emerge. I felt as if I would not, I could not, survive what was happening to me. Finally, after what seemed like a lifetime, it was suddenly over. At first I felt just sort of numb. Shaken. Still halfway between two worlds.

And then, all of a sudden, out of nowhere, something even more extraordinary happened. I suddenly began feeling more alive than I had ever felt before. I began experiencing both an aliveness and a sense of deep peace that I had never before dreamed existed.

I do not mean that I suddenly found myself feeling, *"Oh boy, I'm still alive. I didn't die after all."* There was no verbal content to this experience, just like there had been none to the "death" experience prior to it. Both were nonverbal experiences. It was about having a very different experience of life, a state of being. It was a dimension in which previous concerns seemed unimportant indeed. Another realm of being. A realm beyond the concerns of this world. On the simplest level, I saw things as I had never seen them before.

Afterward, this feeling did not vanish. It persisted into the days that came. I remained far more alive, happy, centered than I had ever been before. The morning light was precious, as was an orange, the smile of an old person, almost any feeling at all. I felt the deepest possible love for my mother. I experienced a new intensity of being in every step I took, every sight I saw, every emotion I experienced. And within, I felt a loosening, a breaking up of fears never before understood.

I realized that I had had a pivotal experience. Before this, I had *intellectually* known, of course, that I would one day die. But it had been an "idea," not an "experience." Actually *experiencing* my feelings about my death had changed everything.

Although it had a powerful impact on my life, transformation did not occur on that one night. I soon fell back into many of my old life-denying ways, living by much of my past conditioning. I often found myself largely reverting to a more automatic way of being, in which I was clearly in denial of death, clearly taking life for granted.

However, this experience did change my life direction. I decided to leave politics and spend the next five years on a spiritual search. Over time, I came to experience an ongoing sense of inner peace and a tranquility that amounted to a transformation of my very experience of life. I found that I could remind myself of the brevity of life, of how precious was what remained, and could draw upon the deep spiritual understandings that I had experienced that night in times of fear or anxiety.

In another interview, a man told the following story:

In 1955, a close friend of mine developed a form of cancer, which at the time was untreatable and had a 100% fatality rate. The doctors informed him that he had only several months, a year at the most, to live. Before the year was up, researchers found a cure for this type of cancer, and my friend was reprieved from his date with death.

Needless to say, this man and his family were overjoyed. The close call with death literally woke him up to his life. He became a different person from the somewhat cynical, sullen young man I had known during high school and college. Previously an inward, brooding and isolated individual, he began to embark on a life of adventure and meaning. Buying a small power boat, he took family and friends on exciting expeditions from the California coast across the often rough 30-mile stretch of open water to the Channel Islands.

Changing careers from his involvement with an unrewarding business enterprise, he became a devoted teacher of educationally handicapped adolescents. He savored life to the fullest, cherished special moments with his wife and children, and remained vulnerable to the poignant, sad feelings he experienced whenever he reflected on his brush with death and his miraculous cure. In time he gradually lost some of his heightened joy in living but the experience continued to have a positive effect on his life.

Negative Reactions

Undoubtedly, there are other people who, like these people, had peak experiences in relation to death, rose to the occasion, challenged habitual ways of living, and went on to live more productive lives. However, it has been our experience that most often people defend themselves against an awareness of death and death anxiety in ways that are adverse to their well-being and harmful to the people closest to them. If a chance confrontation with death disturbs their defense system, temporarily bringing them to life, they gradually return to living their lives as though they will live forever and can afford to throw away their most precious experiences.

Usually encounters with death, illness, or the threat of loss of a loved one predispose adverse emotional reactions that tend to demoralize people. This demoralization typically leads to an intensification of defensive reactions. For example, Aaron and Yvonne's baby daughter, Jody, was born two months prematurely and weighed less than 3 pounds. The couple, frightened and deeply concerned, watched anxiously for signs of improvement in their infant's condition. Finally, the baby slowly began to gain weight and after several weeks, she was released from the hospital. However, both parents found it difficult to form a close attachment to their baby after facing the possibility that they might lose her. When their baby was 6 months old, the couple participated in a workshop attended by other parents who had had similar experiences in caring for a premature infant. In the workshop, Yvonne revealed the feelings she experienced when she brought Jody home from the hospital:

> *Yvonne:* For a long time after I had Jody, I wasn't able to take care of her because she was in the hospital. Then when we brought her home, I didn't have much feeling for her. It's like I knew she was there, and I knew I should do certain things, and that was it. I had no feeling—this is very painful to say— but I felt I had to do the things that had to be done, and that was all that I knew, just do the things I was supposed to do.

> *Aaron:* I remember feeling a sense of panic during that whole period. She looked so small in the incubator, and I prayed that she would make it. After she came home from the hospital, I felt distant from her. I got very involved at work and found myself making excuses for not being available to help Yvonne take care of her.

Yvonne: Somehow I felt like it was my fault, that I had done something wrong for her to have been born early. Even after she gained weight, I was still afraid to pick her up or to feed her. Also I identified strongly with her. She's vulnerable like I am, and it's hard to feel that about myself. Sometimes when I look at her now, I feel very protective of her and my loving feelings start to come back. But then I cut off those feelings almost immediately because it's hard to feel that about myself, that my life is precious, and each moment really matters.

This couple's reaction is not at all unusual. One reason people retreat from close relationships with their mates and their children is their fear of losing their loved one through rejection or death. The fear of object loss is akin to the fear of losing oneself and can trigger a pattern of withholding that limits loving responses and personal involvement. Within couple relationships, partners often distance themselves to protect against the fear of loss. They gradually relinquish the real substance of their life together and retain only the form, a fantasy bond or imaginary connection. This illusion of fused identity imbues them with a sense of immortality. However, these relationships tend to become increasingly hollow and empty and the partners experience considerable guilt and feelings of regret as they grow apart.

There are many different ways that death anxiety affects people's lives and relationships. The problem is reduced to, how can people establish a nondefensive lifestyle that incorporates an awareness of death anxiety yet allows them to maintain a rich and meaningful investment in self and others? An understanding of the defenses that one customarily uses to avoid the fear of death can point the way toward living a more life-affirming existence despite one's limitation in time.

INDIVIDUAL DEFENSES AGAINST DEATH ANXIETY

The arousal of death anxiety[4] generally leads to an increased reliance on defensive behaviors and self-protective lifestyles. Any negative event or reminder of death, such as illness, rejection, accident, or tragedy (or an unusual success or special acknowledgment) can precipitate feelings of death anxiety, which in turn may lead to a retreat to defenses typically used by the person during times of stress.

It appears that the initial reactions of many people to the terrorist attacks of September 11, 2001, were to become more involved in self-protective behaviors and ways of being. For months afterward, we noted a wide range of responses to this painful reminder of death and the fragility of human life. Many individuals reported being more depressed than usual; others revealed that they had reverted to familiar defenses or addictive habit patterns in an attempt to numb or diminish the pain and anguish caused by this horrific event. In other cases, people turned on themselves, experienced a significant increase in self-attacks, and felt cynical and pessimistic regarding the future.

Clinicians may find it difficult to identify defenses specifically related to death anxiety, because defenses are often instituted before the client becomes aware of the anxiety on a conscious level. Regressive trends are activated as an individual suppresses death anxiety. There is a retreat to an earlier stage of development, a level at which the individual was not fully aware of death. These regressive trends may persist throughout a person's life. A number of basic defenses and their specific function in relation to the suppression of death anxiety can be delineated.

Preoccupation With Pseudo Problems

The experience of death anxiety and the reality of a finite existence give rise to a basic paranoia that is then projected onto real-life situations. As noted earlier, paranoia is an appropriate reaction to existential realities, inasmuch as powerful forces are acting on humans that are beyond our control; people are indeed helpless in terms of our ultimate fate. However, many people project this paranoia onto events and interactions in life that do not justify an intense reaction of helplessness and powerlessness. They often react to these events with rage, fear, and panic. For example, Meyer (1975) called attention to the fact that the displacement of problems connected with death is apparent in agoraphobia, fear of cardiac arrest, animal phobias, and, most particularly, claustrophobia. On a nonclinical level, many people appear to be intolerant of a simple, satisfying life and prefer to occupy their minds with melodrama and pseudo problems while shutting off feeling for real issues in their lives. When preoccupied with these concerns, they are tormented by real-life situations but seem to be immune to death anxiety. Moreover, they attend to these situations rather than actually facing their fear of death.

Vanity: An Image of Specialness

Vanity can be defined as a fantasized positive image of the self that an individual uses to compensate for deep-seated feelings of inadequacy and inferiority. It represents remnants of the child's imagined omnipotence and invulnerability that live on in the psyche, always available as a survival mechanism at times of stress or when the person becomes too conscious of the fallibility of the physical nature and the impermanence of life. It expresses itself in the universal belief that death happens to someone else, never to oneself. Zilboorg (1943) described this defense as "specialness" that sets one apart from one's neighbors and gives an individual a feeling of immunity from death: "We must maintain within us the conviction that . . . we, each one of us who speaks of himself in the first person singular, are exceptions whom death will not strike at all" (p. 468).

A compensatory image of exaggerated self-importance often extends to beliefs about marriage and the family. Many people believe that if they are preferred over all rivals, they are somehow special and therefore somehow immune to death. The institution of marriage or commitment to a monogamous relationship can function to support the myth of exclusivity and eternal love. Both men and women tend to have illusions of being special and exempt from death when they feel they are the preferred choice of their partners. Many men are implicitly taught that they should be the ruler of the household, the preferred choice of their mate, the great lover, superior to other males. Whenever this illusion is shattered—for example, by a mate's infidelity, and other slights, real or imagined—the man may feel devastated.

It is interesting to note that women tend to feel more threatened if their mate develops a close, emotionally intimate relationship with another woman than if he becomes involved in a sexual liaison. On the other hand, men appear to feel more threatened when their partners are sexually unfaithful. Evolutionary psychologists have conjectured that these gender-specific threatening scenarios have their basis in the differential sexual strategies developed by men and women over the centuries (Buss, 1994; Daly & Wilson, 1983).

In general, men tend to depend heavily on a woman's support of their vanity. In a succinct passage from *The Female Eunuch*, Germaine Greer (1970/1971) described several subtle techniques used by women to reinforce, in their spouses, the illusion of being preferred, and graphically portrayed the resulting destructiveness to the relationship:

> Every wife who slaves . . . to build up his [her husband's] pride and confidence in himself at the expense of his sense of reality . . . to encourage him to reject the consensus of opinion and find reassurance only in her arms is binding her mate to her with hoops of steel that will strangle them both. Every time a woman makes herself laugh at her husband's often-told jokes, she betrays him. The man who looks to his woman and says, "What would I do without you?" is already destroyed. (p. 157)

Addictive Couple Bonds

Defenses against death anxiety perpetuate the formation of fantasy bonds, and this has an impact on interpersonal relationships that has not been fully recognized. Most people choose debilitating, conventional forms of safety and security over genuine closeness with their loved ones. They maintain a fantasy that they somehow can escape death by merging with another person, but in reality they tend to recreate early painful experiences from childhood in their present relationships. For the most part, people fail to realize that the use of a relationship to obtain security—that is, to secure a lie about life and death from another person—is tantamount to losing that relationship.

According to Kaiser (quoted in Fierman, 1965), people's compelling need to surrender or completely submit their will to another person through a "delusion of fusion" represents the universal neurosis. In his writing, Fromm (1941) described "the tendency to give up the independence of one's own individual self and to fuse one's self with somebody or something outside of oneself in order to acquire the strength which the individual self is lacking" (p. 163). Our observations of marital relationships have shown that most people act out dominant–submissive (parent–child) modes in their coupling. In these cases, one partner becomes the ultimate rescuer, responsible for the other's decisions, happiness, and life. Both partners participate in this harmful collusion, and because the polarization provides an illusion of safety, protection, and permanence, it becomes difficult to disengage from such a relationship.

One of the primary reasons people are afraid of genuine closeness and intimacy is that it paradoxically makes them more aware of their separateness. In addition, some individuals may become sexually withholding to escape an awareness of being connected to their body (Kernberg 1995; Schnarch, 1991). Kernberg (1995), for example, writing about people's fears of erotic love and sexual passion, said, "Orgasm as part of sexual passion may also represent symbolically the experience of dying" (p. 41).

In distancing themselves to protect against fears of loss, rejection, and death, and in using each other for security, many men and women essentially give up their real lives together for an illusion that they will be spared death. The pull to believe that death can be eluded if one is truly loved by another person is irresistible for most people.

Gene Survival

Most parents believe that their children "belong" to them and experience feelings of exclusivity and possessiveness in relation to their offspring. To the extent that children resemble their parents in appearance, traits, and behavior, they are their parents' legacy, imbuing both parents and children with the illusion of immortality. Otto Rank (1936/1972) asserted that this belief leads to guilt in children in relation to separating from their parents and developing their own unique personalities:

> The problem of the neurosis itself is a separation problem and as such a blocking of the human life principle, the conscious ability to endure

release and separation, first from the biological power represented by parents, and finally from the lived out parts of the self which this power represents and which obstruct the development of the individual personality. (p. 73)

The biological power represented by parents referred to by Rank is the special transcendental quality that parents hold out to their children—that is, the possibility of triumphing over death by merging with them. This illusion of fusion is costly, however, because, as Rank emphasized, the child and later the adult feels too guilty to individuate and live his or her own life.

INSTITUTIONAL DEFENSES AGAINST DEATH ANXIETY

The defense patterns[5] of each member of a society are pooled and form social sanctions and institutions that then act back on the individual through negative social pressure. All societies and complex social structures are generally restrictive of individuality and personal expression in the face of existential anxiety, and to some extent all cultural patterns or practices represent a form of adaptation to people's fears of death. Much of people's destructiveness toward themselves and others can be attributed to the fact that they conspire with one another to create cultural imperatives and institutions that deny the fact of mortality (Becker, 1973/1997, 1975; S. Solomon et al., 1991).

There are a multitude of conventional defenses that mitigate against facing the fact of mortality that are used by human beings in an effort to deny and transcend existential finality. Two major forms of defense that have evolved into unique cultural systems are (a) religious dogma, including belief in an afterlife, reincarnation, or union with a universal unconscious (Toynbee, 1968); and (b) group identification and nationalism, idolization of the leader, and allegiance to group cause to the point of mindless conformity.

Religious Doctrine

For the most part, religious doctrine consists of consensually validated concepts of existential truth. Traditional beliefs of both Western and Eastern cultures can be conceptualized as contributing to a collective neurosis whereby defenses against death anxiety reinforce people's tendencies to deny the body or transcend or devalue the self. Misinterpretations of teachings originally meant to enhance the spiritual and humane aspects of life have led to this self-denying, self-sacrificing orientation. Pagels (1988, 1995) noted that theologians since St. Augustine have postulated that the punishment for Adam's act of disobedience in the Garden of Eden was death. They held out the promise that by denying sexual desire and bodily pleasures, one's soul could triumph over the body and survive death. Similarly, many people have misunderstood the Buddhist teachings and assumed that all desire, striving, or "ego" must be relinquished to attain enlightenment (Suzuki, Fromm, & DeMartino, 1960; Watts, 1961).

Religious beliefs that feature life after death fail to completely relieve death anxiety because they represent an altered state of experience that still involves a cessation of life as we know it in our present-day experience. As one of our acquaintances mused, "Who wants to flit around like an angel, in that soft, fluffy world of heaven? Who wants to come back as an animal or different person, who has absolutely no awareness about his former existence?"[6]

In our observation, even when individuals do hold such religious beliefs, they often react strongly to any challenge to their world view. The anxiety aroused by such challenges can even lead to aggression against the perceived threat.

According to several political analysts, the ethnic cleansing that took place in Yugoslavia and Kosovo represented yet another phase in the 600-year-old conflict that began with a religious war during the 14th century. In the six intervening centuries between the original religious war and the more recent bloodshed, with the exception of a few brief interludes, the people involved in the fighting have maintained hatred and animosity based on old forms of logic and reasoning or outdated ideas about each other that no longer have any application to their everyday lives (Moynihan, 1993; Owen, 1993; Puhar, 1993).[7]

Nationalism and Other "Isms"

Nationalism has been defined in various ways. Kecmanovic (1996) has cited two definitions, one by Hayes, who stated that nationalism is a fusion of patriotism with consciousness of nationality, and the other by Shafer (1955), who defined nationalism as being made up of:

> The dogma that the individual lives exclusively for the nation with the corollary that the nation is an end in itself, and the doctrine, too, that the nation (the nationalist's own) is or should be dominant if not supreme among other nations and should take aggressive action to this end. (p. 6)

Nationalism, as well as communism, capitalism, and other "isms" function as a narcotic, a psychic painkiller that fosters dependency in people who are searching for security and relief from existential anxiety. In any system, individuals tend to subordinate themselves in relation to an idea or a principle and experience a false sense of power (Popper, 1945). The illusion of connection that comes from being a part of a patriotic or nationalistic movement is exhilarating and addictive. Fromm (1941, 1950) asserted that existential fears of aloneness and the "terrifying responsibility" compel people to take actions as a group that would be unthinkable to them as individuals:

> There is nothing inhuman, evil, or irrational which does not give comfort provided it is shared by a group. . . . Once a doctrine, however irrational, has gained power in a society, millions of people will believe in it rather than feel ostracized and isolated. (1950, p. 33)

Group identification provides an individual with an illusion of immortality through imagined fusion with the membership. Conformity to the belief system of the group—that is, to its collective symbols of immortality—protects one against the horror of facing the objective loss of self. In merging his or her identity with that of a group, each person feels that although he or she may not survive as an individual entity, he or she will live on as part of something larger that will continue to exist after he or she is gone.

The average person's idolization of the leader, unswerving allegiance to the group's belief system, and denigration of other groups function as defenses against death anxiety. These defenses represent an extension of each individual's idealization of parents and family into a cultural framework. In blocking negative parental characteristics from awareness, people displace them onto other people at the expense of the out-group. Moreover, in idealizing the family, an individual adopts his or her parents' distortions and biases and imitates their negative responses to people who are seen as different. In this way, prejudicial attitudes toward specific groups of people and individuals are transmitted intergenerationally.

When the world view or belief system of a particular group or nation is threatened by outside influences, people are terrified of reexperiencing the pain, anticipatory grief, and dread associated with death. They become extremely defensive and angry at those who disagree with their particular solution to the death problem. Thus, the terror of death drives people to demonize those who hold different world views or beliefs about life and death. Individuals tend to mobilize action against these enemies in a manner similar to medieval crusaders who attempted to impose their fanatical religious beliefs on "heretics" in bloody holy wars. Many people are willing to risk their lives in war and ethnic conflict in an effort to preserve their nation's or religion's ideals in what we interpret as an attempt to achieve a sense of mastery over death.

Data supporting this perspective can be found in findings accumulated over the past two decades by researchers in Terror Management Theory (TMT). For example, S. Solomon et al. (1991) have noted an increased reliance on defense mechanisms to maintain self-esteem as a result of the experimentally manipulated arousal of death anxiety. The TMT model hypothesizes that to maintain self-esteem in the face of increased mortality salience or an awareness of personal death, an individual must bolster and defend his or her world view (consisting of the above-mentioned national or religious immortality ideals). The heightened defensiveness, in turn, increases the individual's liking for groups that validate his or her world view and decreases liking for those that threaten his or her world view.

J. Greenberg et al. (1990) have described how "people's beliefs about reality [and their cultural expressions of such beliefs] provide a buffer against the anxiety that results from living in a largely uncontrollable, perilous universe, where the only certainty is death" (p. 308). These researchers went on to declare that "enthusiasm for such conflicts [religious wars and ethnic conflict] among those who actually end up doing the killing and the dying is largely fueled by the threat implied to each group's cultural anxiety-buffer by the existence of the other group" (pp. 309–310).

More recently, in their discussion of the 2001 terrorist attacks in *In the Wake of 9/11: The Psychology of Terror*, Pyszczynski, Solomon, and Greenberg (2003) commented that, "to our knowledge, no one has yet attempted to place these events in the context of a broad understanding of human motivation: why people behave the way they do" (p. 7). According to these researchers:

> Perhaps the central insight [of TMT] . . . is that human beings attempt to fulfill culturally sanctioned dreams forged to escape the encompassing nightmare, not just of human history but also of human existence itself. Some Islamic terrorists dream of a heaven of dancing virgins overseen by Allah . . . whereas Americans dream of amassing great fortunes, writing that great book, winning Nobel Prizes and Olympic gold medals, their kids' achievements, or entering one of a variety of theologically prescribed versions of heaven. (p. 8)

EMBRACING LIFE IN THE FACE OF DEATH: A CLINICAL PERSPECTIVE

The formulations set forth in this chapter have important implications for psychotherapy. First, the state of vulnerability to death anxiety brought about by dismantling major defenses needs to be taken into account by therapists. When clients move away from illusions of safety and habitual ways of cutting off feeling, they tend to experience their aloneness and separateness. Indeed, the intensity of death anxiety appears to be in proportion to a client's freedom from neurotic propensities. Many clients concerned with the trivialities of life and obsessed with worries about pseudo issues view death with a kind of friendly acceptance. Unless therapists recognize the implications of therapeutic progress related to the arousal of death anxiety, they run the risk of misinterpreting many of their clients' reactions, symptoms, communications, and responses.

Second, therapeutic progress may be disappointing to the client, because it does not lead to a state of prolonged happiness. In fact, by opening clients up to genuine feeling about their lives, improvement gives them a sense of personal freedom that makes them more aware of potential losses. McCarthy (1980) addressed this concern:

> If the goal of the psychoanalytic work is the patient's freedom and autonomy, and the patient retains the unconscious fears that autonomy equals death or the loss of the self, then the positive outcome of the analysis may be as anxiety-provoking as the original inner conflicts. (p. 193)

To some extent, all forms of long-term psychotherapy confront patients' defenses against death anxiety; however, they are often limited by the therapist's own defense system. In many instances, this defense system is supported by the methods and theories that the therapist chooses to apply in his or her practice.

In the following pages, we explore the fundamental issue of choice faced not only by the client who has progressed in psychotherapy but also by every person: whether to reinstate or strengthen defenses, destructive fantasy bonds, and deadening habit patterns in a renewed attempt to avoid pain or to live life fully, with meaningful activity and compassion for oneself and others.

METHODS USED BY PARTICIPANTS IN THE FRIENDSHIP CIRCLE

Can people invest fully in a life they must lose? Is there a remedy for the dread, despair, and anxiety that emerges when one contemplates one's mortality? Are there ways to reduce the devastating impact of death anxiety or prevent some of the more damaging consequences of denial or other defense formations?

For the past 25 years, in their discussion groups and seminars, people in the friendship circle have been considering these questions and exploring their feelings in relation to death. The ongoing communication about existential concerns has allowed them to share their feelings and develop a sense of kinship with others. The high value that each person places on autonomy as well as vulnerability, their emphasis on openness and nondefensive attitudes, and their willingness to experience the sadness associated with the future loss of self and others have helped them challenge and disrupt these defenses.

Identifying Defenses Against Death Anxiety

In their early discussions, the participants identified specific patterns of defense they had adopted in an effort to protect themselves against an acute awareness of death and the associated dread and anxiety. For example, Ryan talked about lying awake many nights as a young boy, pondering questions of infinity and death. He disclosed that later he had gradually grown indifferent to life as a reaction to his evolving knowledge of death's finality. In a discussion group, he revealed,

> *Ryan (35):* From the time I was 7 years old on, I just didn't let anything matter to me. Nothing mattered to me at all. I'd let nothing have any value in my life. I didn't care about school. I wouldn't try to get good grades. I wouldn't take care of anything. I stubbornly refused to let anything or anyone into my life that had any value.

> *Luke (49):* I remember when I was about that age, lying in bed, it seemed night after night, until I resolved this in my mind. I was just tormented by the thought of dying and being dead forever, and I remember going through a logical process, because I knew in my belief system that there was the afterlife, and it was a question of dealing with death through a decision as to whether or not to believe in God. Even as a child I knew that I had that choice, that if I chose to believe in God then I didn't have to worry about death so much. And I chose that. I remember specifically making the decision to relieve myself by believing in God and then I could relax. It fit very nicely into my whole family structure. It was everything that I was supposed to do anyway. The other choice was too hard to even consider, and so I made a decision to believe in God and then I could sleep.

> *Rachel (44):* I really think that each person thinks that they are the one exception to death. On some level, everybody entertains that idea, and whatever the exceptional thing about a person is, that's their key to surviving. Even if it's having children or having a business that will last or writing a book that will last, or whatever. Everybody can find one thing that will assure them that they're the one exception to the rule.

Ryan: I've lived most of my life not being invested in my life at all. I think that only over the last 15 years, I've slowly let things begin to matter to me. My friends are precious to me, things in my life are just extremely valuable to me. And now I have fear—and it feels almost good to have fear. I'm afraid to fly on an airplane, not like white-knuckle, but it feels afraid, I'm afraid of gravity, like it could really kill you. And I like being concerned about my life. I like trying to preserve my body and it *does* matter to me. That level of awareness of my life increases as a direct result of my investing more and more in it.

Malcolm (58): It's like the trivia of our lives distracts us from the reality of death. And I think I am getting closer to some feeling about that for the first time in my life. You know, it sounds corny but when I am in a more open state, like it's a nice day and I'm listening to some music that I love, and I have a feeling that, gee, there will be a time that I'll never be able to hear that music any more or that I'll never feel the sunshine the way that I feel it that day. And it's the first time in my life that I'm starting to feel that. And I know it's because I'm letting things matter more to me.

Ryan: I was thinking about the times when I first become involved with a woman. It makes me feel more about my life than anything. I feel more alive than I've ever felt when I'm in the beginning of a relationship. What I see it turning into, in myself and in 99 percent of the marriages I see, is just the reverse of that. It becomes a mechanism to deny death and to create an atmosphere where your kids are going to be raised to deny death.

Andrea (41): I've talked about my feelings about other people dying in this discussion, but I feel like the most painful thing for me to feel, which I've felt just a few times in my life, is that I have a feeling of loving my life, of loving myself in it. And I feel like I can't stand that feeling because I feel like I would miss being myself so much (cries) and I feel like I can stand the loss of anybody else because I would still be myself, but I can't stand the idea of not being me any more (cries). That's why I think that I start to get into things where I hate myself or I pick at myself or I'm critical of myself, those kind of things, because then I don't have that feeling any more. I remember one time Ricky was talking about dying, little Ricky, and he said "When I die, I won't be Ricky any more." (cries)

Malina (56): I grew up in a society where life and death were totally unexplained. I was very confused. I was very cut off and even when I faced a lot of deaths of people that I knew in my very early childhood from the holocaust and when I was a young teenager in the Independence War in Israel, I didn't have any feelings. I went through the motions, I went to a lot of funerals. I can't believe it, but I didn't feel anything.

The first time in my life that I felt something strong for my life was when I was seriously ill; before the surgery was taking place, I felt something for myself. There were a few thoughts, like it was the first time that I was thinking in these terms, that I was glad that I was born. And that I had a chance to experience life, that I would like to continue to experience life. I didn't want to die. This is really the first time I had a grasp of feeling that I was glad that I was born. I never felt something like this at all. I existed, I lived, there was a lot of agony, some joys. Just today, sitting here, I was thinking also I was so much robbed in my life of reality, of life and the knowledge about death and what can happen. I didn't feel anything.

Malina (to Andrea): I was very touched when you said that you would miss yourself, your life, the fullness of your life, the richness, the happiness. I feel sometimes like this myself. I can't believe that I feel like I would miss myself not being, not existing. And I also have a strong feeling, and this is almost hard to say, that I would be a loss for people who know me because I let them know me some. (sad)

Discussions Regarding Feelings About Death

In the years following the series of discussions described previously, men and women continued to talk about ways of living more fully in spite of one's limitations in time. The process of uncovering and challenging defenses against death anxiety and facing the issue of death squarely appears to have had the effect of shifting people's perspective on the subject in significant ways. In one discussion that took place more recently, the participants described the changes that had occurred in their feeling reactions and philosophical approach to the fact of death.

Andrea (50): I feel like I've changed in relation to the subject of death. We made a film a number of years ago, and in it I had a lot of feelings about myself dying, imagining that. Then three years ago, right around the same time, two people I knew died. I started to have the feelings I always have whenever I had any reminders of death, which were *"This is too terrible. I cannot stand this. I cannot stand it. I hate that it's true. I just cannot stand it! This is absolutely unbearable."* And then for some reason, I had the thought, *"Whose reaction is this that I'm having?"* It crossed my mind that maybe this wasn't even my reaction. Then I remembered that my parents were so absolutely freaked out by the idea of death and so intolerant of the subject, and I could sense it in them, and I could feel the same feelings.

So then I thought, *"Well, how do I really feel about death?"* And I thought that I didn't feel like they did. Even if I still felt panic, it would be *my* feeling. I had never thought about, *"What do I really think about it."* I had some other thoughts. One was concerning what someone said about "accepting death." The Buddhists and other people say, "Accept death." It's such a funny way to put it. It doesn't matter whether you accept it or not, it's there. It's not up to us to accept or not accept. It just is. Whatever my reaction is, it's just there.

Also I had this image. We get so worked up about what's going to happen after death, but whatever it was, was happening before too. I imagined this long, long endless period of nonexistence with this little tiny bump in it, of life. I feel like this little time here is such an incredible gift. That's how I feel. An incredible gift. Every moment I have that feeling. I'm always aware of death, so there's always a sadness in everything that I experience. All the happiness has a poignancy to it. It actually makes it deeper and richer than when it was just "happy."

Robert Firestone (69): That's one of the positive aspects of facing the death issue. It gives a poignant sense of meaning to happiness, which enlarges the experience instead of detracting from it.

Andrea: I thought about the idea of triumphing over death—to me that also seems absurd. Because I am so powerless. But I thought that I can triumph over my defenses about death—I can triumph over the ways that I've defended myself against facing it. So I feel like I've changed and developed.

Robert Firestone: It seems like people are split between an alliance with death or an alliance with life. A lot of voice attacks represent a drive toward death and destruction and a movement away from living, from experience. Or you can ally yourself with living and feeling and embracing life.

Nicole (26): I like what you said, Andrea. It seems that you've come to a level of feeling in your life where you don't feel panicked and you're way more comfortable with the idea of death, although you still experience sad feelings. But for me, I feel like I go in and out of that. At times I feel like, "*You don't live forever, so you've got to challenge everything. You've got to do everything—you should really struggle with the hard things in your life. You should do it because you know that's really living a full life.*" And that does give me inspiration and motivation to live a full life. And then at other times, when I'm feeling the closest I could feel to somebody, I don't feel like hanging in there and staying close, because it is terrifying to realize you're not going to have that person.

Robert Firestone: It's a choice.

Nicole: Yes, it really is.

Robert Firestone: Face the realities and embrace life or turn your back on life and protect against death. I think it's valuable to challenge it, and particularly to talk about it freely.

Nicole: But I have to say, it's definitely a feeling that you go in and out of. Different feelings. To me, I don't feel one way about the whole subject. I have different periods where I feel like struggling. And then I have other periods where it's just sometimes a little too hard.

Robert Firestone: So it's an intermittent experience that you should experience fully. And you can bear it, and you can bear the thought of losing yourself and others too. A lot of people think they can't bear it, so they don't enter a relationship. They're afraid of losing it, so they don't have it. And that's the choosing death over life, whereas the opposite is to embrace life and to take your chances. And you can bear the loss, always.

It's better to love and lose than never to love. It's better to live and die than never to live. But that's not a decision that most people make. A person just drifts into a state of denial and wards off all kinds of emotions and pain in their life at great expense. It's never worth it to take the drug. It's never worth it to kill the pain. That's the key issue. You can bear the pain. And that makes you strong.

Dean (48):   I feel exactly the same way—on both sides of the fence at any given moment. Sometimes so woefully indifferent to the fact that I'm going to die and distant from myself and people. When I wake up from that state, it frightens me because what wakes me up is the awareness that I'm going to die. And when that occurs, it's like, "No, I'm not ready. I want to see that person one more time. I want to take one more boat ride. I want to do something. I'm not ready yet." But during those periods where I'm indifferent, it's really frightening to me, when I wake up out of it. And the thing is it's so tough because it's both—death is both concrete and an abstraction. It's so concrete because it's everywhere. You see it everywhere. People you know die. People on the news die. And yet my own death is such a speculation. Who knows what happens? So in that speculation I can think many things.

I found that my mother dying recently has brought this subject to the surface much more for me. I have so many moments where I think, "What if this was my last moment?" But it doesn't feel morbid to me; it just crystallizes a moment. And because I fly so much, there are a lot of times when I'll be getting on a plane and I'll look around and I'll say, "Well, what if these are the people I'm going to die with?" But it doesn't feel as morbid as it sounds.

Louis (67):   I think that Andrea captured a lot of my feelings, particularly since I have had to face this issue more or less head on in the past year since I was diagnosed with cancer. There's nothing that can be done about it except live what is left. But I loved your description of the long experience and the little dot, an eye-blink. Life is just a eye-blink in that perspective. And you seize the blink or you seize the moment, which is seizing the life. But it's just a moment. It's a precious gift, as you said. It's so momentary in the perspective of things.

Robert Firestone: One other thing, the experience of death leads to a sense of altruism. It really does. I see people living that way here in this group of friends particularly. And it extends beyond our group of friends too, to anybody who crosses our path who needs something or wants something. There's a sense of fulfillment in that that is counter to the death process. A very fundamental part of being alive is being generous and altruistic. I think it's part of our nature.

Louis: We're all in the same boat.

Robert Firestone: There is a feeling of compassion and kinship with other people who are undergoing the same experiences. By remaining vulnerable, people can learn to face the fear of death openly without compensation or defenses and to cope with the sadness of the anticipated loss of self. Their appreciation of life and the human condition gives their lives a poignant meaning in relation to its finality. Recognizing and living with existential truths enhance the precious moments we spend with our loved ones. This awareness can serve to remind us how vital it is *not* to damage the feelings of others, their self-respect, special qualities and desires, and the spirit in which they approach life.

Andrea: I think that in therapy, if it were really a good therapy, the subject of death would come up. Because I think that when a person's defenses are broken down and when they're in touch with their feelings, it has to become an issue. And also when they're not isolated, when they're making contact with another person, I think all of that is conducive to the subject coming up. I think there's also sadness about really feeling yourself and a sadness about the fact that it's finite. I think all of that is happening at the same time.

Robert Firestone: If you really are living a life on the edge in relation to feeling and struggling in relation to other people and really investing in the projects—whatever your life projects are—these issues are inevitably going to arise and they're going to arise in a very powerful way. I think that's what we're doing. Believe me, it pops up every day in every person's mind here. Because they're not living like many other people. This is like an outpost for feeling human beings, a game preserve.

So there is a way of being aware of one's death, dealing with the feelings of sadness or fear openly and honestly, at the same time giving great value to our lives and taking a position philosophically that our uniqueness and our separateness and our creativity are the most essentially human qualities that we have and that these must be protected at all costs. We must strive for that individuality and that sense of self and enhance our lives based on the fact of our death and make our lives more meaningful. I think that's the positive approach to these issues, to live a life of love and truth and of giving great value and commitment to one's life.

CONCLUSION

There is no defense or protection against death, but there is a way to live that is life-affirming rather than life-denying. In an essay, "Life Fear and Death Fear," Otto Rank (1936/1972) asserted that not all anxiety could be overcome therapeutically. Rank was referring to death anxiety in declaring the impossibility of facing the truth of human existence without anxiety.

Although despair is endemic to the human condition, there are ways to ameliorate the anxiety and dread that emerge when one contemplates one's mortality. S. Freud (1915/1957a) shaded his pessimistic view of civilization and the human condition when he suggested that people might benefit from an awareness rather than a denial of their mortality:

> Would it not be better to give death the place in reality and in our thoughts which is its due, and to give a little more prominence to the unconscious attitude towards death which we have hitherto so carefully suppressed? (p. 299)

People can share their feelings about death and dying with close friends and associates and find essential meaning in their existence. Rather than searching outside for the essence or purpose of life, they can shape their lives and give their world form and color according to their own feelings and inclinations. They can maintain a strong sense of self and invest in goals that transcend the narrow focus of their own priorities. It is the nature of humans to develop his or her personal project and maintain his or her unique identity.

There is no way to banish painful memories and feelings from consciousness without losing one's sense of humanity and feeling of compassion for others. However, if people could overcome their personal limitations and embrace life in the face of death anxiety, they would approach their fellow human beings with compassion and a feeling of empathy, because they would realize that people everywhere face the same existential crisis. Such a person would have far less propensity for ethnic hatred or insidious warfare.

With enlightenment on the subject, people could choose to embrace life and live with an awareness of death rather than deaden themselves prematurely. Coming to terms with death as a reality appears to be the only viable alternative to a life of tedium, conformity, and alienation from oneself and others. In choosing to live full and honest lives with a minimum of defense, people can move away from the morbid contemplation of death or its denial toward a life of adventure characterized by freedom of choice, enthusiasm, and optimism.

NOTES

1. Several researchers have investigated the correlations between the early environment, differential attachment patterns, and later preoccupations with death. Mikulincer, Florian, and Tolmacz (1990), who reported results from two such studies, concluded that: "subjects classified as secure in relation to attachment generally experienced less fear of death than did insecurely attached subjects" (p. 278).
2. Tomer and Eliason (1996), in discussing their "working definition" of the concept of death, wrote: "The concept of death anxiety . . . is that of a negative emotional reaction provoked by the anticipation of a state in which the self does not exist" (p. 345).
3. A number of theorists (Becker, 1973/1997; Choron, 1963; Rank, 1936/1972) have argued that the fear of death and the cessation of consciousness affect human beings more than any other existential "given"; however, others, for example Loy (1992), have proposed that the most powerful defenses are those formed against a perception of our groundlessness or the void.
4. Portions of this section are adapted from (1994), "Psychological Defenses Against Death Anxiety," in R. A. Neimeyer (Ed.), Death Anxiety Handbook: Research, Instrumentation, and Application (pp. 217–241). Washington, DC: Taylor & Francis. Reproduced with permission. All rights reserved.

5. Some portions of this section have been adapted from "The Origins of Ethnic Strife" (Firestone, 1996).
6. Pagels (1995) noted that: "Many Christians . . . have believed that they stood on God's side without demonizing their opponents. . . . For the most part, however, Christians have taught—and acted upon—the belief that their enemies are evil and beyond redemption" (p. 184).
7. Interestingly enough, under the influence of a powerful leader and united against a common enemy since World War II, these warring groups lived together in peace.

III

RESTORING INTIMACY
IN RELATIONSHIPS

10

COUPLE RELATIONSHIPS

To love one another truly is to walk in the light, to live in truth, to be truly alive, and perfectly free.
> —R. D. Laing (1989, quoting Paul Parin, 1978)

To fully embrace life it is important for people to develop their capacity for giving and receiving love. Fromm asserted, "The affirmation of one's own life, happiness, growth, freedom is rooted in one's capacity to love" (1956, p. 50, italics deleted). However, the process of learning to love and to be loved is complicated for people who experienced rejection and other hurtful treatment as children. When a hurt person attempts to accept love or let love into his or her life, there is a recurrence of painful feelings from the past. On the other hand, the lover is more likely to experience positive emotional reactions from the process of loving another. In that sense, it is easier to give love than to receive it.

Although other problems in life cause people deep concern—war, poverty, crime, illness, the existential issues of aloneness and death—individuals seem to experience the most pain and distress in relation to the difficulties they encounter in their closest personal associations. The key issues involved in the breakdown of relationships are not usually the explanations typically given: economic hardship, religious differences, problems with in-laws, breakdown of church and family, sexual incompatibility, and many others. Each partner's essential fear of aloneness, vulnerability, abandonment, rejection, and potential loss is at the core of marital and family distress.

RELIVING THE PAST THROUGH SELECTION, DISTORTION, AND PROVOCATION

People who have been damaged in their earliest experiences and are afraid of being hurt or rejected again seek security in repetition. They attempt to recapture the more familiar conditions within the family, the conditions under which they formed their defenses.[1] The more rejected the child, the more desperately he or she clings to the parent and forms a fantasy bond with him or her. In a sense, the rejected child cannot leave home, cannot develop an independent life, and transfers this abnormal dependency to new objects. As a consequence, he or she tends to avoid or reject any experience or person that is not a repetition of the early experience.

To preserve their negative identity, people must modify the responses of their loved ones, in a sense "working them over," in an effort to maintain equilibrium and reduce tension and anxiety. As noted previously, they attempt to recreate the emotional environment that was present in the original family through three major modes of defense: selection, distortion, and provocation.

- *Selection*: People tend to select partners who are similar in appearance, behavior, and defense patterns to one or another family member because they feel familiar and comfortable with this person.
- *Distortion*: People's perceptions of their partners are altered or distorted in a direction that corresponds more closely to a particular member of the family of origin. Not all distortions are negative. Both positive and negative qualities from the past are assigned to significant people in a person's current life. Any misperception, whether an exaggeration of admirable traits or of undesirable qualities, usually generates friction in relationships. People want to be seen for who they are, and being distorted by one's partner arouses hurtful, angry responses.
- *Provocation:* If the first two methods fail to recreate the past and maintain the defense system, partners tend to manipulate each other to elicit familiar parental responses. In this case, their actions provoke reactions similar to those of their parent or parents. For example, partners may incite anger and even rage in each other with thoughtlessness, forgetfulness, incompetency, and other childish, regressive behavior. Frequently, the closest, most tender moments are followed by provocations that create distance between the partners.

Through these three methods, partners are able to externalize the fantasy bond and recreate negative aspects of the original family in their new attachments. They preserve the internalized parent by projecting his or her image onto a new object. In other words, it appears that people prefer to maintain their original defenses rather than adapt to a new set of circumstances, and so they attempt to mold their environment to repeat past conditions.

THE FORMATION OF A FANTASY BOND IN COUPLE RELATIONSHIPS

Individuals often become romantically involved at a point in their lives where they are breaking old dependency ties and experiencing a sense of independence and separateness. In this stage of their development, they tend to seek new friendships and are willing to risk more of themselves emotionally. Other people are attracted to them because of their openness and vitality. At the beginning of their new love relationship, they are living, for a while, in a less defended and more vulnerable state and experience considerable joy and a sense of companionship and closeness.

This state of being in love, although invigorating and exciting, can also be frightening and eventually may precipitate an anxiety state. Fears of rejection, loss, or abandonment and the poignant sadness frequently evoked by loving another and by being loved may become difficult to bear, especially for individuals who have experienced a lack of love in their early lives. At the point where they begin to feel anxious (or perhaps even before anxiety reaches the level of their conscious awareness), they begin to retreat from feeling close and gradually give up the most valued aspects of their relationships. This withdrawal from closeness and intimacy is an outgrowth of the adjustment they made in responding to their early environment. Consider the example of Angela:

> When I was in high school, I was very shy and withdrawn. One summer day, a friend dragged me to the beach with her. While we were there, two guys that I recognized from school came up and started talking with us. At the end of the afternoon they invited us to go out with them that evening. At first I balked but with my friend's encouragement, insistence really, I agreed.
>
> That evening I had the most fun I had ever had on a date. The guy who was interested in me was so warm and funny and relaxed that he put me immediately at ease. I could tell he really liked me. I was so happy, I laughed and joked around, I felt attractive. I could hardly recognize myself. When they dropped me off that night, I was walking on air.
>
> The next afternoon he called me and I was thrilled to hear his voice on the phone. He invited me to an old horror movie that was showing

at the college; it would be fun. Without thinking I heard myself saying, "Oh, no thank you. I don't like horror movies." He hung up, I am sure stinging with the rejection, and I never heard from him again. Meanwhile, I sank back into my familiar life of isolation. To this day, so many years later, I still regret that response to him.

MANIFESTATIONS OF THE FANTASY BOND

As a couple's relationship unfolds, symptoms of the fantasy bond often begin to appear. One early symptom can be observed in a decrease in personal contact between the partners; where they once spent hours in conversation, now they show signs of losing interest in both talking and listening to each other. The partners may become less close and intimate and more superficial and routine in their interactions. Their style of communication tends to become less honest, more duplicitous, and is characterized by small talk, bickering, speaking for the other, interrupting, and talking as a unit. Spontaneity and playfulness gradually dissipate, feelings of sexual attraction may wane, and the couple's sex life often becomes more routine and mechanical. This decline in sexual relating is not the result of familiarity but is of the deadening habit patterns, exaggerated dependency, and negative projections that have developed in each partner. Another early symptom that we have observed is diminished eye contact between the partners; this sign of curtailed relating is indicative of a more impersonal mode of interaction. Both partners may begin to manipulate by playing on the other's guilt or by provoking angry or parental responses.

These signs and symptoms are likely to appear after the partners have made a commitment to one another. The commitment to living together, to marriage, or to starting a family may have been originally based on genuine feelings. On another level, it may be viewed by one or both partners as a guarantee of enduring love and security—external indications of a fantasy of connectedness. For many people, this sense of belonging to another person, of being eternally loved, provides a false sense of security that seems irresistible.

Withholding

As the fantasy bond develops, partners begin to withhold the desirable qualities in themselves that were especially valued by the other (see chapter 7). This form of withholding precipitates feelings of guilt and remorse. As a consequence, both begin to act out of a sense of obligation instead of a genuine desire to be together. In inhibiting actions and holding back traits that are lovable and would evoke tender responses, they manipulate each other to maintain a certain level of comfort and emotional distance instead of continuing to be intimate or personal as they were at the inception of their relationship. By so doing, they inadvertently short-circuit the process of learning how to tolerate the experience of being especially loved and valued.

Polarization of Parent–Child Ego States

In a fantasy bond, individuals often polarize into either a parental or childlike ego state. Some people regress to childish modes of relating in an effort to manipulate others into assuming a parental role and thereby preserve the imagined security of the original fantasy bond with their parents. The partner acting out the parental authoritarian role is often a person whose original fantasy bond involved a strong identification with the aggressor (see chapter 2). In many committed couple relationships, one can observe parent–child modes of interaction, with occasional role reversals. It is rare that both partners relate from an adult ego-state (Willi, 1975/1982).

Idealization/Denigration of the Other

Partners often criticize each other for not living up to their a priori expectations. Their mutual disillusionment and disappointment stem partly from their tendency to idealize their mates as they idealized their parents. Frequently when one partner develops an awareness of the weaknesses, foibles, and vulnerability of the other, he or she becomes angry, bitter, or cynical because this idealization has been broken.

Couples are often hypercritical of each other's traits, attribute blame to their mates for deficiencies in the relationship, and manifest considerable hostility. In spite of their stated attacks, on another level, they strive desperately to maintain an idealized picture of the partner and maintain their illusion of love (Becker, 1973/1997; Firestone, 1985; Rank 1936/1972).[2] In a typical therapy interaction, the wife complains about her husband's lack of communication, coldness, and pattern of compulsive overwork that excludes her, while the husband in turn lists his wife's dependency, childishness, and sexual withholding. It becomes quite apparent that very often both people are accurate in their description of the other's behavior. When asked why they stay together, the typical response is "because we really love each other." In observing interactions with warring couples, it is sometimes difficult to believe their protestations of love for each other.

Loss of Independence

As partners start to sacrifice their interests, friends, and other aspects of their independent functioning to become one half of a couple, their natural attraction to one another is jeopardized. People in a fantasy bond often experience themselves as an appendage of the other person, and the other as an appendage or extension of them, a condition that contributes to the decrease in their feelings of attraction. As partners become increasingly dependent on each other, both in terms of practical functions and psychologically, for example, for their sense of self-worth, they lose much of their assertiveness and vitality and become less appealing in general.

Form Versus Substance

Most men and women who form a fantasy bond appear to be unable to accept the fact that they have lost considerable feeling for each other, that they have become distant and alienated, or that the relationship has deteriorated. To avoid an awareness of this painful truth, they attempt to cover up their lack of feeling with a fantasy of closeness, love, and connection and begin to substitute form for the substance of the relationship. Responses based on conventional form consist of the everyday routines, rituals, customs, cursory conversations, discussions of practical arrangements, and other role-determined behaviors that support their illusion of still being in love. These more habitual responses gradually replace the real substance of the relationship—the genuine love, respect, and affection.

APPLICATION OF VOICE THERAPY TO COUPLE RELATIONSHIPS

More often than not, in a relationship characterized by a fantasy bond, both individuals are listening to and believing what their respective voices are telling them. In a sense, their communications are being filtered through a distorted lens and interpreted through a biased, judgmental point of view that warps their partner's real image. Both partners use rationalizations promoted by the voice to discourage or push away loving responses from the other and to justify their hostility and distancing behavior. In addition, men and women project their specific self-criticisms onto one another and respond as though they are being depreciated by their mates.[3] The goal of voice therapy with couples is to help each partner identify the voice attacks that govern this distancing behavior and create or escalate conflict in the relationship. Through the process of revealing the contents of voice attacks, partners can interrupt even well-established patterns of dishonest communication and reduce the frequency of mixed messages that have characterized their conversations. By identifying self-criticisms as well as judgmental, cynical thoughts about the other, each partner is able to relate more openly and empathically.

In conjoint sessions or couples' groups, individuals usually progress through the following steps in the course of treatment: they (a) formulate the problem each partner perceives as being a barrier to his or her satisfaction in the relationship; (b) learn to verbalize self-critical thoughts and negative perceptions of the other in the form of the voice and release the associated affect; (c) develop insight into the origins of the voice and make connections between past experience and present conflicts; and (d) modify behaviors and communications in a direction that counteracts the dictates of the voice.

The process of identifying negative parental prescriptions regarding self, others, and one's relationship can be facilitated by asking clients to complete an assessment instrument, the Firestone Voice Scale for Couples (FVSC; Firestone & Firestone, 2002a). Items on this self-report questionnaire were gathered from clinical material, from thoughts reported by couples in the friendship circle, and from thoughts and attitudes reported by students enrolled in an undergraduate psychology course. The contents of these internalized voices were either verbalized or written by individuals responding to the question: "What negative thoughts do you have about yourself, your partner, your relationship, and relationships in general?" (See Exhibit 10.1 for sample items.)

In the sessions, both partners are present as each discloses negative thoughts toward him- or herself and the other. Self-critical thoughts are verbalized in the second person "you" (see chapter 8); hostile, cynical attitudes toward the other are expressed in the third person format, as though someone else were imparting negative information to the individual about his or her partner, for example: "*He's* so cold and uncommunicative. *She's* so melodramatic and acts so helpless."

As partners trace the source of their self-attacks and cynical views to early family interactions, they gain perspective on each other's problems and develop more compassion for their mates as well as for themselves. When verbalizing or "giving away" their hostile views of the other, partners strive to be sincere and sensitive and relinquish long-held grudges, even when their cynical attitudes have some basis in reality. Recognizing that their voice attacks are a primary source of their misery, partners stop blaming each other, which takes the pressure off the relationship. The process has a powerful impact on altering and improving partners' attitudes toward their mates and enhances each individual's personal growth.

Voice Therapy Group With Couples

In a series of discussions attended by 10 individuals (five couples) who had been unable previously to maintain long-lasting intimate relationships, the participants focused on identifying, revealing, and analyzing destructive thoughts and attitudes that were causing distress in their relationships. In the

EXHIBIT 10.1
FVSC

Instructions

All people experience thoughts that are critical towards themselves and others. For example, when a person is worried about his/her relationship, he/she might think:

"You'd better hang onto him/her. This may be your last chance. You may never get anybody again."

Or a person might have critical thoughts about a potential partner:

"Don't get involved. You might get hurt because he/she is so unreliable."

Negative thoughts are a part of everyone's thinking process. Please indicate the frequency with which you experience the following thoughts by circling the corresponding number.

1 = NEVER; 2 = RARELY; 3 = ONCE IN A WHILE; 4 = FREQUENTLY; 5 = MOST OF THE TIME

For example, you think or say to yourself:

1 2 ③ 4 5   *"You're unattractive. Why should she/he want to go out with you?"*

1. *You're supposed to be married. If you're not, you're a freak.*	1 2 3 4 5
2. *You've got to put up with a lot to stay involved with a man/woman.*	1 2 3 4 5
3. *You're never going to find another person who understands you.*	1 2 3 4 5
4. *You're so ugly! Why would he/she want to go out with you?*	1 2 3 4 5
5. *Men are so insensitive. They're so opinionated. They won't let you have your own views about anything.*	1 2 3 4 5
6. *Don't get too hooked on him/her.*	1 2 3 4 5
7. *He's/she's so cold and rejecting. Who would want to go out with him/her anyway?*	1 2 3 4 5
8. *You'd better give him/her what he/she really wants so you won't lose him/her.*	1 2 3 4 5
9. *You really owe him/her something now that you've been sexual.*	1 2 3 4 5
10. *You have to take care of a woman. You're nothing except for how you take care of a woman.*	1 2 3 4 5

Used with permission of the Glendon Association.

group sessions, they uncovered internalized voices they had not previously recognized or understood and gained additional insight into defensive behaviors that were interfering with the closeness and intimacy they desired.

Alan and Amanda, who had been involved for approximately six years, reported that they often felt alienated from each other and in conflict. Their problems arose because the defenses of one partner fit in with those of the other. Alan's distrust of women and his tendencies toward isolation and self-denial were exacerbated by Amanda's self-depreciating attitudes and her intrusive, angry reactions to his repeated withdrawals. Recently, as a result of working through many of these problems on an individual basis, the couple had become much closer. The renewed sense of intimacy precipitated intensified self-attacks and cynical attitudes in Amanda.

> Amanda (44): I think that I'm not like other women, that I'm not lovable. I tell myself things like *"You're not lovable. You're not like other women. You're never, never going to have something nice with a man."*
>
> And then it goes on to other people. I don't trust anybody else's relationship either. If I see someone being affectionate I think to myself, *"Just look at them. That's disgusting. It's not real. They're so phony. It's just a big show. They're disgusting. And they're so phony. It's not nice anyway. No one has anything nice!"*

> Dr. Firestone: What about men?

> Amanda: Specifically toward men, it's like, *"What a weak person! He's so desperate. Look at him. He's just such a desperate person. He'll do anything. He crawls over people to get to her. He's disgusting. You could never be attracted to a person like that."* It feels very unfriendly.

> Dr. Firestone: Whose point of view do you think that represents?

> Amanda: Definitely my mother. And that's how I saw my father, too. I think that he was weak. And he never stood up to her, never, ever.

> Dr. Firestone: And that hurt you.

> Amanda: Yes. I had no issues with my father ever. But I was always fighting with my mother. And he threw me out of the house. He's the one who threw me out of the house because he couldn't handle the confrontation between us.

> Dr. Firestone: So he just served her interests. That's the source of his weakness.

> Amanda: Yeah. Ever since I was little I always felt like he liked me, but if it ever came to be an issue where it was her or me, it was always her. But I don't understand now why I feel that way toward men and why I don't have that anger toward women.

Dr. Firestone:	It's like you've incorporated her idea and that's why it's directed toward men. What about yourself? What are your voices toward yourself?
Amanda:	I think that I'm not a woman.
Dr. Firestone:	Say it to yourself.
Amanda:	"You're not a woman. You're not pretty. You're ... "
Dr. Firestone:	Say it with feeling. Really listen to it. Let yourself feel this. It's okay. Just really let yourself feel it.
Amanda:	*"You're not like other women. You're not like them. You're not nice to men. You're not pretty. You're not feminine. You're not lovable. You're not lovable like other women are."* I feel my mother's view of me is *"I hate you. I hate your face. I hate you. You're not right. You don't look right. You don't act right. I'm embarrassed by you. You're not who I want you to be!"*
Dr. Firestone:	You're not what I want.
Amanda:	*"You're not what I want. You don't have the right color hair. You don't have the right kind of hair. You don't have the right looks. You don't fit in. You don't fit into this family. Everyone else is nice. You don't even look like the rest of us. You're not part of this family."* I mean, this is what she actually said. It's hard for me to feel very much, good or bad.
Dr. Firestone:	It looks like you're feeling a lot actually.
Amanda:	It's interesting what you said because one of the attacks that was said to me is that "You're cold. You don't feel anything. You don't care about anybody but yourself."
Dr. Firestone:	What are your voices about Alan, specifically?
Amanda:	I don't have a lot of voices about Alan, that's one of the things that's actually made me feel good recently. But the ones I do have are in relation to his being less aggressive than me. *"He's not going to make things happen. You have to make it happen. You have to plan things out. You have to make it happen. He's not going to stand up for anything. He doesn't stand up for himself. He won't stand up for his rights. He's just too nice. He won't make a big deal about anything."* [To Alan] It's hard to say these voices because I really like you.
Dr. Firestone:	That's nice, too. But look at the negative part for now.

Amanda:	"He's passive. He's nice, but he's passive. He's doesn't make things happen. If you want something to happen you have to do it yourself. He's like the nice guy. He won't ever say what he wants." But I'm not aware of that many voices usually.
Dr. Firestone:	You're totally satisfied.
Amanda:	Except for when I think that he's passive, when he isn't energetic.
Dr. Firestone:	What about you, Alan? What are your voices about yourself?
Alan:	I don't think of them in terms of attacks on myself but I definitely attack the relationship.
Dr. Firestone:	Do you want to say your attacks on the relationship?
Alan:	Lately, for instance she's been expressing her affection by saying that she loves me, and I know that I have a really hard time believing it. I think that she's lying. "She doesn't feel it. She's just saying it for appearances. She's trying to set you up. She's trying to suck you in so you'll believe it. And she's going to drop you. She really doesn't like you. She's saying the words but it's not there. You're getting set up for a big fall." I don't think this part clearly, but I'm pretty sure I don't feel worthy of being loved.
Dr. Firestone:	Say that to yourself. You're not worthy of being loved.
Alan:	It's like, "There's no way somebody could really love you."
Dr. Firestone:	That's right. Go ahead. Like that.
Alan:	"You're no good. How the hell could somebody be interested in you?" [angry, loud voice] "You may be able to fool them for a little while but they're going to find out you're really bad." I know it's there, and I know my mother thought I was a troublemaker, through and through.
Dr. Firestone:	This recapitulates the attitudes of the parent. The attitudes toward yourself are the same feelings that came from your parents' point of view of hating you. Also, your attitudes toward others represent the parents' point of view toward others, particularly toward the opposite sex. It's very important, although I said it with humor, that you need to look at the parent of the same sex as your mate, because you'll see the attitudes toward men acted out by the mother and they'll be pretty much the

same voices that the daughter will have. The same is true for fathers and sons.

Then there's the other part of Amanda's attack, which is directed toward herself, which is her mother's attitude toward her. So she's really living her life based on her mother's attitudes toward her and toward men. They're controlling her whole relationship. The same with Alan. His father's attitudes toward women are one part of his way of thinking, and his parents' attack on him are the other part, his negative attitudes toward himself. Most people believe that these attitudes are based on reality.

[To Amanda] You really do think that you were different and peculiar and disgusting and not right. You really believe it. And it affects your whole relationship and your attitudes toward yourself and toward men, both. In Alan's case, he has his father's total attitude toward women, that he just isn't up to it. He can't give them what they need. He just can't give all that they want. His attitude toward women is that they're demanding and pulling and he has to protect himself like his father protected himself. And he has these terrible attitudes toward himself. Angry. Angry at somebody who would like him because they're tricking him. He knows how bad he is because he was defined that way as a child. So any woman telling him otherwise is a liar and deceiving him. He can't trust her.

Although Amanda and Alan, like the other participants, originally came to the group to improve their relationships, an additional benefit was that each partner became stronger personally, more centered in him- or herself. In the discussions, the participants found that they had been living their lives largely based on destructive thought processes and parental prescriptions rather than on fulfilling their own desires and goals. After they realized the influence of the negative voices, they began to identify and challenge the thought processes that were limiting them and causing distress in their relationships.

The partners participating in the group increased their awareness that they each had suffered to varying degrees in their upbringing. It is valuable for individuals to challenge their negative voices and expose core issues in their relationship. Partners must learn to free themselves of self-defeating, restrictive behavior patterns that cause distress in their relationships. Recognition of an enemy within enables people to develop compassion for themselves as well as empathy for their partner. Each develops the ability to listen to the other with understanding and sensitivity.

OTHER TECHNIQUES FOR UNDERSTANDING AND IMPROVING RELATIONSHIPS

In the context of therapy as well as in their everyday lives, clients can use a number of other methods to enhance their relationships. These methods are based on an understanding of the voice process and how it negatively influences each partner's behavior.

Revealing Destructive Thought Processes to Each Other

In couples therapy, it is valuable for partners to reveal both their negative thoughts toward themselves and about the other in a candid exchange of views. Sometimes the focus will be on one person while the other listens, as was the case in the discussion with Ana and Alan. It is important for each to "give away"—that is, to openly admit and take responsibility for his or her negative attacks in a nonaccusatory style and to not react to the voice statements of the other as personal criticism.

A frequently asked question in training workshops is whether or not the partner feels personally attacked, hurt, or angry when these negative voices are verbalized by the other person. In truth, most people are relieved to hear their partner's hostile statements spoken aloud. In the process of listening to their mate express the cynical, distrusting attitudes, it becomes clear to each partner that these are alien attitudes that neither one agrees with.

Another technique that can be used in psychotherapy by clients who have developed maturity and empathy for each other is for each partner to learn to free associate, to express all their thoughts without the usual censorship, thereby giving the other a unique perspective on his or her inner life. In the session, each individual listens in turn to the entire expression of the other, without interrupting or commenting, except to occasionally reflect an understanding, capture the feeling, or clarify their meaning. Toward the end of the session, the partners describe their reactions and insights. This is a structured format that teaches two skills: empathic listening and self-assertion, the ability to express one's point of view.

Utilizing Journaling to Understand the Voice Process in Couple Relationships

Partners are encouraged to describe in writing what they believe to be their parents' point of view toward them and their partners, and about relationships in general. The person tries to imagine what his or her parent or parents would say about various aspects of his or her life. Most often this description focuses on the attitudes and point of view of the parent of the same sex. Afterward, partners describe their own point of view, generally a more realistic and congenial perspective, on the same topics. The purpose of this exercise is to facilitate separation from negative parental introjects and to strengthen elements of the self system. Individuals are better able to make a clear distinction between the attitudes representative of a parent's point of view and attitudes that reflect their own wants, priorities, and goals for the relationship. In terms of Bowenian Family Systems Theory, this procedure may help elevate an individual's level of self-differentiation. Bowen (1978) believed that:

> The level of differentiation of a person is largely determined by the time he leaves the parental family and he attempts a life of his own. Thereafter, he tends to replicate the lifestyle from the parental family in all future relationships. It is not possible ever to make more than minor changes in one's basic level of self-[differentiation]; but from clinical experience I can say it is possible to make slow changes, and each small change results in the new world of a different lifestyle. (p. 371)

Alicia, 27, and Gary, 48, had been involved for three years and were considering starting a family of their own when Alicia wrote the following descriptions in her journal. Since moving away from her family home, she had gradually succeeded in establishing boundaries between herself and her mother, an intrusive, dictatorial woman who was extremely critical of Alicia's career and friends. On an external level, it appeared Alicia had emancipated herself from the destructive emotional ties she had had with her parents and was maintaining a distant, yet cordial, relationship with them. However, she was very much aware that, on an internal level, she was still strongly influenced by the attitudes and dictates of her mother.

Alicia's journal entry:

What my mother would say about Gary:
> "He is never going to give you what you want. You should be with someone who will give me grandchildren. I should have known you would choose someone who would keep me from having what I want. He is so much older than you. What do you see in him? How can you have anything in common? Aren't you afraid of being with someone who will die before you and leave you alone? You should be with someone who will give you a future."

What I would say to my mother about Gary:
> "Gary is one person I can be myself with. I can be all of me and still feel accepted, which is something that has been hard for me to learn how to do and allow myself to have. I have always felt like I had to hide parts of who I am because I felt they were unacceptable. I love my relationship with Gary because he and I are really friends and when I feel good, we are really lovers. I

feel like I can really be a woman with Gary. He has given me more than what I had wanted. He has given me the opportunity to live such a rich and full life, something deep inside I always was yearning for but never in a million years thought I would have. What he has given me is the opportunity to have love in my life."

What my mother would say about my having a baby with Gary:
"Why are you doing this to me? You know he is not going to support you. How are you going to take care of this baby? With all of your friends? You know they won't help you once they realize what you're really like. You are a bitch. Look at the way you treat me, your own mother, by going off and cutting me out of your life and doing all of these things. You really are a piece of shit! What kind of a mother do you really think you'll be?"

What I would say to my mother about having a baby with Gary:
"I never really considered having a child until now. Even when I got pregnant before and decided to have an abortion, I knew it was because I didn't want to recreate what had happened to me. I remember wanting to die when I found out I was pregnant. Now I feel like I could be a parent, a mother, in a way that I would continue to grow as a person and offer a great life to another person. I never wanted to have a child that would hate me as much as I hate you. But with Gary, and the way I live my life and continue to grow, I think I have a chance at being a mother."

After making this journal entry and several others that were similar in content over the succeeding days, Alicia felt that she had achieved more separation from internalized attitudes she had acquired from her mother.

Setting Goals for the Relationship

We have found that the most powerful deterrent to a negative outcome in a couple relationship lies in the positive personal characteristics and propensities of the individual partners—qualities such as optimal emotional health, a willingness to be vulnerable to another person, and an ability to respect distinct personal boundaries at close quarters. The qualities also include a strong sense of identity; an easy-going, relaxed manner; flexibility; tolerance; and being attuned to one's emotions. It is obvious that these are attributes that people should look for when selecting a potential mate; however, in the context of couple therapy, they are most important in considering each partner's capacity for his or her personal growth and development. Hypercritical attitudes, defensiveness, hostility, superiority, phoniness, sarcasm, dishonesty, and involvement in an addictive habit pattern are poor prognostic signs for a satisfying relationship; these are among the behaviors that partners would need to modify in psychotherapy.

It is productive for individuals to define the personal goals for how they want to be in their relationships in terms of the traits and behaviors they are bringing to their relationships. They would delineate positive personal qualities they like in themselves and list the negative or unpleasant traits and behaviors they wish to eliminate. Next they would outline the steps and specific actions they believe are necessary to accomplish these goals. It is recommended that they track their progress in relation to these goals on a regular basis.

By using all of these techniques, people can discover that they have considerable power in their relationships, not in the sense of changing their mate (which often is the focus of partners in marital therapy) but in terms of having the power and the ability to change themselves. Moreover, as one partner modifies a specific behavior that has caused conflict or distress, the positive movement alters the basic dynamics of the relationship and the style in which the partners interact.

Specific personality characteristics each partner might strive to expand and further develop include,

- *Nondefensiveness and Openness:* Perhaps the most important quality that each partner could bring to a relationship would be a receptivity to feedback, an ability to listen to criticism and to agree or disagree without reacting angrily, crying, falling apart, sulking, or withdrawing. The quality of openness refers to having a genuine interest in learning and growing beyond one's defense system and self-protective routines. Individuals who are open are willing to take more risks in life; they have strong desires to broaden their range of experience rather than follow prescriptions and belief systems imposed from external sources.

- *Honesty and Integrity:* Lies and deception fragment and often completely erode a person's belief in the veracity of his or her perceptions and subjective experience (Bader & Pearson, 2000). Laing (1976) related a tale of deception in *The Facts of Life:*

  A lady of seventy discovers that her husband has had a mistress for the last thirty years. That all her friends knew. . . . She is maybe jealous. But she is quivering, physically, because she says, and I have no reason to disbelieve her, her *whole sense of reality* had been shattered. Her mind runs through all those years: she discovers she has been shrouded in a tissue of deception, all those years. She is past being outraged. She feels desperate because she has been cheated of reality. She has been deprived of truth. I'm sure that truth deprivation can wreak as much havoc to some people as vitamin deprivation. . . . We *need* truth. Truth and reality seem sometimes virtually indistinguishable, sometimes separable, but always most intimately related. . . . To live correctly, my genes need to know what is the case. (p. 145)

The personal qualities of honesty and integrity are vital to the well-being of both partners and the health of the relationship. To achieve integrity and honesty, one must know oneself. Partners must be willing to face aspects of their personality that may be unpleasant and gradually modify defensive behaviors that are limiting both to themselves and to their partner. They also need to learn how to be nonduplicitous in their communications—that is, they must become aware of and challenge any discrepancy that may exist between their words and actions. People can learn to hold themselves to this standard.[4]

- *Physical Affection and Personal Sexuality:* Outward expressions of verbal and physical affection are good prognostic indicators for a long-standing relationship. An "ideal" partner would be comfortable with physical affection, have considerable eye contact with their loved ones, and freely express outwardly feelings of tenderness and love. Internal fantasies or feelings of love on the part of one's mate, without the appropriate external behavioral manifestations, have no value for the recipient other than to disturb his or her reality. In striving to develop themselves, individuals would attempt to cultivate a mature attitude toward sex and not view it as an activity isolated from other aspects of their relationship. They would learn to perceive sexual relating as a fulfilling part of life, a gift, a positive offering of pleasure to their mate and to themselves, and try to overcome withholding patterns that inhibit their natural expressions of affection and sexual desire.
- *Empathy and Understanding:* Understanding implies that partners recognize their differences as well as their commonalities. When individuals talk with respect and feeling for each other regarding their differences, each feels seen for who he or she really is. In contrast, a lack of empathy or understanding between partners has a negative effect on their interactions. When people do not feel listened to, taken seriously, or understood by their mates, they suffer from hurt feelings and increased hostility. Therefore, partners would try to identify and challenge any patterns of chronic misunderstanding that are based on their distorted ways of thinking about themselves or their

partner. This distorted thinking or "voice" manifests itself in two major ways:

1. In negative assumptions about oneself that lead to expectations of rejection. In these cases, the partner may think, "If he(she) really knew you, he (she) would reject you." "Who would love you?"
2. In negative perceptions and distortions of the partner which lead to feeling victimized and angry: "He (she) doesn't treat you right." "He(she) just doesn't understand you."

- *Respect for the Other's Boundaries*: In a genuinely loving relationship, each partner recognizes that the motives, desires, aspirations, and goals of the other are as important as his or her own. Each attempts to support the other's goals, independent of his or her own interests. It is important to recognize that to be close to another person, one has to be separate and autonomous. Only when people are centered in themselves and truly individualistic are they able to sustain relationships in which the personal freedom of both partners is accorded the highest priority.
- *Nonthreatening and Nonmanipulative Behavior*: A healthy relationship is characterized by communications and interactions in which neither partner tries to manipulate or control the other. As clients develop in psychotherapy, they usually become increasingly open in revealing the manipulations and power plays they customarily used to control their partner (see chapter 14). They are able to identify common methods of control that are used by both men and women who, out of insecurity, attempt to establish guarantees of safety and continuing love in a relationship.

The Strategy of "Unilateral Disarmament"

An effective method that partners can use to defuse escalating arguments is that of "unilateral disarmament." Angry exchanges tend to escalate quickly from mild disagreements to outright hostility, verbal abuse, and in serious cases, domestic violence. Yet many times it is possible to interrupt this cycle of accusation and counteraccusation before one or both partners say or do something they regret. It is suggested that when a partner senses that a confrontation is rapidly degenerating into a battle of wills, he or she drops his or her stake in winning and reaches out to the other with an understanding word or an act of physical affection. This strategy is in accord with the goal of developing more closeness and intimacy in the relationship.

It is difficult to maintain one side of an argument when the other has left the field of battle. This technique of "unilateral disarmament" does not at all imply that one partner is surrendering his or her point of view; rather it is an indication that the partner values being close to the other more than winning the argument.

CORRECTIVE SUGGESTIONS USED BY PARTICIPANTS IN THE FRIENDSHIP CIRCLE

In the friendship circle, couples attempt to develop an understanding of a tender, loving way to treat their partners that would extend outward from the couple relationship to their children, other family members, and friends. This style of relating consists of an accepting, nonjudgmental attitude, a recognition of each person as a separate individual, and a concern and respect for boundaries and priorities. The heightened intimacy that results when the love and sexuality between two people who possess these qualities are combined can approach a spiritual level. This kind of love is often expressed in simple ways, in numerous small acts of kindness and consideration, and in actions that contribute to a deep sharing of life experiences.

As couples in the friendship circle have translated these core attitudes into actions and have made them a part of their everyday interactions, they have come to talk with each other in a style that is forthright and candid, yet empathic and sensitive to the other's feelings. Neither partner speaks for the other, and each feels free to express his or her thoughts, feelings, aspirations, attitudes, and opinions about any topic. They are willing to bear their own pain without implicating the other in their internal conflicts and for the most part have given up efforts to "fix" or change the other. They place significant value on building a good relationship with their mate and demonstrate a willingness to cope with the stresses that naturally arise in the course of any close association. They understand that the tender feelings that they experience both toward their loved one and from their loved one often arouse poignant feelings of sadness.

Developing Insight Regarding Defensive Patterns of Relating

Over the past 25 years, individuals in the group of friends have talked openly about the defenses of selection, distortion, and provocation and how acting out these behaviors limited them in their intimate relationships. In the following couples' discussion group, they describe several manifestations of a fantasy bond that they are aware of in their present-day interactions.

They begin by talking about how the partners they selected in the past tended to recapitulate their childhood experiences:

Andrea (48): My father was very judgmental. My mother was very childish, and I tried to duplicate their relationship. I was very much influenced by the way that I saw them relating, and also I tried to duplicate my father's relationship with me. So in my first relationships in college, I would pick people who were judgmental. But in the honeymoon phase, they were judging me that I was a good girl. So it was like getting approval from my father, yet it was completely inappropriate to be an adult in a relationship with someone who was judging me and I was acting like a little kid. So then quickly the relationship turned where there was a lot of disapproval and then I was off and running. I completely recreated my parents' relationship. I had my relationship with my father back again and everything was in its place.

Valerie (45): I identify with that. I grew up feeling unlovable, and the relationship with my father was that he had a hard time or didn't express whatever feelings he had toward me so I always felt desperate toward him, trying to get something from him that wasn't really available. So I took that into my adult life in search of someone that I wanted, but I would always pick someone who was similar in that way where they had a hard time expressing their feelings or they held back. So I was always in relationships where I felt desperate and unfulfilled, and I felt the pain all over again of my childhood. It's reliving that time and time again, which seems hard to break out of.

Robert Firestone (67): So basically you don't feel secure in looking for close relationships. There's a basic insecurity that most of you are talking about, is that right? What's it based on? Why don't you feel that a person would be lucky to meet you?

Ana (43): I feel like I'm not a lovable person, so I feel like no one would feel that way toward me. And if they do, I make it so they don't. That's the pattern. I think I keep recreating that, because I don't believe anyone would love me.

Russell (39): And if you do find someone, you hold on desperately because you feel like if you lose them, you won't be able to find anybody else.

Ryan (45):   In the beginning of a relationship, I think that what the woman really is drawn to originally is my being an outgoing person, being a free person, doing whatever I do naturally. But those are the things I shut down. I take those back. I hold them inside myself and just attach myself to this person, and it's totally meaningless. It doesn't mean anything any more.

Janet (66):   The thing that I feel the most pained about is that I really gave up my independent point of view. When we were first involved, Frank and I would have long discussions. He had a strong point of view. In those days, I was planning my career, I had strong political opinions, and as soon as I was married or even before, I gradually gave up myself as a person. I gave up my point of view, and that was one of the strongest things that I had. And I pretended like Frank always had to have his way or that he knew more than I did.

Ana: In my first marriage, there were a lot of assumptions. There were a lot of shoulds—I should be with him, he should be with me. So I started acting out of guilt a lot of the time. I lost my independence. I didn't think for myself any more. I didn't have ideas. I didn't do anything without first checking in with him, so after a while, I started to hate him.

Brad (57):   I think those assumptions and expectations start really early in a relationship. First of all, I realized that when you start a relationship, from the beginning, let's say, you meet a girl at a party or somewhere, you like her and then you call her up and ask her out and you go out. Then the next time you call her up to ask her out, you don't get her on the phone. So then, you've known her all of 3 days, and when you finally get her on the phone, you say, "I was trying to get you earlier," and then she says, "Oh, I was at such and such a place." I mean the expectations just start with that. Or you might have three Saturday night dates in a row, and then when next Saturday night comes, either she or you or both of you expect to have a date. It's a routine by then.

Robert Firestone: Once you've got something, you have expectations. In the beginning, you have no right to close her in and you talk to her like a person because she still hasn't developed a pattern of "going with you." She's very separate and you talk to her more like a person.

> "Where would you like to go, what would you like to do?"

Ryan: I know that in the past, I always turned a relationship into something to satisfy an emptiness in me. And in that, the person that I was involved with was no longer even a person. It's a hunger being satisfied within myself, rather than just living and cohabiting with someone and sharing your life with someone, enjoying them and them enjoying you, all that was gone. It's just like they became someone else that I had been able to plug into that slot from relationship to relationship my entire life.

By consistently identifying and modifying defensive ways of relating to one another, the people in the group of friends have been able to recapture some of the feelings they initially enjoyed in the beginning stages of their relationships. As a result, free choice rather than obligation now characterizes the majority of the interactions within these couples. Each partner is concerned with his or her own personal growth and well-being as well as that of the other person. Neither takes the other for granted; rather, each appreciates and openly acknowledges the other's acts of kindness, generosity, and the giving of sexual pleasure.

A Personal Account

Over the course of his 14-year relationship with Robyn (41), Dean (described in chapter 1) has developed many of the positive qualities delineated earlier. The couple's interactions are characterized by an unusual degree of honesty, nondefensiveness, and a respect for each other's boundaries. The relationship has offered Dean the opportunity to challenge his distrust of women and to uncover aspects of his personality that he did not know he possessed. In a recent interview, when asked about the history of his relationship with Robyn, he said,

I was very strongly attracted to Robyn many years ago when I first met her. I liked her a lot. We had a kind of off-again, on-again relationship over the years. Eventually we both went our separate ways. She was going through some hard times, and at the same time, I was going through my own difficulties, and we grew apart. Much later, when my ex-wife rejected me, I was really tired of dishonesty and intimidation. Mostly I was deeply hurt by her rejection over the years. It was a painfully classic story. Then Robyn broke up with her boyfriend, and when she first intimated that she wanted to be involved with me, I didn't know what to do because I was really cautious, but at the same time, it was hard *not* to respond to her.

I decided at that point that I would tell Robyn that it would be the one relationship in which I would be absolutely honest to the best of my ability. That if she asked to do something with me and I didn't really want to do it, I would say, "No." I would try to be absolutely honest, and that worked to a large degree. Gradually I found myself preferring her. The relationship itself was helpful to me because it didn't make me feel that I had a pretense going.

I didn't feel like I was wildly in love with her, like the feelings I have felt in the past. But over time, I had this feeling that I can only describe as love and affection, and liking the way she looked. I really enjoyed our time together.

For the most part, it's been easy to talk to her. I've enjoyed offering her a relationship that is not judgmental, that does not impinge on her boundaries. I always notice that it sounds so false to parentally advise her about something, and she has a very negative reaction to it. Like one time, she was in the gym and I offered her some suggestions that might make the workout more beneficial, but she didn't take that too kindly and I had to apologize to her because the way I said it sounded so condescending. So I try not to do that.

I know her so well, and I know how to hurt her, so I choose not to. In a long-term relationship, you know what hurts and what drives them crazy, so I try not to do that. One thing that hurts her is for me to be quiet because then she imagines things more than they are, so I try to tell her things as soon as I know something feels wrong.

We had a hard time when she became addicted to painkillers after an operation. It strengthened the relationship, but it may have hurt it, too. The strength was I didn't get cynical toward her and I allowed her to get through it without the extra pull of feeling like she had ruined the relationship. So that gave us a closeness and a trust. But at the same time, it created a distrust in me again. For a while, it was easier for me to think, *"Be careful, don't let yourself get too close,"* that kind of voice.

My relationship with Robyn is not the only source of my feeling satisfied and good in this area. I also have deep loving feelings for other close women friends, which are fulfilling to me even though we're not involved in a way that would be boyfriend and girlfriend. But what I get from those kinds of relationships is totally fulfilling.

CONCLUSION

There are a number of steps that partners can take to break into the fantasy bond and recapture some of the feelings of friendship and love they experienced in the early phases of the relationship. They can admit to themselves and each other that a fantasy bond exists in their relationship, that they have become distant, and that their behaviors are no longer loving.

It is valuable to learn to be nondefensive and open to this type of feedback. Partners can reveal feelings of anger and withholding behaviors; admit critical, hostile voices toward themselves and their partners; and can face up to the emotional pain and sad feelings involved in trying to restore intimacy. They can expose fears of being alone and separate, including fears of rejection, abandonment, or the loss or death of themselves or their partner. It is important to move toward independence, develop more respect for each other, and attempt to establish equality in the relationship by breaking patterns of dominance and submission. It is helpful to increase interactions with others, friends and family members, to provide a better basis for reality-testing. Finally, if a more extreme solution is necessary, partners can plan temporary or long-term separations, and use the time apart to develop personally.

Once the symptoms of a fantasy bond or addictive attachment between two people have been recognized and altered, a new type of relationship becomes a possibility. The only hope for couples is to break out of the imprisonment of a defensive self-parenting posture. In freeing themselves from destructive ties and moving toward individuation, partners open up the possibility for genuine love and intimacy in the relationship.

The approach to couple relationships described in this chapter suggests that by relinquishing illusions of connection and separating from destructive modes of thinking, men and women can expand their capacity to both offer and accept love. In breaking with defensive programming and pursuing the "good life" in a genuinely loving relationship, people *can* sustain feeling, passion, and meaning in their lives.

NOTES

1. The first author's formulations regarding the repetition compulsion are analogous to S. Freud's (1920/1955) concept in one respect: They both observed the patient going through a repetitive process that is misguided and that cannot have a favorable outcome (Firestone, 1985). However, the first author's understanding of the *purpose* of this compulsion differs from that of Freud's. In contrast to the classical psychoanalytical suggestion that patients repeat the patterns of the past in a futile attempt to obtain gratification, he proposed that patients recreate or provoke situations similar to the past to protect the fantasy of self-sufficiency and to justify their defenses.

2. Otto Rank (1941) asserted,

   As a rule, we find . . . in modern relationships . . . one person is made the god-like judge over good and bad in the other person. In the long run, such symbiotic relationship becomes demoralizing to both parties, for it is just as unbearable to be God as it is to remain an utter slave. (p. 196)

3. See Scharff and Scharff (1991) for an in-depth explanation of partner selection based on the concept of projective identification and Ogden's (1982) discussion in *Projective Identification and Psychotherapeutic Technique*.
4. Canary, Cupach, and Messman (1995) stressed the fact that nonverbal cues often contradict verbal communication between partners. Duck (1994a) cited findings by Gottman (1979) and Gottman and Krokoff (1989) showing that negative messages between partners were conveyed through body language and other nonverbal cues. In these duplicitous communications, it was the negative affect communicated nonverbally that predicted the dissolution of the relationship.

11

SEXUALITY

If our elaborate and dominating bodies are given us to be denied at every turn, if our nature is always wrong and wicked, how ineffectual we are—like fishes not meant to swim.

—Cyril Connolly (1945, p. 28)

Sex is one of the strongest motivating forces in life. It has the potential for creating intense pleasure and fulfillment or causing considerable pain and suffering. A good deal of human misery centers around sexuality and the difficulties most people encounter in attempting to achieve and sustain sexual satisfaction, especially in close interpersonal relationships. People's feelings about their bodies, the acceptance of their sexual identities as men and women, and their experiences in sex are fundamental to their sense of well-being and self-esteem. A healthy orientation to sex is reflected in an individual's level of vitality, overall appearance, and expression of tenderness and compassion. Disturbances in sexual functioning have serious consequences, affecting every aspect of a person's adjustment, including activities and pursuits far removed from sexual functions. The combination of loving, sexual contact and genuine friendship in an intimate relationship is conducive to mental health and is a highly regarded ideal for most people.

TWO VIEWS OF SEXUALITY

People tend to hold two diametrically opposed views of sexuality: a natural, "clean" orientation to sex and a distorted, "dirty" view of sex. From a healthy or clean point of view, sex is perceived as a natural extension of affectionate feelings, rather than as an activity separate from other aspects

239

of a relationship. By contrast, from a dirty point of view, sex is seen as an activity that should be kept hidden and secretive; the human body is seen as shameful, and those parts having to do with sexual functions in particular are given a dirty connotation. This view of sex takes it out of the realm of a natural human function and relegates it to a separate and distinct area of life. As such it is seen as a subject unfit for social conversation or discussion, especially with children.

On a societal level, there is support for the point of view that sex is inherently bad, and this concept still exerts a powerful influence on conventional secular thinking despite the advances achieved by the "sexual revolution" of the 1960s (Calderone, 1974/1977). In some traditional religious belief systems, sex is perceived as an expression of the baser nature of human beings. The damage perpetuated by this attitude is incalculable, because such strict views of morality have repressed children's natural curiosity and aliveness about their sexuality and increased their guilt about sex (Calderone & Johnson, 1989; Gunderson & McCary, 1979). Distorted views of human sexuality have functioned for generations to alienate individuals from their bodily sensations and feelings (Pagels, 1988, 1995; Vergote, 1978/1988).

On an intellectual level, most people would agree that sexual functions are a simple and natural part of human nature. However, on an emotional level, many men and women still retain negative attitudes toward their sexuality. Nearly every individual in our society has been taught to feel shame regarding his or her body, body parts, and sexuality, which has generated a variety of sexual problems and fears related to sexual performance (Calderone & Johnson, 1989; Firestone, 1990b).

PARENTAL ATTITUDES TOWARD SEX AND THE HUMAN BODY

In raising their children, parents are under considerable pressure from within and from society to teach restrictive values and narrow, distorted views of sexuality. As a result, the majority of adults in our society are eventually impaired to varying degrees in their sexual feelings, attitudes, and capacity to enjoy mature sexual relationships. Whether implicit or explicit, these formative influences act to limit almost every individual's capacity for free enjoyment of his or her body. The simple act of sex is contaminated by faulty socialization processes characterized by unnecessary moral restrictions and inhibiting responses that foster self-consciousness and self-attack.

Most people in Western society grew up in families in which they were taught distorted views about sexuality. Subsequently, they pass on both directly and indirectly the attitudes that sex is bad or dirty, that masturbation is vulgar, and that the subject of sexuality is taboo. Some parents refuse to allow their teenagers to attend sexuality education classes, and others insist on limiting the curriculum (Strong, DeVault, & Sayad, 1999). In addition, studies (Fisher & Fisher, 1986) have shown that severe, harsh, or intrusive toilet training is correlated with later emotional and sexual disturbances. Negative views held by parents in relation to nudity and the human body predispose the development of a sense of shame and guilt in children about their bodies and their sexual feelings. These disturbances in one's sexual identity are retained throughout life, causing serious problems in intimate relationships.

There are other ways in which children are damaged in their sexuality. For example, many learn to hold back expressions of affection because their parents find it difficult to accept their warmth and love. Subsequently, they extend this withholding posture to sexual situations and inhibit their positive responses, with little or no awareness of this inhibition.

A distorted perspective in relation to bodily functions and nudity still exists in our society, despite the availability of objective information and open discussions of these issues. Even the so-called sexual revolution of the 1960s had minimal impact on changing basic attitudes of inhibition and prohibition (Szuchman & Muscarella, 2000). Although attitudes toward masturbation appear to have changed over the past several decades, many parents still react severely and punitively when they discover their child masturbating. The guilt engendered by these overreactions can have serious consequences. Many parents still have strong negative responses to sex play among children, rather than recognizing that such play is a natural expression of a child's curiosity. Some families go to the opposite extreme and exploit or overemphasize sex. This focus can be as damaging as the restrictions placed on sexuality in families that are more rigid and repressive.

SOCIETAL ATTITUDES TOWARD SEX

Distorted attitudes toward sexuality acquired by individuals in their formative years are pooled and combine to form cultural attitudes and social mores. Once established, cultural prerogatives based on these defensive attitudes then reflect back on each member of society in the form of negative social pressure. Social conventions reinforce a collective conscience and form the foundation of social relationships. These cultural imperatives permeate every aspect of daily living and, more often than not, are inhibiting and repressive (Foucault 1975, 1980; Goffman, 1967).

In our culture, unnecessarily restrictive codes have inhibited normal sexual expression, predisposing an increase in aggression, sexual abnormality or perversion, sexual molestation, rape, and other crimes (Prescott, 1975,

1996). Paradoxically, in these instances, the overemphasis on sexual morality has "immoral" consequences.[1] People are not basically evil, harmful, or animalistic in their desire for sexual expression. The negative loading on sexuality stems from ignorance, irrational fear, and prejudice that force men and women to turn on themselves and dehumanize the sexual component of their being.

SEXUAL STEREOTYPING

Although there have been changes in the roles of men and women in our society, there are still residuals of stereotypical views that portray men as masterful, powerful, paternalistic, and uncommunicative and women as emotionally responsive and communicative, yet childlike, helpless, and incompetent (Beyer & Finnegan, 1997; Eagly, 1995; Geis, 1993; Lott, 1997; M. Walsh, 1997). Social pressure exerted by these stereotypes and hostile views of both sexes is as damaging to couple relationships as is racial prejudice to the relations of people of various ethnic backgrounds.

Sexual stereotypes confuse people's thinking about the differences between men and women by placing them in artificial categories. Although some sexual stereotypes do correspond to research findings regarding specific gender differences, when these are incorporated into the destructive thoughts and attitudes of the voice process, they take on a connotation of hostility and denigration.[2] These sexist or stereotyped attitudes come into play in many different ways to cut off feelings of sexual attraction and emotional closeness. For example, women may think: "All men want is sex. They don't want a commitment. They don't want to be emotionally close. They can't be trusted." Or men may think: "Women are unreliable. They are so irrational and overemotional. They can't be trusted."

Children assimilate stereotypical views of men and women from their parents, which they then retain throughout their adult lives. Through the process of identification and imitation, they incorporate negative attitudes toward the opposite sex that are held by one or both parents. These hostile and sexist attitudes cause dissension in intimate relationships and complicate couple interactions.

TWO MODES OF SEXUAL RELATING

There are two distinct modes of sexual expression: an outward form of genuine contact that is a natural extension of affection, tenderness, and companionship between two people and an inward, masturbatory style of sexual relating in which sex is used primarily as a narcotic. Characteristics of an outward or positive sexual experience would include close emotional contact with one's partner, a sense of mutual give and take, and feelings of fulfillment and well-being following the experience. There would be an uninterrupted, smooth flow of pleasurable sensations and feelings—that is, a notable absence of inhibition at any point during the process, beginning with the initial expression of physical affection, through foreplay and intercourse, and following the completion of the sex act. This mode of sexual relating can also be described in terms of the behaviors and personality characteristics of the two partners. Ideally, both individuals would have a healthy desire for sex and a positive body image, be unself-conscious and uninhibited in their emotional and sexual responses, and possess congenial attitudes toward the opposite sex that are free of distortion or bias. Schnarch (1991) described this mode of sexuality in terms of an individual's capacity for intimacy and his or her ability to attach "profound emotional meaning to the sexual experience" (p. 19).

On the other hand, the use of sex as a narcotic is directly analogous to physical addictions in that the sexual experience acts like a painkilling drug to cut off or inhibit feeling reactions. It represents a movement away from real intimacy and emotional exchange between two people and toward a reliance on sex as a mechanism for self-gratification that places a limitation on mature genital sexuality.

Sexuality can be conceptualized as ranging along a continuum between these two modes of sexual expression. Sexual experiences are the most emotionally fulfilling when they are the outgrowth of affectionate feelings (Balint, 1952/1985; Carnes, 1997; Kernberg, 1980).[3] During love making, whenever there is a switch from close, emotional contact to a more self-gratifying style of relating, the transformation is hurtful to the well-being of the individuals involved. Many people report feelings of emptiness, a sense of dissatisfaction, and irritability after a sexual experience in which an inward or a less personal mode of relating predominates.

To understand where a client is on the continuum of sexual relating, it is valuable to examine his or her personal history and sexual fantasies because these reveal the person's attitude toward the giving and receiving of love and exchange of products. The quality of a particular sexual encounter is influenced by each partner's mode of sexual relating—that is, whether it is based on a core defense of fantasized self-sufficiency or on the pursuit of a healthy interdependence with another person.

An inward, impersonal style of sexual relating is symptomatic of a fantasy bond. Within this bond, significant deterioration frequently occurs in the couple's sexual relating as well as in both partners' feelings about themselves as men and women. These problems generally can be traced back to disturbances in the original mother–infant dyad (Caplan, 1981; Chodorow, 1978; Friday, 1977; Genevie & Margolies 1987; Kaplan, 1984;

Park, 1995; Rheingold, 1967). Many people encounter difficulties in trying to achieve and sustain sexual satisfaction in their relationships because early in life they adjusted to inadequate sources of external gratification by gratifying themselves internally. Defensive or inappropriate responses to one's partner in a sexual situation vary in intensity according to the degree of deprivation and rejection experienced early in life. By maintaining a pseudoindependent posture in relation to their sexuality, individuals are denying their need for another person or for anything outside the self-parenting system (Firestone, 1985).

MANIFESTATIONS OF ADDICTIVE, SELF-GRATIFYING MODES OF SEXUAL RELATING

A self-gratifying mode of sexual relating is characterized by a number of behavior patterns and associated feeling states: (a) elements of control and sexual withholding in one or both partners; (b) increased reliance on fantasy with corresponding emotional distancing and guilt reactions; and (c) the intrusion of self-critical thoughts or hostile attitudes toward one's partner. These symptoms can become habitual or they can occur intermittently, before, during, or following a sexual experience.

Control and Sexual Withholding

Sexual withholding refers to a holding back or inhibiting of natural sexual desire and its expressions: physical affection, attractiveness, and other aspects of one's healthy sexuality. Withholding in relation to this level of intimacy is especially hurtful in a relationship. As R. D. Laing thoughtfully noted in a number of his workshops, "the bedroom is the most dangerous place on earth." Although this withholding occurs primarily in the privacy of the bedroom, its destructive effects are not confined there. They are widespread and affect every aspect of family life.

Individuals who have become sexually withholding tend to perceive spontaneous sexual interactions and sexual intimacy as threatening to their inward, defended state. As a consequence, they try to regulate or control various aspects of the sex act. They may attempt to dictate the frequency of love making, the time, the place, the conditions, movements, positions, and manner of expressing physical affection.

Example of One Couple

Brandon and Renee, divorced after six years of marriage, provide a poignant example of the consequences of control and withholding. Renee began to hold back her affection and sexual responses early on, and at the same time, she attempted to control every aspect of the marriage. In a session that took place three years following their divorce, the couple, who have remained friends, recalled the history of their relationship:

Renee: In the beginning of our relationship, we were both independent, but pretty quickly I started to control the relationship. I controlled what we did. I controlled where we went. It was my idea. I wanted to be in control, to say where we went to the movies, what movie we saw, who we went to dinner with, what we did every night. I wanted everything to be my way. (to Brandon): I can see over the years that the more I took control, the less attractive you became to me. I felt that in the last few years of our relationship the sexuality was almost terrifying to me because of the way I felt.

Dr. Firestone: How did you feel during sex?

Renee (to Brandon): I always felt that when we went to bed that you would want to be sexual, and I never wanted to. So I decided that I would make love every other day, and you got used to that routine. So if we made love one night, the next night you knew not to bother me. On the nights that I would make love, I felt like the whole act was so routine. It was always the same. And afterward, I was relieved it was over because it was almost like I did my duty. It was a horrible feeling. But I felt like I did what I was supposed to do, and now I was okay—until the last few months when the sexuality was almost terrifying. When you would come on top of me, I would feel almost suffocated, like I wanted to scream. And I wanted to push you off me.

Dr. Firestone: Something you originally were drawn to now was a reprehensible or an unpleasant situation to you. You had a real aversion. How did that happen? What do you think happened? What occurs to you?

Renee: I think two things. One, like I said, I felt so controlling. I felt like I was like your mother in the way I wanted to control you, to tell you what to do, and if you weren't doing the right thing, I felt critical of you. I felt like that took me away from that woman–man relationship and made me feel like your mother. Not like a separate person, but very connected. I think that was part of it, but also in that, I know I gave up my own freedom, my own life.

Dr. Firestone (to Brandon): What do you think happened in relation to this? Did you surrender to her in some way? Did you let her take control of your life?

Brandon: What she said was accurate. I really succumbed to that need to be controlled. I gave up something in myself in looking for direction. I would turn away from my wants and my friends in some sort of need for that direction. I remember that being sexual, I was angry all the time. I was angry that you wouldn't want to make love, and I was angry if you would go to sleep and turn your back on me. Every night I would go to sleep angry. And that's how I lived most nights for that period of time.

Renee: I remember hating you for letting me control you, even though I wanted it so bad. I know it was something I worked at all day long—I was aware of doing it all the time. But every time I hated you for it, still.

Brandon: It's like I lost my point of view about things. If you had asked me, "What do you want to do now?" I didn't know. And it wasn't a conscious thing—it just wasn't there.

Dr. Firestone: What accounted for this? What do you think made you need to control or want to control? What were your fears? What was driving that behavior, do you think?

Renee: Well, it felt like if I didn't control you, that you wouldn't be there. If I didn't control you, you would never choose me. I wasn't going to be likable enough to be chosen. I had to make sure it happened. I had to make sure that you were going to be there, that you would choose me, that you would go to the movies with me that night. But it became life-long. If you were free to know what you wanted to do that night, if you had that much freedom, you would never choose me.

Dr. Firestone: The more invested in him you were, the more you needed to protect your interest and control the situation.

Renee: Right. I felt as though my life depended on it.

Dr. Firestone: Why were you so insecure that you thought he would leave if you didn't tie him to you in some way?

Renee: Because that's exactly how my mother was. The relationship between my parents was like that. That's what my sisters and I learned. Also I hated myself so much, and I felt so unlovable, all the time, that I was surprised I was chosen in the first place. I was thrilled that somebody wanted to be with me that much. (sad) So I had to hold on to it. I didn't think it would ever happen again. I didn't think I was worth somebody choosing me even two days in a row to be with, to even be friendly toward.

And I saw my mother controlling everyone in the family in the same way, to make sure that we would always be there, to make sure that we would always come back and we would always love her or act like we loved her, but I never felt like I was lovable enough to deserve it.

Several months later in treatment, as Renee attempted to gain more insight into the causes of her failed marriage, she recalled that her father had made many seductive, inappropriate sexual advances toward her during childhood and early adolescence. Still later, she began to gradually remember certain details of the sexual games that both parents had engaged in with her at an even younger age. Despite strong resistance against further exploring these memories and their underlying meaning, Renee continued to work through the feelings aroused by her recollections and identified the associated destructive self-attacks and guilt reactions. She came to recognize that her fears of being sexual with her husband originated in a number of sexual abuses that had occurred throughout childhood, and realized that the cumulative effects of this treatment were to make her anxious in intimate situations. On an unconscious level, she had adopted the defenses of control and sexual withholding to deal with her anxiety. In a later session, Renee described the emotional impact of this form of maltreatment:

> I was thinking about all the feelings that I grew up with and how I was treated in my family, especially how my father acted toward me. How he was never sweet toward me. How he never showed me any affection in a nice way. He never said anything like, "You're a valuable child or a valuable girl." He always commented on my looks, or on what I could get for my looks. I know that had a large part to do with my insecurity. I never really learned to like myself, just for myself. And that's why I could never believe that Brandon liked me for myself, because I never did.

Renee's memories were corroborated by two older sisters, who had experienced the same abuses. Although these memories were painful for Renee to face, she realized that experiencing the affect that accompanied the emergence of the memories in the safe environment of the therapy session had helped her develop feelings of compassion for herself.

The Relationship Between Sexual Child Abuse and Sexual Withholding

A number of sexual dysfunctions and disorders of sexual desire have been correlated with childhood sexual abuse (Beitchman et al., 1992; Courtois, 1999; Dorais, 2002; Gartner, 1999; Jarvis & Copeland, 1997; Keane, Young, & Boyle, 1996; Kinzl, Traweger, & Biebl, 1995; McCabe & Cobain, 1998; Sarwer & Durlak, 1996). Herman (1981) reviewed five surveys on the prevalence of sexual child abuse and found that "one fifth to one third of all women reported that they had had some sort of childhood sexual encounter with an adult male" (p. 12). In Finkelhor's (1990) retrospective study, sexual victimization was reported by 27% of the women and 16% of the men.

In elucidating the effects of sexual child abuse, Biller and Solomon (1986) emphasized that "boys who are sexually abused by fathers and stepfathers or other male family members seem to have special difficulty attaining a healthy masculine self-esteem, a comfortable attitude toward their bodies, and successful romantic relationships with females" (p. 108). Herman (1981) reported that in a group of female incest victims she interviewed ($N = 40$),

45% experienced pregnancy in adolescence, 55% had sexual problems, and 35% were promiscuous.

Individuals who have been sexually abused as children may experience fear and an onslaught of other negative affects when they become involved in an intimate relationship, particularly one that combines emotional closeness and sexuality. In many cases, they react to the emergence of these emotions by either withholding their sexual responses or trying to control aspects of the sex act. In most cases, they have little or no conscious awareness of their fear or anxiety before instituting these defensive behaviors. Fragmented memories or flashbacks of earlier sexual abuse often break through to consciousness during the sexual encounter or afterward.

Family Dynamics Related to Control and Sexual Withholding

Both men and women are predisposed to becoming sexually withholding if they suffered from their parents withholding of love and affection, overt sexual abuse, or overt sexualized interest (emotional incest) during their formative years.[4] Children of both genders incur varying degrees of damage in their early relationships with their primary caretaker (usually the mother), the most important figure in their lives at the time when they are the most dependent and vulnerable (Barglow & Schaefer, 1977; Roiphe & Galenson, 1981).

Mothers and Sons. As male children develop, their personalities are affected on a deep level by residuals of maternal deprivation and rejection. We have found that, as a result, many men spend their lives searching for the gratification of these unfulfilled needs and longings, typically seeking new objects in a symbolic attempt to reconnect to the mother. They tend to be self-doubting and are driven by fears of being rejected by a woman. Underlying this hesitancy and distrust is a considerable amount of repressed anger, which may break through to consciousness if the man is sufficiently provoked. Men raised by mothers or caretakers who were withholding are often distrustful or critical of women who are sexually responsive and may avoid forming relationships with them.

Still others suffer from feelings of sexual inferiority and inadequacy because of intrusive or seductive behavior of the part of their mothers. A seductive relationship with the mother often stimulates intense Oedipal rivalry and leads to powerful feelings of inadequacy in the growing boy (Love, 1990; A. Miller, 1979/1981; Park, 1995). This fear of being inadequate in a sexual situation often predisposes sexual withholding or avoidance.[5]

Mothers and Daughters. In a large majority of families, the son, in differentiating himself from the mother, gradually shifts his identification to the father (Chodorow, 1978). The daughter, however, tends to remain finely tuned to the mother. For their part, mothers generally tend to identify with their daughters more than with their sons, and according to Genevie and Margolies (1987) "form this primary relationship more readily with their daughters whom they view as extensions of themselves" (p. 291).

As noted, all parents have both nurturing and hostile tendencies in relation to their children (Badinter, 1980/1981; Bromberg, 1955; Fenchel, 1998; Ferenczi, 1929; Firestone, 1990b; A. Johnson, 1951; Rich, 1976). Joseph Rheingold (1964), whose research focused on maternal behaviors that he believed were the most threatening to the child, argued that:

> It seems to the child more unnatural that the parent who bore him and suckled him should seek to injure him. Further, the child's greater dependency upon the mother causes her attitudes and acts bespeaking rejection to be the more threatening. (p. 19)

Negative aspects in the mother–daughter relationship may be the single most limiting factor in the female child's life and one of the principal factors that contributes to sexual withholding, the need to control, and other sexual dysfunctions in women. For example, a mother who is intolerant of accepting love *from* her daughter may create a feeling in the child that her physical touch is unacceptable or even repulsive. This deep-seated belief can cause the female child to develop a strong feeling of being unlovable, and she ultimately may perceive herself as different from other women, undesirable, or unattractive to men. In addition, reactions of rage because of the early frustration of her desire for physical contact can lead to an immature fixation on the mother or substitute objects and a variety of sexual disturbances. Ironically, the anger generated causes the young woman to rely heavily on repression and to move closer to her mother. This alliance plays a significant role in her sexual withholding as an adult. The psychologist Sirgay Sanger, in a personal communication to Nancy Friday (1977), contended that "the subtle deprivation of physical demonstrations of affection that little girls often suffer from their mothers makes women more vulnerable to fear and the loss of attachment" (p. 58).

Sanger's and Rheingold's observations correspond to our findings regarding the damaging effects of maternal aggression and withholding on children, especially on female offspring. The daughter's peripheral awareness that affection is potentially available causes her to develop powerful longings and emotional hunger for physical contact. Paradoxically, in cases where the daughter was initially loved by her mother, then rejected, she may feel a pull toward her mother to try to reconnect with her, a lure that has an addictive quality. She feels compelled to try to recapture the love she once experienced, and this desperate search persists into her adult life, distorting her relationships with her husband and children.

There are crucial times in women's lives when they are fearful of moving away, symbolically or literally, from the mother: when they pursue a mature sexual relationship with a man, when they marry, when they establish their own household, and when they become mothers. According to Rheingold (1964), "The fear of being a woman may be observed in every biologic 'crisis' of a woman's life, more clearly in the reproductive process with its culmination in the anxieties of motherhood" (p. 142). Dix (1985), in her discussion of postpartum disturbances, asserted:

> When we give birth, all our own infantile instincts and reactions are reactivated. For some women that might mean reliving ambivalence about our mothers that we experienced as infants: the desire to be separate and the need to merge with her. (p. 139)

Each step in the movement toward individuation and separation from the mother can create a sense of fear and guilt. The attainment of sexual maturity often arouses a woman's fear of her mother's jealousy, envy, and vindictiveness, feelings that many women have experienced since childhood. As she matures, a daughter may actually fear retaliation from the mother for seeking adult sexual fulfillment.

Paula Caplan (1981) described how daughters often adjust to their mother's envy: "How does a daughter deal with her mother's competitiveness with her or jealousy of her accomplishments? Often . . . she reduces her efforts to achieve . . . and she puts emotional or physical distance between herself and her mother" (p. 120). Rheingold (1967) also emphasized this point in analyzing his findings from interviews with more than 2,500 women: "In the psychotherapy of women one regularly discovers an association of the masochistic or hostile dependent kind of relationship with the mother and the fear of mutilation and annihilation as punishment for feminine self-fulfillment—indeed, for just being a female" (p. 96).

Many times the powerful emotions that are aroused during these critical periods cause women to retreat to a sameness with the mother, expressed through the acting out of withholding behavior patterns that offer an illusion of safety and have anxiety-reducing properties.[6] Movement toward sexual intimacy with a man also symbolizes the woman's loss of the hope of ever satisfying her longing for maternal love. Thus, it seems that women are necessarily ambivalent about becoming involved in a sexual relationship or marriage; they are drawn to marriage as an imitation of their mothers, yet they fear it as a step toward further individuation and separation from her.

A long-term sexual relationship or marriage has different unconscious connotations for men and women. Shaver and Clark (1994) have called attention to the fact that both men and women tend to base object relations on the primary object relationship to the mother, and the efficacy of this attachment will have a fundamental effect on their satisfaction and security in adult relationships. For men, the relationship can symbolize the fulfillment of their desire for close, affectionate contact with the mother that they have longed for since childhood. The illusion that they are achieving a reunion with the mother is often based more on a childlike fixation than on a healthy, adult desire for companionship and sex, whereas for women, as noted previously, a mature sexual relationship or marriage can symbolize separation from the mother and a loss of dependency, an anxiety-provoking situation.

It must be emphasized that the more painful and frustrating the interactions with a withholding mother, the more the daughter tends to incorporate her mother's toxic attitudes and withholding behaviors through identification with the aggressor. This imitation takes place in spite of the fact that the daughter is frequently critical of these traits in her mother. To the degree that she maintains these characteristics, she suffers from self-hatred and feelings of demoralization that often play a significant part in depression. These dynamics, which include guilt reactions precipitated by the acting out of self-denying behaviors (Rubenstein, 1998), as well as hostile withholding patterns in an intimate relationship, may help explain the higher incidence of depression in married women than in married men (a ratio of 4 to 1).[7]

Fathers and Sons. Studies reviewed by Biller and Solomon (1986) have shown that a positive father–son relationship is correlated with later security and confidence in adult heterosexual relationships, whereas paternal deprivation, father absence, and divorce are correlated with difficulties in developing and maintaining satisfying heterosexual relationships. These researchers observed that:

> The quality of fathering the boy receives is generally the most crucial factor in the positive development of his view of himself as a male. Consistent maltreatment by the father can greatly damage the child's capacity to identify positively with him. (p. 98)

In addition, male children have a serious conflict in relation to their fathers. Desirous of love and nurturance, they also are aware of the times when their fathers has rivalrous and competitive feelings toward them in relation to their mothers. Often they experience covert aggression or hostility directed toward them from their fathers. As adults, they may find it difficult to develop close friendships or associations with other men. In addition, personal or professional success—winning over a male rival—can take on a symbolic meaning of surpassing the father, which triggers intense fear, guilt reactions, and a sense of loss.

The importance of the father as a role model for the male child cannot be overemphasized, especially in relation to the development of patterns of sexual withholding. Sons closely observe and incorporate their father's style of relating to the mother. They identify with and imitate their father's negative attitudes and withholding behaviors in relation to the mother and women in general. They also cannot fail to notice when he is intimidated by her tears or gives in to her control. Many fathers unknowingly support the mother's stereotypical view of men, believing themselves that men are mean and unfeeling, which can lead to their son's developing a tentative approach to women or more passive–aggressive behavior patterns. Park (1995) has emphasized that:

> What the boy needs is a father's help in dealing with the emotional pressures that come from his mother. He needs to learn that there are other views of masculinity than those which she propounds, and that what she says to him has more to do with her own past experiences than with him. (p. 23)

The findings reported by Biller and Solomon (1986) tend to concur in part with Park's hypothesis regarding fathers who are passive in relation to the mother. In their research, Biller and Solomon (1986) stressed the fact that:

> It is the father's sex-role adoption in family interactions that is important [in terms of being a positive role-model for his son], not the degree of masculine behavior he exhibits outside the home. Many fathers have masculine interests and are masculine in their peer and work relationships but are very ineffectual in their interactions with their wives and children. (p. 92)

Fathers and Daughters. In terms of the father's role in helping his daughter develop an acceptance of herself as a woman, Biller and Solomon (1986) noted that the father's "reinforcement of the girl's attempts to emulate her mother's behavior, and the father's general approval of the mother's behavior, seem particularly important" (p. 116). Findings from Biller and Solomon's studies tend to show that fathers treat male and female children differentially more often than do mothers.

In addition, Biller and Solomon (1986) asserted that paternal warmth and involvement in the family are also important factors that influence the development of the daughter's feelings about herself as a woman. They cited findings reported by Lozoff (1974) that suggest "that father–daughter relationships are crucial in the development of women who are able to be successful in both their heterosexual relationships and their creative and professional endeavors" (Biller & Solomon, 1986, p. 125).

Perhaps the finding most relevant to our discussion was reported by Fisher (1973), who:

presented evidence that paternal deprivation in early childhood is associated with infrequent orgasms among married women. ... These women were more preoccupied with fear of not having control than high-orgasmic women were, and this was associated with their lack of security and lack of trust in their fathers during childhood. (Biller & Solomon, 1986, p. 126)

Fantasy, Emotional Distance, and Guilt Reactions

Many men and women put emotional distance between themselves and their partners by fantasizing during love making. The compulsive use of fantasy to enhance sexual excitement indicates a denial of the need for the other person. When these fantasies are kept secret, there is an intensification of guilt feelings associated with fantasizing during a sexual experience. This is particularly true when the fantasies contain incestuous, sadistic, masochistic, or other components unacceptable or ego-dystonic to the person who is fantasizing.

Analyses of sexual fantasies often reveal clients' attitudes toward entering into emotional transactions of giving and taking and the extent to which they have retreated to an inward style of self-gratifying sexuality. The symbolic interpretation of these fantasies can be valuable in understanding each partner's level and style of functioning in interpersonal relationships. It is important to note that the only two direct exchanges of bodily fluids between humans are the breast-feeding of the baby and the depositing of semen from the penis into the vagina. Basic attitudes toward the giving and receiving inherent in sexual intercourse are related to primitive feelings in relation to breast-feeding and other early oral experiences. Often individuals who have been damaged during this phase of development fail to develop basic feelings of trust and may revert to more impersonal, masturbatory modes of relating; use fantasy to enhance their excitement; and lose emotional contact with their partner.

As people choose fantasy gratification, they suffer guilt reactions for betraying their loved ones and existential guilt with respect to their own self-betrayal. When men and women defend themselves against painful feelings aroused by a close personal relationship, they are aware, on some level, that their retreat is hurtful to their loved ones. Attempts to control one's partner, the holding back of affection and sexual responses, and other manipulations that create emotional distance also tend to precipitate strong guilt reactions in the withholding partner.

Intrusion of Negative Thoughts During Love Making

Sexual encounters that are impersonal and self-soothing are characterized by the intrusion of negative cognitions into one's thinking before, during, or following the sex act. Self-depreciating thoughts as well as hostile thoughts toward one's partner can, at any time, disrupt the natural flow of sexuality and generate feelings of self-consciousness. Even minor voice attacks can be a distraction from closeness or can interfere with the ability to perform or take pleasure in making love.

Men and women have internalized voices criticizing their basic feelings about themselves, their bodies, their sexual identity, and their ability to both give and receive sexual gratification and pleasure. This form of inimical thinking creates a view of sex as a performance to be evaluated or judged, rather than an extension of affection and feelings of attraction.

APPLICATION OF VOICE THERAPY TO SEXUALITY

In applying voice therapy techniques to sexual problems in the relationship, partners go through some of the same steps in the therapeutic process described in the previous chapter: (a) each partner verbalizes the problem that he or she has found limits the sexual relationship, while not attributing blame to the other; (b) each partner says his or her self-critical thoughts and negative perceptions of the other, in the form of the voice; (c) each partner releases the anger and sadness associated with the verbalization of the voice; and (d) each develops insight into the origins of the negative thoughts that interrupt feelings during sex and connects past experiences to present-day sexual problems.

Identifying Negative Thoughts That Interfere With Close Sexual Relating

In a couples' group, Ellen disclosed voice attacks she experienced while making love. Ellen had been involved with Glenn for two years and the couple was considering marriage when they began to encounter problems in their sexual relationship:

> *Ellen:* The feeling that I have when I'm sexual is that I really feel awake and in the moment. Then, I feel like I really want something. When I start to feel that, my reaction is to start attacking myself: *"You don't feel anything. You don't like this. You don't feel anything at all. What are you doing?"* And then I get to a point where I don't feel anything, I start feeling cut off. Then I start thinking, *"What do I have to do at work tomorrow? How can I finish all my projects?"* Then I really do feel distracted.
>
> *Dr. Firestone:* Could you get into it? Just say more, as though you were really talking to yourself.

Ellen:	*"You don't feel anything. You shouldn't feel this good. You don't have the right to feel like this. Why do you feel so much? Just stop it. Just stop feeling. You're going to get hurt."* Something like that. (sad)
Dr. Firestone:	You start to get sad.
Ellen:	Just saying it makes me feel really sad, because I can feel a pull not to stay with feeling wanting and feeling alive.
Dr. Firestone:	What do you think that has to do with?
Ellen:	Being afraid of feeling close to someone, feeling alive, feeling that my life is very precious to me. Feeling afraid to really go for the things that I want.
Dr. Firestone:	Do you have any voices about Glenn?
Ellen:	Yes.
Dr. Firestone:	How do they go?
Ellen:	*"He doesn't really want to be with you. You're not the person he wants to be with. You're not really that nice to him. He doesn't feel anything for you."* And that one, when I say it—it's so obvious that it's the opposite that it's really even painful to say and it feels uncomfortable to say.
Dr. Firestone:	Does it affect you anyway, even though it's so irrational?
Ellen:	I'm sure it does. I know that when we start making love and I want things to feel nice, I can feel myself starting to cut off. It feels better to give it away and just say to Glenn, "You know, I felt really alive and really sexual with you and now I feel scared. I feel really scared and I know it's crazy, but the thought in my head is whether you really want to be with me. I know I'm off in thinking that." If I give it away, then I'm still in touch with my feelings. But if I don't give it away, it gets louder and louder.
Dr. Firestone:	And what happens to you?
Ellen:	I cut off. I just feel cut off. It feels mechanical.
Dr. Firestone:	You're not there.
Ellen:	And I hate myself. When it even becomes the slightest bit mechanical like that, then I really get into hating myself. Then I really believe that voice: *"You don't feel anything. You don't have the right to feel anything."*

Later in the group session, Glenn revealed voice attacks that he identified as originating in attitudes he assimilated from both parents:

Glenn: I feel like I hold myself back a lot when we're making love. I couldn't tell whether the voices I had the other night were my mother's voices or my father's voices, and I felt confused. I even wondered if *they* were confused about who was the man in the family themselves. But some of the thoughts I had were that:

"You're just lucky to have any woman who likes you. You don't deserve to even have a woman in your life to be close to, to be sexual with. Where do you get off thinking that you can have a nice woman in your life? That you can have love?"

When I feel especially close to Ellen, I sometimes have the feeling of wanting to have a baby. This feeling is usually followed by a barrage of attacks, like *"What is this crazy thought about wanting to have a baby? You reproduce? I mean look at us, look at me, I can barely function as a human being. How do you think you are going to raise a child? Are you crazy? You are just lucky to have anything. You should just get in the background, go sit in the corner and just hope that nobody notices you. That is the best you should hope for. And look at you, just look at you! You are not attractive, you're short. You are not sensitive."*

At first it was hard to know where these thoughts were coming from. But I know the one that says I can't function as a human being is obviously coming from my father.

Application of Voice Therapy Techniques to Enhance Close Sexual Relating

Clients who have learned to use voice therapy techniques in their sessions can use them to "give away" their voice attacks and maintain personal communication during love making, especially at the point where they begin to lose feeling and become more involved in a cognitive process. The term "giving away" one's negative thoughts, when used in this context, encompasses three processes: (a) honestly admitting that one has negative thoughts; (b) taking responsibility for one's negative thoughts—that is, recognizing that they are not "caused" by the other person; and (c) acknowledging that these thoughts and the associated hostility do not reflect one's real point of view.

Partners can even choose to stop making love temporarily, if necessary, while carrying out this exercise. Partners are encouraged to maintain physical contact while giving away their voice attacks. In other words, they try to not allow their negative thoughts to disrupt the close feelings between them and continue to express physical affection toward each other. This technique can reawaken deep feelings from the past that can be worked through in subsequent sessions.

Several months after identifying her voice attacks in the group session reported previously, Ellen described the results of using this exercise:

> I felt freer since we started talking about the whole subject. I'm more aware of my feelings changing. But I'm able to talk about it with Glenn when it starts happening. That's really making a difference and it's made me feel more for myself. I feel that it's okay when my feelings change. Just some really basic things about letting myself feel whatever is going to happen. That's made me feel so much better and I'm enjoying myself a lot more.

In this type of verbal communication, partners develop a more empathic perspective and experience more compassion for each other. As a result, they are able to overcome many of their anxieties and self-critical attitudes.

Another exercise that is designed to increase clients' tolerance for giving and accepting expressions of physical affection consists of simply allowing each partner, in turn, to do whatever he or she wishes to do to the other. This involves expressing physical affection: touching, kissing, sexual caressing. While in the process of giving or receiving affection, both partners communicate what they are experiencing at the moment.

In developing more closeness sexually and emotionally, partners come to understand how their voices have often interfered with their progress and have led to acting-out behaviors that create distance. They learn that by using self-discipline, they can gradually increase their tolerance for intimacy and not retreat to a more self-gratifying mode of sexual relating. They discover that the anticipatory anxiety involved in following through on a corrective behavior or exercise is frequently more intense than the emotional responses to actually changing one's behavior. If clients are persistent in holding on to the territory they have gained, there is therapeutic movement.

DEVELOPMENT OF A HEALTHY PERSPECTIVE ON SEXUALITY IN THE FRIENDSHIP CIRCLE

Within the friendship circle, there is a strong emphasis on a healthy, active sexual life, whereas in conventional society, there tends to be considerable dishonesty and manipulation in sexual relationships. In attempting to enhance the quality of their relationships, people in the group of friends explored many of the ways they believed they had been affected by their parents' attitudes and traditional social mores.

A Discussion About Various Influences on People's Sexuality

In a series of discussions on sexuality and sexual relationships, men and women in the friendship circle described incidents they experienced in their families as well as societal influences that had deleterious effects on their feelings about their bodies and their sexuality. This particular meeting began with several people talking about their observations of family life and the apparent lack of sexuality between their parents. Rachel described the secrecy that surrounded sexuality in her family:

> *Rachel (41):* By the time I was about 12 or 13, I was looking for signs of sexuality in my house because they were so obviously missing. I would look for signs of birth control, anything, and I never found a thing. I was never aware of my parents being sexual, ever. I have no memory of it, of them ever doing anything that resembled anything sexual between the two of them.

> *Luke (49):* I can't remember ever having a positive or sensitive talk with anyone about anything sexual. It was always "don'ts" or "be carefuls." But there was never anything that indicated that there was a nice part to sex or that it was a mutual situation. So I always felt, and I think to a degree I still feel, that if a woman wants to be sexual with me, there is something in it to be suspicious of and there is something to be careful about. There is something to stay away from. I resent the total absence of my being talked with in a way that would have helped me to understand that part of my life.

Michelle recalled an event that she recognized as having caused her deep humiliation and shame.

> *Michelle (26):* I remember one time—I must have been 10 years old—we had all gotten dressed up to go out to dinner. I remember that I felt pretty, which I never used to feel, but I felt pretty for some reason. I felt happy, and I felt attractive. We were in the restaurant, and I reached up and gave my father a big hug and a big kiss. I remember I felt like I wanted him to think I looked pretty. And my mother pulled me aside and

said, "Nice girls don't kiss their fathers like that in public." I remember that I felt like a pervert, like I had done something so wrong.

Andrea (38): I remember that when I was about 7 years old, I would sleep on top of my pillow at night, climb on top of my pillow. And I think that it felt good. I think that I felt excited. But when I started doing that, my mother, when she would come in to say goodnight, she would see me and just freak out. She said, "get off your pillow, don't do that," but she was very uptight about it. I was sort of confused because I wasn't exactly masturbating. It wasn't something I was totally aware of doing or anything, but I got the message really early that whatever it was leading to that I should stay away from it. I never masturbated, and I think it was because her reaction was so intense.

Robert Firestone (57): Why would anybody want to take an innocent child, who just moves about freely, and teach it to be ashamed of certain parts of its body, as though they're different from other parts, and particularly parts that are potentially joyful or pleasurable and provide some of the greatest pleasure in adult functioning, or even in a child's functioning? What right do we have to stop a boy child from touching his penis, from having access to his own body, or a girl from touching her vagina? What right do we have to intrude on an internal process where a person wants to touch a part of their own body? What right do we have to impose standards on a natural function, a simple, natural pleasurable experience? An innocent, pleasurable activity between oneself and oneself—nobody's business but theirs. What about personal boundaries?

Theo recalled that his parents held many distorted views of the human body, views that he assimilated and that still affect him in his current life.

Theo (30): When I was growing up, there was always a lot of fuss made about me getting dressed and wearing clothes and things like that, just to cover up my body, and even now to this day, say a bunch of friends go skinny-dipping, I'm always really uncomfortable because I think somebody's going to see something about me, but it leaves me feeling really shy in certain situations.

Edgar (60): When I was 4 years old, my mother caught me under the bed with a girl, the two of us touching each other but without any kind of sexual implications—I didn't know anything about sex at that time. It was like having fun. My mother pulled me out from under the bed and beat me with a belt, insinuating that I was dirty, that I shouldn't have done things like that. And I find myself, even today, whenever I am with a woman, the first question that comes to my mind while I am having sex is "does it hurt you?" It's like I'm going to impose pain on the woman by being with her.

Kathy (21): In my family, things were different from many of the stories I've heard here today. From the time I was very young everything was sexual in my mind and my parents didn't have any qualms about telling me about sex. I remember that one of my books when I was a little girl was about "Where Do I Come From," and another one was called something like "I'll Show You Mine If You Show Me Yours."

I think that in my family everything was sexual. I mean everything, and I think that I was treated that way. I remember that my father and mother would go out into the field, the whole family, and he would take pictures of her naked in the field. One of the pictures he took of my mother was hanging in the living room (showing her from the shoulders up), but I felt funny about it. It was like a secret thing to me that she was naked in the rest of the picture.

I thought that every interaction between a man and woman was a sexual interaction. That's how my parents thought, and that's how I thought. I never thought of friendship or of friendliness or even just affection. Sex was the ending and the beginning point; it was the only thing in life, that was how I saw things.

Stephanie related an embarrassing incident that happened to her during her early teenage years. As she reflected on the broader meaning of the event, she discovered that its effects still caused her considerable sadness and pain.

Stephanie (38): When I was about 14, my father was the doctor at a music camp, and so the whole family was at the camp. There was a boy there that I really liked, and we went walking in the woods one day during the rest period. We walked together, and we laid down together and were kissing. But nothing really more than that. Someone saw us, and they made a big thing out of it as though we had been sexual. The boy got expelled from the music camp, and my father had to leave the camp.

I remember that I was so embarrassed that I didn't go to eat in the dining room from the period when the incident happened until my family left the camp, which was about four days. I just sat in the cabin because I felt like I had embarrassed my family enough without going to the dining room. (cries) It's funny, too, because it was so innocent—I didn't know anything. I didn't even really know how a man and a woman made love. I wasn't interested in trying to do anything.

Robert Firestone: Why do you think it's so painful to you today, just in telling the story?

Stephanie: I was surprised because I thought that I would sit here and tell it and have no feeling. I thought I had no feeling about it.

Robert Firestone: What does it mean to you?

Stephanie: I think being misunderstood. I had no vicious feelings toward anyone, and even no goal in mind. Nothing. It was just like talking to someone that you liked. It was nothing. And yet I caused so much trouble. For this boy it was his life, music. He went to Juilliard School of Music later. And for both of my sisters also, it had an effect on both of them, on my father, and on my mother.

Raymond (41): I felt sad when Stephanie said she had no vicious feelings, because throughout my life, especially as a kid, it was always a conflict: I had feelings that seemed totally innocent and yet I felt moralistic toward myself, like I was doing something wrong, or more specifically, that was sinful, and I was going to die and go to hell for it. I think that it had a lot to do with growing up in a family that was religious. I always felt like it was such a sinful thing to feel sexual or to have lustful feelings. And I still carry those kinds of feelings with me.

Robert Firestone: Attitudes toward sex, if you really look at them with any kind of intelligence or perspective, are totally bizarre as people experience them in our culture. Sex is as natural as eating. It's not a separate function. It's not a bizarre thing that people should do secretly and hide. There is no inherent shame in the body. There's nothing essentially ugly or sinful or bad about human beings, about their genitals. The whole thing is absurd. When a man and a woman are together and they're holding each other and they feel love, they touch, they hold each other—it's a tender moment. The sexual touching is no different than any other touching. It's a natural extension to go from caressing an arm, holding hands, to touch a breast, a vagina, to touch a penis. Why wouldn't people just touch each other? There's nothing wrong with that. On a more simple level, the women in many of the countries in Europe are topless on the beaches. They feel wonderful. They feel fine. No one is leaping on anybody. There's no increase in rape. Men are not walking around with giant erections and desperately longing and lurching—there's no chaos. It's just part of a pretty scene, a natural scene. It feels good. It looks good. It's natural.

Intstment In our culture, a whole socialization process is imposed on a natural system, foolishly and stupidly, and in a way that damages people seriously, and it affects other areas of their functioning. In fact, this type of limitation on sexuality, the kinds of crazy limitations and perverse attitudes against it, of making it unclean or peculiar or different from other natural functions, leads to serious states of hostility and often to vicious acts—person against person—totally unnecessary, and based on this bizarre frustration of a very natural and simple system.

Insights About Sexuality That Developed in the Friendship Circle

Over the years the people of the friendship circle have discussed the subject of sexuality with the same openness and candor with which they have addressed other issues. Some of their insights and findings in relation to sexuality include the following:

1. People are the most refractive in their most intimate relations, where there is both an opportunity for an affectionate, feel-

ingful exchange and a sexual, physical response. They tend to pull back or withhold in one area or the other, avoiding the special combination of love, sexuality, and tenderness that is the most rewarding or ideal.

2. Sexual withholding and related insecurities about one's body and sexuality originate from a basic sense of being unlovable. In their discussions, whenever people started talking about sex, more often than not they ended up talking about their desire for love, tenderness, and affection, their attitudes toward themselves as men and women, and their feelings of being undeserving of love.

3. A man's emotional and sexual responses are closely related to a woman's genuine sexual desire. A woman may act interested or aggressive, but without feeling and real desire for the man, her partner will have difficulty responding and find it necessary to resort either to fantasy or a mechanized style of sexual relating for gratification.

4. Men generally blame themselves for sexual failures and tend to deny their mate's influence, even when they are intellectually aware of the woman's negative effect. The times that women in the friendship circle admitted feeling less interested in sex coincided with those times that their partners reported experiencing sexual difficulties.

5. Many women revealed that during pregnancy they felt uncomfortable with the changes in their bodies. It appeared that a husband's decreased sexual response was often related more directly to the woman's feelings about her body than to a diminished interest in sex on his part because of her pregnancy.

6. Most women are attracted, emotionally, aesthetically, and physically, to other women. This attraction is probably based on the strong attraction to the mother and is a natural extension of early physical longings. In their discussions, as women talked more frankly about their feelings toward each other, which included feelings of attraction, they have become better friends. They found that they were drawn to women who were energetic, good-looking, and self-possessed. It appeared that these feelings had sexual components and were similar to men's feelings toward these same women.

7. Although men felt affectionate and warm toward each other, their feelings did not have the same degree of a sexual component as the women's feelings toward each other. It is difficult

to determine whether this finding reflects an essential biological difference between the sexes or is a result of cultural influences with strong prohibitions against physical, affectionate, or sexual contact between men.

8. As women recognized their attraction to other women, they reduced their fear of this attraction and incidentally enhanced their relationships with men. These women have become friendly rivals in the process of supporting each other's freedom and acknowledging competitive feelings.

9. For the most part, men in the circle of friends have given up their insistence on a false build-up and their demand that they be preferred at all times by the woman in their lives. They have come to realize that relationships based on free choice rather than obligation are more satisfying, honest, and often more enduring. They have developed the self-respect and maturity to face themselves realistically rather than relying on images of exaggerated importance or false assurances from women. In challenging their idealization of women, they have abandoned their quest for the "perfect love" based on infantile needs that tended to place unrealistic demands on their partners.

10. Women are more selective in the choice of sexual objects and men are more random. Nevertheless, men in the friendship circle, freed of macho defenses, appear to be as deeply feeling as the women. They have the same desire for developing close long-lasting ties for marriage and for children. They are genuinely concerned about how the women in their lives are feeling and feel happiest when their partners are content.

Findings Related to Competition and Sexual Rivalry

In dealing with sexual rivalry, both men and women in the friendship circle came to realize that competitive feelings are natural. They recognized that all people have legitimate desires for attention, love, affection, and sex, and that anger is aroused in situations where these wants are frustrated. In their discussions, individuals revealed their feelings of possessiveness, jealousy, and competitiveness. As a result of dealing with these feelings in an open forum, they came to the conclusion that a person's sexuality belongs to him- or herself and cannot be assigned to or possessed by another person. In overcoming many of their more primal feelings of jealousy and in learning how to express a healthy, direct competitiveness, they have become closer, and rivals have found that they could also be friends. In fact, honest rivalry appears to enhance genuine friendship, particularly between members of the same gender.

Men and women discovered that feelings of jealousy were often intensified after they had become withholding in a relationship. At these times they would be more inclined toward morbid and jealous brooding over imagined losses. They recognized that in general, jealous feelings disguise the fact that it is often one's own self-denial that prevents one from achieving one's goals, not the presence of a rival or competitor. With respect to other factors that exacerbate jealous reactions in general, Glass and Wright (1988) have observed that "the intensity of a jealous response is not necessarily related to the degree of love felt, but rather to the degree of dependency on the partner for positive self-regard" (p. 341).

It is interesting to note that the women in the friendship circle were the greatest proponents of every form of personal freedom. They, much more than men, had been denied equal status and independence in society and were therefore more sensitive to issues of suppression. As the talks progressed, the character and forthrightness of the women had a significant effect on the men. For example, in one group discussion, a woman who had been married for several years said, "I feel really strongly about this. I see sex simply as another form of communication between two people. So placing limits on another person's sexual freedom would be no different than restricting their freedom of speech. It's inconceivable to me." This woman was not personally defending an extramarital relationship or an intended sexual involvement; she was simply struggling to achieve autonomy in her personal life.

Many diverse opinions and reactions were expressed in these discussions, but at least philosophically speaking, some sort of consensus gradually emerged. In spite of various fears or prejudices, these people believed in freedom and autonomy for their mates and themselves in every area including sexuality. Whatever agreement individual partners eventually came to, they felt that it was imperative that they attempt to live up to it as honest, mature adults. The point of view that they ultimately arrived at is summarized in the next section.

Open Versus Closed Sexual Relationships

The question of having an exclusive or nonexclusive sexual relationship is problematic and complicated for most couples, no matter which decision they eventually make. In general, it is unwise for partners in an intimate relationship to place restrictions on each other, because one or both partners may come to resent such limitations. Yet most people are unable to cope with a partner's sexual freedom without suffering considerable pain. This creates a serious dilemma for most couples. It is of the utmost importance for partners to first agree on a basic policy that is respectful of each other's feelings and desires, and then to live up to their decision. The agreed-on policy or principle should not be violated or, at least, the partners should discuss changing the policy before acting in a way that would modify such an agreement.

Deep and intimate relationships tend to be the most fulfilling when they are not restrictive. Marriages, cohabitation, and other close personal associations that are based on respect for each other's priorities, independence and freedom are continually evolving rather than static.

Although a pledge of fidelity is commonly expected in society at large, one negative effect of such a pledge is that in the process of relegating one's own sexuality to another, a person often becomes less sexually vital. In defining what we mean by "relegating" one's sexuality to another, we are referring to limiting the expression of one's sexuality to one other person in a narrow, constrictive manner that may go against one's natural feelings. As a result of this type of exclusivity, people often report a decline in their sexual desire and a deterioration in their overall sexuality with one another. In fact, this declination in sexuality plagues many couples.

To further complicate matters, many people agree to the principle of fidelity but later violate the agreement. This deception or violation of trust can have a more damaging effect on the relationship than the "sexual infidelity" itself (Glass & Wright, 1997). Affairs cannot be considered to be morally "wrong" if the partners have agreed to accept each other's sexual freedom, are open and honest, and if the affair does not cause any of the parties involved undue distress. On the other hand, an affair can be considered morally wrong when secrecy and deception are involved, because we believe the personal integrity of the individual partners is more important than the sexual issues.

In society at large, monogamous relationships are perceived to offer more security, certainty, and the possibility of long-lasting love than nonexclusive relationships. Many men and women are possessive and try to control their mates in an attempt to compensate for feelings of inadequacy and fears of competition. They act on the assumption that people "belong" to each other because most have been taught early in life that they belong to their families. As a result, they lack a sense of belonging to themselves or feel that they do not have a right to their own lives. In failing to view themselves or their mates as autonomous human beings, they make themselves vulnerable to manipulations that play on their guilt and sense of obligation.

The relinquishment of any personal freedom constitutes a restriction; however, this sacrifice may be worth the price in some cases. For example, if one partner perceives that an affair would cause the other excessive pain in an especially vulnerable area, he or she may wish to remain exclusive.

In general, it is our opinion that the best situation for individuals in a couple relationship is to sustain each partner's freedom of choice and not limit the other by imposing unnecessary rules and restrictions. We believe that restrictive attitudes in marriage violate the policy of supporting the freedom and independence of one's partner and in that sense tend to have a damaging effect on the relationship. However, when there are other positive elements in the relationship, and other personal freedoms are respected, a compromise of choosing monogamy over an open, nonexclusive relationship may still be a viable choice.[8]

CONCLUSION

When sexual love persists and becomes a vital part of a fulfilling long-term relationship, erotic feelings and sexual responses represent an extension of the affection felt by the partners. Indeed, a combination of sexuality and close personal communication represents an ideal in couple relationships. In contrast, defensive patterns of sexual expression manifested by many adults, including sexual withholding, depersonalized sexual relating, and excessive reliance on sexual fantasies, represent a retreat from mature, natural sexuality. In addition, sexist views about the differences between men and women contribute to the battle of the sexes, lead to distortions and misinformation about men's and women's sexual nature, and perpetuate myths that support neurotic dependency or alienation between men and women.

People have both a healthy, "clean" orientation to sex as well as an acquired unhealthy, "dirty," or distorted view of sex that can be verbalized in the form of the voice. When investigated, these internalized voices were found to be associated with considerable sadness and rage toward self and others. Using the procedures of voice therapy to expose voice attacks helps individuals to separate the hostile, attacking part of the self from a more realistic or positive view. By becoming aware of and understanding the roots of sexual dysfunction in destructive thought processes based on negative identification with critical parental attitudes, hostility, and rejection, people can free themselves from these self-defeating, restrictive behavior patterns and significantly improve their sexual relationships.

Finally, a large majority of sexual problems would never arise if there were not other more basic disturbances in the parent–child relationship. Children who grow up in an emotional climate where they feel loved and accepted, especially in relation to their physical nature and bodily functions, would not develop sexual dysfunctions as adults or feel confused about their sexual identity.

NOTES

1. Flora Schreiber's (1983/1984) book, *The Shoemaker: The Anatomy of a Psychotic* relates an especially tragic case history exemplifying the pathological effects on a young boy of his parents' beliefs in the evils of sex and their threats of castration.

2. See discussion of gender stereotyping in chaps. 10 and 11 of *Fear of Intimacy* (Firestone & Catlett, 1999).

3. See Kernberg's (1980) description of a continuum of sexual love. At one extreme on this continuum are "narcissistic personalities who are socially isolated and who express their sexual urges only in polymorphous perverse masturbatory fantasies" (Level 1). At the other extreme (Level 5) is "the normal person who has the capacity to integrate genitality with tenderness and a stable, mature object relation" (p. 278).

4. It appears, however, that women may develop withholding patterns and adopt passive–aggressive means of achieving their goals more than men. We suggest that because women have been subjugated by a patriarchal society (C. Gilligan, 1996, 2002) for centuries, many felt incapable of actively determining the course of their lives. The lack of access to real power led them to adopt indirect or passive techniques in trying to fulfill their human potentiality. Also see *Beyond the Oedipus Complex: Mothers and Daughters*, a Stone Center Working Paper by Irene Stiver (1986) and Attanucci's (1988) observation that after they become mothers, women's identity or subjective experience often becomes confused with or almost completely subsumed by the role of "mother."

5. A seductive relationship with the mother can predispose a number of dysfunctions in adult males' relationships, including avoidance of sex and intimacy, feelings of inadequacy, and overcompliance and submission. According to several psychoanalysts (Kohut, 1977; Masterson, 1985; A. Miller, 1979/1981), children of both sexes who are "used" or exploited in this manner feel compelled to gratify their parents' unconscious primal needs at their own expense.

6. Chodorow (1978) asserted that "for a girl, however, there is no single oedipal mode or quick oedipal resolution, and there is no absolute 'change of object.' . . . A girl never gives up her mother as an internal or external love object" (p. 127). See Welldon (1988) for cogent descriptions of how adolescent girls cope with parental rejection.

7. Hudson and Jacot (1995) described the effects of negative aspects of the mother–daughter bond in women's relationships. They noted that:

   Among the happily married, women are five times as likely to be depressed as men. . . . [it seems that] a significant source of a woman's discontent lies within herself. For women, in other words: Heterosexual intimacy taps automatically into deep reservoirs of unresolved hostility, blame and depression. (p. 9)

8. See Pines's (1998) chapter "Romantic Jealousy in Open Relationships" in her book, *Romantic Jealousy: Causes, Symptoms, Cures*.

12

FAMILY RELATIONSHIPS

What strikes me as a ludicrous fact is that the marriage and family institutions to which such primacy of loyalty and devotion is being taught show anything but optimal health in contemporary society. That most marriages are not deeply satisfying relationships hardly needs documentation. A lot of praise and sanctification floats about us, however, on the matter of families. I think we engage in a lot of repression and denial. Put more simply, we double-pretend: we pretend families are mostly wonderful and then we pretend we are not pretending.

—Robert Harper (1981, p. 5)

The primary function of the family is to nurture the special potentialities of children, facilitate their growth, and enable them to develop, to the fullest extent possible, their autonomy and sense of self. Just as plants and animals need certain basic elements to survive and grow, human beings require specifiable environmental conditions to develop their full potential. Infants need food, water, warmth, shelter, and an optimal amount of audiovisual and tactile stimulation to survive. Young children require contact with empathic, affectionate, mature adults who function as positive role models and help them learn to regulate their affect. In addition, the desire and need for social affiliation is a basic human quality; therefore, living in harmony with family members in an atmosphere of congeniality and personal communication is predominant.[1] The interpersonal environment ideally would provide genuine experiences to enhance the developing child's search for happiness and meaning in life.

DIMENSIONS OF THE IDEAL FAMILY

From our accumulated knowledge regarding environmental factors that have been found to have a negative impact on children, we can contrast those factors with what we might envision as the dimensions of the hypothetical ideal family. In this perfect setting, each family member would be

271

acknowledged, heard, felt, and experienced by the others in such a way as to give the person a sense of his or her unique identity. Children would not be labeled or perceived as having fixed identities; rather, they would be seen as being in a state of change and capable of assuming an active role in their own growth and development. Each person would be valued as a distinctive individual, and his or her sexual identity also would be acknowledged and validated.

The ideal family would embody a spirit of easy sharing and a lack of possessiveness. There would be an open exchange of psychonutritional products, both tangible and intangible, including feelings, thoughts, ideas, good times, and humor. Communication would be straightforward, honest, and compassionate, and everyone would feel free to express any opinion and experience any emotion without self-consciousness. The sense of humor expressed by family members would not be sarcastic or cynical but would reflect the good feelings they have toward each other and an acknowledgment of the human foibles and uniqueness of each member.

Family interactions would be characterized by a lack of role-playing and manipulations through domineering power plays or the passive–aggressive acting out of a victimized position. Ideally, the adults in the family would not rule by force, coercion, or authoritarian means but would operate from an inner strength and authority that would naturally be assimilated and respected by the children. Each family member would be encouraged to pursue his or her special wants and priorities. In giving themselves value and importance, parents and children alike would naturally have respect and show consideration for other family members and their goals.

Overall, the ideal family would provide its members with many advantages: a warm and fulfilling lifestyle; financial security; companionship; the acknowledgment of each person's accomplishments; encouragement of independence; support for each member's development of his or her unique abilities, talents, and careers; and the opportunity for free and open communication—in summary, all of the qualities of a meaningful and fulfilling life.

CURRENT STATUS OF FAMILIES IN SOCIETY

Unfortunately, few families in our society exhibit characteristics that meet the criteria for the "ideal" family just delineated. Yet most people still strongly believe that present-day families are the backbone of a stable society and rigidly adhere to the notion that families contribute to the health and security of their members. Brazelton and Greenspan (2000) called attention to the contradiction between people's beliefs about the family and the reality of intrusive, disrespectful interactions that exemplify most families: "Although consistent nurturing relationships with one or a few caregivers are taken for granted by most of us as a necessity for babies and young children, often we do not put this commonly held belief into practice" (p. 1). Brazelton and Greenspan went on to emphasize that:

> Recent studies have found that family patterns that undermine nurturing care may lead to significant compromise in both cognitive and emotional capacities. Supportive, warm, nurturing emotional interactions with infants and young children on the other hand, help the central nervous system grow appropriately. (p. 1)

Evidence of the widespread incidence of emotional disturbance and child maltreatment in so-called normal families and their profound effects on children (Briere, 1992) has made us question the essential structure of the nuclear family. We do not deny the importance of biochemical or constitutional factors in the etiology of neurosis, but we assert that maladaptive attitudes and behavior manifested in adult individuals are directly related to, and overdetermined by, early environmental components. In light of statistics related to the quality of family life and its consequences, we must concede that what is customarily considered average or normal may have become pathogenic (Felitti, 2002).[2]

It appears that no child enters adulthood without sustaining damage in basic areas of personality development that to varying degrees disturbs psychological functioning and limits his or her ability to maintain satisfying adult relationships. However, while accounting for the roots of this resultant psychopathology, it is important to refrain from focusing blame on parents. Parents who have defended themselves from the emotional deprivation and rejection they suffered in their upbringing cannot help but pass on this emotional pain to their offspring. Both parent and child should be viewed with compassion.

Evidence from studies of attachment theorists and neuropsychiatry (cited in chapter 2) have shown that early trauma and losses in parents' childhoods, especially those revolving around early attachment, are generally reactivated when they have a child of their own. The psychological equilibrium established by those parents in their own childhood, as a defense against painful trauma and loss, is necessarily disturbed by the presence of the infant. Manifestations of this type of disturbance can be observed in the "strong emotions and affective dysregulation" of parents who see themselves as helpless, impotent, and unable to "select, evaluate, or modify their own behavior or that of their children" (George & Solomon, 1999, p. 663). According to a number of attachment theorists (Main & Solomon 1986, 1990), unresolved childhood loss and trauma are correlated with attachment disorganization in the new parent–child relationship. George and Solomon (1999) asserted that:

> In addition to childhood trauma, we propose that the mother's caregiving system may be immobilized because she is afraid of the challenges raised by a particular child or circumstances. (p. 664)

They also noted that

> the activation of the caregiving system, and the resulting caregiving behavior elicited by the baby, appear to be influenced heavily by . . . her own representations [internal working models] of attachment. (pp. 659–660)

Bugental, Brown, and Reiss (1996) also found that parents who believed they had "low-power" in comparison to their children (especially as the children reached middle childhood) justified many of their own behaviors as being self-defense. These parents tended to see themselves as the victims of their children.

Our findings regarding parent–child relations tend to agree with those reported by George and Solomon and Bugental as well as findings of brain researchers regarding the neurochemical basis of disturbed attachment. For example, Perry (1999) observed that:

> Children that are rejected by their parents will have a host of problems including difficulty developing emotional intimacy. In abusive families, it is common for this rejection and abuse to be transgenerational. The neglectful parent was neglected as a child. (p. 6)

Overall, painful experiences of abuse, neglect, and deprivation that parents endured during their formative years lead to serious limitations in their ability to establish secure attachment with their infants.

EFFECTS OF THE COUPLE'S RELATIONSHIP ON THE EMERGING FAMILY

The style of relating that evolves between partners before having children is generally an accurate predictor of the quality and type of attachment they will form with their children.[3] The attitudes and defenses that each partner manifests within the couple tends to determine the attitudes, practices, and interactions within the emergent family. Children born to a couple whose relationship has developed symptoms of a fantasy bond feel excluded and suffer considerably from the lack of emotional sustenance. Furthermore, they are drawn into their parents' world of illusion and pretense. Bowen (1978) contended that:

> The two person relationship is unstable in that it has a low tolerance for anxiety. . . . When anxiety increases, the emotional flow in a twosome

intensifies and the relationship becomes uncomfortable. When the intensity reaches a certain level the twosome predictably and automatically involves a vulnerable third person in the emotional issue. (p. 400)

Most often, that third person is the couple's child.

To the degree that parents are defended, children incorporate their parents' illusions and neurotic behavior patterns. Through the process of imitation, they learn defenses that alienate and isolate family members from each other, yet they are taught to cover up any indication that family members are not close. Children learn to distort their real perceptions and deny the reality that their parents are distant, inward, or self-protective. Boszormenyi-Nagy and Spark (1984) described their observations of this type of distortion that is prevalent in many families:

> Our experience with troubled families has revealed that the child's conflicts are directly connected with the interlocked, collusively unconscious, or denied processes which disrupt and interfere with growth of all the family members. It appears as if, in order to survive emotionally, both parents and children, husbands and wives, do exploit each other and are exploited in their efforts to have unmet dependency needs fulfilled. There is a conscious and unconscious compliance to avoid exposure of the basis of unmet reciprocity between all family members. (p. 251)

Years of clinical experience with families led us to certain unavoidable and painful conclusions about family life and its adverse effect on both children and parents.[4] In our work, we had no intention of challenging the structure of the nuclear family. Our interest was in tracing the pathology of our patients and in trying to understand the meaning of their symptoms and suffering. In tracking down the dynamics of people's resistance to a better life and, in particular, in studying the voice process, we were forced to look at the destructive parental attitudes and responses that were so detrimental to the well-being of individual family members. We discovered that the origins of people's self-defeating behavior and misery were directly traceable to the trauma and abuse they had suffered within the traditional family structure.

Finally, we began to question our earlier thinking about the family. Like most people, we had been resistant to a close examination of this structure, because we had a defensive stake in the sanctity of the family. However, as we explored the lives of our patients, our own personal experiences, and the critical issues raised by parents in the friendship circle, we became increasingly aware that destructive bonds and the organization of defenses around the fantasy bond within the family were important sources of human suffering and primary causative factors in psychopathology (Firestone 1990b, 1997a).

It is not that the nuclear family is inherently detrimental to human growth and development; it is that it has become an institution hurtful to parents and children alike. Only by recognizing this fact and dealing with the issues that make families dysfunctional can we modify or change family life so that it has a more constructive effect on future generations of children.

WHY PARENTS HAVE DIFFICULTY SUSTAINING LOVING RELATIONSHIPS WITH THEIR CHILDREN

Emotional damage to children suffered in the context of family life is a complex phenomenon (Belsky, 1980), and no single circumstance or influence is explanatory. However we can delineate several significant factors that make it difficult for parents to maintain consistent, loving relationships with their children.

Parental Ambivalence

All people are divided in the sense that they have feelings of warm self-regard as well as feelings of self-hatred and self-depreciation (see chapter 2). Therefore, it is not surprising that parents would extend these same contradictory attitudes toward their offspring. Parents' attitudes toward their children are a by-product of their fundamental conflicts and ambivalence toward themselves.

Cross-cultural studies (Rohner, 1986, 1991) encompassing more than 35 primitive and industrialized societies have shown that parents' feelings and attitudes toward their children are both benevolent and malevolent. These conflicting feelings appeared to coexist, in varying proportions, within all of the researcher's (Rohner) subjects. Rohner (1991) conceptualized parents' attitudes as existing on a continuum ranging from parental warmth and acceptance to indifference, rejection, and hostility. On the basis of nearly 40 years of research, he concluded that parental rejection has profound effects on children and that attitudes underlying rejection and perceptions of being rejected can be measured intergenerationally in parent and child, respectively.

Because negative, hostile feelings toward children are usually unacceptable, parents tend to be unaware of or deny aggression toward their children, whether overt or covert. To the extent that they fail to recognize these attitudes toward their children, they will act on them, causing much unnecessary damage to their offspring.[5] Most parents fear that by recognizing negative feelings, they will be more likely to act on them, when in fact the opposite is true.

Threats to Parents' Defenses Posed by the Child's Aliveness and Spontaneity

A significant finding related to parent–child interaction is the phenomenon of parents' remaining insensitive to their children in the areas where they, the parents, are most defended. In general, it appears that a parent unconsciously avoids close personal contact with the child or becomes punishing when the child is going through a specific phase in his or her development where the parent was hurt and forced to build his or her own defense system. Many people have revealed that they became distant from their child during these periods, because contact with the child reminded them of painful events from specific periods in their own childhoods. For example, Gabe was aware that he had become awkward and uncomfortable relating to his son, Darrell, who was approaching his third birthday. In an interview, he described the reasons for this difficulty:

> *Gabe:* I noticed that I can actually have more closeness with adults than I can with Darrell. I have an idea in my mind that when Darrell is older, I'll be able to get closer to him. So I've been searching to find out why I have those two thoughts.
>
> First, I had the thought that I was avoiding Darrell in the same way that I was avoided, and that I wouldn't give to him something that I didn't get for myself. Then I started to remember that my father wasn't there from the time that I was 1 to the time that I was about 4½. He was overseas in the war, but when he got back, he stayed at work every night until very late, and I hardly ever saw him.
>
> *Dr. Firestone:* You made another point in our meeting last week. You said that painful feelings are aroused in you when you treat Darrell differently or feel toward him in a way that is different from the way you were treated, that it leads to a lot of pain for you. It somehow emphasizes the pain that you went through as a child yourself. It's difficult to treat a child with tenderness and sensitivity when in fact it's different from your own experience.
>
> Your father's absence tormented you. You spoke about it, how he avoided the family. And long after he came back from the war, he still used work to avoid any contact, the way you described. In some way, you developed the same pattern in relation to your own family.

Gabe:	It's very rare that I ever have any real interactions with Darrell. Mostly it's the relation of not being there, even when I'm there.
Dr. Firestone:	Even when you're in close quarters, you tend to be insulated, you're saying. Why do you think that is?
Gabe:	Because I won't give to him what I didn't get myself. (tearful)
Dr. Firestone:	And that makes you feel sad.
Gabe:	It's a combination of shame and a wasted sadness. He's there wanting, just like I was there wanting, and there's no real reason. I don't even believe that I'm incapable, but I believe I'm acting irrationally.

Many other parents, like Gabe, have reported that positive interactions and tender, sensitive moments with their children arouse deep, primal emotions they have been avoiding for years. In addition, parents who have grown up with an image of themselves as unlovable are often resistant to having close, tender moments with their children or to having their child look at them with love. When parents cannot bear to feel their children loving them, they respond negatively to them. Books on child-rearing fail to give this phenomenon the importance it deserves. Most parents and many clinicians assume that parents are gratified and thrilled to see their baby's first smiles of happy recognition. Although this is often true on a conscious level, these same expressions can arouse painful feelings of sadness in parents who have spent their lives warding off intimacy and positive interactions. These more painful feelings are usually suppressed before they reach parents' conscious awareness.

In a number of other cases, we found that trauma or unresolved losses from parents' childhoods were often reenacted during interactions with their offspring. Parents who were aware of repeating abusive or overprotective patterns with their children that they had suffered during their formative years experienced considerable guilt and self-recriminations. In the next chapter, we describe interventions that address this repetitive pattern and help relieve parents' guilt.

Parents' Tendency to Confuse Emotional Hunger With Genuine Love

Almost everyone takes for granted that parents, especially mothers, have an innate propensity to love their children (Badinter, 1980/1981; Hrdy, 1999). Unfortunately, this assumption is not necessarily realistic. As noted in chapter 2, many parents confuse intense feelings of need and the subsequent anxious attachment of their offspring with feelings of genuine affection. They are unable to distinguish emotional hunger, an unsatisfied longing for love and care caused by deprivation in their own childhood, from real warmth and concern. They imagine that they love their children at the same time their behavior indicates something different.

Feelings of emotional hunger are experienced by parents as deep internal sensations that range in intensity from a dull ache to a sharp nostalgic yearning. Often, they express physical affection with ostensibly loving gestures toward their child in an attempt to alleviate their own hurt. At these times, they offer affection and love when they feel the need for it themselves and inadvertently take *from* their children rather than give to them. Sustained contact with an emotionally hungry parent is damaging to the child's well-being (Firestone, 1990b; Parker, 1983; Tronick et al., 1986).

The Dependency Load Implied in Assuming
Full Responsibility for a Child

Parenthood symbolizes the end of childhood, and to many this signifies separation from parental support systems and the assumption of a role for which they may not be emotionally equipped (see Leach, 1994, chap. 2, "Mother, Father or Parent?"). Many people taking this significant step feel insecure and self-doubting.

Expectant mothers and fathers often entertain idealistic fantasies of what life will be like after their baby arrives. Reality quickly intrudes when new parents face the responsibilities of 24-hour care for their infant. Reactions to having such fantasies disrupted are varied. Many parents express disappointment, anxiety, resentment, disillusionment, and feelings of being burdened by the care of a new baby. Parents who were deprived or neglected as children discover they have trouble offering security and guidance to their own children. Some immature parents perceive their child as getting the care and attention that they desire for themselves from their spouse, and they have angry reactions or show signs of jealousy.

Parents' Projection of Their Negative Traits Onto Their Children

As described in chapter 2, parents tend to disown their self-hatred and negative voices and project them onto their children. Thereafter, they become overly critical of these projected qualities and traits in the youngsters. Through the process of projection (Bowen, 1978), the child is basically used as a dumping ground; parents deny weaknesses and unpleasant characteristics in themselves and perceive them instead in the child. As a result, many children become imprisoned for life in a narrow, restrictive labeling system that formed their identity early on within the family. As adults, they feel guilty to move away from these definitions, even though they may be inappropriate, negative, or degrading.

This type of projection is prevalent throughout family life (Kerr & Bowen, 1988). The dynamics of this process have been clearly explicated by Murray Bowen (1965):

> [The mother] searches for and diagnoses a defect in the child that best fits her feeling state. . . . She acts toward and treats the child as though her diagnosis is accurate. . . . The projection is fed by the mother's anxiety. When the cause for her anxiety is located outside of the mother, the anxiety subsides. For the child, accepting the projection as a reality is a small price to pay for a calmer mother. Now the child *is* a little more inadequate. Each time he accepts another projection, he adds to his increasing state of functional inadequacy. (p. 225)

Kerr and Bowen (1988) go on to conclude that "those actions [of being inadequate or incompetent] are used by mother to justify her image of the child. The mother is not malicious; she is just anxious. She is as much a prisoner of the situation as the child" (p. 201).

Using One's Child as a Symbol of Immortality

An interesting existential issue often overlooked is that many parents have children for the wrong reason—as a defense against death anxiety. On an unconscious level, these parents believe their children are extensions of themselves and experience feelings of exclusivity, connectedness, and possessiveness in relation to their progeny. However, this defense "works" only to the extent that the child is essentially the *same* as the parents in appearance, personality characteristics, behavior, style of defense, and religious and political conviction. The more the child is different from the parents, the more he or she poses a threat to their illusions of immortality. Indications of nonconformity and individuation in children are perceived as bad and sameness with, or submission to, one's parents is seen as good.

In using the child as a symbol of immortality, parents feel duty-bound to teach their own self-protective coping mechanisms, although these techniques may be distorted, crippling, and maladaptive. They transmit their defenses, beliefs, and values to children both by example and direct instruction. Having been "processed" in this way, children grow up feeling alienated from themselves, as though they have no inherent right to their own point of view as separate human beings.

The Effect of the Child's Developing Unlikeable Personality Traits

Another reason parents face formidable challenges in sustaining affectionate relations with their offspring is that hurt children often develop unpleasant, undesirable personality traits—that is, they become unlikeable. Many deprived or rejected children become desperate, spiteful, unattractive, or hard to be with and inspire further rejection by parents and other people as well. Sometimes the damage occurs in infancy and the ongoing effects are difficult, if not impossible, to reverse. For example, Main (1999) reviewed a number of studies that found "children disorganized with the parent as infants have typically become either controlling and punitive or controlling and caregiving" (p. 861) at 6 years of age.

In addition, children easily take on the parents' disowned and projected traits as part of their own identity and then go on to live up to these negative parental expectations. For example, after expressing his self-critical thoughts in a voice therapy session, a man recalled his father angrily yelling at him, predicting that he would grow up to be "nothing but a bum; a ditch-digger at best." The man recognized that he had essentially fulfilled his father's negative prophecy by failing at successive jobs and sabotaging each career opportunity he had tried to pursue.

THE THERAPEUTIC VALUE OF EXTENDED FAMILY RELATIONS IN THE FRIENDSHIP CIRCLE

In the early years of the friendship circle, participants found that they were experiencing more difficulties and problems in their couple relationships and in interactions with their children than in their friendships. Family members were often insensitive and disrespectful to each other in their expressions and communications; they tended to talk for each other; they interrupted; they avoided really listening; and they tended to blame, mislead, and manipulate through guilt.

In their ongoing group discussions, parents and other adults began to speak about these issues. These talks were accompanied by painful feelings of deep concern on the part of the parents and the other participants for the well-being of all the children. Their concern led to the formation of parenting seminars where they talked openly, in an atmosphere of acceptance, about their difficulties.

In other group discussions, the children were also provided with an opportunity to speak openly about their feelings and perceptions of their parents. As noted in the introduction, a discussion group was formed in 1971 for the older children and adolescents who had become alienated from their parents and who were experimenting with drugs. When these teenagers first met with their parents and talked openly about the emotional pain that they were experiencing in their families, the parents felt deep sadness. Many mothers and fathers previously had had no idea that their children were suffering, often in the same way they had experienced hurt when they were growing up.

A mother recalls the first meeting between the teens and their parents:

As one young girl spoke to her dad about feeling hurt and ignored by him, especially when he would be affectionate to her brother, I started wondering if my daughter had something to say to my husband or to me. I listened while the girl's father, with tears in his eyes, said that he was sorry to have hurt his daughter. Then he said that he had had similar feelings when he was a boy. It seemed that he had longed for *his* father to show him some small sign of affection, but had never had the courage to speak up the way his daughter had.

Later in the conversation, my daughter did talk about the lack of communication in our family. She described how each of us was so isolated, how she and her brother watched TV alone in their own room every night, how the family never shared anything, any fun times, and never talked, and how she felt like she had no one to confide in. It was one of the most painful moments in my life to listen to my daughter and her friends trying hard to say what they really felt.

Talks Between Children and Parents

The primary purpose of the original talks between parents and the teenagers was to provide the opportunity for both to express feelings and opinions to come to understand each other better. Over the years, the democratic exchange of perceptions and sincere expression of feelings that occurred during the meetings gradually dissolved the boundary between the generations. Parental and child roles began to be discarded and the adolescents related to their parents on a more equal basis. Because the group situation put incidental pressure on parents not to talk their children out of their feelings and perceptions but to listen and respond honestly, a great deal was learned about the types of treatment that were hurtful to these adolescents.

This tradition has endured and there are often group discussions with the younger children and their parents. The discussion described next occurred in 1992. Russell (34), one of the participants in the original teenage group, begins by talking with his children, Amelia, 11, and David, 6:

> *Russell:* I remember being in a situation where I was a teenager and we had the idea of talking to our parents and I just remember how valuable it was.
>
> In my relationships with both of you [David and Amelia], I thought that I've been very inconsistent. There have been times where I shared an interest or did things with you or talked with you. But a lot of times after that,

I'll stop doing it. And I think that really has hurt both of you a lot. I just wanted to say that it's not anything to do with you guys—it's nothing wrong with you.

It's because I'm not willing to feel something and it has to do with how I was treated when I was a kid. I didn't really have anybody who was consistently interested in me or who would do things with me or even notice me in a way that was real. And it's very painful for me sometimes to be that way, just to notice you and see the way you are, just in a simple way. A lot of times I don't stay with that feeling and don't keep doing the things with you I was doing.

Amelia: It made me really sad when you said that. I don't know why, but it made me really sad (crying) because for a while every Sunday when we went to the baseball game, you would take me out to breakfast and we would talk and it made me feel really good. I just liked the way you were with me, but after a while you stopped and it made me feel really bad.

Robert Firestone (62): One thing you said is really important, and that is when parents are neglectful or when they don't give you the love that you want and need, you think that there's something bad about you. Children think that there's something bad about them instead of seeing that it really has to do with their parents. And the reason they do that is that they don't want to really see their parents as not perfect.

David: My dad was being really nice to me, but then he stopped being nice to me.

Robert Firestone: That's what he said, too, that he starts being nice and then he stops. He starts and stops and starts and stops. How does that make a person feel, when he starts and stops?

David: I feel bad.

Robert Firestone: Then you start to think nobody loves you, right? Or that there's something wrong with you?

David: Yeah.

Russell: It made me sad to see that because it's so much the way that I felt, like when I saw you get sad,

David, and you, too, Amelia, it just made me sad because I felt so not seen as a kid and particularly with my father, I would feel that happen. Sometimes he would do something with me, play ball or do something, and I just loved doing it with him. And then he would just ignore me for the longest time. So it made me really sad to see you feeling the same way and to be thinking that you're bad or there's something wrong with you. There's nothing wrong with you guys. I'm sorry that I've been like that. I'm sorry that it hurts you.

Robert Firestone: I notice that kids like to make their parents up to be nicer than they are because they want so much to have parents who are nice. If the parents don't treat them nicely, they cling to the parents anyway. Especially when they're really rejected, they tend to hang on desperately to their parents, like they're hungry for their parents to love them. Desperate to get their parents' love, and if their parents don't love them, then they're really not any good. Remember those thoughts you all said last week about being stupid, feeling ugly, feeling that no one likes you? Those thoughts come from feeling that you're bad or there's something wrong with you, instead of facing the fact that some things hurt you when you were growing up.

Lia (14): I notice that in a way I defend my mother a lot.

Robert Firestone: How do you mean?

Lia: I know it goes along with me wanting to believe she's really nice. But sometimes, if I overhear one of her women friends talking about her in a competitive way, putting her down in some way, I get really angry at the woman.

Robert Firestone: You might agree with her otherwise, right?

Lia: Yeah. [to mother] I've really liked spending time with you lately, but I'm still worried that you're going to reject me one of these days because you've been nice to me for a while now.

Marissa (7): Why does everybody always cry in these talks?

Marcus (10): Because they're sad.

Marissa:	But why do they always get sad in these talks? Why didn't they ever get sad before?
Robert Firestone:	That's an interesting question. Anybody want to answer it?
Sam (7):	Maybe because this talk has more feeling than other ones.
Marissa:	It's embarrassing with all the adults here. Not with all the other kids, but I'm embarrassed to say it with all the other adults here.
Lia:	In the kids' talks, we talk about the same issues, but we're not talking directly to our parents. And here you get more emotional because you're telling the one person who could really change that.

Overall Advantages of an Extended Family Situation

From our experience over the past 30 years, we have found that children tend to thrive in a generalized social atmosphere of sharing and congeniality in which they are not solely dependent on one or more specific adults to gratify their needs. Every person in the large group of friends is presently involved in the youngsters' personal development, and the children seem compatible and at ease in their interactions with the adults.

An extended family may be defined as consisting of one or more adults, in addition to the child's natural parents, who maintain consistent contact with the child over a significant period of time. A close friend, a grandparent or other favorite relative, a godparent, an older sibling, a neighbor, or a mentor could be considered to belong to this category.

In addition, close association and friendship with people besides the child's parents help to compensate for parents' fears and inadequacies. The extended family situation offers a variety of inputs, points of view different from those of the parents that expand the child's world and give him or her an enlarged perspective and a more realistic picture of life. This expanded view of life helps disrupt the idealization of and overdependence on parents, thereby providing the child with a more comprehensive and secure base from which to operate. Furthermore, in the case of illness or emotional breakdown in the biological parent, there is a support system already available (Firestone, 1990b; Perry, 1997; D. Siegel, 1999).

An extended family relationship or friendship offers the child an ally, a person in whom he or she can confide, an adult who is relatively unbiased and objective concerning the child's relationship with his or her parents. Children in this setting are also provided with relationships that are generally free of the proprietary interest most parents have in their children. They tend to develop a sense of independence in their interactions with adults, which offers them an alternative to an overly dependent relationship with one or both of their parents. Moreover, other adults are more objective and freer to be a positive influence in the child's life because they are not as prone to guilt reactions or anxieties as the natural parents.

An extended family structure can serve all the functions of the traditional nuclear family: long-standing affection, socialization of children, financial resources available in a crisis, and emotional support and guidance.[6] The pooling of wisdom and understanding in a larger group of people is far richer than what would be available in an individual nuclear family. A nonexclusive and open family structure that includes others benefits all members.

Supportive Findings From Evolutionary Psychology and Neuropsychiatry

One of the major problems confronting the modern nuclear family is that its members are living isolated lives without the support network that was provided in past generations by the extended family. In contemporary Western society, the single-parent family is approaching the statistical norm (U.S. Bureau of the Census, n.d.). The dependency load implied in assuming full responsibility for a child is exacerbated by this lack of a supportive family network or help from other sources.

Evolutionary psychologists conjecture that for most of their evolutionary history human beings lived in small kinship circles or tribes. During the era of environmental adaptation (the two million years in which human beings evolved), this was the environment in which the human brain evolved, in groups where social affiliation was necessary for survival. In other words, social interaction with and stimulation from a small group of individuals probably facilitated the development of the specific brain structures and functions that permitted Homo sapiens to survive as a species. With respect to this hypothesis, several neurological experts in the area of trauma and violence prevention believe that infants and young children need to relate to several adults or older children to promote optimal brain development during the first three years of life.

> Human beings evolved not as individuals, but as communities. Despite Western conceptualizations, the smallest functional biological unit of humankind is not the individual—it is the clan. No individual, no single parent–child dyad, no nuclear family could survive alone. We survived and evolved as clans—interdependent socially, emotionally and biologically. Children *belong* to the community; they are *entrusted* to parents. We have not provided parents with the information and

resources to optimize their children's potential and, when parents fail, we act too late and with impotence to protect and care for maltreated children. (Perry, 1997, p. 144)

According to Perry, the family unit or grouping optimal for healthy brain development would consist of 4.5 adults who are involved with the infant or child.

In *The Developing Mind*, Daniel Siegel (1999) has stressed the evolutionary advantage gained by human beings' ability to make sense of the social world of other minds, to understand "the subtle and rapid signals, both verbal and nonverbal" displayed by other people. In other words, *"the ability to anticipate the behavior of others is dependent upon the ability to understand other minds"* (p. 328). Siegel conjectured that this ability was facilitated by experience in a social or group context:

> Functioning in a complex social network enhances people's capacity to survive as individuals, reproduce, and create a group of like-minded individuals who share such a capacity. This can be seen as a form of interindividual integration, in which an individual becomes a member of a community beyond the dyadic relationships of attachment and friendship. (p. 328)

In addition, research has shown that "resilient" children, those who grew up under extremely traumatic conditions yet were able to survive emotionally, did so because they had a positive relationship with another adult, a teacher, neighbor, or relative, generally a person outside the nuclear family (E. Anthony & Cohler, 1987; Masten & Coatsworth, 1998; McLoyd, 1998; Werner, 1990). In some cases, the child's contact with a significant other was of limited duration, but nonetheless, it had an ameliorative effect on the youngster's well-being. By offering a point of view other than that provided by the parent or parents—that is, a more congenial, accepting attitude toward the child—this person may have provided enough support to avert a psychopathological outcome.

CONCLUSION

The infant at birth is unusually sensitive and vulnerable to sensory inputs (Brazelton & Greenspan, 2000; D. Siegel, 1999; Stern, 1985). From birth (or even before birth), the parental environment has a profound impact on infants, and they respond with their entire body to painful intrusions from the outside world (Gladstone & Beardslee, 2002; Stratton, 1982). As we have seen in chapter 2, if circumstances in the family force young children to deny their sensations, perceptions, and feelings to protect themselves from painful events, they will progressively turn their backs on life. Yet unfortunately, in socializing their children, well-meaning parents obliterate their children's curiosity and creativity, their awareness of the world around them, and their capacity to feel and care deeply for themselves and other human beings.

For this reason, it is incumbent on us as clinicians, and indeed all adults concerned with the well-being of children, to consider the damaging aspects of family life. To *really* protect our children, we must attempt to overcome our prejudices and narrow views of the nuclear family and objectively examine dehumanizing child-rearing practices that characterize most family interactions. As Rheingold (1967) urged, "I believe that we would better serve children if we abandoned the concept of parental love and spoke rather of sensitivity to need, protectiveness, kindliness, respect for the individuality and the dignity of the child, and the reverence for life" (p. 198).

As parents learn to give value to their own lives, they can better allow their children to preserve their human heritage rather than partly taking back the life they gave. They might choose to provide a more nurturing environment for their offspring by including other individuals who could be of potential value to their child, where there would be extended concern for children and where the needs of children would be carefully and conscientiously attended to. Perhaps over many generations, there could be movement toward providing such an environment in which all children could grow and flourish.

NOTES

1. Findings from research in the field of evolutionary psychology stress the importance of these positive qualities and potentialities. According to Robert Wright (1995), researchers have noted that because social cooperation increased primitive man's chances of survival, natural selection must have shaped our minds so that we seek friendship, affection, and trust, tendencies referred to by evolutionary psychologists as reciprocal altruism.
2. For example, approximately 2.8 million child abuse reports were received in 1998 by local child protective services agencies (ChildHelp USA, 2001). Longitudinal evidence (Rohner, Kean, & Cournoyer, 1991) supports the conclusion that parental rejection precedes development of depression, behavior problems, and substance abuse. A recent survey commissioned by Prevent Child Abuse America found that nearly one-half of U.S. parents reported neglecting their child's emotional needs, most on a daily basis (Child Abuse, n.d.).
3. See Belsky's (1999) description of studies related to different attachment styles (secure, avoidant, and resistant or ambivalent) of spouses that were correlated with the type of attachment pattern they formed with their infants.
4. Originally R. Firestone's attention was directed toward families of individuals with schizophrenia (1955–1957); later toward families that contributed to neuro-

ses (1957–1979); and finally, toward an investigation of the effects of the nuclear family on "normal" individuals through observing families in the friendship circle and participating in group and family discussions.

5. Coward (1997) stressed that ignoring the phenomenon of ambivalence while idealizing mothers can sometimes lead to tragic consequences (infanticide and extreme child maltreatment). She also emphasized, "Yet this current idealisation of motherhood denies women the chance to come to terms with the confusing mixture of emotions that motherhood involves. . . . Many women . . . are cheated of ways of recognising when they should go for help" (p. 118).

6. In several cultures, the biological parents are not the primary caregivers for their infants and young children. See James's (1994) introduction to *Handbook for Treatment of Attachment–Trauma Problems in Children*, titled "The Children Belong to All of Us."

13

CHILD-REARING

My experiences have only served to strengthen and confirm my belief that children can be helped through helping their parents. What we do for today's parents has a great bearing on how today's children will live out their lives.

—Vincent J. Fontana (1983, p. xiv)

In our work with patients and in our involvement with individuals in the friendship circle, we have been continually concerned with the toxic aspects of family relationships that contribute to defensive processes in the child and the subsequent development of emotional disturbance in the adult. We recognized how individuals were hurt in their upbringing and how they in turn damage their children, and this understanding has had important implications for child rearing. In identifying the mistreatment and trauma that children suffer, we were able to formulate positive attitudes and philosophical guidelines for child-rearing practices that we felt could minimize the damage. These fundamental principles are analogous to the feeling and tone that we consider essential elements of effective psychotherapy.

First, the therapeutic process is one of inquiry; the therapist suspends judgment while listening with empathy and questioning him- or herself regarding the client and the sources of his or her disturbance. In the same sense, parents who develop a spirit of investigation in relation to their children are interested in and sensitive to the emergence of their unique qualities and behaviors. When their children misbehave, they speculate about what is troubling them rather than automatically punishing their behavior.

Second, the therapist refrains from acting out elements of negative countertransference. Mature clinicians attempt to maintain a neutral or empathic posture and refuse to reject the client for his or her communications, no matter how distorted or negative they may be. It is clear that this task is even more challenging in the parenting situation. Mature parents maintain consistent contact and resist any regressive tendencies within themselves that promote feelings of insecurity and predispose indifference, hostility, or rejecting behaviors toward their children.

Third, in most effective therapies, there is a strong emphasis on freedom of speech and emotional expression. For example, the technique of free association used in psychoanalysis permits the client to let his or her thoughts flow in a stream of consciousness unhampered by the rules of logic or censorship. The client not only learns to think creatively, but also comes to understand, on an emotional level, that any thought or feeling is acceptable. At the same time, the experienced clinician helps clients confront and examine the consequences of their self-defeating or self-destructive behavior. Similarly, good parents accept all of their children's feelings, thoughts, and opinions uncritically, while teaching them to control undesirable, aggressive, or provoking behavior.

Fourth, a good working relationship between the therapist and the client is necessary for a successful outcome. Effective therapy takes place in the context of a respectful, equal therapeutic alliance between two individuals and not within a doctor–patient, role-playing, unequal relationship. The good therapist does not assume a posture of superiority or use his or her expertise to impress the client. The same conditions for a good therapeutic relationship can be applied to parent–child relations.[1] Although children are clearly not the equal of their parents in terms of physical size, power, knowledge, or competence, parents should not use this differential in any way that would make the child feel inferior or weak.

Fifth, a vital dimension of psychotherapy lies in its nonintrusiveness, exemplified in the therapist's acknowledgment of the basic worth of his or her client and his or her right to an individual existence. Similarly, preserving the child's sense of self through respectful treatment is crucial to good parenting.

The ultimate goal of therapy is to facilitate the individuation of the client. In doing so, the therapist encourages the client to challenge his or her inner world of fantasy and to risk seeking satisfaction through goal-directed behavior. In the same sense, the ultimate goal of child rearing is to socialize children in a way that allows them to strive for their goals, shift to a more independent life, and separate from symbiotic ties. Good parents, like good clinicians, take pleasure in observing the unfolding personality of their children as they emerge from dependency and move toward autonomy.

LOVE-FOOD: A NECESSARY INGREDIENT FOR THE CHILD'S EMOTIONAL DEVELOPMENT

To provide infants and children with proper emotional sustenance, parents must be able to sensitively nurture them and be capable of offering them control and direction. Winnicott (1960/1965) used the term *good-enough maternal care* to describe the holding environment needed by the infant for ego development. Previous works (R. Firestone, 1957, 1984) have referred to this function on the part of the primary caretaker as providing love-food. Love-food can be defined as a psychonutritional product whereby the parent has both the *intent* and the *capacity* to gratify the needs of the growing child and help him or her adjust to the socialization process necessary to flourish in a particular culture. Emotional sustenance goes beyond the physical body to the spirit of the child (the self system) and is made up of two qualities: product and intentionality. As noted in chapter 2, love-food is in theory necessary for survival in both the physical and psychological sense of the word.

The ability of parents to provide love-food for their children depends on their motivation as well as their maturity and strength of character. Love from a weak or ineffectual parent is not enough, nor is control without love from a strong or strict parent sufficient to provide for the emotional security of the child. For example, if parents are warm and affectionate yet immature or overly permissive, they fail to teach the child self-control or self-regulation. Conversely, parents who are excessively authoritarian and do not offer kindness and warmth fail to provide the child with the ingredients necessary for a positive life experience. When there is no outward expression of love, children grow up feeling unacceptable and unlovable.

PREREQUISITES FOR OPTIMAL CHILD-REARING

In the healthy or ideal family, as described in the previous chapter, parents would manifest a number of personal qualities that would contribute to the child's well-being and growth into an autonomous person.

Parents' Capacity to Respond Personally to the Child

Parents who provide love-food have attained a level of emotional maturity that permits them to be natural—that is, to "be themselves"—in interactions with their children. In contrast, parents who are defended or are acting out their own negative identity or a parental role inadvertently deprive their children of the experience of knowing them as human and lovable. Children need to be able to feel love for their parents, for the people their parents really are behind the roles. If denied this opportunity, children suffer considerable emotional pain. Many books that offer to teach techniques of "good parenting" can actually be harmful, because specific learned responses or methods inserted into parents' behavioral repertoire are generally not authentic. Often when parents attempt to apply these techniques, they are sending mixed messages that damage the child's capacity for reality-testing.[2]

Many parents talk to children in a patronizing, strategic, or phony manner. Others bombard their children with perfunctory, unfeeling questions. Children can usually sense the indifference underlying these cursory inquiries and frequently respond in kind.[3] This type of questioning is not conducive to building a personal relationship with a child. Children need adults who will listen to them, respond sensitively and realistically to their communications, and who are forthright with them about their own thoughts and feelings.

The Ability to Accept Their Child's Love

Most important, parents need to allow the child to love them, which is perhaps the most difficult task faced by parents. Many adults find it unbearably painful to break through well-established defenses to accept love and to live in harmony with another human being. At times when parents feel a deep love for their children, they feel so much that it actually hurts; it may be emotionally or even physically painful. If parents would choose to bear with these feelings and suffer through this poignant pain along with their children, they could develop a true sense of empathy, thereby opening up the possibility for their children to live and feel for themselves.

The Ability to Relate to the Child as a Separate Person

Parents who treat their children as separate human beings, with respect for their individuality, have a positive effect on their children's development. These children exhibit stronger characters, are centered in themselves, and are more likely to fulfill their unique human potential. Mature parents do not attempt to live their lives through their children or feed off their achievements. They understand that children do not belong to their parents or their families but to themselves. Parents who are respectful of personal boundaries avoid intruding into the lives of their children by identifying too closely with their interests and aspirations or by making them feel that they must report their thoughts, feelings, and behaviors. They do not patronize, categorize, or speak for their children. They refrain from other intrusions, such as going through the child's belongings, reading his or her mail, touching him or her insensitively or excessively, and interfering with his or her personal relationships (Barber, 2002).

Parents' Valuing Their Own Lives

Parents can best help their children not by sacrificing themselves for their children but by attempting to fulfill their own lives. Nothing is more conducive to mental health and a true moral position than people seeking the full development of their potential and pursuing their own goals in a direct manner. When parents are involved in the straightforward pursuit of their own goals, they serve as positive role models for their offspring. To teach their children to live lives of meaning and compassion, parents need to genuinely value themselves, accept their feelings and priorities, and actively participate in their own lives. In contrast, men and women whose lives are insulated, desperate, or self-protective will not inspire their offspring to seek adventure or challenges (Rubenstein, 1998). Parents' level of maturity, their capacity to feel for themselves, and their willingness to invest fully in their own lives have the most profound effect on the personal development and future lives of their children.

AN APPROACH TO PARENTING GROUPS AND PARENT EDUCATION

Voice therapy may be used as an intervention in parenting groups or as part of a comprehensive parent education program. The approach has a dual focus: (a) to allow parents to expose negative attitudes and behavior toward their children in an accepting atmosphere, and (b) to encourage them to remember painful incidents they experienced in their own upbringing. This twofold focus helps parents develop more compassion for themselves by regaining feeling for what happened to them in their own childhoods. Learning to feel for themselves is the key element that enables parents to modify their attitudes toward, and interactions with, their children in a positive direction. The goal in treatment is for parents to develop an empathic understanding of the sources of their limitations and then to see their child from that same perspective—that is, to pass on this sensitive view to their offspring.

The steps in the therapeutic process consists of parents (a) opening up and working on negative feelings and attitudes toward themselves and their children; (b) recalling painful events from their own childhoods; (c) releasing the repressed affect associated with negative experiences in growing up; (d) understanding the connection between their present-day limitations and the defensive patterns set up to cope with early trauma; (e) exposing deficiencies in their families of origin, thereby breaking the idealization of their parents; and (f) developing more compassionate child-rearing practices based on constructive attitude change.

It is important to emphasize that these steps are not discrete, nor do they necessarily occur in the sequence described. These phases tend to evolve as part of a natural process, with parents continually making a transition between talking about interactions with their children and describing their own experiences while growing up. However, it is helpful for the therapist to be cognizant of and sensitive to the steps as the client progresses through each phase of treatment. At each stage, the therapist should be sensitive to situations in which it would be appropriate to suggest that clients use voice therapy techniques—for example, when criticizing themselves as parents or when describing their own parents' attitudes toward them.

Expression of Negative Feelings and Attitudes

It is important to first establish an atmosphere in treatment that is accepting, nonjudgmental, and tolerant—that is, a "holding environment" or "safe place" where parents can talk openly about so-called unacceptable feelings, no matter how ambivalent, hostile, critical, or resentful.

Initially parents present problems in relation to their children that cause them worry or distress. For example, Natalie, 24, an energetic, attractive mother became concerned about her 2 1/2-year-old son, Max, because he had started biting other children.[4] Her friends and other family members saw him as an angry, frustrated child. In addition, the toddler had become increasingly dependent and clingy and cried for his mother whenever there was even a brief separation. According to Natalie, her son had been a happy baby, appeared to be securely attached to both parents, and was friendly and outgoing with other children his age. The symptoms of aggressiveness, pushing, hitting, and biting children had become evident only recently, shortly after Max's second birthday. Natalie was also distressed because the situation with Max was creating tension between her husband and her.

After describing the troubling situation at home, Natalie explored her ambivalent feelings toward her son:

> *Dr. Firestone:* How do you feel about the situation? How do you see Max?
>
> *Natalie:* I feel all kinds of feelings. I feel very mixed up and confused. I'm so worried about him, especially when he cries for me.
>
> *Dr. Firestone:* What are you telling yourself about him at those times?

Natalie:	I tell myself things like: *"Look, he's crying. You've got to make him stop. You've got to make him look okay. You've got to make him look good."* God, I almost feel like my mother.
Dr. Firestone:	How do you mean?
Natalie:	Like she's talking, not me.
Dr. Firestone:	How does it go? What's she saying?
Natalie:	It's very angry sounding, like, *"He's just like you!"* (loud, angry tone of voice) *"He's bad and you're bad. Everyone knows it. Everyone can see it. He's bad because you're bad! You have to make him look good, so they won't see how bad you are!"* Then I start to attack myself even more about how bad I am, not just as a mother, but in every way. I start feeling unattractive and ugly, like a little creep, just like I felt when I was little.
Dr. Firestone:	What are the attacks?
Natalie:	These voices are even more angry, like *"You're ugly. You're so unattractive. You're so unappealing. You have such ugly features. You have a huge nose. It's so embarrassing! You have to hide it. You're too heavy. You're too fat. So you have to walk in a way where it looks attractive. You have to show yourself in a way where it looks good. You have to hold yourself better. You can't just be yourself because you don't look good. And your acne is so disgusting. You have to hide it. You have to put lots of makeup on. Cover up everything. Cover up all those bad points."*

Recall of Painful Events

Often in the course of examining their feelings toward their children, parents recall experiences in their families of origin that had caused them pain and stress. They are encouraged to discuss the specific incidents of abuse, both verbal and physical, to which they were exposed as children and to share their emotions.

Dr. Firestone:	What does this make you think of when you think that way? What does this relate to, these negative thoughts?
Natalie:	It definitely makes me think of how it was when I was growing up. It's so clear to me because it's so much the way I was treated all my life.
Dr. Firestone:	How do you mean?

Natalie: I remember my mother would tell me that I should have plastic surgery when I was old enough. She would say that I looked like my father, but in a way where it was derogatory toward him and toward me. And she was always trying to make me do things to make myself look better. But even more than that, it seemed she had hostility toward me. I think she was really competitive with me. After she got divorced from my father, and when her boyfriends came around, I was at an old enough age where she was very aware of me. She was always noticing just where I was and what I was doing and if they were paying attention to me.

Dr. Firestone: What was the result? What happened to you?

Natalie: I think it really did leave me feeling self-conscious about my looks, but even worse, it left me feeling like I was bad somehow. She always emphasized that appearances were everything, and it was obvious that she thought there was definitely something wrong with me that had to be fixed. There was something really bad about me that embarrassed and disgusted her. Now I feel that same way toward Max. (sad and agitated).

Release of Repressed Affect

From previous clinical work we have learned that most individuals not only tend to deny the validity of early trauma but also to minimize the emotional impact these incidents had on them as children. Therefore, we usually encourage clients to express the feelings associated with the painful events they recall from their childhoods. We believe that in general it is important for parents to experience these feelings to develop compassion for themselves and their children. We focus on methods that lead to a catharsis because catharsis is usually followed by deep insight and new knowledge of self. The expression of emotion is facilitated by giving verbal support—that is, if an individual begins to indicate affect, we say, "Let it out" or "Don't hold back" or "Try to really feel that," or other supportive statements. In some cases, people who have been very defended against remembering events of their childhood or experiencing the deep emotions associated with them are able to recall the incidents in detail after listening to others tell of their experiences.

Natalie: I feel like I'm such a bad mother and his behavior proves it.

Dr. Firestone: Really feel that. Go ahead. Try to get into it.

> Natalie: *"You idiot! Can't you see he's just like you! He's bad! You're bad. Now everybody will know what I've known all along. You're bad. You're a bad seed. No good, Rotten through and through!"* (cries deeply)
>
> Just now I remembered that when my parents got divorced I thought it was my fault. I think she blamed me for the divorce. She implied something about my brother and me being so bad that we drove him away, like she would say, "You're driving your father crazy" and things like that.

Connections Between Present-Day Limitations and Early Defenses

As parents reveal traumatic incidents from their childhoods, they often become aware of almost uncanny parallels between specific incidents of abuse and neglect they suffered in their development and their own faulty patterns of child-rearing. As they come to a deeper understanding of the connection between their presenting problems with their children and painful issues from their own childhoods, they begin to adopt more compassionate attitudes toward themselves and their children.

> Natalie: It's amazing. Here I've been thinking that everyone else thought Max was bad. I thought I was the only one who didn't see him that way. But the opposite is true. The only one thinking he is bad is me! I'm so sure that his "badness" is going to come out that I'm always trying to make him act right. I know he picks up my tension and worry. He has to end up thinking he's bad. (sad)
>
> Dr. Firestone: There seems to be some real pain behind what you just said. What does it make you think?
>
> Natalie: It makes me think that I have that same feeling about myself, that I have a false image of myself which was unnecessarily put on me. It's really sad if I think of it in relation to Max. If I think of that happening to him, it's a painful situation because it's so undeserved.

Exposure of Inadequacies in Their Families

The insights that parents gain into the hurt they suffered as children inevitably challenges the idealized images they hold of their own parents. Most adults have strong tendencies to protect and excuse their own parents and to rationalize the abuses they suffered as children. As clients observe the destructive effects of psychological mistreatment in other group members and feel empathy for them and their limitations, they gradually develop more clarity in relation to their own parents.

Natalie: It's so obvious to me now that my mother had this same attitude toward me, that she saw me as bad. She was always criticizing me, trying to fix me, as I said. I just incorporated her view of me and I've been treating Max the same way. Before talking about this, I didn't want to see how she really treated me, how she thought about me, and how she still thinks of me today.

Two weeks ago, I visited her in San Francisco, and afterward I realized that I was still idealizing her and my childhood on some level. It was a really different visit than I'd ever had with my mother in that we actually talked. I talked about my life and about my past. At one point, she said, "You had a bad childhood." I replied, "Well, compared to a lot of people, it wasn't *that* bad." Then she said, "No, it was. You had a bad childhood."

And then she said something sort of out of the blue, like "one of my biggest regrets was not buying you a prom dress." At the time, her remark totally went over my head. I just said, "Well, actually I have a different memory. I had a dress made for myself." So I didn't even know what she was talking about. But the important thing is that I didn't have any feeling or any response to the fact that she said not buying me the dress was her biggest regret. Out of all the things that happened in my childhood!

When we were talking last week, I realized that in family visits, I always stop feeling the painful things that go on, even in my conversations with her. And so I didn't feel it. I didn't let myself feel anything about what the relationship was then and the way she still feels about me. It was so interesting to see that. I think a lot of people get hurt when they try to make their visits with parents a good visit instead of feeling whatever is going on. I think it's because they still want to see their parents in a good light.

As parents deal with these issues at a deeper level, they may begin to experience the full brunt of the outrage and grief they felt in being limited by these early experiences. Their basic attitude would not be one of blaming but more one of accounting for what happened in their childhoods and reacting emotionally to the discoveries.

Sensitive Treatment of Children

At this point, parents begin to develop a new perspective on child-rearing—that is, they see that they can be different from their own parents. Being sensitive to their children in ways their parents were not sensitive to them tends to break into the idealization of their families. In the process of altering their responses to their offspring, they come to recognize that their parents had abusive or undesirable qualities, that most of the damage they sustained as children could have been avoided.

In identifying the traumatic or painful experiences in their formative years, parents can begin to develop more positive attitudes toward their children and make constructive changes in their child-rearing practices. When parents become more compassionate toward themselves, they often develop a sensitive interest in their children and are able to initiate steps to prevent their child from incorporating a negative self-image. They are more successful in avoiding destructive interactions with their children and can offer them experiences that would enhance their self-esteem as well.

> *Natalie:* Looking back, I can see that both my parents were very self-centered and that they didn't have that much to give. They didn't have loving feelings to give and I think they wouldn't accept my loving feelings toward them So I was kind of left to be by myself, and the whole time I felt that I was a bad person.
>
> I feel so sad right now, and so grateful and so optimistic. I really see myself and Max in a different way. Neither one of us is bad. We are each innocent and lovable. I want to be aware of any time I get that worried, nervous "make him look right" feeling. It's an indication that I'm projecting my old issues onto him.
>
> You know, I *am* worried about the biting, but from a whole different vantage point. Not in relation to how it makes him or me look, but instead, "What does it mean about how he's feeling? Is he angry about something? Is he hurting?" It makes me sad to feel for him and be interested in him in relation to himself, not in relation to what it means to me.

Subsequently, Natalie carried out an exercise that she believed would help her further differentiate her own point of view about herself from her mother's point of view of her. She read the following excerpt from her journal in the parents' group.

> *Natalie:* This is what I wrote about after the session last week. I thought it would be a good exercise and it has turned out to be. I feel much stronger in what I think and feel about Max and myself. I'll read it from my journal.
>
> What my mother would say about my being a mother and what I would say back:
>
> *Mother:* "See, I told you, you can't be a mother. I told you it would be hard. You don't know how to love someone. Now look what you've done. I told you it wouldn't work. Now you know why I am the way I am, and you're just like me. I knew you couldn't do it."

Me: I love Max more than you ever loved me. Sure, it's hard to raise a child, but when I see him, my feelings are always fresh. When I saw you, there were never any feelings. I'm looking into myself and struggling with hard issues to help our relationship and to help him feel better about himself. You always thought that I was the problem and you certainly acted that way.

You always thought I was a bother, but he's not a bother to me, he never was. It's my issues that get stirred up in me. When you felt like I was a bother, you never looked inside yourself to realize that those feelings were internal and had nothing to do with me. You treated me as though I was bad and unlovable. Maybe Max will be spared because I love him and care enough to struggle with these feelings, and hopefully he won't feel bad about himself. So, in my opinion, I am being the best mother I can be.

RELEVANT FINDINGS FROM VARIOUS TREATMENT MODALITIES

Over the past three decades, interventions with a focus similar to our approach have been developed to interrupt the cycle of emotional child abuse by helping parents recall and reexperience painful events in their childhood. In a classic article, "Ghosts in the Nursery," Fraiberg et al. (1980) reported the results of treatment procedures applied in a home setting with mothers and their infants. Introducing the article, Fraiberg et al., wrote,

In every nursery there are ghosts. They are the visitors from the unremembered past of the parents, the uninvited guests at the christening. Under favorable circumstances, these unfriendly and unbidden spirits are banished from the nursery and return to their subterranean dwelling place. (p. 164)

Later, they state that "the parent, it seems, is condemned to repeat the tragedy of his own childhood with his own baby in terrible and exacting detail" (p. 165). Fraiberg et al., in an adaptation of psychoanalytical methods combined with developmental psychology and social work techniques, attempted to help parents "recover the events of the past and undo the morbid effects of the past in the present" (p. 166).[5] The hypothesis developed by these researchers tends to support our thinking regarding effective methods that can be used to interrupt the intergenerational cycle of child mistreatment. Fraiberg et al. concluded, "Our hypothesis is that access to childhood pain becomes a powerful deterrent against repetition in parenting, while repression and isolation of painful affect provide the psychological require-ments for identification with the betrayers and the aggressors" (p. 195).

Building on Fraiberg's model, Lieberman and Pawl (1988, 1990) and Lieberman and Zeanah (1999) have reported their work with parents and their infants within a hospital setting as part of the Infant–Parent Program at the University of California San Francisco:[6]

> Parents are encouraged to recollect their own childhood, and as these memories emerge the therapist looks for and addresses the links between the parents' past experiences and their current feelings and behaviors towards the baby. This technique helps to generate parental insight into the sources of their current difficulties in caregiving, and this insight in turn permits the parents to stop reenacting with their baby the conflicts of their own past. (Lieberman & Pawl, 1988, pp. 339–340)

Recently, Lieberman and Zeanah (1999) described a number of other programs, including the Minnesota Parent–Child Project and the Ann Arbor Approach, which are designed to elicit and reintegrate parents' emotions related to past loss or trauma.

Findings from recent research into early brain development also shed light on the necessity for accessing the *affect* associated with painful child-hood memories to achieve substantive changes in parental attitudes and behaviors. For example, D. Siegel (1999), LeDoux (1996), and Schore (1994) have emphasized that emotion is the organizing process within the brain. In particular, Schore's neurological studies emphasize how early devel-opment of certain brain functions, especially the regulation of affect, is dependent on the environment. (See chapter 2, this volume.) His research has demonstrated that trauma and neglect may result in a loss of, or dimin-ished nerve connection between, the "emotional brain" and the "rational" brain—that is, the higher cortical functions. It may also lead to a reduction in connections that transfer information between the right and left hemi-spheres of the brain. The implications of this research point to the need for interventions that are directed toward reintegration of these two functions of the brain as well as an integration of right-brain and left-brain functions. This type of reintegration is dependent, in part, on the reactivation of repressed or blocked-off affect stored in the emotion-processing parts of the brain.

We hypothesize that until the emotions associated with painful child-hood memories are released from repression and integrated with the higher cortical functions, people who were traumatized or profoundly neglected as children will continue to reenact, in interactions with their children, the destructive behaviors that their own parents acted out on them. The work of a number of other researchers and clinicians (Fosha, 2000; Karr-Morse & Wiley, 1997) tend to support our hypothesis. In recent years, these clinicians have used neurological studies to inform their interventions and have applied an experiential or emotionally focused treatment with disturbed children.

In summary, the format of the parenting groups described in this chapter, which help participants become aware of painful emotions they once experienced as children, may be the most effective form of intervention for both parents and their offspring. Indeed, it appears that only through understanding themselves and the sources of their limitations can parents change the negative attitudes and feelings they express covertly and overtly toward their children.

CHILD-REARING GUIDELINES BASED ON SOUND MENTAL HEALTH PRINCIPLES

In an ideal situation, parents would avoid unnecessary restrictions, rules, and standards. More significant than specific disciplinary measures is the powerful modeling effect derived from the child's living day-in and day-out with parents who themselves consistently behave in a responsible manner. The psychological processes of identification and imitation overshadow parents' verbalizations, rules, and prescriptions for good behavior. Therefore, parents would try to identify and change toxic personality traits within themselves that are not only passed on to their children, but also have detrimental effects on their children's well-being.

When discipline is necessary, it is best practiced with firmness, not cruelty; with understanding, not condemnation. It is important that parents never beat, hit, or physically abuse a child (Firestone, 1990b; Hyman, 1997; Straus, 1994). If restraint is needed, parents can hold the child and talk to him or her with firmness. Clearly, individuals who feel comfortable with their anger are better able to control its expression and are therefore more capable of taking a strong stand in enforcing the rules they have made. However, becoming more accepting of one's anger is a learning process that takes considerable time and requires a high level of emotional maturity. For parents who have problems in handling their anger, experts have recommended that they give themselves a cooling-off period—for example, slowly counting backwards from 20 to 0, then distracting the child with some other activity, or if possible, temporarily leaving the child in someone else's hands.

Overall, discipline should come from an underlying motive of helping the child become not only the kind of person who likes him- or herself but also the kind of person that other people like, respect, and enjoy being with. At the same time, it is important that parents teach children that it is never appropriate to hate themselves for wrong-doing, that it is much more functional and appropriate to change their behavior in the future.

Sensitive parents provide the appropriate amount of care necessary at each successive stage of the child's development, but not a surplus. They show their respect for their children's growing maturity by allowing them to progressively take over their own lives according to their level of capability. In allowing the child the maximum freedom possible at each age level, parents are implicitly expressing a belief in the child's inherent potential for making healthy choices and in his or her capacity for self-regulation.

Parents can help their children develop positive attitudes toward work and discourage attitudes of victimization. Children are capable of entering into productive work in the home at an early age and, as they grow older, they can expand their participation into more and more adult functions. Providing the youngster with a series of jobs serves as a useful discipline that is accepted matter-of-factly by a child who is viewed as a productive member of the family. Here again, it is important for parents to recognize that their attitudes toward work are paramount.

Some specific guidelines include (a) avoiding cynical, judgmental attitudes that create a sense of badness in the child; (b) avoiding making evaluative, judgmental pronouncements about the child's behavior; (c) refraining from categorizing the child or foisting a strict or fixed image on him or her; (d) firmly controlling the child's acting out of hostile, manipulative behavior, such as negative power-plays, helplessness, crying when angry, playing the victim, or having temper tantrums; (e) relying more on rewards than on punishment in guiding the child's behavior; (f) avoiding physical punishment; and (g) avoiding the use of threats of future punishment or loss of their love to enforce their rules.

DEVELOPING CONSTRUCTIVE CHILD-REARING PRACTICES IN THE FRIENDSHIP CIRCLE

Parent–child relations and child-rearing practices became a topic of major concern as more and more children were born into the group of friends. Mothers and fathers and other interested adults have participated in group discussions about these subjects for many years. This has enabled them to observe how child-rearing practices were transmitted through three generations, beginning with the grandparents. In the accepting atmosphere of these discussions, the parents identified and challenged what they considered to be undesirable and potentially harmful behaviors in their interactions with children and altered the attitudes on which they were based, thereby developing more constructive child-rearing practices.

Sharing Child-Rearing Functions

The accumulated knowledge gained from years of talking together about parenting has led to a number of ameliorative measures that have been of enormous benefit to the new generation of children in the friendship circle. These innovative child-rearing practices were not planned in advance but evolved in an informal manner. In many cases, parents asked for help when they realized they were experiencing feelings of nervousness, desperation, or emotional hunger in interactions with their children. Sharing child-rearing functions in this manner is one of the most effective means of helping children achieve their maximum development.

The process of identifying emotional hunger in one or both parents has been valuable in itself and has provided them with a measure of control. For example, when Michelle's (26) baby was two months old, she began to notice that she had two distinct reactions to him, either feeling relaxed and at ease with him or nervous and overly concerned.

> One difference I notice is that when I'm just relaxed, I have contact with a lot of people, no matter where he is or whether I'm holding him or someone else is holding him. The rest of my life goes on. I'm aware of all kinds of things that are happening. When I'm in the other frame of mind, I'm overly focused on him. I'm aware of who's holding him, how they're holding him, if he's fussy. If I'm holding him, I'm looking at him, even if he's asleep. I know it bothers him because he becomes agitated.

After talking about her differential responses to her son, Michelle had the idea of involving a close friend to take care of him at times when she felt anxious, and then initiate contact with him again when she felt more comfortable and easy-going in her responses.

In another group discussion, Brad (49) talked about the expectations he had for his daughter to be perfect or to appear happy:

> With my little girl, it was almost like a compulsion from the start, from the time she was born. I realize that I still look at her very critically. I look at her, and if she isn't looking exactly right, then I know that I feel terrible and I hate myself. I think that it's some kind of a reflection on me and that I'd better fix it up. I'd better make her feel better.

Later, Brad remembered some of the unreasonable expectations his parents had had for him and connected these to situations where he was tense and critical with his daughter. As she grew older, he encouraged her to develop friendships with other adults who did not have perfectionistic attitudes in relation to children.

> I feel like I've been really affected by our discussions about child-rearing, just listening to different people talk about their feelings from their

childhoods and also the feelings that they have toward their kids. Almost everything that each person says about how they feel makes me more aware of my own feelings for my daughter, why I feel that way, and what happened to me in my childhood. It's given me more insight and also I feel that the moves I've made to include other adults in her life has been valuable. For example, when I used to participate in certain activities, like sports, with my daughter, I found myself getting tense and irritable. So now a friend of mine participates with her in many of these activities, and I know it's a better situation. So I feel optimistic that I'm starting to change that pattern and that I can break the chain from generation to generation.

In observing parents who became involved with each other's children, we found that the parent interacting with a friend's child did not manifest the same hungry focus or intrusiveness. Parents came to recognize that although they might still be damaging in some respects to their own child, they were helpful to their friends' children. They saw that the extended family situation, based on adults working together and taking a constructive interest in each other's children, provided better parenting for all the children.

As ties of friendship grew stronger among the parents, they began to share in many child-rearing functions beyond the scope of a simple exchange of babysitting duties. For example, many years ago, several of the children began spending weekends with people other than their parents. Some were taken by friends on ocean crossings and vacation when their parents' work schedules prevented them from traveling. These mothers and fathers were motivated primarily by their desire to extend to their children (and to their friends' children) the social atmosphere that they found so nurturing and adventurous.

Over the years, a number of men and women have gradually become substitute parental figures for their friends' children. In some instances, these friends were primarily responsible for the child's well-being and upbringing for a period of time. In the majority of cases, the children tended to improve significantly; often there were immediate positive results, and the parents were deeply appreciative for their friends' involvement.

The children, including infants and toddlers, have benefited significantly from the contact with empathic, sensitive adults outside of their families. They have received comfort not only from their parents but also from other caring adults who were closely involved with them on an everyday basis. Because of this, the children were not exposed to many of the experiences their parents suffered during their upbringings. As a result, they did not become excessively dependent on self-soothing, self-nurturing mechanisms such as thumb-sucking, pacifiers, blankets, or compulsive routines. They displayed much less self-stimulatory behavior than other children their age.

For example, none of the children were "crib-rockers" nor did they habitually put objects or their fingers into their mouths. Overall, the results noted previously were influenced by an implicit morality toward children and positive attitudes toward child-rearing rather than adherence to calculated practices or techniques.

Although this arrangement is perhaps unique, it can be generalized and modified to accommodate to new circumstances and can play a part in preventive mental health programs. On a preventive level, the concept of parents' exchanging child-rearing functions could be implemented, to varying degrees, among parents in the context of parenting groups networking in the community at large. For a description of this type of arrangement, see Brazelton and Greenspan's (2000) concept of a "Vertical Village" in *The Irreducible Needs of Children* (pp. 167–169).

Selective Separation

In an attempt to help a child who was experiencing serious symptoms, as in the example that follows, parents sometimes chose to take more extreme actions. In this type of "foster parenting," the child was either partially or totally cared for by substitute parenting figures.

For example, Mallory, at 3 months, cried for long periods of time and could not be comforted. Her mother, a quiet, reserved, immaculately dressed woman, treated the little girl as if she were an appendage or a part of her own body. Friends observed that she dressed the infant in stiff, uncomfortable outfits. This mother was not hostile, resentful, or nervous in caring for her new baby, but it seemed that the constant contact without feeling was literally draining the life and vitality from her infant.

At four months, Mallory had not yet begun to smile and had a pinched, dazed expression. She cried pitifully and would not make much eye contact with her parents. She would push hard against the parent who was holding and attempting to calm her.

At this time, Mallory's parents asked a couple they knew well to take care of their daughter, to fulfill the role of substitute parents for her. These friends offered the infant consistent warmth and interest and related to her with affection. The woman had an intuitive understanding of children and consistently intervened when the infant tried to avoid contact. She was able to successfully bring the child out of her withdrawn state through energetic yet nonintrusive intervention and play. The man offered unconditional warmth and affection to the little girl and took great pleasure in caring for her, an attitude that he successfully communicated to the child.

Although Mallory continued to have contact with her parents, her substitute parents were primarily responsible for her well-being and upbringing. The main goal was for her biological parents to gradually reestablish a good relationship with Mallory after working on themselves.

When Mallory became a toddler, the substitute parents had to deal with the problems she had in relating to other children and to adults. The couple firmly controlled her angry, acting-out behavior and rewarded her social responses with affection and tangible rewards. By the time she was 4 years old, Mallory's "real" self began to emerge, and she began to show signs of affection and intelligence. Later, she gradually learned how to appropriately express anger and frustration. As of this writing, she is a lively, attractive 20-year-old young woman, affectionate, creative, and emotionally invested in her life. Her parents remain extremely grateful to these substitute parents.

CONCLUSION

Parents who are defended inadvertently deprive their children of basic human qualities—their feelings, their compassion for others, and even their capacity for rationality, while attempting to spare them the pain that they themselves experienced. In this sense, parent's self-protective defenses are generally harmful to their loved ones. Yet it serves no purpose for parents to hate or punish themselves when they recognize that they are hurtful. It is more constructive for them to attempt to alter their child-rearing patterns—practices that often mirror their own parent's behaviors—than to blame themselves. However, it is difficult for clinicians to interrupt this cycle of guilt in parents and, at the same time, help them see how and why they act out toxic behaviors on their children. The crux of the therapeutic process involves parents' developing insight into the origins of their own defenses and limitations, which incidentally diminishes their guilt reactions and fosters positive movement. In the process of uncovering the source of their aggression and negative attitudes and working through the traumatic episodes endured in their own families-of-origin, parents can recover feeling for themselves and gain control over behaviors that reflected these destructive attitudes.

NOTES

1. See Robert Langs's (1982) *Psychotherapy: A Basic Text*, chap. 4, "A Model of the Therapeutic Process," in which he compared and differentiated the proper functioning of a therapist from that of a parent.
2. In his book *Becoming Attached*, Robert Karen (1994) noted that:

In the self-help literature directed at parents virtually no attention is paid to the emotional upheavals that the parent is likely to face—the disturbing return of long festering feelings, the sense of being driven to behave in ways that one would rather not think about, the haunting sensation of being inhabited by the ghost of one's own mother or father as one tries to relate to one's child. (p. 378)

3. Bugental (1986) found that children (age 7 to 12) were unresponsive to adults who communicated with duplicitous affect, "the polite smile," and other unnatural expressions.

4. In this section, we have condensed a number of meetings that took place over several weeks to illustrate the steps in the therapeutic process.

5. In exploring the etiology of abusive, indifferent, and avoidant behaviors, Fraiberg et al. (1980) observed in high-risk mothers that their "memory for the events of [their] childhood abuse, tyranny, and desertion was available in explicit and chilling detail. *What was not remembered was the associated affective experience*" (p. 195).

6. Also see Lieberman and Pawl's (1990) description of interventions with parents and infants identified as having disorganized patterns of attachment.

IV

PHILOSOPHICAL
CONSIDERATIONS

14

PROTECTING THE RIGHTS OF THE INDIVIDUAL IN COUPLES AND FAMILIES

I am the inferior of any man whose rights I trample under foot.
—Robert G. Ingersoll (1910, p. 202)

Most people underestimate the tyranny that exists in so many couples, families, and in relationships in general. As people in the friendship circle explored the kinds of behavior and emotional climates that are damaging to individuals, they began to formulate an implicit set of values that are enhancing rather than destructive to a person's well-being. In the course of putting these values and ethics into practice, they became increasingly aware that much of the unnecessary harm that people inflict on each other involves violations of individual human rights. They began to alter those behaviors in themselves that they saw as infringements on the rights of others and strengthened their beliefs regarding each individual's personal freedom and equality.

There are a number of ethical principles associated with the preservation of human rights that these people found to be meaningful guidelines for living. In exploring these values and ideals, it is worthwhile to compare the functions of a state or political system with those served by the couple and the family in terms of the extent to which they either enhance or intrude on the rights of the individual. The tyranny, power, and manipulations that exist within social systems can be compared to defensive interactions and inequities existing within traditional couple and family relationships. In both cases, the individual within the system are often seriously impaired.

SOCIAL SYSTEMS

In examining the functions served by a particular social system, it is important to consider the extent to which it provides for the welfare of its constituents. The ideal state would be concerned with economic security for all its members as well as the protection of their personal freedom and basic human rights. Its government would be based on certain philosophical principles that place value on the life of each person over the survival of the system.

In contrast, when protection of the state or political system takes precedence over the individual, the needs of most citizens are not served. Instead, they typically suffer on a personal, economic, and political level.[1] Governments that operate on this philosophy tend to view human rights issues as a low priority, which can set the stage for oppression and tyranny. Totalitarian or authoritarian states that demand conformity and submission impose a wide range of rules and restrictions on their citizens. On the other hand, a truly democratic state allows its citizens more personal freedom and mobility and provides opportunities for the improvement of their economic status.

Although all social systems involve a certain amount of compromise in relation to the rights of the individual, it is a matter of degree. Every modern society, including even the more democratic forms of government, generates social mores and institutions that effectively control the membership (Marcuse, 1955/1966). Foucault (1978) has stressed the emergence of a new form of societal control that coincided with the development of eighteenth-century capitalism. According to Foucault, the growth of capitalism requires the type of power that can "qualify, measure, appraise, and hierarchize [members of a society]" (p. 144).

In general, this type of social control and categorization, as well as conventional attitudes and stereotypical views promulgated by modern society, function to restrict people's thinking, increase their hostility, and negatively affect their behavior toward one another. Emphasizing that mechanisms of social or psychological control exist in all systems, whether small or large, Barber, Bean, and Erickson (2002) argued that "violation of an individual's psychological world is a phenomenon that is not restricted to the parent–child relationship, but . . . appears to be a feature of a variety of different interpersonal relationships, as well as an individual's experience in institutional settings" (p. 282).

In our opinion, instead of challenging or attempting to modify destructive family practices, our society tends to collude with and support the formation of fantasy bonds within the couple and family. For example, the recent emphasis on strengthening divorce laws and the attempt to institute tax reforms to benefit married partners (Crouch, n.d.; McManus, n.d.; Wallerstein, Lewis, & Blakeslee, 2000) may function to preserve the *form* of the couple dyad or family constellation, while disguising the fact that the *substance* or quality has deteriorated.

With respect to the care of children and child welfare, the American society's idealization of the family, regardless of the degree of its dysfunctionality, often helps its members avoid crucial issues that are vital to mental health. In many cases, the rights of the children who are victims of abuse and neglect are disregarded or their trauma is downplayed. According to McFarlane and van der Kolk (1996), the larger society has "a stake in believing that the trauma is not really the cause of the victims' suffering" (p. 27).

COUPLE AND FAMILY SYSTEMS

As described in chapter 12, the ideal couple or family would attempt to gratify the physical, economic, and emotional needs of each individual and enhance the personal development of children. There would be a minimum number of rules and restrictions, allowing for optimal freedom and autonomy. In contrast, the less-than-ideal couple or family tends to function in a manner that exerts excessive control over each person through rules and rituals that favor obligation over choice and image over self. Unnecessary restrictions, manipulations, and power plays, as well as the mystification needed to deny the fact that such controls exist, cause considerable harm. Immaturity, hostility, duplicity, role-playing in couples and families, the illusion of connection between the partners and other family members, and microsuicidal behaviors have devastating effects on the minds and feelings of young people. Each of these behaviors can be viewed ethically as representing an infringement on the child's basic human rights.

In an important sense, it is unethical as well as illogical to place primary value on a social institution or system, whether it be the couple or the family, without considering the well-being of the individual men, women, and children involved. Any system is merely an abstraction, whereas the people involved are real, living entities. Yet many marital and family therapists implicitly endorse this conventional approach and consider "Can this marriage or family be saved?" (M. Rosen, 1994, 2002) rather than "Can these human beings be helped or saved?" as being the most important question to address in their work.

In recent years, there has been a focus of attention on specific forms of interpersonal relationships in which survival of the dyad or system appeared to be valued over the prosperity as well as the physical and emotional health of the individual. Clinicians and theorists have written extensively about destructive elements in dyads and family systems that are similar in many respects to those in a totalitarian state (Ruszczynski & Fisher, 1995b;

Slavik, Carlson, & Sperry, 1998). In introducing the book, *Intrusiveness and Intimacy in the Couple*, Ruszczynski and Fisher (1995a) declared that "sometimes the wish to be close, to be intimate, is associated with a concern for the other. . . . Sometimes, however, the apparent intimacy is an expression of an intrusive determination to control the other" (p. 1). Slavik et al. (1998) described in considerable detail the manipulations and counter-manipulations used by partners in "passive–aggressive couples." "If passive methods fail and anxiety and frustration mount, the individual may switch to angry, emotional outbursts centering on issues of exploitation, unfair treatment, and unappreciation" (p. 300).

A number of studies have delineated suppressive and coercive practices in interactions within these couples and family constellations (Barber, 2002; Tedeschi & Felson, 1994). Their findings indicate that individuals commit the most egregious human rights violations within their couple and family relationships. In fact, marital partners and family members often treat each other in ways they would never treat an acquaintance, coworker, or friend. For example, according to Tedeschi and Felson (1994): "People who rarely if ever use coercion with others make an exception in the case of their children. When these coercive actions are severe, they are often referred to as *child abuse*" (p. 287). These researchers also noted that social mores, cultural attitudes, and the legal system support coercive practices by parents:

> Parental use of coercion is supported normatively and legally by the larger society. Normatively, parents are expected to use some level of coercion with their children. . . . The state also provides legal supports for parents in their use of coercion. . . . The state backs up parental authority over children with its own coercive powers; thus, parents of defiant children can get assistance from juvenile courts. (p. 292)

Barber and Harmon (2002) called attention to several aspects of psychological control exerted by parents including constraining, invalidating, love withdrawal, guilt induction, personal attack on the child, questioning family loyalty, blaming the child for other family members' problems, and erratic emotional behavior on the part of parents who may vacillate between caring and attacking behaviors. A number of other theorists have described couple and family systems that demand loyalty, whether it is deserved or not. In these relationships, control through guilt and a sense of obligation characterizes the interactions between members and supports the perpetuation of destructive family ties (Boszormenyi-Nagy & Sparks, 1984).

To varying degrees, most social systems and institutions ignore important issues of human rights. Similarly many families intrude on and violate the rights of their members to develop as unique individuals. Many parents fail to provide conditions in which the child's real personality and special qualities can naturally emerge. This abuse of personal freedom can eventually evolve into an issue of human rights within the person; the child who is mistreated goes on to mistreat him- or herself in much the same manner. The damage is then perpetuated in new relationships, and perhaps most painfully, in relation to one's children, thereby completing the cycle. Therefore, it appears that a discussion of human rights issues, values, and ethics is essential if we are to adequately explore the dynamics of couples, family relationships, and social structures.

MANIPULATION AND COERCION IN INTERPERSONAL RELATIONSHIPS

Manipulations and coercive power plays are manifested in three important ways in personal relationships: (a) bullying, domination, and the use of force; (b) threats that arouse fear reactions; and (c) maneuvers that trigger guilt feelings in others.

Domineering or authoritarian individuals control other people overtly through aggressive behaviors that reward and punish or indicate approval and disapproval. Sometimes they impose actual physical punishment or act out violent behavior in intimate relationships. Tedeschi and Felson (1994) stressed the fact that:

> Superiority in physical size, strength, and fighting skills may make it more likely that an individual will engage in physical violence. . . . Lack of an ability to achieve influence by noncoercive means increases the likelihood that a person will become involved in a coercive interaction. (p. 361)

In his book *The Batterer,* Dutton (1995a) noted that "although surveys have shown that there are 2.5 million wife assaults in the United States each year, not all of these are of the same gravity" (p. 22). James Gilligan (2001) and Hamish Sinclair (2001) have called attention to what they describe as the "male-role belief system" as being an important factor contributing to domestic and criminal violence. In a remedial program based on "restorative justice" rather than "retributive justice," violent or abusive men learn "how they have been imposing a hierarchical structure on their relationships with people, in which one person (or sex) has to be regarded as superior, and the other as inferior" (J. Gilligan, 2001, p. 127). Delineating the beliefs and assumptions that can lead to domineering, coercive, or violent actions, Sinclair (2001) lists the male's "expectation of services" and "expectation of authority" (male authority) as two major contributing factors. Examples of expectation of services include beliefs such as "She needs to have the house cleaned. . . . She needs to pick me up from the bar when I am ready."

Female violence, although less prevalent than male violence, nonetheless exists in disturbed couple relationships. The psychodynamics of female dominance and aggression as manifested in domestic relations have been delineated by Pearson (1997) and Motz (2001). Motz asserted that women's "acts of violence and offences [are] ... symbols and expressions of earlier conflicts, many of which can be traced to very early experiences in relation to the violent women's own experience ... [of being mothered]" (p. 7).

In a similar manner, these power differentials and superior–inferior roles are acted out in many family constellations, often with little or no awareness on the part of the participants. For example, according to Tedeschi and Felson (1994): "Studies of parent–child interaction in American families reveal high levels of coercive behavior, including bodily force, verbal and physical punishment, physical isolation, and deprivation of resources. ... Physical force is used more often against younger children than older children" (pp. 290–291).

In their studies of coercive actions, these researchers have made a clear distinction between coercion and aggression:

> Coercion is used in an attempt to gain compliance or to administer harm, whereas aggression refers only to acts intended to do harm. Coercive actions refer not only to ... physical abuse of children but also to deprivations or admonishments of parents who punish the misbehavior of their children. (pp. 349–350)

Threats are considered to be coercive actions by Tedeschi and Felson (1994). In their work, these researchers described two types of threats—contingent and noncontingent. "A *contingent threat* is a communication demanding some form of compliance and indicates that the source will impose harm on a target for noncompliance" (p. 169). On the other hand, "A *noncontingent threat* is a coercive action that is usually intended to frighten or humiliate the target person. Fear and humiliation are harms imposed on the target by the threatener; hence, noncontingent threats may be conceived as a form of punishment" (p. 169). Threats of reprisal or loss of economic security by members of a couple or family are clearly intimidating because they arouse fears of punishment and the potential loss of resources in the "target" person.

Abandonment threats are a particularly effective means of control. Many parents use threats of abandonment or sending the child away to promote obedience (Bowlby, 1973). Needless to say, this is destructive because it arouses extreme fear and insecurity as young children are completely dependent on parents for survival. Even though parents typically have no intention of actually carrying out such threats, children tend to take their parents at their word and are not necessarily reassured when they fail to follow through on their threats.

These maneuvers are effective because abandonment fears are experienced with dread by so many people. Even in a bad relationship, if there are threats of being left by an undesirable partner, or if the partner actually leaves, one still suffers emotional trauma. The reason behind this paradox is that being left supports internal thoughts and feelings adverse to the self, feelings that one is unlovable, bad, inadequate, or worthless.

Many marriages and family constellations are characterized by controlling behaviors that are less obvious but nonetheless intimidating. According to Slavik et al. (1998) withholding, controlling, or passive–aggressive behaviors are present in many marriages. These clinicians contended,

> A non-PA [passive–aggressive] partner may feel undermined and resentful. . . . But because resistance is covert, a person using PA methods is able to be nice, soft-spoken, and perhaps even reasonable, whereas a demanding party gets louder, demanding, more shrewish. PA behavior is more effective in a marriage arena than assertive actions would be. (p. 302)

Clearly, these guilt- and anger-provoking responses on the part of one member or another cause considerable harm. There is a kind of terrorism practiced in many personal relationships that makes one individual accountable for the unhappiness of the other. The tyranny of weakness and illness exerted by self-denying or self-destructive individuals clearly has a powerful manipulative effect. For example, tears will frequently establish submission to a person's will. Irrational or microsuicidal behavior is also intimidating. Habitual drinking often controls the behavior of a spouse and family. Threats of self-harm or actual suicide are particularly effective.

Many people unconsciously use self-denying or self-destructive machinations to gain leverage over mates and family members. Although these manipulations are often effective, they are not worth the price to the perpetrators. Indeed, all passive manipulations of control are destructive to both parties. For example, in describing the passive–aggressive couple, Slavik et al. (1998) pointed out the costs inherent in acting out withholding or self-denying behaviors and the powerful resistance to altering such patterns: "Individuals using passive–aggressiveness may decompensate into anxiety and depression in order to delay change and retain a noncooperative relationship" (p. 303).

DEVELOPMENT OF IMPLICIT VALUES REGARDING HUMAN RIGHTS IN THE FRIENDSHIP CIRCLE

Men and women in the friendship circle were deeply concerned about disrespectful and manipulative patterns of interacting with their spouses and children. As a consequence, they devoted themselves to facing these issues honestly and attempted to work through problematic aspects of their relationships. In particular, they increased their awareness of the types of communications and actions that impinged on each other's human rights and personal freedoms.

Within the forum of the ongoing discussions described in the previous chapters, the participants learned more about overt and covert parental aggression. They realized that they had extended their habitual styles of relating within their marriages to their children and that they often felt "connected" and possessive in a proprietary sense. They became increasingly aware of the times they overstepped their children's boundaries and intruded on their privacy. In their talks, they revealed the ways in which they violated the rights of their children to choose their own careers, select their own friends, and develop as separate individuals with their own distinct identities.

By identifying the specific behaviors and manipulations they used to intimidate and restrict their mates and children, they were able to gain control over actions they disapproved of in themselves. For example, in a parenting discussion, Luke recalled the times he had been coercive in disciplining his son, and then remembered being treated in the same manner by his father. Afterward, he felt that he would never again be able to treat his son punitively:

Luke (46): I remembered, because of some of the things we've been talking about, the ways that I've treated my son— not really physically abusing him, although I would spank him. I remember yelling at him and telling him that he had no right to think things, he had no right to feel a particular way. I recall thinking to myself, "what right does he have?" and then I would say something that would deny him his rights.

Remembering those incidents made me feel something, I think for the first time, in terms of my being treated the same way. I remembered my father and uncle saying that to me, that I had no right, but furiously yelling at me and screaming that I had no right to think that or be this or that way. First I felt it in terms of the way that I was with my son, and then I could see that I was treated exactly the same way.

Raymond (38): It's like the children had no rights at all, none. And whatever the parents wanted to do in order to get them to be socialized human beings was justified. I can remember things like "You better watch that. You're gonna spoil that kid." Or when I was a kid, I'd hear "You know better. You know better than to do that," if I did something accidentally. I used to hear that all the time. "You know better."

Louis (52): I think I was that way a lot with my children. Right was on my side, and with a vengeance. I could go after it, I could really bore in, because it's approved; this is the way it's done. But sometimes that veneer would get cracked, and an explosive rage would come out at the kids, and that would be the shocking part, like "What am I, a monster?" And you can't take it back when that happens. But most of the time, right is on your side. I think in a lot of households, there's a lot of these kind of statements: "You've played enough for one day," "It's time for your nap now," "Don't disturb other people." This is the stamp that children have to be put into. Society is a lot on the side of wiping out the rights of children.

Becoming Aware of and Modifying Behaviors That Intrude on the Rights of Others

Individuals in the group of friends have attempted to objectively examine interactions within their couple and family relationships. They have focused on understanding the dynamics of what they considered to be harmful communications and behaviors in all their close associations and made concerted efforts to modify these patterns.

Manipulations Through Guilt and Anger

Men and women found that they often attempted to control the people closest to them through the manipulation of the other person's guilt and anger. This type of manipulation worked because people have been taught early in life that they "belong" to their families. Thus, most people do not have a sense of belonging to themselves or feel that they have a right to their own lives. For these reasons, they are subject to manipulations that play on their guilt. Both partners in a couple learn that they can successfully restrict the lives of their mates. However, these maneuvers are counterproductive because they provoke angry responses and tension in the relationship.

Manipulations through guilt are particularly characteristic of relationships in which people have formed a fantasy bond as a substitute for the love, affection, and friendship that once existed between them. Although restrictions and conventions are often effective in controlling the behavior of each partner, the individuals involved lose a sense of dignity and self-respect. People *can* be badgered or nagged into the desired behavior, but the rewards are short-lived.

The Power Exerted by a Sexually Withholding Partner

A relationship in which the partners' desire for sexual contact is unequal tends to create desperate feelings in one of the partners. We have found that in general both men and women hold back sexually and emotionally from their mates when they revert to a defended stance; however, the tendency to withhold appears to be greater in women. Because men tend to idealize the women in their life (in their attempt to recapture the bliss of the original imagined connection with the mother), the woman's lack of response has tremendous leverage in the relationship. When a man becomes chronically hungry toward a woman, he becomes more passive, desperate, and unattractive. His partner, in turn, becomes further alienated from him because she finds him less appealing and now has justification for rejecting him.

In the friendship circle, as women revealed the basic strategies they used in their relationships with men, we observed that, at the point where women began to reveal their specific patterns of withholding and became open about the underlying anger and resentment, many men reacted angrily. Some of the men used the new insights into this process to support their cynicism and hostility toward women. This reaction strengthened our hypothesis that both men and women have considerable fear and resistance to perceiving women (and their mothers) in more realistic ways.

Male Vanity and Female Control

In discussions about male vanity or macho attitudes, a number of men revealed how they had acted out the belief system of superiority and corresponding belief in the inferiority of women. For example, one man described how he routinely expected his wife to pick him up at the airport on his return from a business trip. In addition, he spoke of the difficulties he was encountering as he attempted to give up a deep-seated belief that it was a woman's job exclusively to keep the house clean and to care for the children.

In the same discussion, many women disclosed how they had played on their mate's need to maintain an image of exaggerated importance. Although they resented men's demand for a validation of this image, they also realized that it gave them leverage and control over the relationship. A divorced woman admitted that during her marriage, she had built up her husband as part of an unconscious contract to ensure that he would take care of her. After their marriage was over, she came to realize that fears and insecurities left over from her childhood had contributed to her compulsion to use this form of control.

> I knew how to listen to him with an enraptured look on my face. I knew how to make him feel that he was the smartest person I knew,

about practically every subject. He had a huge amount of vanity about being a great writer, and I thought to myself, *"I can treat him like a great writer and he'll need me for that."*

I saw all the areas where he was weak and I knew that those were inroads. I knew that I could create dependency in him. Then, as the relationship went on, I hated him when he would say stupid, embarrassing things in public situations. I hated him, but I never once told him. I never once treated him like a person. I never gave him a chance. I was totally involved in this manipulation and hated myself for it.

I knew he would give me anything I wanted as long as I built him up, especially in the areas where he felt weak and that were really important to him. That was the deal, and it's that way in most marriages I see. Men will do anything women want them to do as long as they support the man's vanity. They'll support you, take care of you, and you don't have to do anything.

In general, manipulations that support men's illusions of superiority are debilitating to the men and damage each partner's sense of reality. Often when a woman is more successful or intelligent in an area than the men in her life, she continues to relate as though she were inferior. We have observed that women tend to submit to men's so-called superiority in matters of logic, practicality, and worldliness. When a woman surrenders her individuality and gives up her dignity and self-respect to build up a man's sense of importance, the result is a tragic personal loss for herself and her mate.

A Martyred or Victimized Posture

From the beginning, women in the friendship circle were exceptionally bold and forthright in bringing out the truth regarding passive–aggressive manipulations in couple relationships. At the same time that they were disclosing how they maintained a victimized position in relation to their partners and to men in general, they were fighting for their rights personally, sexually, and vocationally. In their movement toward independence, they no longer saw men as holding them back; instead they perceived their limitations as largely self-imposed, the result of internalizing their mother's passive–aggressive attitudes and often the guilt about surpassing her. The information that women revealed in the group discussions was shared in the spirit of equality. In giving up a victimized posture, they achieved considerable strength and maturity and developed a different perspective on themselves and men. In the same discussions, a number of men also revealed passive manipulations they often used in an intimate relationship, such as complaining, sulking, and withdrawing from communications with their partners.

In general, the tendencies of many women to be passive and to control others through acting weak or helpless appear to result more from suppression and social bias than from biological determinants. Carol Gilligan (1996, 2002) and Jean Baker Miller (1976) have pointed out one important reason that women feel compelled to resort to negative power plays in their relationships: "It is not surprising . . . that a subordinate group resorts to disguised and indirect ways of acting and reacting. While these actions are designed to accommodate and please the dominant group, they often, in fact, contain hidden defiance" (J. Miller, 1976, p. 10).

Over many generations, the internalization of outwardly compliant yet inwardly defiant behavior patterns has become as detrimental to women's development as the social forces that made their use necessary. Passive–aggressive responses result in manipulative behaviors that may only be partially conscious, yet they pose serious obstructions to harmonious relations between men and women.

Threats of Self-Destructive Behavior

To varying degrees, all self-destructive and suicidal behavior has a manipulative element. Self-defeating, self-destructive actions induce feelings of fear, anger, guilt, or alarm in others. All self-denying, self-limiting, dangerous, and risk-taking behaviors have a compelling component that demands a response. Family members are acutely sensitive to covert or nonverbal suicide threats, even though the manifest behavior may or may not be suicidal.

People who are closely involved with a person chronically engaged in self-harming behaviors also experience emotional turmoil and stress. Their loved one's behavior is intimidating for two principal reasons: (a) because of the fear of actual object loss, and (b) because of the guilt inherent in feeling that one is responsible for another person's life or death. Intense feelings of guilt stem from a fear of feeling this heavy burden of responsibility—that is, of being implicated somehow in the destruction of another person.

Families in which one parent abuses alcohol or drugs, is chronically ill or is severely self-destructive are often dysfunctional. However, any family in which one parent is excessively self-denying or feels martyred is also dysfunctional. Manipulations on the part of a self-sacrificing parent or parents who use sickness or threats of falling apart emotionally interfere with the development of autonomy and self-reliance in the children.

In relationships characterized by patterns of manipulation, we found that it was often beneficial for the individuals to separate temporarily and then come together again on a voluntary basis out of a renewed sense of choice and not out of loyalty or obligation. In fact, the only hope for any couple's emotional health is that they sustain their freedom of choice and not limit or place demands on each other through rules and restrictions.

Developing Behaviors That Enhance a Sense of Well-Being in Oneself and Others

As described in the introduction, people in the friendship circle were strongly motivated to conceptualize and then develop qualities and behaviors in themselves that would increase their self-esteem and sense of well-being. They were particularly concerned with building more constructive associations with one another that would meet the needs of each individual and support his or her personal development and movement toward a fulfilling life.

Respect for the Boundaries of One's Partner and Children

Juxtaposed against the background of the traditional family units in which these people were raised were the new forms of family structures and interactions that gradually evolved. As children, many had experienced family life that was characterized by a false sense of togetherness and an image of merged identity, which had been detrimental to their development as separate and autonomous individuals. As Murray Bowen (1978) put it: "In the average nuclear family . . . the spouses are emotionally 'fused' with each other and with the children, and it is difficult to get far beyond the fusion or to do more than react and counter-react emotionally" (p. 545). Many people recalled their parents using phrases and colloquialisms that supported this image of oneness, for example: "Now it's time for *our* nap." "Don't *we* feel happy this morning?" Remembering how they felt in these situations motivated them to refrain from talking to their children in the same disrespectful manner.

People reported boundary violations in which parents had foisted their interests on them or had attempted to live through their accomplishments or performances. For example, Brad, a judge, recognized that the effects of his mother's intrusiveness had persisted into his adult life, limiting his ability to feel socially at ease:

> The more I thought about it, the more I realized that I was abused. It didn't make much difference what type of abuse it was. I was never hit or beaten ever, I mean, never. But I do know that my mother took over my entire life from a very early age, and that I just became a performing object. I was two or three years old, and she was teaching me how to read and giving me dancing lessons. I mean, my entire life was out of my hands. I was always performing. If there was a party and I was asleep, I'd be awakened and called out of my bedroom into the living room, and I'd have to read something or do a dance or whatever it was. I mean, it was an endless succession of performances.
>
> I know that now I can't go into a room with people in it without thinking about what I'm going to do. What am I going to do to please

these people, or what am I going to do to make people like me in some way? Since I've become aware of the way my mother treated me, I've been making a concerted effort not to treat my children in the same way.

Respect for Partner's Freedom and Priorities Separate From Oneself

As men and women in the friendship circle became more independent and self-reliant, those who were in close, committed relationships or who were married began to demonstrate a genuine respect for the boundaries, wants, and priorities of their mates. They recognized that loving implies enjoying the emergence of the other as an individual and a sensitivity to his or her wants. In recognizing that their partner's desires and aspirations were as important as their own, they tried not to manipulate or interfere with activities or friendships that they valued. Instead, they supported their partner's goals and priorities even when these goals were separate from their own.

For example, Amy and Darren had been married a month when Amy had an opportunity to go on an ocean crossing, something she had always dreamed of. She loved sailing and was an active and enthusiastic crew member. However, she was reluctant to go because Darren was unable to take off from work for the two-week voyage. Amy knew that Darren loved sailing even more than she did, and she empathized with his frustration in missing the trip. Darren encouraged Amy to take the trip and said, "I want you to go on that sail and have a great time. I'll miss you a lot, but I know how much sailing means to you." Amy felt touched by Darren's support, and when the couple was reunited, both partners reported feeling closer to each other than they had before the voyage.

Honesty and Integrity in Communication

In recalling interactions within their families of origin, people became more aware that the double messages they had received from parents had constituted a violation of their human rights. The duplicity and dishonesty manifested in many families fracture people's sense of reality, their belief in the veracity of their perceptions, which is essential for maintaining good mental health. In a discussion, a number of people revealed how they had manipulated partners through deception and duplicitous communications. They also disclosed negative voices that influenced them to engage in this form of manipulative behavior. Their understanding of the psychodynamics involved in these duplicitous communications enabled them to be more honest and straightforward in expressing their wants and desires in their intimate relationships:

> *Bill (35):*   I think there are all kind of manipulations be-
> tween men and women, to get what they want

from the other person, I mean subtle ways. Women acting like they're not interested so the man becomes more attentive. The man doing the same thing.

Andrea (46): There's a book about it, "The Code," or something like that, to tell you how to manipulate a man so you can get him. Everything in that book is based on dishonesty.

Bill: I think the deception starts early on in the courtship process where the man or the woman might try to appear more wealthy, look better, put on their absolute best appearance when they meet the person. I had a friend who borrowed my car and alluded to it as his car— he wanted to put his best foot forward—well, more than put his best foot forward, he was putting his best friend's car forward! [laughter] But men will try to cast themselves in a better light, make themselves more attractive, more powerful.

Robert Firestone (65): They lie, actually, or distort the truth about themselves.

Bill: Absolutely, or if they have a terrible past, maybe the man (or the woman) was in jail, he doesn't say it, or they might have a very promiscuous background and they're deceptive about that. In the courtship process I believe there are a lot of lies, a lot of deception, a lot of omissions. And then it continues throughout the relationship.

Russell (37): If there's something about the woman that bothers me, instead of just saying it to her directly, or even hearing things she might say directly to me about something that might not be desirable about me, I have a tendency to kind of filter all that out. And then I say things that are going to keep us together.

Tom (36): There is a feeling that if you get somebody that you like a lot that you probably wouldn't find anybody else. Like *"You'd better hold on to that one because you don't find that many choices that you like that much."*

Andrea: I would act like the man was much more interesting than I thought he was and I would always act like whatever he was saying was just fascinating and brilliant. I'd never disagree, never state my opinions strongly if they were different than his.

Joanna (28): I did that, too. I acted as if my boyfriend was the world to me. I gave that impression by falling apart. If I didn't get all his attention, I would fall apart. That was a deception because I had a whole life of my own, my own interests, before I met him, so it was a deception to act like he was my whole life.

Andrea: I didn't want to admit that it mattered to me, that it matters to me to be loved.

Robert Firestone: So you have kind of a defense of "I don't need anyone."

Julia (21): For me, if I show a man that he's really important to me and that I really do love him, as soon as I have that thought, even, I don't even have to say it, but as soon as I have that thought, I think to myself, "Don't say it, just don't show it, don't let him see how you really feel."

Robert Firestone: Why?

Julia: "Because as soon as you say it, as soon as you let him know, then everything's going to come down on you. The ax is going to fall."

Robert Firestone: What would he do? Why wouldn't he just appreciate it?

Julia: "You see, if you keep him hanging, then you'll always be able to keep him. But as soon as you let him know how you feel, you become vulnerable, then he might not like you that much any more. You're not that appealing."

Andrea: You don't want to feel the pain that you used to feel. I really believe that.

Robert Firestone: You don't want to be hurt again, is that right? You don't want to be vulnerable to be hurt again.

Treating Children as Equals Rather Than With Condescension

In our work with parents and children, we have been impressed with the mistaken notions many people have about adults as distinguished from children. Most people perceive adults as more mature emotionally than children, based on the assumption that adults have somehow outgrown or transcended the fears, turmoil, and pain of their childhoods. This supposition is generally false; residuals of the hurt child exist in every person and are acted out in petty arguments, in expressions of intense jealousy, and in desperate moves to preserve dependent, symbiotic relationships. Yet most adults treat children in a condescending manner and with a good deal of role playing that is not authentic or appropriate. Much of what is passed on to the child, based on parents' experience and so-called emotional maturity, is dishonest and demeaning to the child.

In their talks with the teenagers and later with the younger children, the adults in the friendship circle have all but dispensed with patronizing ways of treating and communicating with children. It is accurate to say that the adolescents in the original teenage discussion group took the lead in a movement that led to bridging the generation gap. They challenged the hypercritical, judgmental attitudes that they had grown up with and spoke out against condescending and disrespectful treatment. They began to ask for, and earn and inspire, real acknowledgment and respect from their parents.

When the parents of these teenagers were first challenged to relate to their children more as equals, with mutual respect, many of them felt threatened. When their children started to call them by their first names rather than mom or dad, they felt as if they were losing something vital and basic to the relationship. As the group discussions progressed, however, the parents realized that they were losing the form of their parental roles but were gaining the substance of a real relationship with their children. Through honest relating, they were breaking down a fantasy of connection that had actually kept them apart. They became aware that, because of this change, their children no longer *belonged* to them in that sense, but were becoming their friends. Since then, the children (who are now adults) have maintained these friendships and have actively sought out their parents' company for the past 25 years.

CONCLUSION

The ethical principles in the small society of the friendship circle were shaped by a key concept from which all other values flowed: All people should be free to speak their minds, without inhibition, even if they speak the unspeakable. The manner in which this right was protected for each person is what separates the internal dynamics of this group from traditional family and cultural practices that are unnecessarily restrictive. The society that emerged is based on the American ideal of democracy but also contains a powerful emotional bill of rights that has been fiercely protected. The overall result has been an expansion of self-knowledge and understanding of other people, enlightenment about relationships, and a movement toward personal freedom that is uncharacteristic of the society at large.

In a certain sense, the people in the friendship circle have redefined the concept of power, particularly as manifested in couple and family relationships. Dispensing with definitions of a power differential in terms of "might makes right" or dominance and submission in a relationship, they defined *personal power* as knowledge and integrity within oneself and the capacity to honestly pursue one's personal goals in life while maintaining a compassionate, respectful view of others. In other words, they favored honest selfishness over dishonest selflessness and viewed the accumulation of this form of personal power and self-respect as an ideal pursuit in life. Their experiences and personal successes in living more honestly have validated the truth that individuals concerned with the proper pursuit of personal power tend to respect the rights and personal freedom of others and that this pursuit leads to a more satisfying life.

NOTE

1. Simone Weil (1949/1952) would add spiritual suffering to the damage incurred by individuals living within a nondemocratic or authoritarian state. Weil also asserted that "it may happen that the obligation toward a collectivity which is in danger reaches the point of entailing a total sacrifice. But it does not follow from this that collectivities are superior to human beings" (p. 8).

15

SOCIETAL FORCES:
MALEVOLENT AND BENEVOLENT

The principles of the good society call for a concern with an order of being . . . where it matters supremely that the human person is inviolable, that reason shall regulate the will, that truth shall prevail over error.

—Walter Lippmann (1955, p. 165)

In pursuit of a more fulfilling life, individuals are besieged by destructive forces both from without and from within. They are assaulted by negative social pressures that work together with their own defenses, and the resulting feedback system makes the project of becoming a person, a unique and autonomous human being, extraordinarily difficult.

THE EXTENSION OF INDIVIDUAL DEFENSES INTO A MALEVOLENT SOCIAL SYSTEM

As described in previous chapters, people form defenses to cope with excessive conditions of stress experienced in growing up. These individual patterns combine to produce cultural attitudes and social mores that shape a society. Once established, cultural prerogatives and social institutions based on defense formation reflect back on each of us (Billig, 1987; Billig et al., 1988; Mead, 1934/1967), interfering with our movement toward individuation and depriving us of vital experiences necessary for pursuing our personal freedom and reaching our true potential (J. Henry, 1963). Marcuse (1955/1966) described this collusive, reciprocal relationship between individuals and an oppressive society as follows: "The struggle against freedom reproduces itself in the psyche of man, as the self-repression of the repressed individual, and his self-repression in turn sustains his masters and their institutions" (p. 16).

The Function of the Family in Socializing the Child

In performing its function of socializing the child, the family imparts the values, mores, and belief systems of the culture. Despite the fact that each family has its own unique lifestyle and distinctive set of beliefs, there are many general attitudes, behaviors, roles, and routines in a given society that most people accept uncritically and attempt to convey to their children. These social mores are transmitted, along with parents' defensive habit patterns, through instruction, reward, and punishment, as well as through nonverbal cues and the process of imitation. Unfortunately, the socialization process in the nuclear family categorizes, labels, and puts the stamp of conformity on most children. Faulty child-rearing practices impose a negative voice, a self-punishing, self-regulating system, on children that cuts deeply into their feeling reactions and conditions their thoughts and behaviors to meet certain accepted standards.

Children are first exposed to parents' defenses and affected by the idiosyncratic child-rearing practices in the family in which they are raised (Montgomery, 1988). As they expand their boundaries into the neighborhood, the school, and the larger society, they continually encounter new imprinting and socialization processes. For centuries, people in all cultures have created increasingly complex institutions, conventions, and belief systems in an attempt to adapt to interpersonal pain and death anxiety by dulling feeling and awareness and by limiting the life experience. Each generation has been raised by people whose ancestors were themselves reared by parents who experienced personal suffering, feared death as a reality, and defensively retreated from investing in their lives. Each succeeding generation has added its own building blocks to the system of denial and accommodation, contributing to the increased rigidity and power of the defensive process. Although there have been uprisings and challenges to the status quo along the way, over time there appears to have been a negative trend toward increased suppression of feelings.

The Individual in Society

Most adult members of society remain prisoners of their own internal programming while supporting the socialization processes that damaged them. Negative social pressures exerted by other defended individuals, wielded by the power structure, and perpetuated through contemporary mores and practices generally have a delimiting effect on each person's personal freedom, healthy sexuality, integrity, and the natural drive for affiliation with others.

The larger society today has become saturated with contradictory messages, banalities, and updated myths that continually distort and reconstruct our sense of reality, with drastic consequences. The trivialization of real experience through the simulation of experience presented in the media-saturated televisual culture destroys an individual's sense of uniqueness by blurring the distinction between appearance and reality. Images of pseudo-sexuality collide with images of dying AIDS victims, images of lifestyles of abundance collide with images of starving children, images of terrorist attacks and genocide collide with the bland and deathless images of sitcoms and movies of the week.

Society is in collusion with the self-parenting process in each individual and supports the preference for choosing self-nourishing fantasies and habits over real experience and real relationships. We are asked to consume a meaningless series of commodities that we are conditioned to need, in spite of the fact that most of them are addictive, trivial, or simply useless. The culture presents us with images in place of experiences, data in place of wisdom, spectatorship in place of participation. It appears that we are progressively forfeiting much or our humanness, losing contact with feeling, embracing self-deception, and accepting substitute gratifications that destroy the real self in favor of merely provisional roles technologically guaranteed to make us "feel better."

Marcuse (1964) has labeled the conditioned needs described as "false needs." In his essay, "One Dimensional Society," he argued that:

> The intensity, the satisfaction and even the character of human needs, beyond the biological level, have always been preconditioned. Whether or not the possibility of doing or leaving, enjoying or destroying, possessing or rejecting something is seized as a *need* depends on whether or not it can be seen as desirable and necessary for the prevailing societal institutions and interests. (p. 4)

Why do most individuals continue to accept the status quo, comply with conventional restrictions, and conform to accepted prejudicial and stereotypical attitudes? The answers are complex and multidetermined and, in part, can be traced back to the basic assumptions and beliefs that are held by members of a social system. These assumptions include (a) the belief that human beings are basically inadequate or deficient in and of themselves, that they are born bad and require rehabilitation, cleansing, and purification; (b) the presumption that an individual is abnormal unless he or she preserves the couple, family, or accepted social norms; (c) the notion that freedom necessarily leads to anarchy and chaos, and that therefore rules and restrictions are essential; and (d) beliefs about the nature of love, that it is constant and invariant and that parents have unconditional love for their children (Badinter, 1980/1981; Hrdy, 1999).[1] These assumptions are reinforced through a variety of mixed messages and social pressures that assault people throughout their lifetime. Although it is possible for people to work their way free of these assumptions, messages, and pressures, doing so requires an understanding and recognition of how deeply they influence most individuals in our society.

The Mixed Messages of Society

An accurate perception of reality is central to an individual's well-being; to mislead or confuse another person's perception of the world is extremely destructive (Bateson, 1972). Mixed messages are pervasive throughout our culture. The hypocrisy and duplicity inherent in these double messages begin with the individual and extend first to the couple, then to the emerging family, and finally spread to society at large. For example, *people are encouraged to compete in every area of life, yet at the same time successful people are often viewed with suspicion and disapproval*—"How many people did they have to step on to get where they are?"—and this sets up an essential conflict. If people continue to pursue their goals in a competitive situation, they experience considerable guilt in relation to their rivals, whereas if they retreat from competing, they experience a painful form of existential guilt for turning their backs on their own wants and desires. They may attempt to rationalize their withdrawal by proclaiming that they are still pursuing personal and career goals, and this leads to duplicitous communications. This lack of integrity further intensifies their guilt.

Within the couple, partners often try to maintain a fantasy that they really love each other long after the romance, affection, and sexuality have deteriorated. Men and women who have formed a fantasy bond find it difficult to face the reality of their lack of feeling for each other. This denial of reality within the couple has a fundamental effect on the family and the society at large. The need to protect this fantasy leads to a collusion within the family that is entered into by society.

Cynical attitudes are widespread in our society, yet personal happiness and fulfillment are the stated goals. Everyone claims to want happiness and many people try to act as though they are seeking it. Yet if happiness were truly being sought, the search would interrupt one of our most well-established defenses: the hundreds of cynical thoughts we entertain about the world, about ourselves, and about other people.

"There are no honest politicians."
"You can't fight city hall."
"Lawyers are just out to get your money."

"The rich and powerful must be corrupt."

"People are poor just because they don't want to get out and work."

"Teenagers are only interested in taking drugs and having a good time."

"It's ridiculous to pursue a romantic relationship after a certain age."

"You can't change human nature."

"It's stupid to get attached to someone because you'll just get hurt."

These cynical attitudes have an insidious effect because they reinforce each individual's defense system. Social pressure to conform to societal mores and expectations based on the fallacies just listed help preserve the status quo.

Social Pressure

Social pressure is a strong pull from important people in one's family, and from society in general, to imitate the behavior of others. It has been demonstrated that individuals are influenced more by actions than by spoken words—that is, through the process of imitation, modeling, or observational learning (Bandura, 1975; Berkowitz, 1962; N. Miller & Dollard, 1941). Social pressure has a profound influence because there are strong tendencies in people toward conformity (Basic Behavioral Science Task Force, 1996; Cialdini, 1984; Wood, Pool, Leck, & Purvis, 1996).[2]

Social pressure from self-denying family members or friends exerts a strong pull on us to unconsciously deprive ourselves of much that we value in life to stay in step with them. For example, a woman whose roommate complained about being unhappy and lonely felt guilty about her own happiness and joy in life. She found herself holding back her excitement about a new romance out of guilt and concern about hurting her roommate. Within a family, any member who is self-denying or self-hating is able to exert enough pressure to control the entire family through guilt and fear.

The philosophy of self-denial and selflessness instilled in children by most families is propagated by society's institutions. Some religions support critical self-evaluations and hostile attitudes toward the body and foster a posture of self-denial. Often religious prohibitions lead to the very immorality that they are trying to avert. By denying natural outlets for physical affection and sexuality and a positive regard for the self, they increase hostility and therefore contribute to destructive antisocial behavior. The recent revelations of sexual misconduct by some members of the Catholic clergy may be, at least in part, explained by this dynamic (Dillon, 2002).

Within society, there are also social pressures against the expression of feeling, especially in public or formal settings. Many people believe that a display of feeling is somehow shameful or degrading, whereas appearing stoic or unemotional is admirable. This form of social pressure lends support to the kind of nonfeeling, inward state in which many individuals exist.

Societal institutions and conventional beliefs that exert negative social pressures on people represent a malevolent force in their lives, whereas a social order that is supportive of each person would be considered ideal, a benevolent force in human affairs.

A BENEVOLENT SOCIAL SYSTEM: AN IDEAL

A benevolent social system would stand in contrast to the malevolent societal forces discussed previously and place its highest value on both the psychological and material welfare of every individual. It would be a society that emphasizes each member's autonomy, personal freedom, and economic well-being (Rawls, 1971; Rorty, 1998, 1999).

In a benevolent society, people would be considered as an "end in themselves" and never as a means to serve an outside entity. Havel (1990) stated this concept succinctly in an interview: "The most important thing is that man should be the measure of all structures, including economic structures, and not that man be made to measure for those structures" (p. 13). Giving the individual preeminence rather than the state or its institutions is logical as well as ethical because systems are merely hypothetical, whereas people are actual living beings.

Individuals living within such a system would teach their children that all human beings are born with a great potential for living peacefully and behaving with generosity toward one another. They are not angry or destructive by nature, and these negative emotions can be understood and controlled. Children would be taught that the human body is a natural, healthy organism about which there is no reason to feel guilt or shame. Morality would be based on emulating the positive behavior of adult role models rather than being forced to conform to moralistic rules based on the assumptions that human beings are essentially immoral. And there would be an ethic of mutual respect for all people, regardless of their ethnicity, race, religion, gender, age, or sexual identity.

A benevolent social system would also be characterized by realism regarding love and relationships. People would understand that it is natural to both love and hate, and like and dislike, one's parents, partners, or friends, and they would learn to tolerate ambivalent feelings toward their fellow human beings. Individualism and seeking one's own path—including the kinds of relationships one pursues and how one chooses to behave at various ages of one's life—would be encouraged. People would be aware of the natural tendency of a group to impose conformity on its members and actively seek to counter this by promoting individuality and personal growth.

SOCIAL, POLITICAL, AND ECONOMIC DIMENSIONS OF THE FRIENDSHIP CIRCLE

The friendship circle can be viewed as a microcosm of the society at large. The experiences of the men, women, and children in this small society demonstrate that it is possible to move in the direction of creating a benevolent social system. Historically, the group originated with a few families who enjoyed sharing life's experiences in close friendship. As noted, there was never a plan to form an extended group or create a new society. As these people led a life of adventure and enterprise, they met others who were compatible and the group gradually increased in numbers. Its growth was spontaneous; there was no sense of in- or out-group differentiation, nor was there an element of exclusivity. There never was any attempt to proselytize or increase the membership. People gradually formed the close ties that have persisted for many years.

Although there was no master plan—a positive way of life simply emerged—looking back, one can perceive an orderly progression. During years of close, personal communication in the discussions, individuals developed a shared concern for one another that transcended family lines and extended not only to their friends but encompassed a compassionate feeling for people everywhere.

We describe in more detail this way of life and the nature of this society that eventually developed into a unique social paradigm. The structure and various dimensions of this social system are explained by demonstrating how they actually work within the friendship circle and in the members' lives. It is valuable to reflect on the politics and economics of this unusual aggregation when considering the concept of a more fulfilling life. In describing the specifics of this social milieu, there are six major categories that are considered: (a) ethics, (b) politics, (c) economics, (d) personal development, (e) social security, and (f) the children.

Ethics

A benevolent social system has a minimum number of rules but a high standard of ethics. People in the group of friends have developed a tacitly understood set of values and have the courage to question those values of the larger society that are inherently damaging to individuals. Their values are defined in terms of those that help, support, or create positive conditions for the development of the individual and the evolution of a humanistic society.

It is important to emphasize that this understanding of a benign social order grew out of the study and development of sound principles of human behavior. Over the course of the evolution of the circle of friends, and even before that, we and our colleagues were assembling and documenting much information regarding the emotional damage that people sustained as children and how their specific defenses perpetuated their suffering throughout their lives. As noted, our investigations led to certain conclusions about both the type and quality of experience that are conducive to the well-being of individuals, as well as those experiences that are limiting and destructive. From this pool of knowledge, certain ethical principles emerged that indicated a better way to live. Thus, the implicit ethical code that gradually evolved is based on solid mental health precepts, not on rules, authoritarian codes, or parental prescriptions.

The values and ideals endorsed by the individuals in this group were derived from their understanding of the deepest human needs and wants: the desire for affection and attention, to be seen as one really is, and to not be intruded on. In a humane social system such as the friendship circle, power is invested for the "good," with good being defined as what nurtures human qualities in general and the unique traits specific to each individual. People place a high value on expressions of personal power—that is, the direct, honest, decent pursuit of one's goals—and disapprove of expressions of surplus power, status moves, and unnecessary control or domination of others. Manipulation through weakness is also viewed as a destructive power play. There is a concern for human rights violations within individuals as well as between them; self-destructive behavior and other attacks on the self are challenged. For example:

Justin (18): I think it's really important to set a standard for the way you want to live your life and really live it that way and be the kind of person you want to be. I think it's important to be happy with the way you are toward yourself and toward other people. And to be kind to other people—it makes me feel better about myself.

Lia (21): Right now I'm involved in taking care of my little sister, and it's made me feel better about myself just to help another person and to be able to teach her morals. Not like in a lesson, not like talking down to her, but wanting to help her to be the best person she could be. Just to be nice to another person makes me feel good about myself.

A benevolent social system also condemns all forms of sexual stereotyping, racism, and prejudice. There is a minimum of sexist attitude, no racism or distinctions along color lines or religion, and an absence of a disrespectful generation gap in the treatment of young or old people. Although the people in this group hold strong values regarding human rights issues and have put them into practice in their everyday lives, their approach is nonintrusive. In other words, there is no mandate to change oneself. One is "left alone" in the best sense of the word to pursue one's life. In a similar spirit, the advantages and benefits of this lifestyle are not imposed on any individual, they are simply available to all. It is also important to point out that these ethical principles do not represent a *group* philosophy; in discussing their values, the friends respect diverse and individual views and strive to protect these views from any encroachment of a "group consensus."

Politics

A humanitarian political system is characterized above all by a commitment to allowing individuals to govern themselves and giving each person a right to be heard. It is particularly important that individuals be encouraged not only to discuss issues but the feelings underlying them. The friendship circle is not a political institution or society; however, it has several unique qualities that can be compared to an experimental culture or political system. One observer, a philosopher and social theorist, commented that the friendship circle appeared to be an experiment in trying to live a nonauthoritarian life. It can be conceptualized politically as a social democracy because individuals have the right to govern themselves and each person has a right to be heard.

Because of the groups' shared vacations, common interests, and mutual concerns, a committee is elected each year to plan and manage the variety of activities and to deal with any conflicts or problems that might arise. Out of more than 100 people, 15 men and women and 1 chairperson are elected to represent their friends. They are selected based on their value to the group and their interest in serving; however, all people are encouraged to participate in the committee meetings any time they wish. Interestingly enough, very few problems arise. The committee rarely meets, and when it does it is usually for the purpose of helping someone in need, to plan future distributions of funds, as discussed later in this chapter, or to consider other acts of generosity.

Economics

Justin (18): The important thing about getting money is obviously that it gives you freedom, which is what money means most to me. It means you can travel around the world or have a nice boat. Or you can help pay for your friends to travel or do whatever they want. There was a time in this circle of friends when people didn't have as much money, obviously, as they do now, but they were still very happy. So I wouldn't say money is absolutely necessary, but it is nice to be able to have freedom.

Bill (39): I realize how fortunate I am to have other people to give to. It's like my life is full of opportunities to be generous to other people, to give to children. But not just giving monetary things, but being generous with yourself and your time. Taking time to take a walk with a kid, or teaching someone how to drive a car or ride a bicycle. There are so many opportunities.

A benevolent social system is characterized by an extensive sharing of resources, though on a voluntary, not obligatory basis, and derived from mutual feeling and a desire to give on the part of those who can afford to do so. A sense of community and deep feeling of friendship for one another has led to a form of distributive justice (Rawls, 1971) whereby resources are provided to the least advantaged because better-off members naturally wish to share their good fortune.

In society at large, of course, such an economic system has been hard to achieve. In general, capitalistic economies are characterized by significant inequity.[3] Socialistic experiments in coercing greater equality have generally been proven ineffective. Our experience indicates that a voluntary sharing of resources can occur, however, in smaller communities such as the friendship circle. The key for such sharing seems to be that people know and care for each other and that a practice of generosity is consciously cultivated as a mental health principle. People in such a system are aware that being generous is one of their highest sources of satisfaction. They are thus generous for "selfish" reasons, because it makes their own lives more meaningful, and not because they are "supposed" to do so or will meet with disapproval if they do not.

Generosity is one of the most prominent characteristics of the friendship circle. To convey how it is practiced, it is important to emphasize that generous or altruistic acts are not a function of wealth. These people have been voluntarily sharing resources since the beginning, when their means were quite modest. The group of friends routinely cares for people's health needs and shares the profits of its businesses and other resources for a wider variety of needs. This arrangement has been more than adequate in meeting the individual physical, economic, and psychological needs of all members for more than two decades. In addition, specific monetary gifts are given to individuals to meet special needs or desires.

The altruism manifested among the friends is unique; there are equal exchanges between people—a mutual give-and-take—a generosity and a willingness to accept what one is offered. The ability to give and take is a fundamental psychological principle. There are no charity cases because each person has contributed in some way to the ongoing lifestyle and business success, and each individual is valued for his or her particular contribution.

There are countless examples of small and large acts of kindness on the part of individuals in the friendship circle. One woman was given a new car because her friends were worried about the condition of her old car and were seriously concerned about her safety. An aspiring writer was given a new computer and word-processing software, and a physician was presented with a new leather bag for house-calls after his friends noticed the poor condition of his old one. A substantial sum of money was loaned to another individual who was deeply in debt and threatened by bankruptcy. One of the teenagers who was musically inclined was presented with a set of drums and given money for lessons. A woman who secretly believed no one ever remembered her birthday was deeply moved when her friends threw a large surprise party for her. In several instances, people with poor employment records have been given a chance to work in one of the businesses, helped to overcome unproductive work habits, and encouraged to find their own niche in the company.

In the business ventures, each employee is valued. The bottom line is one measure of success, but human concerns have a higher priority. People are rewarded according to what they have contributed, yet there is a basic standard of fulfilling everyone's economic needs. Each person is provided with the means to travel and to participate in the vacations, which are extensive and include world travel. No matter what their income, people are able to enjoy the same lifestyle as their friends. The only advantage of being well-off is that one is able to give more, which brings more pleasure.

Considerable assistance has also been offered on an individual basis to people who are not members of the friendship circle. For example, a man who had occasionally played in the friends' weekly baseball game was wrongly accused of a crime and threatened with prison. When members of the team learned of this man's plight, they provided him with financial aid for legal fees, as well as with legal representation, on a pro bono basis, from one of the friends who is a trial lawyer. In several other cases, they have offered their funds to help acquaintances who were ill or injured.

Personal Development Through Honest and Compassionate Communication

Every social system has a core set of practices.[4] One of the core practices of a truly democratic society is open and honest communication in which information is shared, secrecy is at a minimum, and people are encouraged to voice negative feelings so that they do not act them out.

Because information is power, sharing information is critical to creating a decent society. A community seeking to meet people's psychological as well as material needs must place a particularly high value on honest communication, because avoiding dealing with difficult feelings inevitably leads to manipulation, power plays, and unhappiness. For people to open up about their true feelings, however, there must be as high a value placed on a practice of kindness and compassion as there is on honesty and forthrightness. Honest and empathic communication is a core practice needed to create and sustain a benevolent society.

The friendship circle demonstrates how straightforward, direct, and compassionate communication can operate. Underlying the personal development of the people in the friendship circle and the ease with which they interact is a style of communication that evolved from the original discussion groups. The honest dialogue in these talks has been at the heart of people's successes, and the tradition has been passed on to the young people and children. Children and adolescents talk regularly to interested adults, aside from their parents, participate in their own groups, and have learned that their opinions are valued. According to Lia (20):

> In our talks, we talk about different things, and people say things they're embarrassed about. There are a lot of things people want to change about themselves, different struggles they're having. And no one is hiding anything in those talks, that's why they're so interesting. That's why I love them so much because you go to a talk and it is so honest. It's like there's nothing that isn't said. Sometimes the talks go on for three hours just because everybody is so inspired to talk.

Social Security

A benevolent society does more than provide for the material needs of its senior citizens. It also acknowledges the value of their long years of experience, discourages expectations that they should behave in a certain way because they are older, and above all offers seniors ongoing opportunities for productive work.

In the friendship circle, for example, older people are supported in their later years. They are cared for according to their needs, and funds for health problems are made available to them whenever necessary. They are encouraged to remain active in intellectual activities, sports, and travel. Thus, they have continued their involvement in the energetic lifestyle and most are still engaged in productive work. People who are temporarily unemployed are also supported through their career crises, and medical expenses for individuals of all ages that are not covered by insurance are paid for collectively by members of the community as a whole.

The Future: The Children

The quality of a social system and its future potential lies in its children. The ultimate measure of a society, therefore, is its commitment to its children. There is no greater cause for concern about society today than the high rates of disaffection, drug use, suicide, violence, and alienation among young people. Leading a more meaningful life requires above all creating an environment that nurtures young people in developing their creativity, nondefensiveness, potential for kindness and love, skills, and unique path to personal growth.

The friendship circle provides one example of how such a child-oriented community can operate. The friends have offered their children an environment that supports the development of their unique potential, with a minimum of "programming" or unnecessary, destructive aspects of the socialization process. The values and ethical principles of the adults are being passed on to the children, but not through lectures or moral lessons. The youngsters have simply imitated the decency, honesty, and kindness of their parents and have rarely, if ever, been physically punished or coerced into behaving appropriately. The guiding principle for raising children has been that they owe us nothing, while we owe them everything. We brought them into the world and are responsible for their existence; therefore, we must try to further their needs and never interfere with the emergence of their uniqueness and their true nature.

As the children have grown older they have maintained strong friendships with their peers in addition to sustaining long-standing associations with favorite adult friends. The lack of discrimination in terms of age has contributed to the children's feeling more comfortable in stating their opinions forthrightly and relating to adults on a more equal basis than do their counterparts in the larger society. They have rarely felt disrespected nor have they been treated as second-class citizens. Therefore, they lack much of the rage that disenfranchised and disrespected children in Western culture often express through their music and sometimes in their actions.

The children and adolescents are supported in their aspirations and their special interests, and people try to facilitate the attainment of their goals in life. The children are not forced into a mold or influenced in their interests or choice of careers but are allowed to choose their own path in life. So far, some have chosen to pursue careers in the arts and in music, several elected to go to college and seek advanced degrees, and others chose to go directly into business. According to Natasha (19):

> I think that in many families there is a set way the parents want their kids to turn out. They want their kids to go to college, to become a

doctor, dentist, whatever. But I feel like for me I never felt that pressure. I felt that I could do whatever I wanted. Whatever my interests were, they were supported, just because they were my interests.

Overall, this small society provides a forum, an opportunity, and the atmosphere for the energetic pursuit of personal development, self-improvement, life-long learning, and education according to each person's ability and interest. The group process is almost always pure—that is, uncontaminated by negative elements such as an individual's hidden agenda, which often interferes with the group process in the larger society. There is invariably support for personal freedom and valuing of self in each participant. The environment that these people have allowed to evolve is warm and responsive to individuals who are struggling for a better life and fighting for themselves. In the midst of a conventional and largely unfeeling society, it has become a refuge for living a feelingful existence.

CONCLUSION

Insight into faulty assumptions about human nature and mixed messages that proliferate throughout our culture could help to challenge the abuses of power that exist in contemporary society and in many families. Becoming more aware of the double messages in society can diminish the effects of negative social pressure in people's lives. However, there is strong resistance to perceiving destructive elements that operate to varying degrees within society and within the family. This resistance, as well as the failure to recognize the rights of children, go hand in hand with the myth that parents have unconditional love for their children and therefore know best how to raise them. In supporting this myth and protecting parents' rights over those of their children, society unwittingly condones the harm done to children "for their own good."

We must seriously reconsider our priorities in relation to social and family values. The goal is not to dismantle the family or our social institutions but to build more constructive associations between people that, like the true democratic system exemplified in the friendship circle, would meet the needs of all people and enhance their personal development and their pursuit of a better life.

Only by becoming aware of the serious and painful issues described can we begin to change these patterns on both the familial and the societal level. We are optimistic with regard to this possibility. Because this group of friends has been able to create a better way of life for themselves and their children, other people might well be inspired to challenge their own defenses, to not conform to damaging social mores and conventional thinking, and to go on to fulfill their own destiny in life, rather than living out the life prescribed for them by their families and by society.

Overcoming negative social pressures requires above all that people challenge their *individual* defenses against leading a feelingful life. To lead a life of meaning and compassion, individuals need to develop their capacity to feel; cope with anger and victimization; move away from addictive life-styles; develop genuine friendships; move beyond fantasy; encourage generosity, aesthetics, and adventure; and challenge their self-destructive tendencies and defenses against death anxiety. Individuals wishing to lead a better life must first become aware of the personal demons they carry from the past, see how these influences affect their adult lives, and take measures to progressively free themselves of this negative influence. Then they will be able to deal with societal issues.

In closing, these words, written by Robert Firestone, are from a documentary film (Parr, 2002) about the friendship circle:

> Part of the good life involves a concern for other people,
> Starting with your own family,
> Giving value and respect to other human beings,
> Serving others, wanting to better the world you live in,
> To help, to heal, to share,
> Making your life the best story possible.

NOTES

1. Sarah Hrdy (1999) took an evolutionary psychological perspective in discussing the assumption that maternal love exists as a natural predisposition in all mothers. She concluded that "small downward adjustments of maternal priorities regarding a given infant, which cumulatively amount to life-or-death decisions, have had an enormous impact on the direction of human evolution. Degree of maternal commitment was itself a selection pressure impinging on each newborn" (p. 380). Hrdy's explanations regarding the evolutionary basis of maternal ambivalence tend to agree with our observations and Rohner's (1986) cross-cultural research on the continuum of parental acceptance and rejection of children.
2. There are cultural differences in the extent to which individuals tend to conform or adjust to societal standards or seek to influence them. See Morling, Kitayama, and Miyamoto's (2002) article "Cultural Practices Emphasize Influence in the United States and Adjustment in Japan."
3. Richard Rorty, in *Achieving Our Country* (1998), noted that in American society, "economic inequality and economic insecurity have steadily increased" (p. 83). We are likely to wind up with an America divided into hereditary social castes" (p. 86). Also see Barbara Ehrenreich's (2001) *Nickel and Dimed: On [Not] Making It in America.*
4. See Ullman's (1965) definition of "culture" as "a system of solutions to unlearned problems, as well as of learned problems and their solutions, acquired by members

of a recognizable group and shared by them" (p. 5). Duck (1994b) defined culture as follows:

> *Culture as code* refers to an organized system of beliefs or values; *culture as conversation* emphasizes the patterning of lived experience that is created in normal conversation; *culture as community* emphasizes the sharing of identity based on a communal ordering of memories. (p. 57)

16

PSYCHOTHERAPY: PAST, PRESENT, AND FUTURE?

The very existence of the therapist as a humanist, as a social activist, as a systemic thinker is under attack. We must challenge the institutions that oppress our field in order to preserve not only the right to freely practice therapy, but also the right of clients to freely choose therapy without medication and even the right to freedom of thought.
—Cloe Madanes (1999, p. 57)

From the 1950s to the 1970s, psychoanalysis and depth psychotherapy were flourishing and had a prominent place in the foreground of a cultural revolution. At that time, the majority of clinical psychologists considered it a virtual necessity to experience their own depth analysis to better understand the patients they would be treating. There was a spirit of optimism and idealism that permeated the mental health profession and a deep investment in the psychological approach to emotional maladies.

During much of this time, millions of young people were fighting for their ideals in a valiant attempt to find a better life. The youth movement was characterized by sentiments that opposed the Vietnam War; challenged the status quo materialism of the American scene; favored self-development, self-expression, and sexual freedom; exposed the weaknesses and hypocrisy in the traditional family; and put a high price on individuality and human decency. This movement and its aspirations were thwarted by the fact that its positive thrust was accompanied by an extraordinary guilt and fear reaction that led to the ever-increasing use of drugs and alcohol. These young men and women simply could not cope with their personal demons, reflections of their childhood trauma. It is our belief that their misguided attempt

Portions of this chapter have been adapted from Robert W. Firestone (2002), *The Death of Psychoanalysis and Depth Psychotherapy, Psychotherapy,* 39(3), 223–232. Used with permission of the American Psychological Association.

347

to quiet the emotional pain and anxiety of breaking symbolic dependency bonds and seeking autonomy weakened them and eventually led to the demise of their movement.

During this period of experimentation and upheaval, people more than ever before were concerned with their personal psychological development. The existential–humanistic movement represented by Abraham Maslow (1968) and Rollo May (1983), the "antipsychiatry" campaign reflected in the work of R. D. Laing (1967, 1960/1969) and Thomas Szasz (1974, 1978), and the influence of Eastern thought (Suzuki et al., 1960; Watts, 1961) generated a process of change that affected the culture at large. In *The Repression of Psychoanalysis*, Jacoby (1983) observed that "there was an obvious affinity between youthful rebellion and psychoanalysis" (p. 39). He also noted,

> The youth movement of the first and seventh decades of the twentieth century resembled each other. Both advanced a slogan of "youth culture"; both rebelled against the style, content, and conformism of bourgeois life; and both placed Eros and nature above work and artificiality. (p. 48)

At that time, many psychologists were involved in sensitivity-training groups, marathons, workshops, and encounter groups—procedures that broke out of the narrow confines of the psychotherapy office setting and extended into the business arena, education, and even international relations. People were challenging the status quo in every aspect of their psychological lives and were willing to look at painful issues.

In the course of these events, many important but disturbing truths were being revealed. The hidden aspects of family life and the bedroom were brought into sharp focus, and people's most cherished defenses were threatening to be uncovered. Nothing was considered too sacred to be exposed to scrutiny. The pattern of honest exposure was also characteristic of the humor of those times.

Although the truth may eventually promote healing, when it first manifests itself, it generally inspires terror. Something had to be done about the discomfort. This same story has echoed throughout time. Of course there was the expected counterattack, and it affected both the youth movement and the practice of psychotherapy.

In this chapter, we are not primarily concerned with the efficacy or nonefficacy of psychotherapy or psychoanalytical treatment or the correctness or incorrectness of its theoretical precepts. There are mixed reviews about the therapeutic value of depth therapy, but a generally positive consensus (Beutler, 1995; Roth & Fonagy, 1996; Sandell et al., 2000; Seligman, 1995; Spiegel, 1999; Wampold, 2001).[1] What we are concerned with is the decline in the use of methodologies such as free association, dream analysis, feeling-release therapies, and group encounters. These approaches represented unique psychological processes that brought into daylight the previously hidden content of our most intimate thoughts and memories. They were valuable resources, windows into the unconscious mind and an illumination of previously unavailable psychological phenomena.

The discoveries made possible by these methods revealed deep-seated secrets of family dynamics. By their essential nature, the resulting insights were threatening to the status quo in the social milieu. The forthcoming reaction of society was predictable, and eventually the menace was for the most part effectively extinguished.

The bulwarks of society, initially outraged by these new developments, gradually, under pressure, swallowed up some of the ideology. This partial ingestion and later backlash was more effective than a direct confrontation. At that time, everyone spoke in psychological terms, the jargon of self-help and self-actualization ran rampant, and people mouthed the platitudes of the freedom movement until they became banal. Then, subtly at first, and later with increased momentum, there was an insidious conservative backlash that invalidated much of what was learned.

In our opinion, the subsequent decline of psychoanalysis and depth psychotherapy over the past 30 years can be attributed in large part to this reactionary movement that sought, among other things, to deny the veracity of insights achieved by both patients and therapists in the treatment modality. According to psychoanalyst John Gedo (2000):

> Today it has become evident that American social conditions do not favor the acceptance of psychoanalytic ideas (p. 39). In North America the resistance to its message has penetrated the psychoanalytic community itself, so that depth psychology has been watered down and replaced by mythic variants. . . . This is, indeed, the twilight of our profession in the New World. (p. 52)

Like other attempts that have been made throughout history to suppress knowledge and insight, these efforts are on a par with book-burning and brainwashing. When this type of revelation is stifled, in spite of all of our amazing technological advances, we are thrown back into the dark ages.

To summarize, malevolent societal forces have succeeded in almost completely suppressing important knowledge concerning the widespread incidence of emotional, physical, and sexual child abuse and other destructive practices in "normal" families and their long-term harmful effects on adult individuals. Currently, cultural attitudes of indifference and denial continue to exert a powerful influence on the field of psychotherapy and have, in large part, transformed it from a creative, compassionate enterprise to a weak and frightened community of mental health professionals dispensing drugs and quick fixes that support the status quo.

A BRIEF HISTORICAL REVIEW

As noted, society represents, in part, a pooling of individual psychological defenses that reflect back on individual personality development. Therefore, theories and methodologies that threaten psychological defenses will necessarily come under attack. Only the sturdiest can survive the outrage. S. Freud (1896/1962) himself shied away from his seduction theory and subsequently rejected his original hypotheses concerning the etiology of hysteria. It is significant that both he and Jung failed to survive the vehemence of the public attack that greeted their initial findings (A. Miller, 1981/1984b, 1988/1990). Each theorist went on to repudiate his own clinical evidence, material that suggested that the source of the neuroses lay in the sexual and physical abuse of children. In *Thou Shalt Not Be Aware*, Alice Miller (1981/1984b) asserted,

> The concealment of a previously recognized truth in the case of both famous thinkers of our century is tragic, but it is all too understandable in view of the strong influence their upbringing had on them. . . . Consequently, the children who are mistreated and abused in their earliest years ultimately disappear in the forest of Jungian archetypes and the collective unconscious, just as they do in Freud's drive theory. (p. 202)

Madanes (1999) summarized the history of a repetitive cycle of progress and exposure followed by reactionary suppression of the truth:

> More than a century ago, Sigmund Freud shocked the medical establishment of his day by suggesting that mental illness was caused by childhood physical and sexual abuse. . . . Six years after his professional colleagues blasted his paper on the long-term psychological damage stemming from real injuries inflicted by parents on their own children, Freud recanted. (p. 44)

Subsequently, S. Freud (1905/1953) developed his theory of infantile sexuality, the Oedipal complex, and the death instinct to explain his data (Masson, 1985; Miller, 1981/1984b). In this revision of his original seduction theory, hysteria and other emotional disturbances were conceptualized as originating in children's fantasies about *imagined* sexual and physical trauma.

Later, during the 1950s and 1960s, family therapists in America began to develop innovative treatment approaches based on psychoanalysis and developmental psychology and "treated families from a predominantly historical, analytical, or *transgenerational* perspective" (Seaburn, Landau-Stanton, & Horwitz, 1995, p. 5). Once again, "personal relationships—between parents and children, wives and husbands" were seen as "the key to understanding human emotional life" (Madanes, 1999, p. 46).

Today, the so-called radical ideas of psychoanalysis and the truths that were revealed during these years of fruitful exploration have once again been effectively concealed. The sanctity of the family and family values stands above criticism and exposure, to the detriment of all concerned.

In *Banished Knowledge*, Alice Miller (1988/1990) described how Freud's drive theory, combined with the intellectual defenses of many psychoanalysts, has contributed to the continued suppression of the truth about abusive child-rearing practices and other damaging aspects of family life:

> Psychoanalysts protect the father and embroider the sexual abuse of the child with the Oedipus, or Electra, complex, while some feminist therapists idealize the mother, thus hindering access to the child's first traumatic experiences with the mother. Both approaches can lead to a dead end, since the dissolving of pain and fear is not possible until the full truth of the facts can be seen and accepted. (p. 79)

INCREASED MEDICALIZATION OF PSYCHOLOGY

Over the past decade, the biomedical approach to psychopathology, partially valid in its own right, has swept away and effectively eradicated the psychological approach. The medical model conceptualizes the patient as ill, or as possibly suffering from a disease or biochemical imbalance. As such, it dehumanizes and compartmentalizes an individual by emphasizing symptoms rather than the whole person. Anthropologist Tanya Luhrmann (2000) has described the increasing medicalization of psychiatry and psychology in her book, *Of Two Minds: The Growing Conflict in American Psychiatry*, and deplored its potential consequences: "We are so tempted to see ourselves as fixable, perfectible brains. But the loss of our souls is a high price to pay" (p. 293).

In conjunction with the ascendance of the biomedical approach, the use of antidepressants has had an explosive increase, and an alarming number of children have been treated with Ritalin, with one estimate suggesting that as many as five million school-aged children may currently be taking stimulant drugs (Breggin, 2000). Zito et al. (2003) called attention to the fact that from 1987 to 1996, "Total psychotropic medication prevalence for youths increased two- to three-fold and included most classes of medication" (p. 17). In fairness, concern has been registered about this practice in the recent literature. In an editorial in the *American Journal of Orthopsychiatry*, Carlos Sluzki (2001) warned that in our society:

> We endure an era of "mindless mental health," in which everything is referred back to brain functioning, and psychiatric disorders and human miseries of all kinds are dealt with by the, after all, not-so-magic bullet of this or that designer medication. (p. 149)

Several clinicians have called attention to their colleagues' excessive reliance on drugs in the treatment of mental illness and have criticized their refusal to use even those psychotherapy techniques whose effectiveness has been empirically validated. These "dissident" voices include Breggin (1991) in *Toxic Psychiatry* and Valenstein (1998) in *Blaming the Brain: The Truth About Drugs and Mental Health*. In condemning the *DSM-IV*'s (American Psychiatric Association, 1994) reductionistic, dehumanizing categorization of patients, psychologist Paula Caplan (1995) challenged another damaging element associated with the increased medicalization of psychology.

In contrast to the relatively generous remuneration they allow consumers for the cost of drugs prescribed by psychiatrists, health care providers allow for only limited opportunities for psychotherapy, often no more than four to six sessions. Current practice is largely limited to a variety of brief treatment programs or medications that can never replace or even begin to cope with the myriad of emotional problems that are debilitating for so many individuals. In the restricted time allotted for mental health care, the attempt to find shortcuts is inevitable, but these efforts are by their very nature insufficient.

A number of psychoanalysts and researchers have documented the rise of medical psychiatry and the corresponding decline of their profession, including Bornstein (2001), Masling (2000), de Schill (2000), and de Schill and Lebovici (1999). However, there appears to be confusion regarding the factors responsible for this trend. For example, in "The Impending Death of Psychoanalysis," Bornstein (2001) attributed the problem to internal factors, arguing that "Psychoanalysis is suffering primarily because it has been mismanaged by its adherents for too many years" (p. 7). He delineated several characteristics of psychoanalysis that he considered as contributing to its demise, including the exclusiveness and insularity of analysts, the inaccuracy and irrelevance of Freudian theories, and the inefficiency of psychoanalytical methods.[2]

Masling (2000) asserted that "if psychoanalysis is not going to be consigned to Trotsky's 'dust bin of history,' it must join the modern world's acceptance of science as a method for determining the validity of ideas" (p. 682). Although we agree that the need for empirical research is of great importance in the mental health field, we disagree that the lack of scientific validation of psychoanalytical constructs is the core problem afflicting present-day psychoanalysis and depth psychotherapy. There is a wealth of research data demonstrating the effectiveness of a variety of psychotherapies (Beutler, 1995; Hollon, Shelton, & Davis, 1993; Horvarth & Luborsky, 1993; Jacobson, 1993; Weisz, Weiss, & Donenberg 1992), and at least one survey (Seligman, 1995) has shown that a majority of clients feel that they benefit from psychotherapy.

Similarly, although the "internal" factors described by Bornstein have undoubtedly undermined psychoanalytical practice, they are not the factors primarily responsible for its decline. For example, other reasons for the increased use of pharmacological rather than psychoanalytical approaches in treating mental or emotional disturbance were cited by Karon (2002) in a commentary on Bornstein's article:

> The federal government has stopped subsidizing clinical psychology and psychiatry programs. A great deal of the current opposition to psychoanalysis and psychoanalytic therapy has to do with the marketing of medication (often disguised as education or continuing education) and the fact that medicating pays better than doing psychotherapy. (p. 568)

And in "A Mark of Decline," Stoller (2000) declared,

> Although most analysts are deeply concerned about the present state of analysis, they hope that the tree itself, still growing vigorously, can be properly shaped by trimming and pruning a piece of theory here and there. . . . *Other analysts, who do not believe all is so sound, feel analysis has been wounded from the outside—that society, as it changes, is unwilling to live in the heady atmosphere of truth required of the person committed to analysis.* (p. 59; italics added)

We believe that the demise of psychoanalysis and depth psychotherapy is closely related to a cultural phenomenon determined to deny the truth of human experience. Of course this is an extremely dangerous trend for members of society, because how can we hope to develop better family life if we do not honestly scrutinize the dynamics of present-day family interactions? We must effectively account for adolescent suicide, violence in our schools, the widespread use of drugs, and a myriad of other symptoms of emotional disturbance in our young people.

THE FALSE MEMORY SYNDROME MOVEMENT

One of the most insidious attacks on psychology and psychotherapy has come from proponents of the "false memory syndrome" movement. Psychologists and psychotherapists have been accused of putting negative thoughts into the heads of their clients, influencing them to resent their families and loved ones and inciting them to reject all familial ties (Loftus & Ketcham, 1994).[3] An extremist movement among dissenters has sprung up to harass psychologists who have revealed the truth of destructive family practices, which include the widespread behaviors that relate to incest, sexual abuse, and the physical abuse and verbal abuse of children. Some psychologists have been threatened with physical retaliation; many more have been troubled by real or potential lawsuits, or, in the least, suffered from an unfair prejudicial atmosphere and have had their offices picketed (Pope & Brown, 1996). Indeed, fears of such lawsuits have made some psychologists reluctant to undertake treatment with clients manifesting symptoms of posttraumatic stress disorder or other dysfunctions that have been shown to be related to a history of child abuse.

Psychotherapists working with children are afraid to manifest any form of physical affection toward their clients for fear that their motives will be misinterpreted and subjected to legal action. The atmosphere of suspicion and distrust has had many other detrimental effects on therapist–client relationships and has tended to dehumanize their contact. Society has blatantly and irrationally identified the messenger with the message. Paradoxically, psychotherapists, often attacked by their clients for their therapeutic silence and refusal to offer advice, have been erroneously blamed for their clients' negative reactions to their spouses and family members.

Has anyone ever raised the question of why mental heath professionals would make up lurid descriptions of family life or possibly have a stake in them? Actually, psychologists are just as likely to idealize their families as lay persons are. Indeed, they are an integral part of the greater culture and are usually representative of the same defensive reaction patterns.

In recent years, many professionals and experts in child development have moved in the direction of deemphasizing or even negating the important link between early childhood trauma and subsequent maladaptive behavior in adult patients (A. Miller, 1981/1984b, 1990/1991; Plomin, 1989; Rosenfeld, 1978). This trend has contributed to the atmosphere of doubt and controversy surrounding the validity of adults' recollections of being sexually, physically, and psychologically abused as children (Briere, 1992; Conte, 1994; Courtois, 1999; Masson, 1985; Whitfield, 1995). In her book, *Betrayal Trauma: The Logic of Forgetting Childhood Abuse*, Freyd (1996) asserted,

> Profound amnesia (as opposed to other symptoms of PTSD) is a likely result in cases involving a betrayal of trust that produces conflict between external reality and social dependence. . . . In other words, in order to survive in cases of core betrayal (abuse by a trusted caregiver on a dependent victim) some amount of information blockage is likely to be required. (p. 75)

In addressing the "recovery of repressed memories" controversy in *Memories and Abuse*, Whitfield (1995) called attention to the tendency to block out information in his fellow psychotherapists:

> After Freud's retraction of the seduction-trauma theory, with few exceptions—such as psychoanalyst Sandor Ferenczi—we continued to deny the abuse. For most of the 20th century we also maintained the myth of "The Family" as being always ideal, private and sacrosanct, even in the face of the obvious abuse of millions of children and adults. (p. 56)

DEFINITION OF PSYCHOTHERAPY

A previous work (Firestone, 1990c) defined psychotherapy as representing:

> A unique human relationship, wherein a devoted and trained person attempts to render assistance to another person by both suspending and extending him or herself. Nowhere in life is a person listened to, felt, and experienced with such concentrated sharing and emphasis on every aspect of personal communication. As in any other human relationship, this interaction may be fulfilling or damaging to either individual. To the extent that a new fantasy bond or illusion of connection is formed (for example, doctor–patient, therapist–client, parent–child), the relationship will be detrimental; whereas in a situation that is characterized by equality, openness, and true compassion, there will be movement toward individuation in both parties. (p. 68)

PREREQUISITES FOR AN EFFECTIVE PSYCHOTHERAPY

Although all forms of psychotherapy challenge defenses to varying degrees and in general have positive results (Seligman, 1995), there are certain elements that are crucial to an effective psychotherapy and successful outcome. First, the therapeutic process must support the truth and place it above any form of protecting false assumptions about the family, society, or human beings. Therapists must be willing to experience painful realities that their patients reveal and refuse to place social conformity over the personal interests of patients. Because there is a great deal of controversy in our field and a limited state of empirical knowledge about the most effective methods of psychotherapy, the least the therapist can offer the patient is an honest interaction, marked by personal integrity, strength of character, and moral courage to challenge the status quo, if necessary. The therapeutic process offers the patient a renewed opportunity for personal development that transcends virtually any other mode of experience. Therefore, this opportunity for growth must not be limited or interfered with by the therapist's defenses or tendencies to deny unpleasant truths that may be uncovered by the patient over the course of treatment.

PERSONALITY CHARACTERISTICS
OF AN EFFECTIVE THERAPIST

The personality of the therapist largely determines the emotional quality of the interaction that takes place between patient and therapist. Research has shown that a number of specific personality characteristics of the therapist are correlated with the ability to form and sustain a constructive therapeutic alliance (Bachelor & Horvath, 1999; Beutler & Clarkin, 1990; Beutler, Machado, & Neufeldt, 1994; Bongar & Beutler, 1995; Stolorow, 1992; Wampold, 2001). The effective therapist would be skilled in helping patients reconnect to themselves and to their lives; he or she would be more like an artist than a scientist or technician. With the sensitivity of an artist, the therapist would be in tune with a person's real feelings, qualities, and desires and would be able to distinguish these from internalized voices or psychological defenses that prevent the patient from achieving his or her full potential as a human being.

To be honest and straightforward with patients implies more than simply trying to tell the truth. The clinician would need a good deal of self-knowledge and an objective view of both negative and positive qualities in his or her own personality. Ideally, therapists would exhibit strength of character and serve as role models for their patients. They would not set themselves apart from their patients but would demonstrate, through their implicit and explicit responses and behavior how to struggle against destructive forces within the personality and how to live less defensively. They would resist regressive trends in their own personalities so that they would be able to cultivate a feeling of security and trust in their patients. As facilitators and catalysts for change, they would be sensitive to the entire range of defensive patterns manifested by the patient and have the courage and strength to challenge and interrupt these patterns.

Effective therapists would not attempt to fit their patients into a particular theoretical framework or model; rather, they would try to learn from them and gradually develop a uniquely personal psychological theory for each individual. As Otto Rank (1936/1972) stated in *Will Therapy:*

> In each separate case, it is necessary to create, as it were, a theory and technique made for the occasion without trying to carry over this individual solution to the next case. . . . The essential factor remains always the capacity to understand the individual from himself, in which process the common human element, certainly not to be denied, can constitute only the hypothesis, not the content of the understanding. (pp. 3–4)

Therapists would be nonintrusive in their interpretations and would suspend judgment regarding the patient's communications, while exploring the relationship between past experience and present disturbances. Although strong in their optimism and belief in the possibility of personal growth and change, they would not underestimate the strength of a person's defense system and would be sensitive to the fear underlying resistance.

As noted in chapter 4, therapists can be conceptualized as "transitional objects" in that they provide a genuine relationship for the patient during the transition from depending on self-nurturing processes to seeking satisfaction in real relationships in the external world. In serving this function, therapists would remain human—that is, they would be interested and warm as well as direct and responsible. This would temporarily "hold" or sustain the patient as he or she moved away from fantasy gratification toward authentic relationships and the pursuit of personal and vocational goals.

LIMITATIONS POSED BY THERAPISTS' DEFENSES AND VIEWS OF THE DEFENSE SYSTEM

Psychoanalysts and psychotherapists are the products of the same processing that their patients were subjected to in their childhoods. They will continue to unintentionally process their patients, unless they themselves are emancipated. Unfortunately, therapists who are sensitive to the destructiveness of defenses and have compassion for themselves and others are in the minority. In his critique of current psychoanalytical practice, de Schill (2000) asserted that "quite a few expert clinicians have estimated that only about 15 percent of psychodynamic psychotherapists can be considered accomplished professionals" (p. 428). Indeed, many therapeutic failures can be attributed to limitations imposed on the patient by the therapist's own defense system. Negative personality traits, such as narcissism, phoniness, and hostility, are particularly detrimental to the patient.[4]

In this sense, the key issue in training successful therapists is the selection process. Candidates for training in psychotherapy or psychiatry are drawn primarily from the fields of clinical psychology and medicine. Those who come from the field of medicine are often dogmatic, parental, and pedantic in their approach to patients and act out the doctor–patient dichotomy, whereas those from clinical psychology, with its focus on research, are often too intellectual or analytical. As a result, many trainees and interns appear to lack sufficient empathy, concern, or intuitive understanding of people and human behavior.

Although certain behaviors, attitudes, and qualities can be learned or developed by therapists during training or in supervision, basic elements of personality are often highly resistant to change. In fact, training and supervision may have negative effects on an intern's or a novice therapist's personality and basic attitudes (W. Henry, Strupp, Butler, Schacht, & Binder, 1993; Siqueland et al., 2000). For example, researchers W. Henry et al. (1993) investigated the impact of training on 16 experienced therapists working in the context of time-limited dynamic psychotherapy and found that:

At the same time therapists were becoming more intellectually sensitized to the importance of in-session dyadic process, they were actually delivering a higher "toxic dose" of disaffiliative and complex communications. ... After training, therapists were judged to be less approving and supportive, less optimistic, and more authoritative and defensive [possibly based on a certain anxiety and defensiveness]. ... We frequently observed that therapists' posttraining interventions seemed somewhat mechanical or ill-timed. (p. 439)

Therapists who tend to be intellectually defended and removed from their feelings often experience discomfort when patients express strong emotions. By their response or lack of response, they often unintentionally inhibit further expression of feelings, causing their patients to become increasingly alienated from, rather than closer to, themselves. Essentially, by their responses, therapists are either supporting their patients' defenses and cut-off emotional states or they are challenging their patients' defenses by helping them expose their self-attacks and express the accompanying feelings of anger, sadness, and grief.

Another major factor limiting the effectiveness of psychotherapy is the fact that its practitioners often have a misunderstanding of core defensive processes. At the time of seeking therapy, most people are frequently in a state of anxiety or depression because their defenses are no longer effective or workable. In some sense, their symptoms can be conceptualized as manifestations of potentially positive change, a possible movement toward emotional health rather than deterioration. Conventional therapies that attempt to restore patients to their premorbid anxiety-free state by strengthening their defenses inadvertently do these patients a disservice. In trying to relieve their patients' pain and help them reestablish psychological equilibrium, proponents of these therapies are condemning their patients to a limited life experience. In this case, patients' defenses will continue to restrict them and interfere with their lives even though they may feel more comfortable.

By preserving core aspects of the patient's defense system, therapists, in effect, are facilitating their patients' reentry and readjustment to society. According to Rollo May (1983):

> The kind of cure that consists of adjustment, becoming able to fit the culture, can be obtained by technical emphases in therapy. ... Then the patient accepts a confined world without conflict, for now his world is identical with the culture. And since anxiety comes only with freedom, the patient naturally gets over his anxiety; he is relieved from his symptoms because he surrenders the possibilities which caused his anxiety. (pp. 164–165)

Any attempt to support dishonest defenses or misperceptions that temporarily reduce a person's discomfort does a serious injustice to both the patient and the therapist in the long run. Adjustment or even "feeling good" may be very inappropriate to circumstances in life that are intolerable and unacceptable. Indeed, fitting into a pathogenic society may represent a form of psychopathology. Every therapist faces a dilemma in his or her practice, whether to serve the interests of society or those of his or her patient. Just as the physician upholds the oath of Hippocrates, the therapist should be devoted to helping his or her patient above all other considerations, both personal and social.[5]

Last, although many therapists are cognizant of the destructive effects of trauma in an individual's life history and personality development, they often do not fully recognize that positive circumstances and favorable events later on can also be equally threatening. Positive events foster anxiety states, and some degree of stress invariably accompanies positive movement in therapy. As Ernest Becker (1973/1997) asserted, "Not everyone is as honest as Freud was when he said that he cured the miseries of the neurotic only to open him up to the normal misery of life" (p. 271). In addition, therapists may have a limited awareness of the extent to which clients have incorporated the defense systems of their parents and how resistant they are to living their lives without these defenses. Preserving the defense system serves as the core resistance to positive therapeutic outcome, and many people choose to lead an inferior (more defended) existence rather than struggle through the anxiety associated with positive growth.

THE ESSENTIAL PARADOX OF PSYCHOTHERAPY

It is obvious that a nondefensive approach to life has its disadvantages as well as its advantages. The problems involved in retaining an open and vulnerable orientation have been addressed by a number of clinicians. Wolberg (1954), in writing about the dilemma of psychotherapy, stated that "society itself imposes insuperable embargoes on certain aspects of functioning. It supports many neurotic values which necessitate the maintenance of sundry defenses for survival reasons" (p. 554).

Although it is true that defenses have probably had a selective adaptive advantage for human beings in the evolutionary scheme, it is also true that cruelty and injustice are an outgrowth of defended patterns of thinking and living that preclude people's feeling for themselves and arouse hostility toward others. There is an essential paradox in relation to childhood psychological defenses: Although these defenses protected the infant and young child from debilitating anxiety states or, in some cases, ego disintegration, ultimately these very same defenses are generally harmful in later life. Defenses function to dull psychological pain, but like a drug, there is a price to be paid in terms of limiting one's capacity for achieving one's full potential in life.

Many patients mistakenly believe that improvement in therapy will make them less sensitive to the pain of everyday living and more impervious to distress arising from failure, rejection, or loss. In general, our findings indicate an opposite trend. Emotionally healthy individuals are acutely sensitive to events in their lives that impinge on their sense of well-being and adversely affect the people closest to them. They appear to be *more* responsive, not less, to emotionally painful situations than they were before therapy. However, more important, by fully experiencing their feeling reactions, they are better able to cope with anxiety and stress and are far less susceptible to regression and neurotic symptom formation.

It is inevitable that therapeutic progress or improvement leads to a heightened sense of awareness and a new level of vulnerability. Before therapy, patients' defensive patterns served the function of numbing them to the pain inherent in everyday living. Positive developments in therapy disrupt these patterns, freeing patients to feel more of both the joy and pain of living.

As patients move away from the imagined safety of familiar support systems, they experience their true state of aloneness and often feel considerable guilt and fear in relation to separating from illusions of connection with family and home. Although more capable of sustaining genuinely close and intimate relationships, they tend to find themselves in a high-risk situation. In their personal interactions, they may feel more hurt by retaliation and rejection from loved ones who are defended and cannot accept their love, generosity, and acknowledgment. On a broader level, there is a great deal of unavoidable suffering and anguish inherent in living a relatively undefended life. People who have progressed in therapy are more, not less, sensitive to external issues such as crime, poverty, economic recession, illness, and the potential threat of a nuclear or biochemical holocaust. For a feeling person, a typical news broadcast will cause a good deal of emotional pain.

In addition, most people are unaware of how much they are afraid, even terrified, of freely pursuing their goals, attaining personal power, and finding satisfaction in loving interactions. The majority underestimate the difficulty and the pain and anxiety involved in establishing a new identity and developing long-lasting, close relationships that are free of fantasy elements. Finally, all people are confronted with an insurmountable problem in life—the fact that they are imprisoned in a body that will eventually deteriorate and die. Recovering aspects of their child selves and emotional vitality makes them more poignantly aware of the inevitable loss of self and consciousness through death. As S. Freud (1930/1961) remarked,

We are threatened with suffering from three directions: from our own body, which is doomed to decay and dissolution and which cannot even do without pain and anxiety as warning signals; from the external world, which may rage against us with overwhelming and merciless forces of destruction; and finally from our relations to other men. (p. 77)

Who wants to live with this new awareness, this heightened vulnerability to rejection, loss, and death? Therein lies the dilemma, for how can the therapist symbolically influence the patient to embrace life fully in the face of a predictable future with an ultimately negative outcome?

To summarize, the essential dilemma of therapeutic improvement or "cure" may be stated as follows: The patient who progresses in therapy faces an increased awareness of death and possibly intensified feelings of death anxiety. As he or she reaches out to embrace life, there is a greater realization of a finite existence. The problem facing the patient is basically no different from that faced by every human being. As one studies the situation, the alternatives become clear: Without challenging destructive aspects of ourselves, we will gradually submit to an alien, inimical point of view and shut down on our authentic self and unique outlook; on the other hand, disrupting powerful, self-protective defenses intensifies our awareness of life's tragic dimensions and threatens at times to overwhelm us with feelings of helplessness and dread.

A patient's fears of change are related to each dimension of life described earlier: an increased potential for feeling both happiness and distress, the problematic nature of intimate relationships, the circumstances of a troubled world and destructive societal forces, and the fear of losing through death everything gained through expanding one's boundaries. Juxtaposed against this fear is the knowledge that only by abandoning defenses and fantasy bonds can one avoid inflicting incidental damage on other individuals, especially one's children and loved ones. In addition to expanding opportunities for personal gratification and becoming better adjusted, remaining vulnerable and undefended becomes an ethical choice, given the alternatives.

Ideally, an effective psychotherapy would enable the patient to discover an implicit ethical or moral approach toward him- or herself and other human beings. It would facilitate an attitude of exploration and investigation wherein patients would be able to uncritically accept and examine their most irrational thoughts and feelings, while at the same time viewing others and the world with curiosity and concern.

In conclusion, when one considers the paradoxical aspects of psychotherapy practice and its effects in relation to a culture characterized by denial, it is easy to understand the resistance to psychoanalysis and depth therapy. Societal forces combined with individuals' resistance have effectively extinguished this unique form of inquiry and conspired to shut it down as a source of insight and illumination.

THE FUTURE?

Over the years, science has repeatedly threatened our most precious illusions and self-confidence. In *The Origin of Species*, Darwin (1859/1909) argued that we are simply products of evolution rather than beings created by God. Freud taught that motives and choices in life, believed to be manifestations of free will, are largely governed by unconscious motives. In our investigations, we have found that not only are we driven by unconscious forces, but we have internalized an alien aspect of our personality in the form of destructive voices that are basically suicidal in intent and diametrically opposed to our happiness and well-being. As a result of faulty child-rearing patterns, we have an enemy within that extends normal parenting practices. Often, we are motivated by forces that are self-destructive and, under certain conditions, potentially life-threatening.

We believe that the future of psychotherapy lies in facing these essential truths about human beings and their personal interactions in their families of origin. There is hope in identifying the internalized destructive aspects of the personality and in learning to re-route our behavior in directions that are more productive (Firestone, 1989). One hopes that in the future the field of psychology would become more cognizant of the true source of emotional pain and suffering and develop better techniques to cope with hostile elements in the personality. Ideally, by counteracting the dictates of inimical thought processes and disrupting illusions of connection, psychotherapy could offer people a unique opportunity to fulfill their human potential (Firestone, 1997a).

It is possible for psychoanalysis and depth psychotherapy to survive and find a resurgence if courageous individuals in and outside the field of psychotherapy are willing to challenge cultural attitudes and illusions that cause so much personal damage. Energy must be directed toward understanding and improving emotional interactions within the family system.

Education is crucial for achieving this goal: We must expand our awareness of the malevolent forces in society that function to stifle information, develop a more objective view of present-day family life, and critically evaluate dehumanizing child-rearing practices. As Luhrmann (2000) asserted,

> The idea of the unconscious carries with it the implication that life is harder than we realize, because we act not only in accord with visible circumstances but against fears and angers we find so alarming that we refuse even to acknowledge them. And so psychoanalysis also admires

the courage to look with unflinching curiosity at oneself, to attempt not to be a turtle with its head pulled in. (p. 290)

For psychoanalysis and depth psychotherapy to remain vital, clinicians need to become familiar with new information and scientific data, especially the new findings relevant to child development. Recently research from neuropsychiatry and attachment theory is suggestive of an empirical basis for psychoanalytical formulations, and these findings need to be integrated into current-day psychoanalysis and object relations systems. According to Hobson and Leonard (2001), "Science has learned a lot about the brain. This knowledge has shed a powerful light on mental ills that besides pushing back the darkness has revealed much about how to combine medication, therapy, monitoring, and other features of sound treatment" (pp. 266–267).

The impressive findings derived from research conducted by Perry (1997), van der Kolk et al. (1996), Schore (1994, 1999, 2001), and D. Siegel (1999, 2001) concerning the development of the brain during the first three years of life are crucial. Their studies of trauma using brain-imaging techniques tend to support our hypotheses that early experiences are crucial in determining an individual's personality, mental health, and ways of coping with stress throughout the life span.

In addition, therapists should be cognizant of recent studies conducted by attachment theorists and researchers Main and Hesse (1990), J. Solomon and George (1999), Fonagy et al. (1995), and others, as well as the work of Fraiberg (1982), Fraiberg et al. (1980), and Lieberman and Pawl (1988, 1990) demonstrating that early attachment sets the stage for a life-long pattern of personal relationships. Their clinical investigations and follow-up have led to positive interventions that access the patient's emotions and that have proved effective in averting negative outcomes in high-risk infants and toddlers.

These disciplines offer hope for a better understanding of psychological trauma and favor psychotherapeutic interventions that involve accessing patients' emotions associated with the trauma (Fosha, 2000; S. Johnson, Hunsley, Greenberg, & Schlinder, 1999; S. Johnson & Whiffen, 1999; Neborsky, 2001; Plutchik, 2000; Rothschild, 2000; Samilov & Goldfried, 2000; Westen, 2000). As LeDoux (1995) has suggested, "The role of therapy may be to allow the cortex to establish more effective and efficient synaptic links with the amygdala," which research has shown is "an important part of an aversive emotional memory system" (pp. 225, 227). Thus, it appears that forms of treatment that involve accessing emotions associated with early trauma could have a potentially positive effect on the future of psychoanalysis and depth therapy.

It is obvious that clinical work and psychotherapy that help people express these affects are time-consuming and require a good deal of emotional investment on the part of patients. Only in depth psychotherapy or in a comprehensive treatment program that uses experiential as well as cognitive–behavioral methodologies can these affects be accessed and worked through.

Without this resurgence, much important meaning in life will be sacrificed, a uniquely valuable therapeutic tool will be lost, the future will be bleak for those individuals suffering from emotional distress, and a powerful methodology to help humankind move toward a truly compassionate and moral approach to life will have been abandoned. However, as Lothane (2002) emphasized in his critique of Bornstein (2001), "As long as human-kind remains what it still is, in spite of the proliferation of the technologies of television, cyberspace, and even the culture of listening to Prozac, there will be a need for listening to a person" (p. 577).

CONCLUSION

Only the truth can set us free. From this perspective, it becomes a moral imperative to revive the disciplined study and practice of depth psychotherapy and integrate the important data of human experience derived from this source. We must rise to the challenge despite the threat to our most precious illusions and defenses. We are convinced that the tens of thousands of individuals who have benefited in life from depth psychotherapy share this concern.

NOTES

1. See Wampold's (2001) chapter titled "Relative Efficacy: The Dodo Bird Was Smarter Than We Have Been Led to Believe," for a review of efficacy studies beginning with Eysenck (1961).
2. In the same article, Bornstein (2001) asserted, "Numerous long-standing psycho-analytic treatment techniques are of questionable value (e.g. free association, dream analysis), yet they continue to be taught in analytic training institutes primarily because they always have been" (p. 10). Although it is currently impossible to prove or disprove the effectiveness of techniques such as free association, the important point is that the techniques did reveal aspects of couple and family life that were unpalatable and that needed to be suppressed. See *Psychoanalytic Psychology* (Reppen, 2002) for critiques of Bornstein's (2001) article.
3. It should be noted that Loftus and Ketcham (1994) carefully qualified their remarks when they stated, "We are not challenging the reality of childhood sexual abuse or traumatic memories" (p. 141). However, they also went on to say that "We are only questioning the memories commonly referred to as 'repressed'—memories that did not exist until someone went looking for them"

(p. 141), therefore implying that the concept of "repression" has no scientific basis. These researchers' use of language appears at times to be unprofessional and inflammatory, as exemplified in their labeling trauma therapists as "true believers" and their own staff as a "skeptic."

4. See "A Review of Therapist Characteristics and Techniques Negatively Impacting the Therapeutic Alliance" (Ackerman & Hilsenroth, 2001).

5. There is one notable exception that applies to the condition in which a patient could be considered to be a danger to him- or herself or to other members of the community.

17

THE THERAPEUTIC VALUE
OF FRIENDSHIP

Without friends no one would choose to live.

—Aristotle

Neurosis originates through a social process and can potentially be altered in a social milieu. Individuals in the group of friends, through their shared endeavors and friendships, have created a new social environment that counters neurotic tendencies to relive the past in present-day relationships. In the process, they found that it was virtually a necessity to share their struggle with friends who were supportive of their individuality and personal freedom. The long-lasting friendships they have forged and sustained over three decades have been a major factor in their achieving a more life-affirming existence.

These people have shared every aspect of their lives, including child-rearing, business ventures, travel, and adventure on the high seas. In their talks, they have discussed their deepest concerns and revealed their inner lives. They have helped and supported each other through their darkest moments. For these people, achieving a more meaningful life involved years of struggle and a strong commitment to coping with their own personal defenses. For however long their associations may last, it would be satisfying to remember that there was a place that existed not as a fantasy but as a place where many people could share life in harmony together, with a high level of honesty and deep feeling.

Friendship, which stands in opposition to a fantasy bond, has therapeutic value. It provides companionship that is nonintrusive and nonobligatory, qualities that lead to self-awareness and encourage a person to emerge from an inward posture. We have found that meaningful interaction with a close friend on a daily basis diminishes voice attacks and significantly interferes with the propensity to be self-denying and self-hating. It is also important to have friends who possess the qualities to which one aspires. Emulating the qualities of an admirable person and using him or her as an ally is a significant step toward developing one's own sense of values and transcendent goals.

Self-disclosure and honest communication have been cited as important elements for maintaining friendship over the long-term. According to Fehr (1996), friends use a number of strategies to maintain the relationship, including "engaging in self-disclosure [and] providing support and assurance" (p. 172). Yet, in society, it is rare to achieve an adult level of communication between people on personal subjects. A respectful dialogue or mutual self-disclosure about real issues, without coercion, manipulation, or parent–child role-playing, is difficult to come by. When people are defended, adult communication, uncomplicated by phoniness, dishonesty, and efforts to make points, becomes almost impossible.

Often, when people come together to work on a common project, especially during times of distress such as wars and disasters, they are able to transcend their defenses and work together efficiently, with a spirit of real cooperation. These times are treasured in spite of adversity and have special therapeutic effects. In fact, if one had to choose whether to create a community based on psychological principles or one based on a work project, shaped by friendship, equality, and an honest division of labor, there would be more chance of success with the latter.

An aggregate based on sound practical principles that challenge a person's defended posture, with goals that supersede one's petty preoccupations, has real therapeutic potential. One woman, in describing what friendship meant to her, said, "It means being honest with each other, talking openly. I mean, you can cure yourself. You can have a life. You can experience your children. The therapeutic idea of friendship—you have no idea of the ways you defend yourself, ways you guard against your life, ways you protect yourself that limit your life so incredibly and your spirit."

THE RELATIONSHIP BETWEEN FRIENDSHIP, PHYSICAL HEALTH, AND EMOTIONAL WELL-BEING

The need and desire for social affiliation are basic human potentialities. Researchers Ryan and Deci (2000) identified "relatedness" as one of the three basic needs that are "innate, essential and universal" in human beings:

By our definition, a basic need, whether it be a physiological need . . . or a psychological need, is an energizing state that, if satisfied, conduces toward health and well-being but, if not satisfied, contributes to pathology and ill-being. We have thus proposed that the basic needs for competence, autonomy, and relatedness must be satisfied across the life span for an individual to experience an ongoing sense of integrity and well-being. (pp. 74–75)

The need for close emotional ties with a number of other individuals appears to have had a selective adaptive advantage for human beings. Evolutionary psychologists have emphasized the fact that social relationships enhanced our ancestors' chances for survival. "Groups shared food, provided mates, and helped care for children. . . . Facing enemies, there was strength in numbers" (Myers, 2000, p. 62). Thus, it is likely that our desire and need for social affiliation are genetically determined. The evolutionary basis of the need for close social ties "helps explain why epidemiologists, after following thousands of lives through time, have consistently found that close, intact relationships predict health" (p. 62).

Buss (2000) has noted other advantages of friendship in small kinship groups: "Ancestral humans relied on their friends and relatives to seek justice, to correct social wrongs, to deal with violence inflicted on them from others" (p. 16). Contrasting ancestral tribal life with present-day living, Buss asserted that "in modern America, for example, kin members often scatter in the pursuit of better jobs and promotions, yielding a social mobility that removes the social support of extended kin and makes social bonds [friendships] more transient" (p. 17).

Block (1980) analyzed the results of a survey of 2,063 individuals about their friendships over the life span and concluded that:

The experience of friendship . . . is not a mere luxury. For optimal functioning, it is an imperative. . . . Childhood friends are the first link with the world outside our family. They help us begin the process of separation from our parents; they teach us by their reactions acceptable social behavior; through friends we become introduced to the world of sex, and friends as well as parents contribute to our moral development. (pp. 211–212)

However, surveys documenting the actual occurrence or prevalence of long-term friendships in society show that many people are not benefiting from the enhanced mental and physical health associated with nonfamilial relationships. Block (1980) reported, for example, that "although most survey respondents recall a close special friend during their teen and preteen years, many reported being in and out of friendships frequently" (p. 213). House, Landis, and Umberson (1988) called attention to the fact that "just as we discover the importance of social relationships for health, and see an increasing need for them, their prevalence and availability may be declining" (p. 544).

In society at large, it is unusual for a person to maintain close friendships over the life span. According to Fehr (1996), friendship, particularly between a man and a woman, is atypical. In summarizing his findings, Block (1980) noted the dearth of cross-gender friendships and compared the free choice inherent in friendship to the restrictiveness of many marital relationships:

> Less than one-third of married respondents regarded their mates as friends! . . . These findings warn against the extreme demand for marital togetherness sanctioned by our society. Instead of a code of bonding, most of us have been indoctrinated with one of bondage. . . . How many couples in our society freely allow each other strong individual friendships outside marriage? Very few indeed. (pp. 216–217)

DIMENSIONS OF FRIENDSHIP THAT HAVE THERAPEUTIC VALUE

The aspects of friendship that we have found to be of special therapeutic value include support for pursuing one's priorities and goals in life; opportunities for truthful, open dialogue; and the sharing of projects and activities. In the following pages, we delineate the various dimensions of friendship that have had significant effects on the personal development of participants in the group of friends.

Lack of Exclusiveness and Possessiveness

In contrast to a fantasy bond within a couple or family relationship, a genuine friendship between two mature adults is characterized by a lack of exclusiveness and possessiveness. Acting out of choice rather than obligation leads to feelings of joy and happiness, while at the same time diminishing anger, resentment, and self-criticism. In a friendship, each person is respectful of the other's boundaries, goals, and aspirations. An authentic friendship, which involves closeness without illusions of security, enables a person to feel the truth of his or her separateness.

Friendships are often more rewarding than family relationships, perhaps precisely because they tend to be based on free choice rather than obligation. Friends are chosen on the basis of positive likable qualities, mutual respect, compatibility, and similar interests, whereas in many cases family members engage in role-determined behavior and activities in an unpleasant, disrespectful atmosphere that injures all parties.

Equality Versus Polarization of Parent–Child Modes of Interaction

In a genuine friendship, people relate to each other as independent individuals with considerable give and take in terms of reciprocal need gratification. Friends refrain from imposing rules and role restrictions on the friendship; as a consequence, each person is left alone, in the best sense of the word, to pursue his or her own goals. There is a lack of judgmental, parental role-playing and childlike responses, and each person respects the other's point of view. In contrast to a fantasy bond, friendship between two emotionally mature individuals is characterized by equality and respect for each other's boundaries.

Self-Disclosure and a Forum for Honest Communication

Underlying the ease with which participants in the friendship circle interact is a style of communication that evolved from the original group discussions described in the introduction. People's devotion to personal self-disclosure within the context of these discussions have played a significant role in sustaining personal relationships between couples and family members and overall friendship of the participants. It would have been impossible for a significant number of people, however well-intended, to succeed in sailing across oceans in a large group without friction, compete in the business world, mix work with friendship, survive as partners, raise their children in close proximity, and remain friends for more than 25 years without learning to cope effectively with their emotions.

The discussions have a town hall atmosphere—a genuine sense of democracy in which all people can speak their minds freely. The situation goes well beyond the town hall analogy because not only are free speech and the right to be heard without censure acceptable, they are fundamental. There is not only freedom to express ideas, but each person can express feelings as well. Emotional responses of every variety are not merely tolerated, they are cherished. The focal point of the group discussions is the communication of feelings, and people come with the expectation that they will get closer to their emotions and thereby closer to themselves. By the act of participating, people are asking for honest feedback and will listen to all that is said without taking offense or retaliating. The feedback in this group process is sensitive and empathic and rarely comes from an attacking orientation. Years of this sort of open and direct conversation have helped people to become unusually nondefensive.

The style of communication has enabled people to live and work together in a remarkably harmonious way. The normal, routine bickering of everyday life has been diminished to a considerable degree. In ongoing dialogue between the friends, hostility and anger are not acted out but are openly revealed. Negative perceptions, disappointments, and hurt feelings are dealt with, without holding grudges. In contrast to Hellmuth Kaiser's (Fierman, 1965) descriptions of neurotic patients who are unable to share their problems with other people, the people in the friendship circle have consistently shared their deepest concerns and personal stories with each other and have found this mutual self-disclosure to be highly beneficial.[1]

In spite of the active and varied pursuits that occupy the friends— sailing, business, travel—they value their participation in these talks more than any other activity. People's involvement in the intellectual discussions and compassionate encounters is a vital part of their lives, and the talks have been the principal agent of change for many.

Sharing Projects and Activities

Friendship cannot exist in a vacuum. In this group of friends, the process of sharing adventure, travel, and work projects was undoubtedly essential to people's maintaining their long-standing friendships. As noted, the expansion of this friendship circle encompassed three areas of endeavor: the rebuilding of a sailing schooner, which led to sea voyages and eventually to a circumnavigation; the sharing of business ventures; and the search for a more meaningful and richer emotional life. The projects and activities that initially brought these people together have helped solidify their friendships. In addition, the circumnavigation typified the kind of lifestyle that many people had originally sought—a life of calculated risk—of taking chances without being self-destructive, a life that heightened their consciousness of being alive and that represented a healthy balance between living life fully and spontaneously, while maintaining safety precautions.

By sharing the adventure of sailing, working together and pooling their resources, these people found that they could achieve far more than any one of them could have accomplished alone. The shared projects were far more rewarding than singular accomplishments because of the exceptional joy of team involvement.

CONCLUSION

Most people have been taught to turn away from the basic strivings that are essential for living a meaningful life. For many people, their curiosity, their search for self-knowledge, their desire to live congenially with others, and their ability to form their own values and ideals have been damaged to varying degrees in the process of growing up. Most have "adjusted" to a life directed by internalized voices and external values and are content to lead less than a fully realized existence.

Admittedly, it is difficult for people to be inspired to take an interest in themselves once they have disconnected from their feelings. However, understanding the sources of people's resistance, creating a social process to cope with them, and keeping them in the foreground of awareness can have a powerful and broadening effect on people's lives. Among the friends, the toxic behaviors that many individuals previously acted out in close personal interactions have been diminished to a marked degree. As a consequence, these people have a positive influence on each other rather than a detrimental effect. Through their shared endeavors and close friendships, these people have attempted to change generation on generation of thought within the brief span of their own lives and are currently involved in a complex process of acculturation. Having inadvertently evolved into a new culture, they are learning to live in it and to accommodate to the vast difference between their new world and the world they knew as children.

Finally, the uniqueness of this group of people as a living psychological laboratory lies in the style of open discussion that deepened their friendships and in the sustained observation of three generations of family life. In their talks over the years, people have revealed the dynamics of their inner lives and their dreams, innermost secrets, and feelings. At the same time, their outward behavior has been visible, providing systematic objective data. Thus, it has been possible to study the full extent of a neurotic or maladaptive psychological function. For example, if a person were passive, all the dimensions of his or her passivity could be discerned—in work, in personal interactions, in intimate relationships, and in other situations. His or her personality dynamics and problematic style of interacting with others could be elucidated in the context of a total life experience. From this wealth of information, we have been able to develop and further elaborate a number of hypotheses that we believe to be generally valid for human behavior in the larger society.

SOME OF OUR PERSONAL IMPRESSIONS

The growth of the circle of friends has been organic in the sense that events just happened and friendships developed, and the sharing that we have done has extended itself into many different areas. It is difficult to describe all of the remarkable effects that we have had on one another and what has been accomplished. The friendships have enhanced each person's individual development and helped people to achieve far-reaching goals, both personal and vocational. We believe that none of this would have been possible if it were not for the open and honest communication of thought and feeling. The discussions, which provided the medium for self-expression, were extended to the children in their developmental years and persisted when they grew up and eventually had children themselves.

Our movement toward a new society of warmth and friendship and the sharing of activities, adventure, and projects has been extremely stimulating. We have taken a serious interest in understanding the dynamics of people in both family constellations and their interactions in the social milieu. It has added powerful dimensions to our understanding of human beings.

In concluding this chapter, we would like to share some of our personal impressions and poignant incidents of everyday life among this group of friends. Try to imagine:

A crowd of happy people in a large living room, all laughing and good-natured before a serious talk. The faces of three adorable two-year-old youngsters, peering at us from the glassed-in porch. Friends sitting in couples and clusters, scattered all over restaurants around the world, obviously involved in important personal communication. Our friend Bill, leading the little kids around on horseback. Seven or eight children climbing, swinging, and playing happily together.

Wild scenes at sea; huge frightening waves, violent motion, the powerful force of the wind on the sails and the heel of the boat as she rushes through the water. Fog so thick that we could not see the end of the ship. Individuals working together, plotting courses, navigating through dangerous waters and struggling to take down sails during stormy conditions. Checking squalls on the radar as they move across the path of our vessel. Huddling together in the wheelhouse at night as we bounce along the big waves. The ship at anchor in a quiet, scenic harbor. Men, women, and children, jumping gleefully off the bow or swinging into the sea holding onto the spinnaker halyard, the onlookers laughing and cheering them on.

The thrill of business successes and the torment of business reversals. The joy of business growth and the pain of cutting back. Sweating together over business problems. Racking our brains for new ideas and new ventures. Shared projects, where we revel in each other's accomplishments.

The deep respect for one another and the painful disillusionment at those times when friends are stubborn, defensive, or rejecting. The anguish we all experience when a person reveals a particularly painful childhood episode. The incredible compassion and empathy that we observe all around us when someone is suffering. So many faces etched in pain and so many tear-streaked faces. The hurt, angry moments, the rage at past and present misunderstandings. The terror we sometimes feel when someone we care about is acting in a self-destructive manner. The guilt we feel when someone uses feedback badly instead of rising to the challenge. The hurt we feel when a person reacts with suspicion and distrust when we are generous or loving. The embarrassment we feel when we are confronted with negative information about our behavior and challenged about our self-deception. The feelings of sadness and rejection when someone we cared about leaves. The torture of losing close friends through sickness or death.

The joy and exaltation we feel when we observe a person breaking out of a life-long defensive pattern, witness a courageous individual overcoming a deep-seated fear reaction, overhear a sensitive, caring comment or truly supportive remark, feel the tenderness and insight of our comrades, or experience a remarkable release of feeling. The great moments when everyone present is enlightened. The surge of energy when repressions are lifted, our minds are clear, and we feel strong and centered in ourselves. The unbridled enthusiasm as we approach life armed with increased self-knowledge. The happiness we all share when we see real improvement in a person's life and recall our own personal gains. The nostalgia and the gratitude we feel when looking back we realize how impoverished our lives would have been if we had never met.

These images depict the advantages of friendship and its therapeutic value. More important, they suggest that there are numerous ways that therapists and their clients, outside this friendship circle, can expand their own lives.

NOTE

1. An analogy can be made between the characteristics of a genuine friendship and an effective therapeutic relationship as described by Hellmuth Kaiser (quoted in Fierman, 1965). Kaiser's model of therapy makes a distinction between authentic relating and those communications and behaviors (on the patient's part) that support a "delusion of fusion":

   Patients are lonely persons. Many of them are literally isolated and have few contacts with people, but even those who move in a circle of friends, have wives and children, parents and other relatives around them, are at least alone with their neurotic problems, because these problems cannot be shared with other people. (p. xix)

18

SPIRITUALITY, MYSTERY, AND THE SEARCH FOR MEANING

Death-tinged sadness—lovers parting, life ending, cherry blossoms falling—is inseparable from and an evocation of the larger life process.
—Robert Jay Lifton (1979, p. 28)

A critical component in pursuing the good life involves developing our sense of the sacred, enhancing the spiritual dimensions of our experience, exploring the mysteries of existence, and seeking meaning in life. In our search for meaning, we believe it is important to reach our own conclusions—that is, to develop our own beliefs and speculations about the vital questions in life based on our own personal experiences rather than on ideas and beliefs mediated through diverse religious or secular systems.

Harvard scientist E. O. Wilson (Petzinger, 2000) has emphasized that "the predisposition to religious belief is the most complex and powerful force in the human mind, and in all probability an ineradicable part of human nature" (p. R16). Yet today more than ever before, science has made a powerful intrusion on religious belief systems. Mounting evidence of human beings' evolution has made an incisive attack on the Judeo–Christian tradition of creation. People in Western society at large have become increasingly cynical about an all-powerful God, conceived of in traditional parental terms, often behaving in a vindictive and punitive fashion, who has allowed for so much human suffering. In some way, it appears that people created God in an image that fulfilled their desperation for a parent in the sky to protect them from death.

Wilson goes on to say,

Quoted material from T. Petzinger (2000, Jan. 1), Talking About Tomorrow: Edward O. Wilson. *Wall Street Journal*, pp. R16, R18, used by permission.

The expansion of human knowledge with science and technology, especially neuroscience, genetics and evolution, renders traditional religious belief less and less tenable, more and more difficult to justify and argue logically. The more we understand from science about the way the world really works, all the way from subatomic particles up to the mind and on to the cosmos, the more difficult it is to base spirituality on our ancient mythologies. (quoted in Petzinger, 2000, p. R16)

According to Wilson:

The conflict over the origin of humanity and ethics—whether they were in some way ordained by a divine will or are natural in the universe, whether they are transcendental or a material production of evolution—this will be the struggle for men's souls in the 21st century. . . . It's more likely to tip gradually toward the empiricists. The great religions of the world will continue to evolve, as they have been for many years, toward a more secular view of the world, with an inner core of spirituality preserving the psychologically most powerful rituals and rites. (p. R16)

We agree with Wilson when he emphasizes that "whatever we feel in our hearts, we need to believe that there is some ultimate measure of sacredness, whether you perceive it as secular in origin through the organic evolution of humanity, or whether you perceive it as God-directed" (p. R16). He has suggested that we must be "proactive in seeking it and defining it instead of reactive in the traditional manner of taking the sacred texts and beliefs handed down to us and trying to adapt them to an evolving culture" (p. R16). Some seek the sacred in nature, in our natural surroundings, others in music and the arts, and some find it in love. Indeed, if death anxiety is conceptualized as the poison, then love may well be the antidote. Wilson goes on to describe the spiritual celebration of nature as being:

The celebration of the full complexity of the world that is, that exists, and particularly the living world, which reveals itself as to be splendid beyond anything in any of the sacred texts when you begin to understand it. We need to create in a new epic based on the origins of humanity. . . . We are justified in having a great deal of species pride, and then devising a new spirituality based on what we actually know about our own origins across millions of years of evolution, and thence on into our historical origins, too. Homo sapiens have had one hell of a history! And I am speaking both of deep history—evolutionary, genetic history—and then added on to that, and interacting with it, the cultural history recorded for the past 10,000 years or so. It is just an amazing epic. If we somehow can formulate it correctly and honestly, it could be as inspiring as anything that traditional mythology now offers us. (pp. R16, R18)

One of the fundamental challenges to achieving a humanitarian-based and personal spirituality lies in our confronting those traditional religious beliefs and practices that deny the body—and our sexuality, sensuality, and aliveness. Challenging traditional belief systems opens the door to allow for every individual to choose his her own path in life. In the pursuit of an enriching lifestyle, people can define their own individualized, personal goals and values. When values and ethics are developed from within rather than outer-directed, a person can charter the course of his or her life in a manner that is harmonious and well-integrated. He or she will exhibit a clear and distinct point of view, manifest internal consistency, avoid self-deception, dishonesty, and compartmentalization, and maintain a powerful sense of self.

CONVENTIONAL DEFENSES AGAINST DEATH ANXIETY

People's fear of death has a profound effect on the formation of pathological defensive processes that play a significant role in every form of psychopathology and limits human experience in a manner that threatens each person's opportunity to pursue the good life. Defenses against death anxiety are varied and complex but each form of defensive illusion takes its toll on life, and the cost is dear. Usually conventional religious beliefs offer the hope of a life after death, in many ways at the expense of forsaking a real life in the present, a trade-off of the body that must die for the surviving soul. Alive sensual fulfillment and the capacity for genuine feeling may become a willing sacrifice in exchange for a disconnected life of the mind that has no flesh or physical component and therefore cannot be lost. In that sense the disembodied life offers the promise of immortality.

The first author recounts a conversation with a deeply religious woman, who asked, "Are you not frightened to be without faith in relation to your own personal death?" Without hesitation he answered that indeed he was, but the fact that he was disconcerted did not necessarily lead him to a belief system that would seem to him to contradict all of the scientific discoveries that human beings have labored to uncover. It had always puzzled him why people of equal intelligence and sensibility arrive at different conclusions in regard to the matter of faith. Why do some believe and others find it unacceptable? Also, why do some believers so strongly assert that even other believers in God who do not share precisely their version of God are going to Hell?

THE MYSTERY OF EXISTENCE AND
EXPERIENCE OF THE SACRED

Even after considering the impact on belief systems caused by scientific advances in understanding the origin of Homo sapiens and the development of life on the planet earth, one cannot rule out faith, for much is still unknown. Aristotelian logic and modern science not only fail to explain existence, they preclude its possibility. All that we know in the scientific sense points to the fact that something cannot come from nothing; even if one postulates a God, one is burdened by the question of where could that essence have come from. Faced with this preposterous logical contradiction, we are left with a hypothetical problem that goes beyond human intelligence and intellect. In the vernacular we are faced with a mind-blowing problem of immense proportions. We are forced to accept the blow to our vanity and face the painful truth of our intellectual limitations, but there is a consolation. We are left with the fact of mystery, free to contemplate the awesome spectacle of existence of all varieties, and we are left open to form our own conclusions about life and meaning.

In spite of skepticism about extrasensory phenomena, precognition, psychokineses, auras, and the like, there is a body of generally disregarded experimental data and experiential evidence that is at the least suggestive that there is more to life than we usually consider. There is still magic in the world. We are not likely to find the answer to the riddle of life in absolute systems, rhetoric, or dogma, as though the truth may be hidden under a rock somewhere. Like Buddha, who taught that we should all find God in ourselves, we must seek our own spiritual solutions and not succumb to outside pressures. Paradoxically people have made a God out of Buddha, and we believe that points out our great weakness. In our fear we sacrifice our personal strength and power and subjugate ourselves to other persons and ideologies in a desperate bid for dependency and security. We forsake reality for illusion, choose symbols in place of really living, sacrifice individuality for a costly fantasy of fusion, and reject our unique and separate identity for a life of conformity and submission. In a subservient life, we not only mistake the map for the territory but actually prefer the map to the territory, thereby giving up the only life that we know about for sure. When we experience emotional pain or become afraid, we divest ourselves of real experience, choose fantasy over our sensations and feelings, prefer inwardness over genuine relating, depersonalize, and pretty much turn our backs on our human heritage.

THE SEARCH FOR MEANING

A human being's search for meaning and purpose is as fundamental as his or her physical drives for self-preservation. Without this core, he or she functions on a subhuman level, lacks a center, and suffers from a form of emotional poverty. Kierkegaard (1954) conceived of despair as endemic to the human condition, but considered the despair about being unaware of that despair to be a more horrifying state, a condition worse than the contemplation of death itself.

There are a myriad of ways that people find meaning in life and there are countless avenues in which to approach the good life. Although the concept of personal goal-directed investment is of the utmost importance to a person's well-being, with the exception of cases of brutality and human rights violations, one cannot place a value judgment on the form that the investment takes. Some people find meaning in contributing to the arts, others may find it in business enterprises, scientific pursuits, medical research, charitable acts, or other people concerns. No matter which direction is chosen, personal involvement is essential, and it is a fundamental aspect of a healthy emotional existence. When thinking about finding personal meaning in life, the first author is reminded of a patient in psychotherapy, an engineer and scientist who suffered from an obsessive–compulsive disorder with paranoid ideology. This man found himself in a great deal of pain and was nearly overcome by depression, yet his consuming interest in working on a NASA project at Cape Canaveral (in those early, glamorous days of rocket science) virtually saved his life. Working closely with others on a common goal that transcended a narrow view of his personal life had a profoundly positive effect on his psyche.

We agree with Victor Frankl (1946/1959), in his book, *Man's Search for Meaning*, when he emphasized that one cannot seek happiness directly, but rather that happiness is a by-product of being responsive to transcendent goals that give meaning to life. In *Freedom and Destiny*, Rollo May (1981) made an important distinction between happiness and joy:

> Happiness is finding a system of rules which solves our problems; joy is taking the risk that is necessary to break new frontiers. . . . Joy is the experience of possibility, the consciousness of one's freedom as one confronts one's destiny. In this sense despair, when it is directly faced, can lead to joy. After despair, the one thing left is possibility. (p. 242)

A person cannot selectively cut off feeling. When we try to block out psychological pain, we shut down our capacity to feel happiness as well. In relation to death anxiety, we might do well to mourn the tragic passing of our existence rather than trying to deny or escape from the existential dilemma. Lifton (1979) referred to this as a feeling of the " 'sad beauty' or 'suchness' of existence. . . . The feeling is often used to express one's involvement in and, in a sense, passive acceptance of the slow, sad truths of life and nature" (p. 28). Feeling sadness openly and permitting its free expression allows us to savor the experience of living. Men and women who face up to issues of death and dying, rather than living a life of denial, experience richer, fuller lives and generally do not infringe on the rights of others. There is a sense that all human beings are fragile, life is precious, and that we are all in the same boat. These people place humanistic concerns above nationalistic interests and are unlikely to act out hostility or aggression on their neighbors.

In contrast, those who hold absolutist views are threatened by people who adhere to different belief systems. They are anxious and punitive when their traditional defenses against death anxiety are questioned or scrutinized and tend to judge others and lash out.

ETHICAL ISSUES

Although it is worthwhile for people to develop an ethical frame of reference, there are countless ways of addressing the subject of values, and an individual must seek his or her own guidelines. Without wishing to prescribe for others, we will attempt to outline the implicit set of ethics and values based on sound mental health principles that has evolved in the friendship circle. Aware of the forces that had caused them pain and suffering in the course of their development, these friends were able to identify toxic personality traits as distinguished from behaviors that were positive or reinforcing of good feelings. As they were increasingly cognitive of negative behaviors that were detrimental to the well-being of others, they gradually came to articulate their code of values in more explicit terms. Without moralizing, becoming prescriptive, or making excessive rules, people came to adopt these standards as a way of life, and there was a minimum of friction or disharmony in their interactions. As a result, even people who casually come into contact with members of the friendship circle or meet their children are immediately impressed with their eye contact, kindness, and geniality.

People's values in the friendship circle do not appear to differ significantly from traditional religious beliefs based on the golden rule. These people live by their values and are uncomfortable with any form of hypocrisy, and these values extend beyond the more familiar considerations. There is a powerful emphasis on generosity and compassion that is unique among people anywhere else. They have learned to say "yes" to one another in a way that shows deep respect and concern for each other's goals and aspirations. There is an incredible respect for the individual and a deep concern about human rights issues in personal relationships, and this is uniquely evident in relation to the children. There is a special valuing of each person's freedom and independence and a strong support for individual pursuits.

People place an unusual emphasis on personal honesty, open expression of feelings, kindness and affection, a sense of humor, a willingness to give and take in emotional transactions, personal competence, courage, a sense of responsibility for self and one's companions, and a joy in living. On the other hand, there are negative attitudes toward behaviors that are critical or demeaning of others, such as dishonesty, manipulation, high-handedness, sarcasm, hostility, or cynicism. In addition, all forms of manipulative power plays or attempts to control through either weakness or domination are frowned on. People have developed unique methods to deal with anger, competitive feelings, and other aggressive tendencies, making hostility and outbursts of nastiness practically nonexistent. They have learned to talk about their feelings freely in an open forum. They concluded that, generally speaking, whereas all feelings are considered acceptable, actions, even verbal actions, must be scrutinized in relation to one's personal goals and moral considerations. They came to understand that we all have competitive feelings and possessive feelings and experience anger when we are frustrated in reaching our personal goals. Yet they learned that these feelings are not catastrophic for adults to experience. We can cope with rivalry and frustration without manifesting aggression, becoming manipulative, controlling, or restrictive of our loved ones. When we are angry in personal relationships we have learned that it is better to talk about our angry feelings rather than assaulting the other verbally or physically. Such expressions of anger merely arouse anger in the other, and this is not usually the aim.

In conclusion, living with these standards, people have learned to share an enjoyable lifestyle while in close proximity, with a minimum of negative interactions, secrecy, or duplicity. They are able to cope with and triumph over competitive feelings, successfully deal with rivals at close quarters, and communicate their feelings in an honest fashion. They have found it worthwhile to formulate values and ethical standards based on a sensitive understanding of human nature and an awareness of the destructive forces that impinge on a healthy psychological adjustment. They have come to realize that ethical training imposed from a judgmental, moralistic point of view suffers in comparison to values and attitudes toward life that are based on example.

LOVE

Early in this chapter, we referred to love as the antidote to existential despair, an alternative to the void that offers real hope and fulfillment. Raised to its highest level, love and loving become the core, the center, the essence of spiritual life. But what is it that we mean by love, and what is it not? It is most certainly not the fantasy of fusion or fantasy bond, whereby one speaks about love but merely implies connection or illusion while behaving in a manner that completely defies any reasonable definition of the word. We are not talking about an abstract sentiment that has no observable or operational connotation in the real world. In fact, very often people speak of love while their actions imply the opposite.

R. D. Laing (1967) stated that:

> Love and violence . . . are polar opposites. Love lets the other be, but with affection and concern. Violence attempts to constrain the other's freedom, to force him to act in the way we desire, but with ultimate lack of concern, with indifference to the other's own existence or destiny. (p. 58)
> Perhaps men and women were born to love one another, simply and genuinely, rather than to this travesty that we call love. If we can stop destroying ourselves we may stop destroying others. We have to begin by admitting and even accepting our violence, rather than blindly destroying ourselves with it, and therewith we have to realize that we are as deeply afraid to live and to love as we are afraid to die. (p. 76)

Laing implied some optimism in a rather bleak formulation:

> Yet within all this, I do not preclude the occasions when, most lost, lovers may discover each other, moments when recognition does occur, when hell can turn to heaven and come down to earth, when this crazy distraction can become joy and celebration. (p. 75)

If love must have an external manifestation, those behavioral operations that would constitute a loving process must be defined. Generally speaking, they would include such observable signs as the expression of affection, usually inclusive of a physical aspect, respectful treatment, kindness, sensitivity, and a desire for ongoing companionship and friendship. Where there is real love, one values the other separate from one's selfish interest in the love object and places his or her goals on a par with one's own.

Up to this point, love has been referred to within the context of couple relationships, but love is more extensive and far reaching—not to underplay the importance of *romantic love* or its function in the good life. Unfortunately, love is hard to find because it requires a certain level of emotional maturity. Furthermore, as difficult as love is to find, it is even more difficult for people to tolerate. Most everyone says that they want love and lasting ties in their lives, but most often love and special personal recognition challenge defenses that maintain psychological equilibrium and therefore predispose anxiety. People are generally refractory to the love that they claim to desire, and the beloved often rejects or aggresses against the lover, thereby maintaining a safe amount of emotional distance. Indeed, love reminds us that we are truly alive and really do exist, and in embracing life and love we are forced to be cognizant of our personal death as well. Giving value to our existence makes us poignantly aware of our mortality.

CONCLUSION

The people of the friendship circle have found profound meaning in their love for one another, a love that expresses itself in countless examples of sensitivity, kindnesses, and generosity, big and small. We are deeply touched as we observe them sharing their appreciation of nature and love of life as they experience a sunrise or sunset at sea, sit silently before talking personally in group discussions, and laugh and cry together about the exigencies of life. The remarkable compassion and empathy in these group meetings gives rise to a transcendent feeling that makes each person aware of his or her uniquely human heritage and communion with his or her fellows. At these moments, there is an unusual combination of joy and exaltation together with an acute sensation of existential anguish. People never feel more together or more alone. It is at these times in particular that one approaches a true spiritual sense of oneself in relation to the interpersonal world and the universe at large.

EPILOGUE

In the spring of 2001, we completed the first draft of this manuscript. That summer we sailed to Europe with our families and friends. In the midst of the most glorious summer imaginable, we experienced an event that made us all acutely aware of the pain involved in choosing an invested and meaningful life. After the episode, our friends gathered on the sailboat to talk. We were very moved and affected by this conversation and the ones that took place during the weeks that followed. One of our friends, Richard, who keeps a journal, also wrote of his feelings and reactions during this time.

We decided to include partial transcripts from the talks as well as excerpts from the journal as an epilogue to this book. We feel that they are not only enlightening and insightful in relation to the subjects discussed in this book, but that they offer the reader an opportunity to experience the way these people live, how through their honest communication, compassion, caring, acceptance of feeling, and understanding of life's painful issues, they have developed an awareness of what it means to live the "good life."

ISSUES OF LIFE AND DEATH:
LIFE-AFFIRMING DEATH AWARENESS

In this book, we have spoken about the essential dilemma of life, whether to face the existential reality of our basic aloneness, eventual deterioration, and death or to choose a defensive existence characterized by fantasy and denial, the use of painkillers, and other self-protective mechanisms and the increased probability of psychopathology. The first option lends itself to an honest life and potential movement in the direction of personal freedom, integrity, and autonomy, yet there is considerable pain in experiencing the full depth of the human condition. The second helps to deflect psychological pain but there is a price to pay in that like other addictions, reliance on psychological defenses precludes the possibility of living a full life, hurts our personal relationships, reduces the capacity to feel, and ultimately tends to be self-destructive.

In this chapter we will describe a particularly painful episode that best illustrates the problems encountered in choosing an invested and meaningful life. Furthermore, the incident reveals that in coming face to face with death, most people experience powerful regressive tendencies, tend to turn against themselves, and distance themselves from their loved ones.

Our group of more than 40 friends and family members were touring the Mediterranean ports aboard a large motor-sailer. Each day was magnificent, swimming in the sea, exploring picturesque ports, tasting the foods of the region, and shopping for meaningful gifts for friends and relatives. For most, the summer was the happiest of our lives because although we had vacationed together in the area many times before, over the years we had developed our appreciation of the experience to a fine point. Our frequent group talks and personal exchanges were the highlight of the trip.

One day, the day after a particularly wonderful night of celebration in Venice, Louis, a beloved man of 70, suddenly collapsed at the rear of the boat, fell against the teak bar, and hit his head. He had no pulse; it appeared that his heart had stopped, and those who witnessed the horror were afraid that he was dead. Luckily there happened to be a paramedic aboard who rendered aid and resuscitated him, and he was rushed by boat ambulance to the hospital. Although the man was suffering from cancer, after extensive tests the doctors found nothing else wrong. Several days later, he was discharged from the hospital and returned to the trip. It was thought that the episode was related to heat exhaustion and overexertion.

Everyone aboard was deeply affected by the incident, because Louis was a much loved and important member of the friendship circle. In the early days he played a significant part in the formation of the group, inspired the young people, and taught everyone about navigation and sailing. He was instrumental in the group's first circumnavigation. His intelligence and wise counsel were much appreciated, and he was a close friend to many people.

About two weeks after Louis rejoined the travelers, there was a group talk that took place in the large salon on the ship. After the crowd had gathered, there was the usual silence as people switched from the social talk and activity to more serious personal considerations. Louis's son Richard (48) was among the participants. The first man to speak was Brant, a tall, bearded man with a sad expression.

Brant (52):	I feel guilty to bring this up but since the day that you got sick, Louis, I've been feeling really bad. My life has been really nice on this trip. Things with Lynn and my daughter are unbelievable, but I feel more and more troubled, sort of a feeling of futility and a depression coming back.
Robert Firestone (70):	Since Louis fell and his life was threatened very directly, it's been my observation that

almost everyone has felt bad. I certainly did, and almost everybody I know felt worse personally. And it's not just that we felt bad about Louis. I think the reason everyone felt worse was because it supported their voices about the futility of life. And it's a tragic truth. It's difficult to turn it around and feel good again. On an intellectual level, it's easy for me to affirm life based on what happened. But emotionally, I've turned on myself in a lot of different ways. In the beginning of the summer, I especially wanted not to lose myself in activity and stay close to my feelings. But I have felt more lost and cut off, and so has almost everybody I know. Strangely, people who weren't even particularly close to the situation had that reaction. They pulled away from people they were close to.

Even though intellectually, I support the exact opposite response, and maybe in the long run, I'll bounce back with even more feeling, but the immediate effect, to be truthful, was negative because it supported my voices. It's a sad truth. I started really worrying about myself in a hypochondriacal way, concerned about my age and worrying that I might die soon. A lot of attacks like that.

Tom (41):   I know that's true. We were making a lot of plans for the future, for how to improve our lives, but they feel dull now. My voice attack was, *"What's the use?"* and I know I wove that into what happened when the storm hit in Korkula. That felt like a similar type thing, like it was a surprise. An hour before, the kids had been playing ball in the cockpit, and then suddenly, it was a nightmare. I know I tied that into the thing with Louis—it was sort of the same thing. In Venice the night before, we had the party, we were dancing in that same area, then the next day there was that nightmarish scene. It's hard to enjoy life after that.

Robert Firestone: It's a hard thing to fight. There's a sense of turning on yourself. I think man is turned on himself because he knows that he'll die. He hates himself for that. He has a bitter hatred of himself because he's fragile and he'll die, and he's tempted not to invest in his life, not to really care about it. It's hard to turn that around. And that's why people's defenses are so intense about death. They want to deny it or they want to make up solutions that alleviate that tension. Also in making up those solutions and warding off the anxiety, and in the process of denial, they become far more destructive, far more turned on themselves and other people, too.

Stacey (54): When I was young, I realized that people ignored the subject of death, that people were going around as though there was no such thing, and it puzzled me how much denial there was. The world seemed insane because of the lack of realization of the reality of life and death.

Dean (50): I'm reminded of that story Robert wrote about his grandfather.

Robert Firestone: Yeah, I shared a room with my grandfather when I was young. When he would cough or he would seem to be close to death, it scared me. I saw him as unaware in some way, sort of living on a vegetative level, and I didn't want to be lulled into a life without awareness. I wanted to have a meaningful life.

But still the death issue is so amazing. When I was young, I thought there would be time to learn a lot about it, to understand it, but I haven't gotten anywhere. It's still a gigantic puzzle. You see millions of people all over the world, living and dying. You just wish there was some meaning to all of that, some sense to it—to understand this meaningless thing.

Tom: It's a tragic situation that we're all faced with. I was very excited about the ideas of change, I still am. I still intend to do all the things that I intended to do, but there's no heart in it, for the moment. There's no excitement.

Robert Firestone: So you turn away from the self that will be destroyed ultimately. That's the tragedy. And that's why people are so insensitive and unfeeling. And they don't even know how to get back to feeling. So even if things were perfect in growing up, you would not have a person free from destructive voices toward him- or herself. I've always emphasized that there are two major sources, the interpersonal pain that we go through and the existential despair that's inevitable. Both tend to make us defended and removed from feeling and make us turn on ourselves. Both lead us to punish ourselves. This is a tragic truth; I know it's true.

Andrea (52): Early in the summer, I felt that feeling I talked about in the last talk, the sadness and poignancy that are connected to my feeling that life was limited. It made my time more valuable to me and I was more aware of things, the beauty of the trip, but when the thing happened with Louis, I just plunged into a feeling of hopelessness that was so familiar to me, on a deeper level. I had an awareness of death that was enhancing my life, but then when the fact of death actually hit me, it was hard to stay with it.

Robert Firestone: Sometimes it gets so hard. To me, it's very touching because when we heard the news about Louis, we were playing tennis. Everybody stopped and was sad and cried. [sad] Everybody felt so sad. There were a lot of our friends watching the tennis and we just stood there feeling the grief. It's just that you can't win. And that adds to the personal loss. The personal loss of a friend you can deal with, and the sadness, but the futility of life is more difficult.

Andrea: Everything had a *"what's the use"* feeling to it. *"What's the point?"*

Robert Firestone: I didn't really think that. I don't think that way at all, but on a subtle level, that type of thing takes hold.

Brant: I felt so bad seeing you in Venice, Louis. I have a lot of feeling about it. It was ironic that Richard [Louis' son] and I came to the intensive care unit at the same time. Like we were both your sons. I always wanted to be close to my own father and you were like a substitute father to me, teaching me things and all. I leaned down and I hugged you and kissed you. (deep sadness). I felt so embarrassed about kissing you. (cries deeply).

(After a long pause) I feel better saying this and feeling my feelings, I feel in my own skin again. I wonder why I always resist feeling sad. It always makes me feel better after I feel it.

Robert Firestone: Sometimes that's the only way to get back to yourself. There are a thousand ways to cut off feelings, to remove yourself from pain, but the only way to feel yourself is to experience your sadness. Otherwise you're removed from yourself and the people in your life.

Brant (to Louis): When you were lying on the deck and you weren't conscious at that point, it's a wild thing, but I had such a strong feeling that I was glad that I was there. It was like a similar feeling like when Lia was born. It's strange: birth and death.

Louis: The first day in the hospital I felt sweet and close to you all, especially Robert and Andrea. But the very next day I felt cut off and unfeeling. I'm happy to be back on the boat and have a chance to talk about my struggles. (pauses) But there is something that I have been afraid to say. It's to you, Ilena [Louis's wife]. I feel guilty to be bringing this up, like it's morbid or too morbid. But I have to say it. The fact is I really am dying, my systems are shutting down, the cancer. Recovering from the incident in Venice was only a temporary respite.

[There was a stunned silence in the room after Louis's comment. Everyone felt deeply sad. Tears streaked every person's face as they felt the full impact of Louis's statement.]*

Robert Firestone: When you spoke, Louis, it hit me deeply and I felt admiration for your courage. I've observed that you were dying but your words hit full force. It's brave to be so direct, so forthright.

---

*Transcripted statements made by Louis Catlett; used by permission.

Franz (59): I have to say I respect you, Louis, for the way you're living your life, facing your death. It should be an example to all of us. The way you look benign and accepting, so genial and upbeat.

Louis: I'd like to talk about what I felt when I fell. The first part was the anger at being waked up. Fury, like *"Leave me alone!"* I don't know where that came from really, but it was just like someone shaking me from a deep sleep and that was pretty momentary, I think. Then I felt really, really sad to see everybody. I couldn't stop the tears, I didn't want to. Then I saw the people on the boat around me and then you all came to the hospital. Then through the day, I just felt so sad. I also felt a lot of irony in the situation. I kept thinking sort of jokes, humor.

Brant: That helps to get through it.

Louis: But then, the next day, I found myself down and dull, but I think I've gotten back to feeling somewhat, getting back on the trip. Roger said something to me yesterday that blew my mind almost. He said, "You know, one of the paramount memories of my visit here is seeing how much you're loved." But it startled me. I told him that it was hard for me to feel that.

Robert Firestone: It's hard to feel that you're loved for yourself.

Louis: When Brant and Richard came to the hospital, I felt very sad. But I had that sweet feeling toward everyone I saw. Sad but sweet. You guys—the feeling is so hard to hold on to.

Robert Firestone: The despair leads to the cutting off of feeling, so the next day it was harder for you to feel. So theoretically, just to sum it up, focus on the death issue led to primal feelings for most of us about our own death, which led to an inward process that left us removed, and many of us tended to be self-critical and self-destructive. And the way out of that is to get into the deep feelings associated with the issue. But typically there is resistance to overcome in order to do that. It's very hard to get to those feelings, even though you'd like to. The easier part is to feel for the other person; the hardest part is to feel for your very own circumstances.

Theo (44): Louis, when I heard what happened to you, I thought back through the years when we first started sailing the boat. I just realized what effect you've had on my life. I felt so bad that you could die (cries) and I wouldn't be able to tell you that. The huge effect you've had on my life.

Joyce (69): When I was very young, every day I felt dread and hopelessness. But I noticed that people grew up and left home and that gave me a glimmer of hope. But then when I was 5, my father left and at the same time I figured out about death. The two things happened around the same time. So my glimmer of hope was lost and I sank into despair and depression. But even before I figured out about death, I had developed inward habits to try to help myself, going alone to my room to read or to cry, fantasizing, different defenses, so after that, I just went more into those behaviors.

Robert Firestone: That's right, the death issue reinforced the defenses.

Andrea: I really believe one of the things that would have helped me when I was young and facing the issue of death would have been to be allowed to feel about it in my family. It wouldn't have resolved it but I would have been better.

Robert Firestone: But the reason you're not allowed to feel it is because it's threatening to people.

Andrea: Right, right, but it was so unacceptable to feel anything, especially anything about death.

Robert Firestone: But viewing all this in terms of the changes in our lifestyle that Tom was referring to, basically they're changes directed against the cutting off of feeling in various ways, finding distractions, anything that takes you further away from yourself, anything that makes you less of a feeling person, these are the things we want to address. We want to live a life that supports getting into feeling and dealing with these issues. When we cut off pain, we cut off life as well.

Bill (40): Robert, you said there were all kinds of voices that come up that make people disengage, move away from life, embrace death.

Robert Firestone: Exactly, voices that support self-limiting or self-destructive attitudes and behavior, which means moving away from closeness and intimacy personally, finding substances to cut off pain, finding distractions that lead you away from your life, moving toward isolation, distancing yourself from people, becoming more angry and parental and critical, acting out hostile or childish manifestations. All of these kind of responses that cut you off from feeling, that support your being more cynical, all these are reactions that you can expect in a person who is siding with the voice, siding against themselves, siding with death.

AN EXAMPLE OF REGRESSION IN FACE OF THE DIRECT ENCOUNTER WITH DEATH

Richard (49): Since Louis's collapse, I had some interesting things happen to me. Louis, when you were lying on the ground, your eyes were shut for a second and then you opened them—you looked at me and reached up and grabbed my arm and I grabbed your hand. That felt very good to me, that was a very touching experience. But at the same time, you had this look of fury in your eyes that I hadn't seen in a long time and it was something I used to see all the time. It was the same kind of anger, sort of mindless rage, that you directed at me when I was a kid. That's one thing that happened.

Then when I was going to the hospital, I was in this water taxi by myself and I was going through the most beautiful place on earth and I'm thinking, "I cannot believe that this is going to be the last place I'm going to see Louis." And the contrast between what was happening and what I was seeing, it was just tearing my insides out.

Then I calmed down some when I saw you that evening. Later I had a good time. Brant and I talked about our feelings about the incident and I liked that a lot. . . . But then, what has happened in the time since then is that I always think that men are angry at me. I think that they hate me, that they absolutely despise me. I see it in their faces. This has happened to me my whole life.

After that happened with you [Louis], I saw that same look that I saw in your eyes in all my male friends' eyes, that fury. I don't quite understand what that's about but my theory is that in defending what happened to me in my family, I have to color the rest of the world as being angry. I really wanted to love you, Louis, but in order to love you when you were mean to me, I had to see the world as an angry, terrible place.

Robert Firestone: That's how it works. In order to hold on to the fantasy bond or imaginary connection to the parent, you idealize the parent on a certain level, but you have to dispose of the traits, their negative characteristics, and so you project those onto the world at large. You see the world in those terms. You can't maintain that distortion, the idealization process, without projecting the negative qualities outward, on to the world or seeing them in yourself for that matter.

Richard: It was interesting to me how clearly I understood that at that moment. I wanted to love you, Louis, and feel for you, which I do, but on the other hand, I could tell that's what was going on with me as a kid all the time. I perceived the world as an angry, terrible place.

But I haven't felt that bad way since I figured this out; I feel better since I had that realization. It's also good to talk it over with your friends and find out if they are pissed off. They usually say, "No." (Laughter). When I heard that you (Brant) had the same feelings that I had, that was interesting.

Robert Firestone: If you make the projection that we're talking about to maintain the idealization process, then you act accordingly and you provoke reactions in the other person. You actually succeed in provoking angry reactions. If you act strange, obviously sheepish, or you act hostile, you keep people distant or hostile back toward you.

Brant: The day before was my favorite day on the trip. It was the day we took the new boat to the Venice airport. It was just so much fun. The camaraderie, a lot of joking going on. It's like I wish we were still driving it.

Robert Firestone: What I would say, summing it up in relation to not denying the death issue, is what Andrea said, that if there's not a direct confrontation, basically you can maintain a soft feeling.

Andrea: It does enhance your life to be aware of it.

Robert Firestone: It does enhance your life, but if it hits you too hard, it really supports the voice process and tends to turn you against yourself. And that makes you more alienated from yourself, more cut off and in that state, you tend to isolate yourself more and tend to be more inward and get more into your head, negative thoughts. And it's hard to maintain contact. See, it's the most difficult thing to have feeling for people when you're faced directly with the fact of death and the futility of life.

Rachel (53): I feel so appreciative for what everyone said because I understood exactly what happened. I've been torturing myself with my own thoughts and I've isolated myself more, but I know what it's from.

Robert Firestone: So many people did that. You remind yourself that you're going to die in a sort of savage, mean way. It's almost like a rehearsal for death, making it more desirable. You become a friend of death instead of a friend of life. There are so many examples.

Rachel: All my life, I've fought these kinds of battles, but I know I've sided with the wrong side since Louis fell.

Robert Firestone: The issue would promote or strengthen this inward pattern of turning against yourself, just in and of itself. This is probably why people have such a destructive impact on children, because we built these defenses originally and then they have a destructive effect on others. The interpersonal pain leads you to become defensive and the existential despair leads you to become even more defended. Both converge to make you cut off, not want to feel, or be hopeful or excited, and to turn against yourself and others to some extent. When you're inward and self-critical, you hurt the people closest to you.

Richard: Down through the generations.

Robert Firestone: In fact, that's what happened throughout human history. As people came to understand what was going to happen to them, they erected more serious defensive barriers. People fight over these defenses, they will kill over them. They go to war over them, over differences, as though those differences had to do with immortality. Ethnic issues are vitally serious because you have to kill others with different belief systems, with different defenses against death anxiety, because these differences threaten you.

Brant: Death issues are probably the first thing people defended against.

Robert Firestone: That's why humans are so full of aggression, too. Part of our natural anger and the natural destructiveness comes from the death issue.

Andrea: One thing that I kept thinking about myself was there was something old and familiar about what I was feeling during the days after Louis got sick. When I was little and first figured out that my parents were going to die, and figured out the whole thing about death, this was the feeling that must have come over me, this horrible, sinking despair. I think that as an adult, I can cope with death even though there's no escape. I was having a primal reaction to the situation, like a kid, and that just didn't feel right.

Stacey: Yes, it's an old subject that goes way back.

Andrea: What I'm saying is that I think I could have had all the same feelings but something about my "sinking" was primal. I could have felt more like I did at the beginning of the summer, still enjoying life despite the pain of death.

Robert Firestone: That makes sense. The sadness about life and the poignancy, you can deal with. The essential despair is old and painful and difficult and hits on a level beneath that, which is primal. Remember Stuart Boyd's "The Last Cricket Match," where he says that he had the feeling of what a gun meant to a child. It felt familiar, immediately familiar, because it's part of where that aggression comes from and the essential horror and the siding with death. This is where Freud's death instinct comes into this, not as an instinct, but as a reaction. His data is right and in one sense, he's not necessarily wrong, it's just that there's no real evidence for the instinctual aspect.

	Feelings about death are intensified particularly when things are going well; if things are going bad, the attitude toward the death issue is familiar. Death is not such a problem when you're feeling really wretched—it's more acceptable.
Jenny (31):	What do you mean, death is more acceptable?
Robert Firestone:	Here's the thing: when you're feeling really shitty about life, you don't mind the thought of dying that much. When you're really happy, or excited, you're in love, everything is pretty, you hate to lose it, then it's painful.
Stacey:	That's why, Jenny, when you get scared about the thought of dying, like Robert was saying, it stimulates a lot of voices that attack your life and put you in a state that you don't care that much.
Robert Firestone:	Let me give you an example with you, Jenny. (Laughter). You feel in love and are having an especially happy time and you trust in your love, and then on some level, you're aware that you're going to die. Then, whether you realize it or not, you pull back so it won't hurt. You color the original situation with the elements of despair that were related to the death issue and you get distrustful of Josh (her fiancé) and you pull away from him. You get angry at him and get insecure and demand proof of his love. You give up your life, that's how you protect yourself. Then you're siding with the death part more, cutting off your life, and you don't give a damn. You want to get away, you feel hopeless and so on. It's an adaptation to the death issue; you get rid of some of the pain temporarily but you lose your good feelings about life in the process.
Russell (42):	I was at home when I heard about Louis and the episode in Venice. A couple of days after I got the news, I turned on myself. All of a sudden, I'm attacking myself and I'm overworking and I'm beating myself up.
Robert Firestone:	This data is overwhelming to me. One person after another reporting the same phenomenon. If you don't think this is a part of life, you're crazy. That's all I can tell you. (Laughs) So many of our friends attacked themselves and distanced themselves and many became somewhat depressed. They depersonal-

ized to some extent and were no longer centered in themselves. Who wants to be centered in a self that's going to die? In other words, to avoid pain, we remove ourselves from ourselves whether it's emotional pain or despair about dying.

Monica: I really like this talk. I feel like I'm getting back to my feelings.

Robert Firestone: It's very good that Brant brought this up.

Monica: I realized that there is a block of time and in only a second you could be gone.

Robert Firestone: That's right, it's very impersonal. Death is impersonal.

PERMISSION TO FEEL SAD ABOUT DEATH

Brant: I still wonder why good feelings make me so sad. But when I feel sad, then I feel good again.

Robert Firestone: To be real, you have to feel the sadness about life and in some sense, mourn your own death and the potential death of those you love. If you don't, you cut off from yourself and the people you love the most.

Adam (39): Absolutely. I feel like this talk is helpful to me. I had a chance to feel.

Andrea: I feel much better. The way I felt before was being childish. Now I feel really sad, in a good way. It's really worth it to live, in spite of it being sad.

Robert Firestone: You can deal with the sadness.

Andrea: Yes, there was something about the primal part that made me feel like I couldn't deal with it.

Robert Firestone: In a way, for some reason, you don't get a chance to deal with it. That's the problem. Something interferes with the normal depth of sadness or else you'd get out of it, and then get back into a regular mood. That's the value of funerals. I don't really like funerals but I remember when my father died, that sharing the pain and feeling was a relief.

Andrea: It's like at an Irish wake, a place to really feel the grief.

Louis: Or a place to get loaded and forget it. (Everyone laughs.)

Andrea:	I think that the fact that most people lead isolated lives prevents them from dealing with deep issues like death. Isolation is such a perfect situation for the voice process to flourish, and the voice process attacks feeling. When you start to feel good about yourself or sad, then you attack yourself for feeling it. *"You're being self-centered, you don't have any feeling for anybody but yourself."* But in our group talks, the environment is just the opposite, it's a place where we let ourselves feel.
Robert Firestone:	The question is: why is genuine sadness so unacceptable in "normal society"? Why, even though it is acceptable among our friends, is it so problematic even here, and why is it even more difficult to feel it in isolation?
Brant:	I cried for Louis when I was alone.
Robert Firestone:	True, but it was difficult to feel for yourself or you might not have gotten depressed.
Brant:	But also I didn't feel the permission to feel it that I do here.
Robert Firestone:	That's partly the answer.
Brant:	If I would go off alone, I would cry.
Robert Firestone:	Yes, but it didn't get you back to yourself as much as this talk for some reason. That's something to investigate. I don't know the answer, but that's part of it, that there's a sense of permission. Or let's put it the other way: typically there's a sense of nonpermission to feel the deep sadness. I think that is the usual state. However, here in our group talks, I think we are able to get to our deep feelings because there is a sense of permission.
Brant:	In my family, they absolutely disapproved of feeling sad and approved of not showing it. When my grandfather died and was dying for a month, I wasn't allowed to go see him. When he died, my family kept trying to talk me out of my sadness and I had to lock myself in my room to feel it. (sad)
Robert Firestone:	It's interesting, even if there is feeling for others, like this permission to feel the sadness about Louis, there is a taboo against feeling about ourselves. So that's where we cut off. We definitely felt feelings about losing him, somebody we loved, or the potential loss.

We felt it and it was immediate and simple. We got to that sadness and it just came out. But when it came to the existential despair, the issue of our own death, we couldn't feel it so easily. Instead, many people regressed and got into this critical, self-destructive thinking.

The most I've gotten out of this whole talk is there's a sense of nonpermission to feel the sadness about your own life and death. I remember my father telling me when I raised issues like that, "Why do you trouble yourself about things like that? Why do you think those kinds of things? Why do you go deeply into things?" He was angry at the probing into painful subjects. Most people are. So there is a sense of nonpermission to feel the sadness about your own situation. It's also associated with this whole thing that you're selfish if you think about yourself. You shouldn't be selfish, self-centered, concerned about yourself. All these kinds of issues are tied to this, too.

Franz: So far you emphasized the fact that death awareness and separation anxiety often lead to defensive reactions, regression, self-attacks, and the like, but what about the positive side of facing death as a real issue in life versus denial?

Robert Firestone: Well, so far it appears that our reactions to Louis's situation have been primarily negative. People have felt worse, more depressed, but the talks are helping and it's difficult to predict what the final outcome will be. I do know that over the past 25 years, our awareness of death has made us softer, kinder people, more compassionate. The fact is that people can go either way with it. We wouldn't be what we are as a group if we had dodged these issues. It's led to a life that is more gentle and real.

RICHARD'S JOURNAL*

For the last two summers I have been the captain of a sleek and elegant 80-foot motor yacht in the Mediterranean. This job provided me with the unique privilege of seeing hundreds of ports and countless exotic islands from a seaman's perspective. The months of voyaging gave me experience

---

*Used by permission of Richard Catlett.

and, at 49, it sometimes seemed to me that my life was starting over. My 20 years of running my business from behind a computer screen had vanished, and I was often surprised to see that what had once seemed my destiny of working my life away was gone and instead I was a seasoned captain in the Mediterranean, tanned and strong from my months at sea, armed with a newfound youthfulness in my perspective of the world. The boats I traveled on carried many of my friends and family members. One of those was my father, and, although there are so many stories about these last two years, this is about him.

"Fool's Gold"

I am in Venice. The sole passenger in a beautifully finished water taxi. Finding peace in my appreciation of the vessel's fine lines, flawless glistening varnish, and thoughtful construction. Winding through the smaller canals, then back to the more cluttered popular sections, beneath ancient and magnificent bridges cluttered with tourists clicking photos of their children, then lost again in tiny waterways where residents' laundry is suspended over the canals and vaguely fluttering in an attempt of a breeze. The hint of movement in the air does nothing to take the blunt weight of heat away. Still, in spite of the hot Italian afternoon, such beauty.

I am following in the muddy wake of the ambulance boat that is carrying my father to the hospital, and I am guilty of being seduced by my incredible surroundings when the rhythm of his heart had become quiet a few minutes ago and soon could be forever silent. *"What kind of son are you?"* I think. *"To spend this time relishing this wondrous city in the face of death?"* I notice my eyes occasionally clouding with tears; somehow, whenever I am sad, I always have a profound clarity and appreciation of my surroundings. A special peace where, for that moment, my world is set right, everything fits, like an orchestra that is perpetually out of tune suddenly begins to play in a perfectly pleasing harmony.

Sadness is an illusive thing to me. But once it finds me, its effects are never limited to what finally drew it out of me. When I feel sadness, its dimensions are never limited to sadness. Depth and personal integrity are added to all my feelings, to everything I see, hear, smell, touch. I am sad for my father and what he is facing alone in the ambulance boat. Alone, not because there is no one there with him. Alone because I realize that it is something we all will face alone. Connected to no one but ourselves. Maybe I am drinking in as much of my surroundings as I can because I keep thinking that this may be the last day Louis [my father] will ever see. I shudder at my inability to digest this thought.

By the time we are docking at the hospital entrance my father has already been wheeled inside and I am left alone at the entrance. I watch as the taxi driver pulls away and is lost in a collage of boats. I make my way through an impressive white high-ceiling entrance and finally find a small waiting room where several of his and my friends are waiting. They look concerned and lost in thought but all stand to greet me. I am glad to see them and know that they are glad to see me. But still the thought persists, *"What kind of son are you? How can I feel so alive, glad that I am alive, have senses so enhanced, when my father is on the verge of losing all of this?"* Still, there are worse thoughts. *"I am so glad that it is not me lying in there with doctors over me,"* but in that I know that someday it will be me. I am just so glad that it isn't me now. *"What kind of son are you?"*

My father did not think I was a good son. This is something that I have always known intuitively. I don't know how he feels these days but I am aware that we view each other through a clouded lens. We are unable to see each other simply. These things have always caused me trouble for reasons that are foggy and vague. They belong in my past where many of the events that occurred there have tangled and blended into milky clarity and, although I do not see them clearly, the feelings I see when I look back often have a strong kinship with how I feel now, as a man of 49, and in that I sometimes see that there is unresolved sadness I wrestle with, I have always wrestled with, but mostly, have run madly from.

I run from sadness as if it is an angry dog. I have used all my energy to avoid it as if sadness is linked with death. Keep these things tucked away. Locked behind steel, encased in cement—rarely questioning what possessed me to build elaborate defenses. What happened to cause so much sadness? It is not often that I want to sift through scraps of memory to piece together my past. Finding the reasons that I built these thick walls will surely just let the sadness out. Best keep it locked up. There are times I suspect there is a scream imprisoned in me that sounds like it comes from a person who has lost his soul. It is confined in a space far too small and the pressure sometimes threatens to burst my walls from the inside out. But still I work only harder to incarcerate whatever rage is unresolved inside me.

Sadness is a persistent force, though, always struggling to surface with the noble dedication of an unsaid truth. As much as I have protected myself from feeling it, another part of me is always looking for times to experience it. When I feel it, I relish it washing over me and find myself calm and refreshed in its afterglow. As if I am able to discard everything I believe about myself for a moment, a noise stops in my mind and I can think clearly, like a cool breeze blowing through a hot closed room. In those moments I am an honest person.

I have lived pretending that death is a myth. Logically I have always known I will die, but the reality has no place in my mind. Death is an emotionally sterile fact that I do not attach to. It is beyond thinking. But at this moment it is real and personal. Death has meaning and my surroundings are affected by this glaring view of my father's mortality. When I look at my friends in this waiting room I see they also feel the closeness of death. Touched that my father's life could imminently end, they are probably more aware that the same will someday happen to them. In that thought, I love and cherish them, have compassion for them, and for the smallest of seconds, feel the same for myself.

When I was a kid, my father was the threat of death to me. I learned how to avoid him in order to survive and when I became an adult, applied the same lessons to my life and remained in many ways unnecessarily a survivor. These skills were not only things I learned through personal trauma in my relationship with him; they were also an adoption of the lessons and fears he learned from his own father. A sort of emotional DNA that was passed down from father to son, to son's sons, that contained methods to bend our lives out of shape, to drastically limit our experiences, to keep sadness and any personal acknowledgment of mortality far away.

I learned that one of the best ways to avoid my father's wrath was to remove myself from me. As if I was in a closet hiding, looking out through a crack at me playing in my room. The person playing in the room was vulnerable to my father coming in at all times and if something happened to that person, I would not be affected because I was no longer in my skin. I think that most people I see around me have adopted versions of this same tool— we are all one step removed from ourselves and death is going to happen to the person playing just beyond the closet door and not to us. I think that my sadness is the result of occasionally reattaching to myself.

But my father's eyes have changed slowly in the years since he first learned about his cancer. Something has shifted as if he has quietly abandoned everything he thought he knew about himself, is content to not know who he is, and is fascinated in continually finding out who he is. When he talks to people these days, he looks at them with regard—instead of cold scrutiny—as if he is simply appreciating who they are. There is openness and warmth always present that I caught only rare glimpses of as a child.

Until recent years I had spent the bulk of my life in search of countless ways to avoid sadness and death. Hundreds of places to hide in, methods to numb myself, and have chased them down like they were the most precious metal in the world. I had little time for anything else. In this waiting room I realize how ridiculous and futile my search was. I believe most people search for the same thing, their own precious metal, and strive to exist as if they will never die. What a strange thing to spend your life avoiding something that will be as real as it has ever been at the end of your life.

Imagine life ending and realizing with your last breath, that in limiting your life to avoid death, your life went unlived. That you had basically spent your life underground mining your own brand of precious metal that would keep you one step removed from yourself. At our last conscious moment we would know that whatever we had thought we had found did nothing to protect us from death, it did not work at all, there was no rare ore, it never existed.

It was only a fool's gold.

* * *

The next day, I take another water taxi to visit Louis in the hospital. He is better and I am happy about that. But I feel changed and troubled in knowing that what occurred was merely a preview of the inevitable. I know the ripples of this event will continue to affect me in the days ahead in many unforeseen ways.

I am tired and look into the evening sky trying to gauge what the morning's weather will be like. The fading sun paints the Grand Canal and surrounding buildings a powerful orange. I am glad to have this time to look across the city, the gondola pilots negotiating traffic and countless bridges, and finally into the incredible sky. It is no wonder that a person would be tempted to believe in a God when they look into the Italian sky. There is something so beautiful about it that it seems to touch a part of your soul in a way that makes you strangely sad, aware of your existence, and a part of yourself that in a funny way seems to extend well beyond and before the time you were even born. A person knows instantly that this incredible sky is timeless and, in that, you become aware of how brief a time you are really here to view it. But somehow, for that moment, it is all okay.

Louis is sitting up in bed reading a *Time* magazine. I sit next to him for a while talking and telling him that the weather is probably going to be good enough for me to leave early the next morning. I reach for his hand to say goodbye and am struck by how tired and fragile he looks. I remember at that moment how he looked when he was younger and strong and wish he could have all that back, now, when his life, for a very strange reason, seems in complete perspective and makes sense to him. There is still that awkwardness between us, but whatever roles we have both played in our times together have all but faded away over time, and the awkwardness seems more of a pleasant evaluation of who we each might really be.

We say our good-byes and I walk back to where the water taxi is docked and gaze into the darkening sky where the first stars are beginning to show. *"What will it be like to never see another day, another sunset, another evening sky again?"* I wrestle with this thought as I step on board the water taxi.

CONCLUSION

There have been many talks since the incident where Louis fell and later commented on the fact that he was dying from cancer. Gradually people dealt with the different issues that were stirred up and began to cope with their own death anxiety. There were many ups and downs and mood swings among the friends. Sometimes people remained soft and vulnerable and at other times, they were hardened, cynical, and defensive. Overall, the talks were constructive and helped people to stay close to their feelings. In the long run, it appears that the subject left us with the feeling that people all face the same fate, life is fragile, and that there is a good deal of sadness in a feelingful existence. We were more vulnerable, respectful of one another, less judgmental and more compassionate, and it helped us to sort out what was meaningful in life and what problems were relatively insignificant.

REFERENCES

Ackerman, S. J., & Hilsenroth, M. J. (2001). A review of therapist characteristics and techniques negatively impacting the therapeutic alliance. *Psychotherapy, 38*, 171–185.

American Psychiatric Association. (1994). *Diagnostic and statistical manual of mental disorder* (4th ed.). Washington, DC: Author.

Anderson, R. H., Bikson, T. K., Law, S. A., & Mitchell, B. M. (Eds.). (1995). *Universal access to e-mail: Feasibility and societal implications*. Santa Monica, CA: Rand.

Anthony, E. J., & Cohler, B. J. (Eds.). (1987). *The invulnerable child*. New York: Guilford Press.

Anthony, S. (1973). *The discovery of death in childhood and after*. Harmondsworth, UK: Penguin Education. (Original work published 1971)

Arieti, S. (1974). *Interpretation of schizophrenia* (2nd ed.). New York: Basic Books.

Aristotle. (1931). *Ethicanicomachea* (W. D. Ross, Trans.). London: Oxford University Press.

Arlow, J. A. (1989). Psychoanalysis. In R. J. Corsini & D. Wedding (Eds.), *Current psychotherapies* (4th ed., pp. 19–62). Itasca, IL: F. E. Peacock.

Attanucci, J. (1988). In whose terms: A new perspective on self, role, and relationship. In C. Gilligan, J. V. Ward, & J. M. Taylor (Eds.), *Mapping the moral domain: A contribution to women's thinking to psychological theory and education* (pp. 201–224). Cambridge, MA: Harvard Graduate School of Education.

Auerbach, J. S. (1993). The origins of narcissism and narcissistic personality disorder: A theoretical and empirical reformulation. In J. M. Masling & R. F. Bornstein (Eds.), *Psychoanalytic perspectives on psychopathology* (pp. 43–110). Washington, DC: American Psychological Association.

Bach, G. R., & Deutsch, R. M. (1979). *Stop! You're driving me crazy*. New York: Berkley Books.

Bachelor, A., & Horvath, A. (1999). The therapeutic relationship. In M. A. Hubble, B. L. Duncan, & S. D. Miller (Eds.), *The heart and soul of change: What works in therapy* (pp. 133–178). Washington, DC: American Psychological Association.

Bader, E., & Pearson, P. T. (with J. D. Schwartz). (2000). *Tell me no lies: How to face the truth and build a loving marriage.* New York: St. Martin's Press.

Badinter, E. (1981). *Mother love: Myth and reality: Motherhood in modern history.* New York: Macmillan. (Original work published 1980)

Balint, M. (1985). *Primary love and psycho-analytic technique.* London: Maresfield Library. (Original work published 1952)

Bandura, A. (1975). *Social learning through imitation.* New York: Holt, Rinehart, and Winston.

Bandura, A., & Walters, R. H. (1963). *Social learning and personality development.* New York: Holt, Rinehart, and Winston.

Barber, B. K. (Ed.). (2002). *Intrusive parenting: How psychological control affects children and adolescents.* Washington, DC: American Psychological Association.

Barber, B. K., Bean, R. L., & Erickson, L. D. (2002). Expanding the study and understanding of psychological control. In B. K. Barber (Ed.), *Intrusive parenting: How psychological control affects children and adolescents* (pp. 263–289). Washington, DC: American Psychological Association.

Barber, B. K., & Harmon, E. L. (2002). Violating the self: Parental psychological control of children and adolescents. In B. K. Barber (Ed.), *Intrusive parenting: How psychological control affects children and adolescents* (pp. 15–52). Washington, DC: American Psychological Association.

Barglow, P., & Schaefer, M. (1977). A new female psychology? In H. P. Blum (Ed.), *Female psychology: Contemporary psychoanalytic views* (pp. 393–438). New York: International Universities Press.

Basic Behavioral Science Task Force of the National Advisory Mental Health Council. (1996). Basic behavioral science research for mental health: Social influence and social cognition. *American Psychologist, 51,* 478–484.

Bateson, G. (1972). *Steps to an ecology of mind.* New York: Ballantine Books.

Baumeister, R. F., Bratslavsky, E., Finkenauer, C., & Vohs, K. D. (2001). Bad is stronger than good [Electronic version]. *Review of General Psychology, 5,* 323–370.

Beavers, W. R. (1977). *Psychotherapy and growth: A family systems perspective.* New York: Brunner/Mazel.

Beavers, W. R., & Hampson, R. B. (1990). *Successful families: Assessment and intervention.* New York: Norton.

Beck, A. T. (1978a). *Beck Depression Inventory.* San Antonio, TX: Psychological Corporation.

Beck, A. T. (1978b). *Beck Hopelessness Scale.* San Antonio, TX: Psychological Corporation.

Beck, A. T. (1991). *Beck Suicide Inventory.* San Antonio, TX: Psychological Corporation.

Beck, A. T., Rush, A. J., Shaw, B. F., & Emery, G. (1979). *Cognitive therapy of depression*. New York: Guilford Press.

Beck, A. T., Steer, R. A., Beck, J. S., & Newman, C. W. (1993). Hopelessness, depression, suicidal ideation, and clinical diagnosis of depression. *Suicide and Life-Threatening Behavior, 23*, 139–145.

Beck, A. T., Wright, F. D., Newman, C. F., & Liese, B. S. (1993). *Cognitive therapy of substance abuse*. New York: Guilford Press.

Beck, J. S. (1995). *Cognitive therapy basics and beyond*. New York: Guilford Press.

Becker, E. (1975). *Escape from evil*. New York: Free Press.

Becker, E. (1997). *The denial of death*. New York: Free Press. (Original work published 1973)

Beitchman, J. H., Zucker, K. J., Hood, J. E., Dacosta, G. A., Akman, D., & Cassavia, E. (1992). A review of the long-term effects of child sexual abuse. *Child Abuse & Neglect, 16*, 101–117.

Belsky, J. (1980). Child maltreatment: An ecological integration. *American Psychologist, 35*, 320–335.

Belsky, J. (1999). Modern evolutionary theory and patterns of attachment. In J. Cassidy & P. R. Shaver (Eds.), *Handbook of attachment: Theory, research, and clinical applications* (pp. 141–161). New York: Guilford Press.

Belsky, J., Taylor, D. G., & Rovine, M. (1984). The Pennsylvania infant and family development project, II: The development of reciprocal interaction in the mother–infant dyad. *Child Development, 55*, 706–717.

Berger, K. S., & Thompson, R. A. (1995). *The developing person through childhood and adolescence* (4th ed.). New York: Worth.

Berke, J. H. (1988). *The tyranny of malice: Exploring the dark side of character and culture*. New York: Summit Books.

Berkowitz, L. (1962). *Aggression: A social psychological analysis*. New York: McGraw-Hill.

Berkowitz, L. (1989). Frustration–aggression hypothesis: Examination and reformulation. *Psychological Bulletin, 106*, 59–73.

Bettelheim, B. (1979). Individual and mass behavior in extreme situations. In *Surviving and other essays* (pp. 48–83). New York: Alfred A. Knopf. (Original work published 1943)

Beutler, L. E. (1995). The germ theory myth and the myth of outcome homogeneity. *Psychotherapy, 32*, 489–494.

Beutler, L. E., & Clarkin, J. (1990). *Systematic treatment selection: Toward targeted therapeutic interventions*. New York: Brunner/Mazel.

Beutler, L. E., & Harwood, T. M. (2000). *Prescriptive psychotherapy: A practical guide to systematic treatment selection*. New York: Oxford University Press.

Beutler, L. E., Machado, P. P., & Neufeldt, S. (1994). Therapist variables. In S. L. Garfield & A. E. Bergin (Eds.), *Handbook of psychotherapy and behavior change* (4th ed., pp. 259–269). New York: John Wiley.

Beyer, S., & Finnegan, A. (1997, Aug.). *The accuracy of gender stereotypes regarding occupations*. Paper presented at the 105th Annual Convention of the American Psychological Association, Chicago.

Biller, H. B., & Solomon, R. S. (1986). *Child maltreatment and paternal deprivation: A manifesto for research, prevention, and treatment*. Lexington, MA: Lexington Books.

Billig, M. (1987). *Arguing and thinking: A rhetorical approach to social psychology*. Cambridge: Cambridge University Press.

Billig, M., Condor, S., Edwards, D., Gane, M., Middleton, D., & Radley, A. (1988). *Ideological dilemmas: A social psychology of everyday thinking*. London: Sage.

Bilodeau, L. (1992). *The anger workbook*. Center City, MN: Hazelden.

Black, C. (1981). *It will never happen to me!* Denver: M.A.C..

Blatt, S. J., Auerbach, J. S., & Aryan, M. (1998). Representational structures and the therapeutic process. In R. F. Bornstein & J. M. Masling (Eds.), *Empirical studies of the therapeutic hour* (pp. 63–107). Washington, DC: American Psychological Association.

Blatt, S. J., & Erlich, H. S. (1982). A critique of the concepts of resistance in behavior therapy. In P. L. Wachtel (Ed.), *Resistance: Psychodynamic and behavioral approaches* (pp. 197–217). New York: Plenum Press.

Blatt, S. J., McDonald, C., Sugarman, A., & Wilber, C. (1984). Psychodynamic theories of opiate addiction: New directions for research. *Clinical Psychology Review, 4*, 159–189.

Bloch, D. (1978). *"So the witch won't eat me": Fantasy and the child's fear of infanticide*. New York: Grove.

Block, J. D. (1980). *Friendship*. New York: Macmillan.

Blumberg, M. L. (1974). Psychopathology of the abusing parent. *American Journal of Psychotherapy, 28*, 21–29.

Bocknek, G., & Perna, F. (1994). Studies in self-representation beyond childhood. In J. M. Masling & R. F. Bornstein (Eds.), *Empirical perspectives on object relations theory* (pp. 29–58). Washington, DC: American Psychological Association.

Bollas, C. (1987). *The shadow of the object: Psychoanalysis of the unthought known*. New York: Columbia University Press.

Bongar, B., & Beutler, L. E. (Eds.). (1995). *Comprehensive textbook of psychotherapy: Theory and practice*. New York: Oxford University Press.

Bornstein, R. F. (1993). Parental representations and psychopathology: A critical review of the empirical literature. In J. M. Masling & R. F. Bornstein (Eds.), *Psychoanalytic perspectives on psychopathology* (pp. 1–41). Washington, DC: American Psychological Association.

Bornstein, R. F. (2001). The impending death of psychoanalysis. *Psychoanalytic Psychology, 18*, 3–20.

Boszormenyi-Nagy, I., & Spark, G. M. (1984). *Invisible loyalties: Reciprocity in intergenerational family therapy*. New York: Brunner/Mazel.

Bowen, M. (1965). Family psychotherapy with schizophrenia in the hospital and in private practice. In I. Boszormenyi-Nagy & J. L. Framo (Eds.), *Intensive family therapy: Theoretical and practical aspects* (pp. 213–243). New York: Harper and Row.

Bowen, M. (1978). *Family therapy in clinical practice*. New York: Jason Aronson.

Bowlby, J. (1973). *Attachment and loss: Vol. II. Separation: Anxiety and anger*. New York: Basic Books.

Bowlby, J. (1980). *Attachment and loss: Vol. III. Loss: Sadness and depression*. New York: Basic Books.

Brazelton, T. B., & Cramer, B. G. (1990). *The earliest relationship: Parents, infants, and the drama of early attachment*. Reading, MA: Addison-Wesley.

Brazelton, T. B., & Greenspan, S. I. (2000). *The irreducible needs of children: What every child must have to grow, learn, and flourish*. Cambridge, MA: Perseus.

Breggin, P. R. (1991). *Toxic psychiatry*. New York: St. Martin's Press.

Breggin, P. R. (2000). Peter R. Breggin, MD, testimony September 29, 2000, before the Subcommittee on Oversight and Investigations, Committee on Education and the Workforce, U.S. House of Representatives. Retrieved Feb. 15, 2003, from http://www.breggin.com/congress.html

Briere, J. N. (1992). *Child abuse trauma: Theory and treatment of the lasting effects*. Newbury Park, CA: Sage.

Briere, J., & Runtz, M. (1987). Post sexual abuse trauma: Data and implications for clinical practice. *Journal of Interpersonal Violence, 2*, 367–379.

Bromberg, N. (1955). Maternal influences in the development of moral masochism. *American Journal of Orthopsychiatry, 25*, 802–812.

Brooks, R., & Goldstein, S. (2001). *Raising resilient children: Fostering strength, hope, and optimism in your child*. New York: McGraw-Hill Contemporary Books.

Broussard, E. R. (1979). Assessment of the adaptive potential of the mother–infant system: The neonatal perception inventories. *Seminars in Perinatology, 3*(1), 91–100.

Brown, J., Cohen, P., Johnson, J. G., & Smailes, E. M. (1999). Childhood abuse and neglect: Specificity and effects on adolescent and young adult depression and suicidality. *Journal of the American Academy of Child & Adolescent Psychiatry, 38*, 1490–1496.

Brown, S. L., Nesse, R. M., Vinokur, A. D., & Smith, D. M. (in press). Providing social support may be more beneficial than receiving it: Results from a prospective study of mortality. *Psychological Science*.

Bugental, D. B. (1986). Unmasking the "polite smile": Situational and personal determinants of managed affect in adult–child interaction. *Personality and Social Psychology Bulletin, 12*, 7–16.

Bugental, D. B., Brown, M., & Reiss, C. (1996). Cognitive representations of power in caregiving relationships: Biasing effects on interpersonal interaction and information processing. *Journal of Family Psychology, 10*, 397–407.

Buss, D. M. (1994). *The evolution of desire: Strategies of human mating*. New York: Basic Books.

Buss, D. M. (2000). The evolution of happiness. *American Psychologist, 55,* 15–23.

Calderone, M. S. (1977). Eroticism as a norm. In E. S. Morrison & V. Borosage (Eds.), *Human sexuality: Contemporary perspectives* (2nd ed., pp. 39–48). Palo Alto, CA: Mayfield. (Original work published 1974)

Calderone, M. S., & Johnson, E. W. (1989). *The family book about sexuality* (Rev. ed.). New York: Harper and Row.

Canary, D. J., Cupach, W. R., & Messman, S. J. (1995). *Relationship conflict: Conflict in parent–child, friendship, and romantic relationships*. Thousand Oaks, CA: Sage.

Caplan, P. J. (1981). *Between women: Lowering the barriers*. Toronto: Personal Library.

Caplan, P. J. (1995). *They say you're crazy: How the world's most powerful psychiatrists decide who's normal*. Reading, MA: Perseus Books.

Carnes, P. (1991). *Don't call it love: Recovery from sexual addiction*. New York: Bantam Books.

Carnes, P. (1992). *Out of the shadows: Understanding sexual addiction* (2nd ed.). Center City, MN: Hazelden.

Carnes, P. (1997). *Sexual anorexia: Overcoming sexual self-hatred*. Center City, MN: Hazelden.

Cavaiola, A. A., & Schiff, M. (1988). Behavioral sequelae of physical and/or sexual abuse in adolescents. *Child Abuse and Neglect, 12,* 181–188.

Chadwick, P., Birchwood, M., & Trower, P. (1996). *Cognitive therapy for delusions, voices and paranoia*. Chichester, UK: John Wiley.

Chang, E. C. (Ed.). (2001). *Optimism and pessimism: Implications for theory, research, and practice*. Washington, DC: American Psychological Association.

Chernin, K. (1985). *The hungry self: Women, eating, and identity*. New York: Times Books.

Chess, S., & Thomas, A. (1999). *Goodness of fit: Clinical applications from infancy through adult life*. Philadelphia: Brunner/Mazel.

Child abuse rises in the face of lower U.S. crime trends. Retrieved November 11, 2001, from http://www.childabuse.com/incabuse.htm

ChildHelp USA. (2001, March). Child abuse statistics. Retrieved November 11, 2001, from http://www.childabuse.com/newsletter/stat0301.htm

Chodorow, N. (1978). *The reproduction of mothering: Psychoanalysis and the sociology of gender*. Berkeley: University of California Press.

Chodorow, N. J. (1999). *The power of feelings: Personal meaning in psychoanalysis, gender, and culture*. New Haven, CT: Yale University Press.

Choron, J. (1963). *Death and Western thought*. New York: Collier Books.

Chu, J. A., & Dill, D. L. (1990). Dissociative symptoms in relation to childhood physical and sexual abuse. *American Journal of Psychiatry, 147,* 887–892.

Cialdini, R. B. (1984). *How and why people agree to things*. New York: William Morrow.

Cicchetti, D., & Toth, S. L. (1995). Child maltreatment and attachment organization: Implications for intervention. In S. Goldberg, R. Muir, & J. Kerr (Eds.), *Attachment theory: Social, developmental, and clinical perspectives* (pp. 279–308). Hillsdale, NJ: Analytic Press.

Clance, P. R., & Imes, S. A. (1978). The impostor phenomenon in high achieving women: Dynamics and therapeutic intervention. *Psychotherapy: Theory, Research, & Practice, 15*, 241–247.

Claude-Pierre, P. (1997). *The secret life of eating disorders: The revolutionary approach to understanding and curing anorexia and bulimia*. New York: Vintage Books.

Comte-Sponville, A. (2001). *A small treatise on the great virtues: The uses of philosophy in everyday life* (C. Temerson, Trans.). New York: Metropolitan Books. (Original work published 1996)

Connolly, C. (1945). *The unquiet grave*. New York: Harper and Row.

Conte, J. R. (1988). The effects of sexual abuse on children: Results of a research project. *Human sexual aggression: Current perspectives. Annals of the New York Academy of Sciences, 528*, 310–326.

Conte, J. R. (1994). Child sexual abuse: Awareness and backlash. *Future of Children, 4*, 224–232.

Conte, J. R., & Schuerman, J. R. (1987). The effects of sexual abuse on children: A multidimensional approach. *Journal of Interpersonal Violence, 4*, 380–390.

Coons, P. M. (1986). Child abuse and multiple personality disorder: Review of the literature and suggestions for treatment. *Child Abuse and Neglect, 10*, 455–462.

Cooper, A., Scherer, C. R., Boies, S. C., & Gordon, B. L. (1999). Sexuality on the Internet: From sexual exploration to pathological expression. *Professional Psychology: Research and Practice, 30*, 154–164.

Courtois, C. A. (1999). *Recollections of sexual abuse: Treatment principles and guidelines*. New York: W. W. Norton.

Coward, R. (1997). The heaven and hell of mothering: Mothering and ambivalence in the mass media. In W. Hollway & B. Featherstone (Eds.), *Mothering and ambivalence* (pp. 111–118). London: Routledge.

Crouch, J. (n.d.) *Divorce reform page: Limiting no-fault divorce; covenant marriage*. Retrieved October 22, 2002, from http://www.divorcereform.org

Csikszentmihalyi, M. (1990). *Flow: The psychology of optimal experience*. New York: Harper Perennial.

Dalai Lama. (2000). *Transforming the mind: Teachings on generating compassion*. London: Thorsons.

Daly, M., & Wilson, M. (1983). *Sex, evolution, and behavior* (2nd ed.). Boston: Willard Grant Press.

Darwin, C. (1909). *The origin of species*. Danbury, CT: Grolier. (Original work published 1859)

Death row, U.S.A., The statistics. Retrieved August 31, 2001, from http://Arctic.st.usm.edu/-lmlewis/drowinfo.html

deMause, L. (2002). The evolution of the psyche and society. *Journal of Psychohistory, 29,* 238–285.

de Schill, S. (2000). *Crucial choices—Crucial changes: The resurrection of psychotherapy.* Amherst, NY: Prometheus Books.

de Schill, S., & Lebovici, S. (Eds.). (1999). *The challenge for psychoanalysis and psychotherapy: Solutions for the future.* London: Jessica Kingsley.

Diamond, D., Blatt, S. J., Stayner, D., & Kaslow, N. (1991). *Self–other differentiation of object representations.* Unpublished manuscript, Yale University, New Haven, CT.

Dillon, S. (2002, July 12). Role of bishops is now a focus of grand juries [Electronic version]. *New York Times.* Retrieved October 20, 2002, from http://www.nytimes.com

Dinwiddie, S. H., & Bucholz, K. K. (1993). Psychiatric diagnoses of self-reported child abusers. *Child Abuse & Neglect, 17,* 465–476.

Dix, C. (1985). *The new mother syndrome: Coping with postpartum stress and depression.* New York: Pocket Books.

Dodge, K. A., Pettit, G. S., & Bates, J. E. (1997). How the experience of early physical abuse leads children to become chronically aggressive. In C. Cicchetti & S. L. Toth (Eds.), *Developmental psychopathology: Developmental perspectives on trauma, Vol. 9, Theory, research and intervention* (pp. 263–288). Rochester, NY: University of Rochester Press.

Dorais, M. (2002). *Don't tell: The sexual abuse of boys* (I. D. Meyer, Trans.). Montreal, Canada: McGill-Queen's University Press.

Doucette-Gates, A., Firestone, R. W., & Firestone, L. A. (1999). Assessing violent thoughts: The relationship between thought processes and violent behavior. *Psychologica Belgica, 39,* 113–134.

Drotar, D. (Ed.). (1985). *New directions in failure to thrive: Implications for research and practice.* New York: Plenum Press.

Drotar, D., Eckerle, D., Satola, J., Pallotta, J., & Wyatt, B. (1990). Maternal interactional behavior with nonorganic failure-to-thrive infants: A case comparison study. *Child Abuse & Neglect, 14,* 41–51.

Duck, S. (1994a). *Dynamics of relationships.* Thousand Oaks, CA: Sage.

Duck, S. (1994b). *Meaningful relationships: Talking, sense, and relating.* Thousand Oaks, CA: Sage.

Durkheim, E. (1951). *Suicide: A study in sociology* (J. A. Spaulding & G. Simpson, Trans.). New York: Free Press. (Original work published 1897)

Dutton, D. G. (with S. K. Golant). (1995a). *The batterer: A psychological profile.* New York: Basic Books.

Dutton, D. G. (1995b). *The domestic assault of women: Psychological and criminal justice perspectives* (Rev. ed.). Vancouver, Canada: University of British Columbia Press.

Eagly, A. H. (1995). The science and politics of comparing women and men. *American Psychologist, 50,* 145–158.

Egeland, B., & Sroufe, A. (1981). Developmental sequelae of maltreatment in infancy. *New Directions for Child Development, 11,* 77–92.

Ehrenreich, B. (2001). *Nickel and dimed: On (not) getting by in America.* New York: Henry Holt.

Ellis, A. (1973). *Humanistic psychotherapy: The rational-emotive approach.* New York: Julian.

Ellis, A., & Harper, R. A. (1975). *A new guide to rational living.* North Hollywood, CA: Wilshire Book.

Emerson, S., & McBride, M. C. (1986). *A model for group treatment of adults molested as children.* Las Vegas: University of Nevada. (ERIC Document Reproduction Service No. ED 272814)

Ensink, B. J. (1992). *Confusing realities: A study on child sexual abuse and psychiatric symptoms.* Amsterdam: VU University Press.

Epstein, M. (2001). *Going on being: Buddhism and the way of change: A positive psychology for the West.* New York: Broadway Books.

Epstein, S. (1994). Integration of the cognitive and the psychodynamic unconscious. *American Psychologist, 49,* 709–724.

Epstein, S. (1998). *Constructive thinking: The key to emotional intelligence.* Westport, CT: Praeger.

Eysenck, H. J. (1961). The effects of psychotherapy. In H. J. Eysenck (Ed.), *Handbook of abnormal psychology* (pp. 697–725). New York: Basic Books.

Fairbairn, W. R. D. (1952). A revised psychopathology of the psychoses and psychoneuroses. In W. R. D. Fairbairn, *Psychoanalytic studies of the personality* (pp. 28–58). London: Routledge and Kegan Paul.

Farberow, N. L. (1980). Introduction. In N. L. Farberow (Ed.), *The many faces of suicide: Indirect self-destructive behavior* (pp. 1–12). New York: McGraw-Hill.

Feeney, G. F. X., Young, R. M., Connor, J. P., Tucker, J., & McPherson, A. (2001). Outpatient cognitive behavioural therapy programme for alcohol dependence: Impact of naltrexone use on outcome. *Australian and New Zealand Journal of Psychiatry, 35,* 443–448.

Fehr, B. (1996). *Friendship processes.* Thousand Oaks, CA: Sage.

Felitti, V. J. (2002). The relation between adverse childhood experiences and adult health: Turning gold into lead. *Permanente Journal, 6*(1), 44–47.

Felitti, V. J., Anda, R. F., Nordenberg, D., Williamson, D. F., Spitz, A. M., Edwards, V., et al. (1998). Relationship of childhood abuse and household dysfunction to many of the leading causes of death in adults: The Adverse Childhood Experiences Study. *American Journal of Preventive Medicine, 14,* 245–258.

Fenchel, G. H. (Ed.). (1998). *The mother–daughter relationship: Echoes through time.* Northvale, NJ: Jason Aronson.

Ferenczi, S. (1929). The unwelcome child and his death-instinct. *International Journal of Psycho-Analysis, 10,* 125–129.

Ferenczi, S. (1955). Confusion of tongues between adults and the child. In M. Balint (Ed.), *Final contributions to the problems & methods of psycho-analysis* (E. Mosbacher & others, Trans., pp. 156–167). New York: Basic Books. (Original work published 1933)

Field, T. (1987). Interaction and attachment in normal and atypical infants. *Journal of Consulting and Clinical Psychology, 55*, 853–859.

Fierman, L. B. (Ed.). (1965). *Effective psychotherapy: The contribution of Hellmuth Kaiser.* New York: Free Press.

Finkel, K. C. (1987). Sexual abuse of children: An update. *Canadian Medical Association Journal, 136*, 245–252.

Finkelhor, D. (with Araji, S., Baron, L., Browne, A., Peters, S. D., & Wyatt, G. E.). (1986). *A sourcebook on child sexual abuse.* Beverly Hills, CA: Sage.

Finkelhor, D. (1990). Early and long-term effects of child sexual abuse: An update [Electronic version]. *Professional Psychology: Research and Practice, 21*, 325–330.

Firestone, R. W. (1957). *A concept of the schizophrenic process.* Unpublished doctoral dissertation, University of Denver.

Firestone, R. W. (1984). A concept of the primary fantasy bond: A developmental perspective. *Psychotherapy, 21*, 218–225.

Firestone, R. W. (1985). *The fantasy bond: Structure of psychological defenses.* Santa Barbara, CA: Glendon Association.

Firestone, R. W. (1986). The "inner voice" and suicide. *Psychotherapy, 23*, 439–447.

Firestone, R. W. (1988). *Voice therapy: A psychotherapeutic approach to self-destructive behavior.* Santa Barbara, CA: Glendon Association.

Firestone, R. W. (1989). Parenting groups based on voice therapy. *Psychotherapy, 26*, 524–529.

Firestone, R. W. (1990a). The bipolar causality of regression. *American Journal of Psychoanalysis, 50*, 121–135.

Firestone, R. W. (1990b). *Compassionate child-rearing: An in-depth approach to optimal parenting.* Santa Barbara, CA: Glendon Association.

Firestone, R. W. (1990c). Voice therapy. In J. Zeig & W. Munion (Eds.), *What is psychotherapy? Contemporary perspectives* (pp. 68–74). San Francisco: Jossey-Bass.

Firestone, R. W. (1990d). Voices during sex: Application of voice therapy to sexuality. *Journal of Sex & Marital Therapy, 16*, 258–274.

Firestone, R. W. (1993). The psychodynamics of fantasy, addiction, and addictive attachments. *American Journal of Psychoanalysis, 53*, 335–352.

Firestone, R. W. (1994). Psychological defenses against death anxiety. In R. A. Neimeyer (Ed.), *Death anxiety handbook: Research, instrumentation, and application* (pp. 217–241). Washington, DC: Taylor and Francis.

Firestone, R. W. (1996). The origins of ethnic strife. *Mind and Human Interaction, 7*, 167–180.

Firestone, R. W. (1997a). *Combating destructive thought processes: Voice Therapy and separation theory*. Thousand Oaks, CA: Sage.

Firestone, R. W. (1997b). *Suicide and the inner voice: Risk assessment, treatment, and case management*. Thousand Oaks, CA: Sage.

Firestone, R. W. (2000). Microsuicide and the elderly: A basic defense against death anxiety. In A. Tomer (Ed.), *Death attitudes and the older adult: Theories, concepts, and applications* (pp. 65–84). Philadelphia: Brunner-Routledge.

Firestone, R. W. (2002). The death of psychoanalysis and depth therapy. *Psychotherapy. Psychotherapy, 39*(3), 223–232.

Firestone, R. W., & Catlett, J. (1999). *Fear of intimacy*. Washington, DC: American Psychological Association.

Firestone, R. W., & Firestone, L. (1996). *Firestone Assessment of Self-Destructive Thoughts*. San Antonio, TX: Psychological Corporation.

Firestone, R., & Firestone, L. (2002a). *Firestone Voice Scale for Couples*. Unpublished work.

Firestone, R., & Firestone, L. (2002b). Suicide reduction and prevention. In C. Feltham (Ed.), *What's the good of counselling & psychotherapy: The benefits explained* (pp. 48–80). London: Sage.

Firestone, R. W., Firestone, L., & Catlett, J. (2002). *Conquer your critical inner voice: A revolutionary program to counter negative thoughts and live free from imagined limitations*. Oakland, CA: New Harbinger.

Firestone, R. W., & Seiden, R. H. (1987). Microsuicide and suicidal threats of everyday life. *Psychotherapy, 24*, 31–39.

Fisher, S. F. (1973). *The female orgasm: Psychology, physiology, fantasy*. New York: Basic Books.

Fisher, S., & Fisher, R. L. (1986). *What we really know about child-rearing: Science in support of effective parenting*. Northvale, NJ: Jason Aronson.

Fleming, J., Mullen, P., & Bammer, G. (1997). A study of potential risk factors for sexual abuse in childhood. *Child Abuse & Neglect, 21*, 49–58.

Fonagy, P. (2001). *Attachment theory and psychoanalysis*. New York: Other Press.

Fonagy, P., Steele, M., Steele, H., Leigh, T., Kennedy, R., Mattoon, G., et al. (1995). Attachment, the reflective self, and borderline states: The predictive specificity of the Adult Attachment Interview and pathological emotional development. In S. Goldberg, R. Muir, & J. Kerr (Eds.), *Attachment theory: Social, developmental, and clinical perspectives* (pp. 233–278). Hillsdale, NJ: Analytic Press.

Fontana, V. J. (1983). *Somewhere a child is crying: Maltreatment—Causes and prevention* (Rev. ed.). New York: New American Library.

Fosha, D. (2000). *The transforming power of affect: A model for accelerated change*. New York: Basic Books.

Foucault, M. (1975). *Discipline and punishment: The birth of the prison*. London: Allen Lane.

Foucault, M. (1978). *The history of sexuality: Vol. 1, An introduction* (R. Hurley, Trans.). New York: Vintage Books.

Foucault, M. (1980). *Power and knowledge.* Brighton, UK: Harvester.

Fowler, R. D. (Ed.). (2000). Positive psychology [Special issue]. *American Psychologist, 55*(1).

Fraiberg, S. (1982). Pathological defenses in infancy. *Psychoanalytic Quarterly, 51,* 612–635.

Fraiberg, S., Adelson, E., & Shapiro, V. (1980). Ghosts in the nursery: A psychoanalytic approach to the problems of impaired infant–mother relationships. In S. Fraiberg (Ed.), *Clinical studies in infant mental health: The first year of life* (pp. 164–196). New York: Basic Books.

Frankl, V. E. (1959). *Man's search for meaning* (Rev. ed.). New York: Washington Square Press. (Original work published 1946)

Frankl, V. E. (1967). Group psychotherapeutic experiences in a concentration camp. In V. E. Frankl, *Psychotherapy and existentialism: Selected papers on logotherapy* (pp. 95–105). New York: Simon and Schuster. (Original work published 1954)

Freud, A. (1966). *The ego and the mechanisms of defense* (Rev. ed.). Madison, CT: International Universities Press.

Freud, S. (1953). Three essays on the theory of sexuality. In J. Strachey (Ed. and Trans.), *The standard edition of the complete psychological works of Sigmund Freud* (Vol. 7, pp. 135–245). London: Hogarth. (Original work published 1905)

Freud, S. (1955). Beyond the pleasure principle. In J. Strachey (Ed. and Trans.), *The standard edition of the complete psychological works of Sigmund Freud* (Vol. 18, pp. 7–64). London: Hogarth Press. (Original work published 1920)

Freud, S. (1957a). Thoughts for the times on war and death. In J. Strachey (Ed. and Trans.), *The standard edition of the complete psychological works of Sigmund Freud* (Vol. 14, pp. 273–302). (Original work published 1915)

Freud, S. (1957b). Some character-types met with in psycho-analytic work. In J. Strachey (Ed. and Trans.), *The standard edition of the complete psychological works of Sigmund Freud* (Vol. 14, pp. 311–333). (Original work published 1916)

Freud, S. (1959). An autobiographical study. In J. Strachey (Ed. and Trans.), *The standard edition of the complete psychological works of Sigmund Freud* (Vol. 20, pp. 7–75). London: Hogarth. (Original work published 1925)

Freud, S. (1961). Civilization and its discontents. In J. Strachey (Ed. and Trans.), *The standard edition of the complete psychological works of Sigmund Freud* (Vol. 21, pp. 64–145). London: Hogarth. (Original work published 1930)

Freud, S. (1962). The aetiology of hysteria. In J. Strachey (Ed. and Trans.), *The standard edition of the complete psychological works of Sigmund Freud* (Vol. 3, pp. 191–221). London: Hogarth. (Original work published 1896)

Freyd, J. J. (1996). *Betrayal trauma: The logic of forgetting childhood abuse.* Cambridge, MA: Harvard University Press.

Friday, N. (1977). *My mother/my self: The daughter's search for identity*. New York: Delacorte Press.

Fromm, E. (1941). *Escape from freedom*. New York: Avon Books.

Fromm, E. (1950). *Psychoanalysis and religion*. New Haven, CT: Yale University Press.

Fromm, E. (1956). *The art of loving*. New York: Bantam.

Gallwey, W. T. (2000). *The inner game of work: Focus, learning, pleasure, and mobility in the workplace*. New York: Random House.

Garbarino, J. (1999). *Lost boys: Why our sons turn violent and how we can save them*. New York: Free Press.

Garbarino, J., & Gilliam, G. (1980). *Understanding abusive families*. Lexington, MA: Lexington Books.

Garbarino, J., Guttmann, E., & Seeley, J. W. (1986). *The psychologically battered child*. San Francisco: Jossey-Bass.

Gartner, R. B. (1999). *Betrayed as boys: Psychodynamic treatment of sexually abused men*. New York: Guilford Press.

Gedo, J. E. (2000). A time of discontent: Contemporary psychoanalysis in America. In S. de Schill, *Crucial choices—Crucial changes: The resurrection of psychotherapy* (pp. 39–54). Amherst, NY: Prometheus Books.

Geis, F. L. (1993). Self-fulfilling prophecies: A social psychological view of gender. In A. E. Beall & R. J. Sternberg (Eds.), *The psychology of gender* (pp. 9–54). New York: Guilford Press.

Genevie, L., & Margolies, E. (1987). *The motherhood report: How women feel about being mothers*. New York: Macmillan.

George, C., & Solomon, J. (1999). Attachment and caregiving: The caregiving behavioral system. In J. Cassidy & P. R. Shaver (Eds.), *Handbook of attachment: Theory, research, and clinical applications* (pp. 649–670). New York: Guilford Press.

George, C., West, M., & Pettem, O. (1999). The adult attachment projective: Disorganization of adult attachment at the level of representation. In J. Solomon & C. George (Eds.), *Attachment disorganization* (pp. 318–346). New York: Guilford Press.

Gerson, R. (1995). The family life cycle: Phases, stages, and crises. In R. H. Mikesell, D. Lusterman, & S. H. McDaniel (Eds.), *Integrating family therapy: Handbook of family psychology and systems theory* (pp. 91–111). Washington, DC: American Psychological Association.

Ghent, E. (1999). Masochism, submission, surrender: Masochism as a perversion of surrender. In S. A. Mitchell & L. Aron (Eds.), *Relational psychoanalysis: The emergence of a tradition* (pp. 211–242). Hillsdale, NJ: Analytic Press. (Original work published 1990)

Gilbert, P. (1989). *Human nature and suffering*. Hillsdale, NJ: Erlbaum.

Gillham, J. E. (Ed.). (2000). *The science of optimism and hope: Research essays in honor of Martin E. P. Seligman*. Philadelphia: Templeton Foundation Press.

Gilligan, C. (1982). *In a different voice: Psychological theory and women's development.* Cambridge, MA: Harvard University Press.

Gilligan, C. (1996). The centrality of relationship in human development: A puzzle, some evidence, and theory. In G. G. Noam & K. W. Fischer (Eds.), *Development and vulnerability in close relationships* (pp. 237–261). Mahwah, NJ: Erlbaum.

Gilligan, C. (2002). *The birth of pleasure.* New York: Alfred A. Knopf.

Gilligan, J. (1996). *Violence: Our deadly epidemic and its causes.* New York: G. P. Putnam's Sons.

Gilligan, J. (2001). *Preventing violence.* New York: Thames and Hudson.

Gladstone, T. R. G., & Beardslee, W. R. (2002). Treatment, intervention, and prevention with children of depressed parents: A developmental perspective. In S. H. Goodman & I. H. Gotlib (Eds.), *Children of depressed parents: Mechanisms of risk and implications for treatment* (pp. 277–305). Washington, DC: American Psychological Association.

Glass, S. P., & Wright, T. L. (1988). Clinical implications of research on extramarital involvement. In R. A. Brown & J. R. Field (Eds.), *Treatment of sexual problems in individual and couples therapy* (pp. 301–346). Costa Mesa, CA: PMA.

Glass, S. P., & Wright, T. L. (1997). Reconstructing marriages after the trauma of infidelity. In W. K. Halford & H. J. Markman (Eds.), *Clinical handbook of marriage and couples interventions* (pp. 471–507). New York: John Wiley.

Goffman, E. (1967). *Interaction ritual.* Garden City, NY: Anchor Press.

Gootnick, I. (1997). *Why you behave in ways you hate: And what you can do about it.* Granite Bay, CA: Penmarin Books.

Gordon, R. M. (with L. Aron, S. A. Mitchell, & J. M. Davies). (1998). Relational psychoanalysis. In R. Langs (Ed.), *Current theories of psychoanalysis* (pp. 31–58). Madison, CT: International Universities Press.

Gottman, J. M. (1979). *Marital interaction: Experimental investigations.* New York: Academic Press.

Gottman, J. M., & Krokoff, L. J. (1989). Marital interaction and satisfaction: A longitudinal view. *Journal of Consulting and Clinical Psychology, 57,* 47–52.

Gove, W. R., & Hughes, M. (1980). Reexamining the ecological fallacy: A study in which aggregate data are critical in investigating the pathological effects of living alone. *Social Forces, 58,* 1157–1177.

Greenberg, J., Pyszczynski, T., Solomon, S., Rosenblatt, A., Veeder, M., Kirkland, S., et al. (1990). Evidence for terror management theory II: The effects of mortality salience on reactions to those who threaten or bolster the cultural worldview. *Journal of Personality and Social Psychology, 58,* 308–318.

Greenberg, L. S., & Safran, J. D. (1987). *Emotion in psychotherapy: Affect, cognition, and the process of change.* New York: Guilford Press.

Greer, G. (1971). *The female eunuch.* New York: McGraw-Hill. (Original work published 1970)

Gunderson, M. P., & McCary, J. L. (1979). Sexual guilt and religion. *Family Coordinator, 28,* 353–357.

Guntrip, H. (1969). *Schizoid phenomena object-relations and the self.* New York: International Universities Press.

Hall, S. M., Havassy, B. E., & Wasserman, D. A. (1990). Commitment to abstinence and acute stress in relapse to alcohol, opiates, and nicotine. *Journal of Consulting and Clinical Psychology, 58,* 175–181.

Harper, R. A. (1981). Limitations of marriage and family therapy. *Rational Living, 16*(2), 3–6.

Harre, R., & Parrott, W. G. (Eds.). (1996). *The emotions: Social, cultural and biological dimensions.* London: Sage.

Hassler, J. H. (1994). Illnesses, failures, losses: Human misery propelling regression, therapy, and growth. In A. Sugarman (Ed.), *Victims of abuse: The emotional impact of child and adult trauma* (pp. 213–222). Madison, CT: International Universities Press.

Havel, V. (1990). *Disturbing the peace: A conversation with Karel Hvizdala* (P. Wilson, Trans.). New York: Alfred A. Knopf.

Henry, J. (1963). *Culture against man.* New York: Vintage Books.

Henry, W. P., Strupp, H. H., Butler, S. F., Schacht, T. E., & Binder, J. L. (1993). Effects of training in time-limited dynamic psychotherapy: Changes in therapist behavior. *Journal of Consulting and Clinical Psychology, 61,* 434–440.

Herman, J. (with L. Hirschman). (1981). *Father–daughter incest.* Cambridge, MA: Harvard University Press.

Herman, J. (1992). *Trauma and recovery.* New York: Basic Books.

Hewlett, S. A. (1991). *When the bough breaks: The cost of neglecting our children.* New York: Basic Books.

Hobson, J. A., & Leonard, J. A. (2001). *Out of its mind: Psychiatry in crisis: A call for reform.* Cambridge, MA: Perseus.

Hollon, S. D., Shelton, R. C., & Davis, D. D. (1993). Cognitive therapy for depression: Conceptual issues and clinical efficacy. *Journal of Consulting and Clinical Psychology, 61,* 270–275.

Holmes, T. H., & Rahe, R. H. (1967). The social readjustment rating scale. *Journal of Psychosomatic Research, 11,* 213–218.

Horvath, A. O., & Luborsky, L. (1993). The role of the therapeutic alliance in psychotherapy. *Journal of Consulting and Clinical Psychology, 61,* 561–573.

House, J. S., Landis, K. R., & Umberson, D. (1988). Social relationships and health. *Science, 241,* 540–545.

Hrdy, S. B. (1999). *Mother nature: A history of mothers, infants, and natural selection.* New York: Pantheon Books.

Hudson, L., & Jacot, B. (1995). *Intimate relations: The natural history of desire.* New Haven, CT: Yale University Press.

Hyman, I. A. (1997). *The case against spanking: How to discipline your child without hitting.* San Francisco: Jossey-Bass.

Ingersoll, R. G. (1910). *Prose-poems and selections from the writings and sayings of Robert G. Ingersoll* (9th ed.). New York: C. P. Farrell.

Jacobson, N. S. (1993). Introduction to special section on couples and couple therapy. *Journal of Consulting and Clinical Psychology, 61,* 5.

Jacoby, R. (1983). *The repression of psychoanalysis: Otto Fenichel and the political Freudians.* Chicago: University of Chicago Press.

James, B. (1994). *Handbook for treatment of attachment-trauma problems in children.* New York: Free Press.

Janov, A. (1970). *The primal scream: Primal therapy: The cure for neurosis.* New York: Putnam.

Jarvis, T. J., & Copeland, J. (1997). Child sexual abuse as a predictor of psychiatric co-morbidity and its implications for drug and alcohol treatment. *Drug & Alcohol Dependence, 49*(1), 61–69.

Johnson, A. M. (1951). Some etiological aspects of repression, guilt and hostility. *Psychoanalytic Quarterly, 20,* 511–527.

Johnson, S. M. (1999). Emotionally focused couple therapy: Straight to the heart. In J. M. Donovan (Ed.), *Short-term couple therapy* (pp. 13–42). New York: Guilford Press.

Johnson, S. M., Hunsley, J., Greenberg, L., & Schlinder, D. (1999). Emotionally focused couples therapy: Status and challenges. *Clinical Psychology Science and Practice, 6,* 67–79.

Johnson, S. M., Maddeaux, C., & Blouin, J. (1998). Emotionally focused family therapy for bulimia: Changing attachment patterns. *Psychotherapy, 35,* 238–247.

Johnson, S. M., & Whiffen, V. E. (1999). Made to measure: Adapting emotionally-focused couple therapy to partners' attachment styles. *Clinical Psychology Science and Practice, 6,* 366–381.

Kaminer, Y. (2000). Contingency management reinforcement procedures for adolescent substance abuse. *Journal of the American Academy of Child and Adolescent Psychiatry, 39,* 1324–1326.

Kandell, J. J. (1998). Internet addiction on campus: The vulnerability of college students. *CyberPsychology & Behavior, 1,* 11–17.

Kaplan, L. J. (1984). *Adolescence: The farewell to childhood.* New York: Simon and Schuster.

Karen, R. (1994). *Becoming attached: First relationships and how they shape our capacity to love.* New York: Oxford University Press.

Karon, B. P. (2002). Psychoanalysis: Legitimate and illegitimate concerns. *Psychoanalytic Psychology, 19,* 564–571.

Karpel, M. (1976). Individuation: From fusion to dialogue. *Family Process, 15*(1), 65–82.

Karpel, M. A. (1994). *Evaluating couples: A handbook for practitioners.* New York: W. W. Norton.

Karr-Morse, R., & Wiley, M. S. (1997). *Ghosts from the nursery: Tracing the roots of violence.* New York: Atlantic Monthly Press.

Kasl, C. D. (1989). *Women, sex, and addiction: A search for love and power.* New York: Harper and Row.

Kastenbaum, R. (1974, Summer). Childhood: The kingdom where creatures die. *Journal of Clinical Child Psychology,* 11–14.

Kastenbaum, R. (1995). *Death, society, and human experience* (5th ed.). Boston: Allyn and Bacon.

Kaufman, E. (1974). The psychodynamics of opiate dependence: A new look. *American Journal of Drug and Alcohol Abuse, 1,* 349–370.

Kaufman, J., & Zigler, E. (1987). Do abused children become abusive parents? *American Journal of Orthopsychiatry, 57,* 186–192.

Keane, F. E. A., Young, S. M., & Boyle, H. M. (1996). The prevalence of previous sexual assault among routine female attenders at the department of genitourinary medicine. *International Journal of STD & AIDS, 7,* 480–484.

Kecmanovic, D. (1996). *The mass psychology of ethnonationalism.* New York: Plenum Press.

Kempe, R. S., & Kempe, C. H. (1978). *Child abuse.* Cambridge, MA: Harvard University Press.

Kempe, R. S., & Kempe, C. H. (1984). *The common secret: Sexual abuse of children and adolescents.* New York: Freeman.

Kennedy-Moore, E., & Watson, J. C. (1999). *Expressing emotion: Myths, realities, and therapeutic strategies.* New York: Guilford Press.

Kernberg, O. F. (1980). *Internal world and external reality: Object relations theory applied.* Northvale, NJ: Jason Aronson.

Kernberg, O. F. (1984). *Severe personality disorders: Psychotherapeutic strategies.* New Haven, CT: Yale University Press.

Kernberg, O. F. (1995). *Love relations: Normality and pathology.* New Haven, CT: Yale University Press.

Kerr, M. E., & Bowen, M. (1988). *Family evaluation: An approach based on Bowen theory.* New York: Norton.

Keys, A., Brozek, J. Henschel, A., Mickelsen, O., & Taylor, H. L. (1950). *The biology of human starvation* (Vol. 2). Minneapolis: University of Minnesota Press.

Khantzian, E. J., Mack, J. E., & Schatzberg, A. F. (1974). Heroin use as an attempt to cope: Clinical observations. *American Journal of Psychiatry, 131,* 160–164.

Kierkegaard, S. (1954). *The sickness unto death* (W. Lowrie, Trans.). New York: Doubleday.

Kinkade, K. (1994). *Is it Utopia yet? An insider's view of Twin Oaks Community in its 26th year.* Louisa, VA: Twin Oaks.

Kinzl, J. F., Traweger, C., & Biebl, W. (1995). Sexual dysfunctions: Relationship to childhood sexual abuse and early family experiences in a nonclinical sample. *Child Abuse & Neglect, 19,* 785–792.

Klein, M. (1964). *Contributions to psycho-analysis 1921–1945*. New York: McGraw-Hill. (Original work published 1948)

Kohut, H. (1977). *The restoration of the self*. New York: International Universities Press.

Kotelchuck, M. (1980). Nonorganic failure to thrive: The status of interactional and environmental etiologic theories. *Advances in Behavioral Pediatrics, 1*, 29–51.

Kotulak, R. (1996). *Inside the brain: Revolutionary discoveries of how the mind works*. Kansas City, MO: Andrews McMeel.

Kozak, M. J., & Foa, E. B. (1997). *Mastery of obsessive–compulsive disorder: A cognitive–behavioral approach: Therapist guide*. San Antonio, TX: TherapyWorks.

Kozol, J. (1995). *Amazing grace: The lives of children and the conscience of a nation*. New York: Crown.

Kramer, R. (Ed.). (1996). *Otto Rank: A Psychology of Difference: The American Lectures*. Princeton, NJ: Princeton University Press.

Kraut, R., Patterson, M., Lundmark, V., Kiesler, S., Mukopadhyay, T., & Scherlis, W. (1998). Internet paradox: A social technology that reduces social involvement and psychological well-being? *American Psychologist, 53*, 1017–1031.

Laing, R. D. (1967). *The politics of experience*. New York: Ballantine.

Laing, R. D. (1969). *The divided self*. London: Penguin Books. (Original work published 1960)

Laing, R. D. (1972). *The politics of the family and other essays*. New York: Vintage. (Original work published 1969)

Laing, R. D. (1976). *The facts of life: An essay in feelings, facts, and fantasy*. New York: Pantheon.

Laing, R. D. (1989). *The challenge of love*. Unpublished manuscript.

Laing, R. D. (1990). Foreword. In R. W. Firestone, *Compassionate Child-Rearing: An in-depth approach to optimal parenting* (pp. vii–xi). Santa Barbara, CA: Glendon Association.

Langs, R. (1982). *Psychotherapy: A basic text*. New York: Jason Aronson.

Lasch, C. (1984). *The minimal self: Psychic survival in troubled times*. New York: W. W. Norton.

Leach, P. (1994). *Children first: What society must do—And is not doing—For children today*. New York: Vintage Books.

Leahy, R. L. (2001). *Overcoming resistance in cognitive therapy*. New York: Guilford Press.

LeDoux, J. E. (1995). Emotion: Clues from the brain. *Annual Review of Psychology, 46*, 209–227.

LeDoux, J. (1996). *The emotional brain: The mysterious underpinnings of emotional life*. New York: Simon and Schuster.

LeDoux, J. (2002). *Synaptic self: How our brains become who we are*. New York: Viking.

Lerner, H. G. (1985). *The dance of anger: A woman's guide to changing the patterns of intimate relationships*. New York: Harper and Row.

Lester, D. (1970). Relation of fear of death in subjects to fear of death in their parents. *Psychological Record, 20,* 541–543.

Levenkron, S. (1991). *Obsessive–compulsive disorders: Treating & understanding crippling habits.* New York: Warner Books.

Levy, D. M. (1943). *Maternal overprotection.* New York: Columbia University Press.

Lieberman, A. F., & Pawl, J. H. (1988). Clinical applications of attachment theory. In J. Belsky & T. Nezworski (Eds.), *Clinical implications of attachment* (pp. 327–351). Hillsdale, NJ: Erlbaum.

Lieberman, A. F., & Pawl, J. H. (1990). Disorders of attachment and secure base behavior in the second year of life. In M. Greenberg, D. Cicchetti, & E. M. Cummings (Eds.), *Attachment in the preschool years: Theory, research, and intervention* (pp. 375–397). Chicago: University of Chicago Press.

Lieberman, A. F., & Zeanah, C. H. (1999). Contributions of attachment theory to infant–parent psychotherapy and other interventions with infants and young children. In J. Cassidy & P. R. Shaver (Eds.), *Handbook of attachment: Theory, research, and clinical applications* (pp. 555–574). New York: Guilford Press.

Lifton, R. J. (1979). *The broken connection: On death and the continuity of life.* New York: Simon and Schuster.

Lippmann, W. (1955). *Essays in the public philosophy.* Boston: Little, Brown.

Loftus, E., & Ketcham, K. (1994). *The myth of repressed memory: False memories and allegations of sexual abuse.* New York: St. Martin's Griffin.

Lore, R. K., & Schultz, L. A. (1993). Control of human aggression: A comparative perspective. *American Psychologist, 48,* 16–25.

Loring, M. T. (1994). *Emotional abuse.* New York: Lexington.

Lothane, Z. (2002). Requiem or reveille: A response to Robert F. Bornstein (2001). *Psychoanalytic Psychology, 19,* 572–579.

Lott, B. (1997). Cataloging gender differences: Science or politics? In M. R. Walsh (Ed.), *Women, men, and gender: Ongoing debates* (pp. 19–23). New Haven, CT: Yale University Press.

Love, P. (with J. Robinson). (1990). *The emotional incest syndrome: What to do when a parent's love rules your life.* New York: Bantam Books.

Loy, D. (1992). Avoiding the void: The lack of self in psychotherapy and Buddhism. *Journal of Transpersonal Psychology, 24,* 151–179.

Lozoff, M. M. (1974). Fathers and autonomy in women. In R. B. Kundsin (Ed.), *Women and success* (pp. 103–109). New York: William Morrow.

Luhrmann, T. M. (2000). *Of two minds: The growing disorder in American psychiatry.* New York: Alfred A. Knopf.

Lyons-Ruth, K., & Jacobvitz, D. (1999). Attachment disorganization: Unresolved loss, relational violence, and lapses in behavioral and attentional strategies. In J. Cassidy & P. R. Shaver (Eds.), *Handbook of attachment: Theory, research, and clinical applications* (pp. 520–554). New York: Guilford Press.

Lyons-Ruth, K., & Zeanah, C. H., Jr. (1993). The family context of infant mental health: I. Affective development in the primary caregiving relationship. In

C. H. Zeanah, Jr. (Ed.), *Handbook of infant mental health* (pp. 14–37). New York: Guilford Press.

Madanes, C. (1999, July/August). Rebels with a cause: Honoring the subversive power of psychotherapy. *Family Therapy Networker*, 44–49, 57.

Main, M. (1999). Epilogue: Attachment theory: Eighteen points with suggestions for future studies. In J. Cassidy & P. R. Shaver (Eds.), *Handbook of attachment: Theory, research, and clinical applications* (pp. 845–887). New York: Guilford Press.

Main, M., & Hesse, E. (1990). Parents' unresolved traumatic experiences are related to infant disorganized attachment status: Is frightened and/or frightening parental behavior the linking mechanism? In M. T. Greenberg, D. Cicchetti, & E. M. Cummings (Eds.), *Attachment in the preschool years: Theory, research, and intervention* (pp. 161–182). Chicago: University of Chicago Press.

Main, M., & Solomon, J. (1986). Discovery of an insecure-disorganized/disoriented attachment pattern. In T. B. Brazelton & M. W. Yogman (Eds.), *Affective development in infancy* (pp. 95–124). Norwood, NJ: Ablex.

Main, M., & Solomon, J. (1990). Procedures for identifying infants as disorganized/disoriented during the Ainsworth strange situation. In M. T. Greenberg, D. Cicchetti, & E. M. Cummings (Eds.), *Attachment in the preschool years* (pp. 121–160). Chicago: University of Chicago Press.

Maltsberger, J. T. (1986). *Suicide risk: The formulation of clinical judgment*. New York: New York University Press.

Marcuse, H. (1964). *One-dimensional man: Studies in the ideology of advanced industrial society*. Boston: Beacon Press.

Marcuse, H. (1966). *Eros and civilization: A philosophical inquiry into Freud*. Boston: Beacon Press. (Original work published 1955)

Maris, R. W., Berman, A. L., Maltsberger, J. T., & Yufit, R. I. (Eds.). (1992). *Assessment and prediction of suicide*. New York: Guilford Press.

Masling, J. (2000). Empirical evidence and the health of psychoanalysis. *Journal of the American Academy of Psychoanalysis, 28*, 665–685.

Maslow, A. H. (1968). *Toward a psychology of being* (2nd ed.). New York: Van Nostrand Reinhold.

Masson, J. M. (1985). *The assault on the truth: Freud's suppression of the seduction theory*. New York: Penguin Books.

Masten, A. S., & Coatsworth, J. D. (1998). The development of competence in favorable and unfavorable environments. *American Psychologist, 53*, 205–220.

Masterson, J. F. (1985). *The real self: A developmental, self, and object relations approach*. New York: Brunner/Mazel.

May, R. (1981). *Freedom and destiny*. New York: Dell.

May, R. (1983). *The discovery of being: Writings in existential psychology*. New York: Norton.

McCabe, M. P., & Cobain, M. J. (1998). The impact of individual and relationship factors on sexual dysfunction among males and females. *Sexual & Marital Therapy, 13,* 131–143.

McCarthy, J. B. (1980). *Death anxiety: The loss of the self.* New York: Gardner.

McClearn, G. E., Plomin, R., Gora-Maslak, G., & Crabbe, J. C. (1991). The gene chase in behavioral science. *Psychological Science, 2,* 222–229.

McClure, L. (2000). *Anger and conflict in the workplace: Spot the signs, avoid the trauma.* Manassas Park, VA: Impact.

McCormack, C. C. (2000). *Treating borderline states in marriage: Dealing with oppositionalism, ruthless aggression, and severe resistance.* Northvale, NJ: Jason Aronson.

McFarlane, A., & van der Kolk, B. A. (1996). Trauma and its challenge to society. In B. A. van der Kolk, A. C. McFarlane, & L. Weisaeth (Eds.), *Traumatic stress: The effects of overwhelming experience on mind, body, and society* (pp. 24–46). New York: Guilford Press.

McIntosh, J. L. (1995). Suicide prevention in the elderly (age 65–99). In M. M. Silverman & R. W. Maris (Eds.), *Suicide prevention: Toward the year 2000* (pp. 180–192). New York: Guilford Press.

McLoyd, V. C. (1998). Socioeconomic disadvantage and child development. *American Psychologist, 53,* 185–204.

McManus, M. (n.d.). *The politics of marriage: Alliance for Marriage press coverage of the August 2000 marriage poll.* Retrieved 10/17/02 from http://www.allianceformarriage.org/press/McManusColumn.htm

Mead, G. H. (1967). *Mind, self, and society: From the standpoint of a social behaviorist.* Chicago: University of Chicago Press. (Original work published 1934)

Meissner, W. W. (1986). *Psychotherapy and the paranoid process.* Northvale, NJ: Jason Aronson.

Menninger, K. (1938). *Man against himself.* New York: Harcourt, Brace and World.

Meyer, J. E. (1975). *Death and neurosis* (M. Nunberg, Trans.). New York: International Universities Press.

Mikulincer, M., Florian, V., Birnbaum, G., & Malishkevich, S. (2002). The death-anxiety buffering function of close relationships: Exploring the effects of separation reminders on death-thought accessibility. *Personality and Social Psychology Bulletin, 28,* 287–299.

Mikulincer, M., Florian, V., & Tolmacz, R. (1990). Attachment styles and fear of personal death: A case study of affect regulation. *Journal of Personality and Social Psychology, 58,* 273–280.

Miller, A. (1981). *Prisoners of childhood: The drama of the gifted child and the search for the true self* (R. Ward, Trans.). New York: Basic Books. (Original work published 1979)

Miller, A. (1984a). *For your own good: Hidden cruelty in child-rearing and the roots of violence* (H. Hannum & H. Hannum, Trans., 2nd ed.). New York: Farrar, Straus, and Giroux. (Original work published 1980)

Miller, A. (1984b). *Thou shalt not be aware: Society's betrayal of the child* (H. & H. Hannum, Trans.). New York: Farrar, Straus and Giroux. (Original work published 1981)

Miller, A. (1990). *Banished knowledge: Facing childhood injuries* (L. Vennewitz, Trans.). New York: Doubleday. (Original work published 1988)

Miller, A. (1991). *Breaking down the wall of silence* (S. Worral, Trans.). New York: Meredian. (Original work published 1990)

Miller, H. (1941). *The wisdom of the heart*. New York: New Directions.

Miller, J. B. (1976). *Toward a new psychology of women*. Boston: Beacon Press.

Miller, N. E., & Dollard, J. (1941). *Social learning and imitation*. New Haven, CT: Yale University Press.

Minuchin, S. (1974). *Families & family therapy*. Cambridge: Harvard University Press.

Montgomery, B. M. (1988). Quality communication in personal relationships. In S. W. Duck, D. F. Hay, S. E. Hobfoll, W. Ickes, & B. Montgomery (Eds.), *Handbook of personal relationships: Theory, research and interventions* (pp. 343–362). New York: John Wiley.

Morling, B., Kitayama, S., & Miyamoto, Y. (2002). Cultural practices emphasize influence in the United States and adjustment in Japan. *Personality and Social Psychology Bulletin, 28,* 311–323.

Motz, A. (2001). *The psychology of female violence: Crimes against the body*. East Sussex, UK: Brunner-Routledge.

Moynihan, D. P. (1993). *Pandaemonium: Ethnicity in international politics*. New York: Oxford University Press.

Mrazek, D. (1993). Psychosomatic processes and physical illness. In C. H. Zeanah, Jr. (Ed.), *Handbook of infant mental health* (pp. 350–358). New York: Guilford Press.

Myers, D. G. (2000). The funds, friends, and faith of happy people. *American Psychologist, 55,* 56–67.

Myss, C. (1996). *Anatomy of the spirit: The seven stages of power and healing*. New York: Three Rivers Press.

Nagy, M. H. (1959). The child's view of death. In H. Feifel (Ed.), *The meaning of death* (pp. 79–98). New York: McGraw-Hill. (Original work published 1948)

Nakken, C. (1996). *The addictive personality: Understanding the addictive process and compulsive behavior* (2nd ed.). Center City, MN: Hazelden.

Neborsky, R. J. (2001). Davanloo's method of intensive short-term dynamic psychotherapy. In M. F. Solomon, R. J. Neborsky, L. McCullough, M. Alpert, F. Shapiro, & D. Malan (Eds.), *Short-term therapy for long-term change* (pp. 16–53). New York: W. W. Norton.

Neborsky, R. J., & Solomon, M. F. (2001). Attachment bonds and intimacy: Can the primary imprint of love change? In M. F. Solomon, R. J. Neborsky, L. McCullough, M. Alpert, F. Shapiro, & D. Malan (Eds.), *Short-term therapy for long-term change* (pp. 155–185). New York: W. W. Norton.

Nelson, F. L., & Farberow, N. L. (1982). The development of an indirect self-destructive behaviour scale for use with chronically ill medical patients. *International Journal of Social Psychiatry, 28,* 5–14.

Noyes, R., Hoenk, P. R., Kuperman, S., & Slymen, D. J. (1977). Depersonalization in accident victims and psychiatric patients. *Journal of Nervous and Mental Disease, 164,* 401–407.

Oaklander, V. (1978). *Windows to our children: A gestalt therapy approach to children and adolescents.* Moab, UT: Real People Press.

Oatley, K. (1996). Emotions: Communications to the self and others. In R. Harre & W. G. Parrott (Eds.), *The emotions: Social, cultural and biological dimensions* (pp. 312–316). London: Sage.

Ogden, T. H. (1982). *Projective identification and psychotherapeutic technique.* New York: Jason Aronson.

Ogden, T. H. (1989). *The primitive edge of experience.* Northvale, NJ: Jason Aronson.

Orbach, I., Shopen-Kofman, R., & Mikulincer, M. (1994). The impact of subliminal symbiotic vs identification messages in reducing anxiety. *Journal of Research in Personality, 28,* 492–504.

Ornish, D. (1998). *Love and survival: 8 pathways to intimacy and health.* New York: Harper Perennial.

Owen, D. (1993). The future of the Balkans: An interview with David Owen. *Foreign Affairs, 72,* 1–9.

Pagels, E. (1988). *Adam, Eve, and the serpent.* New York: Random House.

Pagels, E. (1995). *The origin of Satan.* New York: Random House.

Palazzoli, M. S., Boscolo, L., Cecchin, G., & Prata, G. (1978). *Paradox and counter-paradox: A new model in the therapy of the family in schizophrenic transaction* (E. V. Burt, Trans.). New York: Jason Aronson. (Original work published 1975)

Parin, P. (1978). *Furchte deinen Nachsten wie dich Selbst* [Fear thy neighbor as thyself]. Frankfurt, Germany: Suhrkamp.

Park, J. (1995). *Sons, mothers and other lovers.* London: Abacus.

Parker, G. (1983). *Parental overprotection: A risk factor in psychosocial development.* New York: Grune and Stratton.

Parr, G. (Producer and director). (1983). *Voyage to understanding* [Videotape]. Santa Barbara, CA: Glendon Association.

Parr, G. (Producer and director). (1987). *Of business and friendship* [Videotape]. Santa Barbara, CA: Glendon Association.

Parr, G. (Producer and director). (2002). *Friendship: A life of meaning and compassion* [Videotape]. Santa Barbara, CA: Glendon Association.

Parrott, W. G., & Harre, R. (1996). Overview. In R. Harre & W. G. Parrott (Eds.), *The emotions: Social, cultural and biological dimensions* (pp. 1–20). London: Sage.

Paykel, E. S. (1974). Recent life-events and clinical depression. In E. K. Gunderson & R. H. Rahe (Eds.), *Life stress and illness* (pp. 134–163). Springfield, IL: Charles C. Thomas.

Pearson, P. (1997). *When she was bad: How and why women get away with murder*. New York: Penguin Books.

Perry, B. D. (1996). Neurodevelopmental adaptations to violence: How children survive the intragenerational vortex of violence. Cybrary version of a chapter in *Violence and childhood trauma: Understanding and responding to the effects of violence in young children* (pp. 67–80), Gund Foundation, Cleveland, OH. Retrieved October 4, 2000, from http://www.bcm.tmc.edu/cta/vortex_violence.htm

Perry, B. D. (1997). Incubated in terror: Neurodevelopmental factors in the "cycle of violence." In J. D. Osofsky (Ed.), *Children in a violent society* (pp. 124–149). New York: Guilford Press.

Perry, B. D. (1999, October). Bonding and attachment in maltreated children: Consequences of emotional neglect in childhood. Draft. *Child Trauma Academy Parent and Caregiver Education Series*, *1*. Retrieved Dec. 14, 1999, from http://www.bcm.tmc.edu/civitas

Perry, B. D. (2000). Violence and childhood: How persisting fear can alter the developing child's brain. A Special Child Trauma Academy Website version of "The neurodevelopmental impact of violence in childhood." Web Version draft. Houston, TX: Child Trauma Academy.

Perry, B. D., & Marcellus, J. (1997). The impact of abuse and neglect on the developing brain. *Colleagues for Children*, *7*, 1–4.

Person, E. S. (1995). *By force of fantasy: How we make our lives*. New York: Basic Books.

Petry, N. M. (2000). A comprehensive guide to the application of contingency management procedures in clinical settings. *Drug and Alcohol Dependence*, *58*, 9–25.

Petry, N. M., Tedford, J., & Martin, B. (2001). Reinforcing compliance with non-drug-related activities. *Journal of Substance Abuse Treatment*, *20*, 33–44.

Petzinger, T., Jr. (2000, January 1). Talking about tomorrow: Edward O. Wilson. *Wall Street Journal*, pp. R16, R18.

Pines, A. M. (1998). *Romantic jealousy: Causes, symptoms, cures*. New York: Routledge.

Plomin, R. (1989). Environment and genes: Determinants of behavior. *American Psychologist*, *44*, 105–111.

Plutchik, R. (2000). *Emotions in the practice of psychotherapy: Clinical implications of affect theories*. Washington, DC: American Psychological Association.

Pope, K. S., & Brown, L. S. (1996). *Recovered memories of abuse: Assessment, therapy, forensics*. Washington, DC: American Psychological Association.

Popper, K. R. (1945). *The open society and its enemies, Vol. 1, The spell of Plato*. London: Routledge and Kegan Paul.

Post, R. M. (1992). Transduction of psychosocial stress into the neurobiology of recurrent affective disorder. *American Journal of Psychiatry*, *149*, 999–1010.

Potter-Efron, R. (1994). *Angry all the time: An emergency guide to anger control.* Oakland, CA: New Harbinger.

Prescott, J. W. (1975, November). Body pleasure and the origins of violence. *Bulletin of the Atomic Scientists,* 10–20.

Prescott, J. W. (1996). The origins of human love and violence. *Journal of Prenatal & Perinatal Psychology & Health, 10*(3), 143–188.

Puhar, A. (1993). Childhood origins of the war in Yugoslavia: I. Infant mortality. *Journal of Psychohistory, 20,* 373–379.

Putnam, F. W., Guroff, J. J., Silberman, E. K., Barban, L., & Post, R. M. (1986). The clinical phenomenology of multiple personality disorder: Review of 100 recent cases. *Journal of Clinical Psychiatry, 47,* 285–293.

Putnam, R. D. (1995, January). Bowling alone: America's declining social capital. *Journal of Democracy, 6,* 65–78.

Pyszczynski, T., Solomon, S., & Greenberg, J. (2003). *In the wake of 9/11: The psychology of terror.* Washington, DC: American Psychological Association.

Raimy, E. (1979). *Shared houses, shared lives: The new extended families and how they work.* Los Angeles: J. P. Tarcher.

Rank, O. (1941). *Beyond psychology.* New York: Dover.

Rank, O. (1972). *Will therapy and truth and reality* (J. Taft, Trans.). New York: Knopf. (Original work published 1936)

Rawls, J. (1971). *A theory of justice.* Cambridge, MA: Harvard University Press.

Reppen, J. (Ed.). (2002). [Complete issue.] *Psychoanalytic Psychology, 19*(3).

Rheingold, J. C. (1964). *The fear of being a woman: A theory of maternal destructiveness.* New York: Grune and Stratton.

Rheingold, J. C. (1967). *The mother, anxiety, and death: The catastrophic death complex.* Boston: Little, Brown.

Rich, A. (1976). *Of woman born: Motherhood as experience and institution.* New York: W. W. Norton.

Richman, J. (1986). *Family therapy for suicidal people.* New York: Springer.

Richman, J. (1993). *Preventing elderly suicide: Overcoming personal despair, professional neglect, and social bias.* New York: Springer.

Roberts, M. S. (1995). *Living without procrastination.* Oakland, CA: New Harbinger.

Rochlin, G. (1967). How younger children view death and themselves. In E. A. Grollman (Ed.), *Explaining death to children* (pp. 51–85). Boston: Beacon Press.

Rohner, R. P. (1986). *The warmth dimension: Foundations of parental acceptance-rejection theory.* Newbury Park, CA: Sage.

Rohner, R. P. (1991). *Handbook for the study of parental acceptance and rejection.* Storrs: University of Connecticut.

Rohner, R. P., Kean, K. J., & Cournoyer, D. E. (1991). Effects of corporal punishment, perceived caretaker warmth, and cultural beliefs on the psychological adjustment of children in St. Kitts, West Indies. *Journal of Marriage and the Family, 53,* 681–693.

Roiphe, H., & Galenson, E. (1981). *Infantile origins of sexual identity.* New York: International Universities Press.

Rorty, R. (1998). *Achieving our country: Leftist thought in twentieth-century America.* Cambridge, MA: Harvard University Press.

Rorty, R. (1999). *Philosophy and social hope.* London: Penguin Books.

Rosen, K. S., & Rothbaum, F. (1993). Quality of parental caregiving and security of attachment. *Developmental Psychology, 29,* 358–367.

Rosen, M. D. (Ed.). (1994). *Can this marriage be saved? Real-life cases from the most popular, most enduring women's magazine feature in the world.* New York: Workman.

Rosen, M. D. (Ed.). (2002). *Seven secrets of a happy marriage: Wisdom from the annals of Can This Marriage Be Saved.* New York: Workman.

Rosenfeld, A. (1978, April 1). The "elastic mind" movement: Rationalizing child neglect? *Saturday Review,* pp. 26–28.

Ross, C. A., Miller, S. D., Reagor, P., Bjornson, L., Fraser, G. A., & Anderson, G. (1990). Structured interview data on 102 cases of multiple personality disorder from four centers. *American Journal of Psychiatry, 147,* 596–601.

Roth, A., & Fonagy, P. (1996). *What works for whom? A critical review of psychotherapy research.* New York: Guilford Press.

Rothschild, B. (2000). *The body remembers: The psychophysiology of trauma and trauma treatment.* New York: W. W. Norton.

Rubenstein, C. (1998). *The sacrificial mother: Escaping the trap of self-denial.* New York: Hyperion.

Ruszczynski, S., & Fisher (1995a). Introduction. In S. Ruszczynski & J. Fisher (Eds.), *Intrusiveness and intimacy in the couple* (pp. 1–9). London: Karnac Books.

Ruszczynski, S., & Fisher, J. (Eds.). (1995b). *Intrusiveness and intimacy in the couple.* London: Karnac Books.

Ryan, R. M., & Deci, E. L. (2000). Self-determination theory and the facilitation of intrinsic motivation, social development, and well-being. *American Psychologist, 55,* 68–78.

Safran, J. D. (1999). Foreword. In E. Kennedy-Moore & J. C. Watson, *Expressing emotion: Myths, realities, and therapeutic strategies* (pp. xi–xii). New York: Guilford Press.

Samilov, A., & Goldfried, M. R. (2000). Role of emotion in cognitive–behavior therapy. *Clinical Psychology: Science and Practice, 7,* 373–385.

Sandbek, T. J. (1993). *The deadly diet: Recovering from anorexia & bulimia* (2nd ed.). Oakland, CA: New Harbinger.

Sandell, R., Blomberg, J., Lazar, A., Carlsson, J., Broberg, J., & Schubert, J. (2000). Varieties of long-term outcome among patients in psychoanalysis and long-term psychotherapy. *International Journal of Psychoanalysis, 81,* 921–942.

Sanders, B., & Giolas, M. H. (1991). Dissociation and childhood trauma in psychologically disturbed adolescents. *American Journal of Psychiatry, 148,* 50–54.

Sarwer, D. B., & Durlak, J. A. (1996). Childhood sexual abuse as a predictor of adult female sexual dysfunction: A study of couples seeking sex therapy. *Child Abuse & Neglect*, 20, 963–972.

Schakel, J. A. (1987). Emotional neglect and stimulus deprivation. In M. R. Brassard, R. Germain, & S. N. Hart (Eds.), *Psychological maltreatment of children and youth* (pp. 100–109). New York: Pergamon Press.

Scharff, D. E., & Scharff, J. S. (1991). *Object relations couple therapy*. Northvale, NJ: Jason Aronson.

Schnarch, D. M. (1991). *Constructing the sexual crucible: An integration of sexual and marital therapy*. New York: W. W. Norton.

Schore, A. N. (1994). *Affect regulation and the origin of the self: The neurobiology of emotional development*. Hillsdale, NJ: Erlbaum.

Schore, A. N. (1999, April 9–10). Early trauma and the development of the right brain. Presented at the Psychological Trauma: Maturational Processes and Therapeutic Interventions Conference, Boston.

Schore, A. N. (2001). The relevance of developmental neuropsychoanalysis to the clinical models of Sandor Ferenczi and Wilfred Bion: Introduction. *Psychologist/Psychoanalyst*, 21(1), 12–13.

Schreiber, F. R. (1984). *The shoemaker: The anatomy of a psychotic*. Harmondsworth, UK: Penguin Books. (Original work published 1983)

Schwartz, B. (2000). Pitfalls on the road to a positive psychology of hope. In J. E. Gillham (Ed.), *The science of optimism and hope: Research essays in honor of Martin E. P. Seligman* (pp. 399–412). Philadelphia: Templeton Foundation Press.

Schwartz, J. M. (with B. Beyette). (1996). *Brain lock: Free yourself from obsessive–compulsive behavior*. New York: Regan Books.

Seaburn, D., Landau-Stanton, J., & Horwitz, S. (1995). Core techniques in family therapy. In R. H. Mikesell, D. Lusterman, & S. H. McDaniel (Eds.), *Integrating family therapy: Handbook of family psychology and systems theory* (pp. 5–26). Washington, DC: American Psychological Association.

Searles, H. F. (1979). *Countertransference and related subjects: Selected papers*. Madison, CT: International Universities Press.

Seiden, R. H. (1984). Death in the west: A regional analysis of the youthful suicide rate. *Western Journal of Medicine*, 140, 969–973.

Seixas, J. S., & Youcha, G. (1985). *Children of alcoholism: A survivor's manual*. New York: Harper and Row.

Seligman, M. E. P. (1975). *Helplessness: On depression, development, and death*. New York: Freeman.

Seligman, M. E. P. (1990). *Learned optimism*. New York: Alfred A. Knopf.

Seligman, M. E. P. (1995). The effectiveness of psychotherapy: The *Consumer Reports* study. *American Psychologist*, 50, 965–974.

Shafer, B. C. (1955). *Nationalism: Myth and reality*. New York: Harcourt, Brace.

Shaver, P. R., & Clark, C. L. (1994). The psychodynamics of adult romantic attachment. In J. M. Masling & R. F. Bornstein (Eds.), *Empirical perspectives* on object relations theory (pp. 105–156). Washington, DC: American Psychological Association.

Shengold, L. (1989). Soul murder: The effects of childhood abuse and deprivation. New Haven, CT: Yale University Press.

Shneidman, E. S. (1966). Orientations toward death: A vital aspect of the study of lives. International Journal of Psychiatry, 2, 167–200.

Shneidman, E. S. (1973). Deaths of man. New York: Quadrangle/New York Times.

Shorter, E. (1997). A history of psychiatry: From the era of the asylum to the age of Prozac. New York: John Wiley.

Siegel, D. J. (1999). The developing mind: Toward a neurobiology of interpersonal experience. New York: Guilford Press.

Siegel, D. J. (2001). Toward an interpersonal neurobiology of the developing mind: Attachment relationships, "mindsight," and neutral integration. Infant Mental Health Journal, 22, 67–94.

Siegel, R. K. (1994). Whispers: The voices of paranoia. New York: Crown.

Silverman, L. H., Lachmann, F. M., & Milich, R. H. (1982). The search for oneness. New York: International Universities Press.

Simon, L., Greenberg, J., Harmon-Jones, E., Solomon, S., Pyszczynski, T., Arndt, J., et al. (1997). Terror management and cognitive–experiential self-theory: Evidence that terror management occurs in the experiential system. Journal of Personality and Social Psychology, 72, 1132–1146.

Sinclair, H. (2001, February 21). Movement and action transform trauma: A community action response to violence prevention. San Francisco: Manalive Violence Prevention Programs.

Singer, J. L. (1998). Daydreams, the stream of consciousness, and self-representations. In R. F. Bornstein & J. M. Masling (Eds.), Empirical perspectives on the psychoanalytic unconscious (pp. 141–186). Washington, DC: American Psychological Association.

Siqueland, L., Crits-Christoph, P., Barber, J. P., Butler, S. F., Thase, M., Najavits, L., et al. (2000). The role of therapist characteristics in training: Effects in cognitive, supportive–expressive, and drug counseling therapies for cocaine dependence. Journal of Psychotherapy Practice and Research, 9, 123–130.

Skodol, A. E. (Ed.). (1998). Psychopathology and violence crime. Washington, DC: American Psychiatric Press.

Slavik, S., Carlson, J., & Sperry, L. (1998). The passive–aggressive couple. In J. Carlson & L. Sperry (Eds.), The disordered couple (pp. 299–314). Bristol, PA: Brunner/Mazel.

Sluzki, C. E. (2001). Editorial: Drug-company influence on medical education in the U.S.A. American Journal of Orthopsychiatry, 71, 148–149.

Snyder, C. R., & Lopez, S. J. (Eds.). (2002). Handbook of positive psychology. New York: Oxford University Press.

Solomon, J., & George, C. (1999). The place of disorganization in attachment theory: Linking classic observations with contemporary findings. In J. Solomon

& C. George (Eds.), *Attachment disorganization* (pp. 3–32). New York: Guilford Press.

Solomon, M. F. (1989). *Narcissism and intimacy*. New York: W. W. Norton.

Solomon, M. F., Neborsky, R. J., McCullough, L., Alpert, M., Shapiro, F., & Malan, D. (Eds.). (2001). *Short-term therapy for long-term change*. New York: W. W. Norton.

Solomon, S., Greenberg, J., & Pyszczynski, T. (1991). A terror management theory of social behavior: The psychological functions of self-esteem and cultural worldviews. *Advances in Experimental Social Psychology, 24,* 93–159.

Spiegel, D. (Ed.). (1999). *Efficacy and cost-effectiveness of psychotherapy*. Washington, DC: American Psychiatric Press.

Sproull, L., & Kiesler, S. (1991). *Connections: New ways of working in the networked organization*. Cambridge, MA: MIT Press.

Stanton, A. L., Danoff-Burg, S., Cameron, C. L., Bishop, M., Collins, C. A., Kirk, et al. (2000). Emotionally expressive coping predicts psychological and physical adjustment to breast cancer. *Journal of Consulting and Clinical Psychology, 68,* 875–882.

Steele, B. F. (1990). Some sequelae for the sexual maltreatment of children. In H. B. Levine (Ed.), *Adult analysis and childhood sexual abuse* (pp. 21–34). Hillsdale, NJ: Analytic Press.

Stern, D. N. (1985). *The interpersonal world of the infant: A view from psychoanalysis and developmental psychology*. New York: Basic Books.

Stern, D. N. (1995). *The motherhood constellation: A unified view of parent–infant psychotherapy*. New York: Basic Books.

Stettbacher, J. K. (1991). *Making sense of suffering: The healing confrontation with your own past* (S. Worrall, Trans.). New York: Meridian. (Original work published 1990)

Stiles, W. B. (1999). Suppression of continuity-benevolence assumptions (CBA) voices: A theoretical note on the psychology and psychotherapy of depression. *Psychotherapy, 36,* 268–273.

Stiver, I. (1986). Beyond the Oedipus complex: Mothers and daughters. *Work in Progress, 26,* 1–17. Wellesley, MA: Stone Center Working Paper Series.

Stoller, R. J. (2000). A mark of decline: The abuse of language in psychoanalysis and psychotherapy. In S. de Schill, *Crucial choices—Crucial changes: The resurrection of psychotherapy* (pp. 59–77). Amherst, NY: Prometheus Books.

Stolorow, R. D. (1992). Closing the gap between theory and practice with better psychoanalytic theory. *Psychotherapy, 29,* 159–166.

Stratton, P. (Ed.). (1982). *Psychobiology of the human newborn*. Chichester, UK: John Wiley.

Straus, M. A. (with D. A. Donnelly). (1994). *Beating the devil out of them: Corporal punishment in American families*. New York: Lexington Books.

Straus, M. A., & Gelles, R. J. (1986). Societal change and change in family violence from 1975 to 1985 as revealed by two national surveys. *Journal of Marriage and the Family, 48,* 465–479.

Strong, B., DeVault, C., & Sayad, B. W. (1999). *Human sexuality: Diversity in contemporary America* (3rd ed.). Mountain View, CA: Mayfield.

Suzuki, D. T., Fromm, E., & DeMartino, R. (1960). *Zen Buddhism and psychoanalysis.* New York: Harper and Row.

Szanto, K., Prigerson, H., Houck, P., Ehrenpreis, L., & Reynolds, C. F. (1997). Suicidal ideation in elderly bereaved: The role of complicated grief. *Suicide and Life-Threatening Behavior, 27,* 194–207.

Szasz, T. S. (1974). *The myth of mental illness: Foundations of a theory of personal conduct* (Rev. ed.). New York: Harper and Row.

Szasz, T. (1978). *The myth of psychotherapy: Mental healing as religion, rhetoric, and repression.* Syracuse, NY: Syracuse University Press.

Szuchman, L. T., & Muscarella, F. (Eds.). (2000). *Psychological perspectives on human sexuality.* New York: John Wiley.

Tart, C. T. (1994). *Living the mindful life.* Boston: Shambhala.

Tedeschi, J. T., & Felson, R. B. (1994). *Violence, aggression, & coercive actions.* Washington, DC: American Psychological Association.

Toch, H. (1992). *Violent men: An inquiry into the psychology of violence* (Rev. ed.). Washington, DC: American Psychological Association.

Tolle, E. (1999). *The power of now: A guide to spiritual enlightenment.* Novato, CA: New World Library.

Tomer, A. (1995). Personal identity and death concern: Philosophical and developmental perspectives. In J. Kauffman (Ed.), *Awareness of mortality* (pp. 91–107). New York: Baywood.

Tomer, A., & Eliason, G. (1996). Toward a comprehensive model of death anxiety. *Death Studies, 20,* 343–365.

Toynbee, A. (1968). Changing attitudes towards death in the modern western world. In A. Toynbee, A. K. Mant, N. Smart, J. Hinton, S. Yudkin, E. Rhode, et al. (Eds.), *Man's concern with death* (pp. 122–132). London: Hodder and Stoughton.

Trevarthen, C. (1990). Growth and education of the hemisphere. In C. Trevarthen (Ed.), *In brain circuits and functions of the mind* (pp. 334–363). Cambridge: Cambridge University Press.

Tronick, E. (1980). Infant communicative intent. In A. P. Reilly (Ed.), *The communication game: Perspectives on the development of speech, language and non-verbal communication skills* (pp. 4–9). Skilmer, NJ: Johnson and Johnson.

Tronick, E. Z., Cohn, J., & Shea, E. (1986). The transfer of affect between mothers and infants. In T. B. Brazelton & M. W. Yogman (Eds.), *Affective development in infancy* (pp. 11–25). Norwood, NJ: Ablex.

Turkle, S. (1997). *Life on the screen.* New York: Simon and Schuster.

Ullman, A. D. (1965). The framework. In A. D. Ullman (Ed.), *Sociocultural foundations of personality* (pp. 1–6). Boston: Houghton Mifflin.

United States Bureau of the Census. (n.d.). *Family structure and children's living arrangements*. Retrieved October 20, 2002, from http://www.census.gov/population/www/socdemo/child/la-child.html

Valenstein, E. S. (1998). *Blaming the brain: The truth about drugs and mental health*. New York: Free Press.

Valliant, L. M. (1997). *Changing character: Short-term anxiety-regulating psychotherapy for restructuring defenses, affects, and attachment*. New York: Basic Books.

van der Kolk, B. A., Greenberg, M., Boyd, H., & Krystal, J. (1985). Inescapable shock, neurotransmitters, and addiction to trauma: Toward a psychobiology of posttraumatic stress. *Biological Psychiatry, 20*, 314–325.

van der Kolk, B. A., McFarlane, A. C., & Weisaeth, L. (Eds.). (1996). *Traumatic stress: The effects of overwhelming experience on mind, body, and society*. New York: Guilford Press.

Vergote, A. (1988). *Guilt and desire: Religious attitudes and their pathological derivatives* (M. H. Wood, Trans.). New Haven, CT: Yale University Press. (Original work published 1978)

Vitalari, N. P., Venkatesh, A., & Gronhaug, K. (1985). Computing in the home: Shifts in time allocation patterns of households. *Communications of the ACM, 28*, 512–522.

Wachtel, P. L. (Ed.). (1982). *Resistance: Psychodynamic and behavioral approaches*. New York: Plenum Press.

Waddell, M. (1998). *Inside lives: Psychoanalysis and the development of the personality*. New York: Routledge.

Wallerstein, J., Lewis, J., & Blakeslee, S. (2000). *The unexpected legacy of divorce: A 25 year landmark study*. New York: Hyperion.

Walsh, C., MacMillan, H., & Jamieson, E. (2002). The relationship between parental psychiatric disorder and child physical and sexual abuse: Findings from the Ontario Health Supplement. *Child Abuse & Neglect, 26*, 11–22.

Walsh, M. R. (Ed.). (1997). *Women, men, and gender: Ongoing debates*. New Haven, CT: Yale University Press.

Wampold, B. E. (2001). *The great psychotherapy debate: Models, methods, and findings*. Mahway, NJ: Erlbaum.

Watts, A. (1961). *Psychotherapy East and West*. New York: Vintage.

Weil, S. (1952). *The need for roots: Prelude to a declaration of duties towards mankind* (A. F. Wills, Trans.). London: Routledge. (Original work published 1949)

Weisz, J. R., Weiss, B., & Donenberg, G. R. (1992). The lab versus the clinic: Effects of child and adolescent psychotherapy. *American Psychologist, 47*, 1578–1585.

Welldon, E. V. (1988). *Mother, madonna, whore: The idealization and denigration of motherhood*. London: Free Association Books.

Werner, E. E. (1990). Protective factors and individual resilience. In S. J. Meisels & J. P. Shonkoff (Eds.), *Handbook of early childhood intervention* (pp. 97–116). Cambridge: Cambridge University Press.

West, M. L., & Keller, A. E. R. (1991). Parentification of the child: A case study of Bowlby's compulsive care-giving attachment pattern. *American Journal of Psychotherapy, 45,* 425–431.

Westen, D. (2000). Commentary: Implicit and emotional processes in cognitive–behavioral therapy. *Clinical Psychology Science and Practice, 7,* 386–390.

Wexler, J., & Steidl, J. (1978). Marriage and the capacity to be alone. *Psychiatry, 41,* 72–82.

Whitaker, C. A., & Malone, T. P. (1953). *The roots of psychotherapy.* New York: Brunner/Mazel.

Whitfield, C. L. (1995). *Memories and abuse: Remembering and healing the effects of trauma.* Deerfield Beach, FL: Health Communications.

Willi, J. (1982). *Couples in collusion: The unconscious dimension in partner relationships* (W. Inayat-Khan & M. Tchorek, Trans.). Claremont, CA: Hunter House. (Original work published 1975)

Winnicott, D. W. (1958). *Collected papers: Through pediatrics to psycho-analysis.* London: Tavistock.

Winnicott, D. W. (1965). The theory of the parent–infant relationship. In D. W. Winnicott, *The maturational processes and the facilitating environment: Studies in the theory of emotional development* (pp. 37–55). Madison, CT: International Universities Press. (Original work published 1960)

Wolberg, L. R. (1954). *The technique of psychotherapy.* New York: Grune and Stratton.

Wong, P. T. P., & Fry, P. S. (Eds.). (1998). *The human quest for meaning: A handbook of psychological research and clinical applications.* Mahwah, NJ: Erlbaum.

Wood, W., Pool, G. J., Leck, K., & Purvis, D. (1996). Self-definition, defensive processing, and influence: The normative impact of majority and minority groups. *Journal of Personality & Social Psychology, 71,* 1181–1193.

Wright, R. (1995). The evolution of despair. *Time,* pp. 50–54, 56–57.

Yalom, I. (1980). *Existential psychotherapy.* New York: Basic Books.

Young, K. S. (1998). *Caught in the net: How to recognize the signs of Internet addition— And a winning strategy for recovery.* New York: John Wiley.

Zerbe, K. J. (1993). *The body betrayed: A deeper understanding of women, eating disorders, and treatment.* Carlsbad, CA: Gurze Books.

Zilboorg, G. (1943). Fear of death. *Psychoanalytic Quarterly, 12,* 465–475.

Zito, J. M., Safer, D. J., DosReis, S., Gardner, J. F., Magder, L., et al. (2003). Psychotropic practice patterns for youth: A 10-year perspective. *Archives of Pediatric Adolescent Medicine, 157*(1), 17–25.

Zohar, J., & Insel, T. R. (1997). Obsessive–compulsive disorder: Psychobiological approaches to diagnosis, treatment, and pathophysiology. In D. J. Stein & M. Stone (Eds.), *Essential papers on obsessive–compulsive disorder* (pp. 277–303). New York: New York University Press. (Original published 1987)

AUTHOR INDEX

Numbers in italics refer to listings in the reference section.

Kozol, J., 16, *426*
Kramer, R., 61, 85n, *426*
Kraut, R., 15, 34n, *426*
Krokoff, L. J., 237n, *422*
Krystal, J., 44, *439*
Kuperman, S., 49, *430*

Lachmann, F. M., 56n, *436*
Laing, R. D., 37, 40, 42, 49, 107, 110,
    112, 137, 149, 213, 228, 244,
    348, 384, *426*
Landau-Stanton, J., 350, *435*
Landis, K. R., 369, *423*
Langs, R., 309n, *426*
Lasch, C., 16, 137, *426*
Law, S. A., 15, *409*
Lazar, A., 348, *434*
Leach, P., 279, *426*
Leahy, R. L., 61, 85n, *426*
Lebovici, S., 352, *416*
Leck, K., 335, *440*
LeDoux, J. E., 41, 44, 110, 303, 363, *426*
Leigh, T., 363, *419*
Leonard, J. A., 363, *423*
Lerner, H. G., 128n, *426*
Lester, D., 39, *426*
Levenkron, S., 92, *426*
Levy, D. M., 42
Lewis, J., 315, *439*
Lieberman, A. F., 303, 310n, 363, *427*
Liese, B. S., 106n, *411*
Lifton, R. J., 377, 381, *427*
Lippmann, W., 331, *427*
Loftus, E., 353, 364n, *427*
Lopez, S. J., 11n, *436*
Lore, R. K., 148n, *427*
Loring, M. T., *427*
Lothane, Z., 364, *427*
Lott, B., 242, *427*
Love, P., 249, *427*
Loy, D., 208n, *427*
Lozoff, M. M., 253, *427*
Luborsky, L., 352, *423*
Luhrmann, T. M., 351, 362, *427*
Lundmark, V., 15, 34n, *426*
Lyons-Ruth, K., 44, 68, 85n, *427*

Machado, P. P., 356, *411*
Mack, J. E., 91, *425*

MacMillan, H., 36, *439*
Madanes, C., 347, 350, *427*
Maddeaux, C., 106n, *424*
Main, M., 40, 44, 56n, 68, 273, 281, 363,
    428
Malan, D., 120, *436*
Malishkevich, S., 186, *429*
Malone, T. P., 68, 85n, *440*
Maltsberger, J. T., 183n, *428*
Marcellus, J., 43, *432*
Marcuse, H., 314, 331, 333, *428*
Margolies, E., 243, 250, *421*
Maris, R. W., 183n, *428*
Martin, B., 95, *432*
Masling, J., 352, *428*
Maslow, A. H., 348, *428*
Masson, J. M., 350, 354, *428*
Masten, A. S., 287, *428*
Masterson, J. F., 269n, *428*
Mattoon, G., 363, *419*
May, R., 348, 358, 381, *428*
McBride, M. C., 37, 40, *417*
McCabe, M. P., 248, *428*
McCarthy, J. B., 199, *428*
McCary, J. L., 240, *422*
McClearn, G. E., 42, *428*
McClure, L., 150, 151, *429*
McCormack, C. C., 136, *429*
McCullough, L., 120, *436*
McDonald, C., 91, *412*
McFarlane, A., 56n, 315, 363, *429, 439*
McIntosh, J. L., 174, *429*
McLoyd, V. C., 287, *429*
McManus, M., 314, *429*
McPherson, A., 95, *417*
Mead, G. H., 331, *429*
Meissner, W. W., 135, 136, 137, *429*
Menninger, K., 165, 166, *429*
Messman, S. J., 237n, *414*
Meyer, J. E., 138, 192, *429*
Mickelsen, O., 56n, *425*
Middleton, D., 331, *412*
Mikulincer, M., 56n, 186, 208n, *429, 431*
Milich, R. H., 56n, *436*
Miller, A., 35, 37, 40, 43, 63, 64, 115,
    249, 269n, 350, 351, 354, *429*
Miller, H., 15, *430*
Miller, J. B., 324, *430*
Miller, N. E., 21, 335, *430*
Miller, S. D., 56n, *434*
Minuchin, S., 37, *430*

Mitchell, B. M., 15, *409*
Mitchell, S. A., 113, *422*
Miyamoto, Y., 345n, *430*
Montgomery, B. M., 332, *430*
Morling, B., 345n, *430*
Motz, A., 133, 318, *430*
Moynihan, D. P., 196, *430*
Mrazek, D., 115, *430*
Mukopadhyay, T., 15, 34n, *426*
Mullen, P., 36, *419*
Muscarella, F., 241, *438*
Myers, D. G., 369, *430*
Myss, C., 11n, *430*

Nagy, M. H., 39, 53, *430*
Najavits, L., 357, *436*
Nakken, C., 87, *430*
Neborsky, R. J., 85n, 120, 363, *430, 436*
Nelson, F. L., 170, *430*
Nesse, R., 158
Neufeldt, S., 356, *411*
Newman, C. F., 106n, *411*
Newman, C. W., 173, *411*
Nordenberg, D., 41, 45, 55n, *417*
Noyes, R., 49, *430*

Oaklander, V., 37, 62, *430*
Oatley, K., 108, *431*
Ogden, T. H., 134, 237n, *431*
Orbach, I., 56n, *431*
Ornish, D., 11n, *431*
Owen, D., 196, *431*

Pagels, E., 195, 208n, 240, *431*
Palazzoli, M. S., 37, *431*
Pallotta, J., 55n, *416*
Parin, P., 213, *431*
Park, J., 244, 249, 253, *431*
Parker, G., 42, 279, *431*
Parr, G., 11n, 86n, 345, *431*
Parrott, W. G., 108, 120, *423, 431*
Patterson, M., 15, 34n, *426*
Pawl, J. H., 303, 310n, 363, *427*
Paykel, E. S., 115, *431*
Pearson, P., 128n, 133, 228, 318, *410, 431*
Perna, F., 56n, *412*

Perry, B. D., 43, 44, 45, 55n, 56n, 274, 285, 287, 363, *431, 432*
Person, E. S., 84n, *432*
Peters, S. D., 45, *418*
Petry, N. M., 95, *432*
Pettem, O., 85n, *421*
Pettit, G. S., 128n, *416*
Petzinger, T. , Jr., 377, 378, *432*
Pines, A. M., 269n, *432*
Plomin, R., 42, 354, *428, 432*
Plutchik, R., 129n, 363, *432*
Pool, G. J., 335, *440*
Pope, K. S., 353, *432*
Popper, K. R., 196, *432*
Post, R. M., 44, 56n, *432, 433*
Potter-Efron, R., 128n, *432*
Prata, G., 37, *431*
Prescott, J. W., 242, *432*
Prigerson, H., 170, *438*
Puhar, A., 196, 242, *432*
Purvis, D., 335, *440*
Putnam, F. W., 56n, *433*
Putnam, R. D., 16, *433*
Pyszczynski, T., 39, 55n, 195, 197, 198, *422, 433, 436, 437*

Radley, A., 331, *412*
Rahe, R. H., 151, 152, *423*
Raimy, E., 11n, *433*
Rank, O., 36, 85n, 101, 152, 194, 207, 208n, 217, 236n, 356, *433*
Rawls, J., 336, 340, *433*
Reagor, P., 56n, *434*
Reiss, C., 274, *413*
Reppen, J., 364n, *433*
Reynolds, C. F., 170, *438*
Rheingold, J. C., 110, 244, 250, 251, 288, *433*
Rich, A., 250, *433*
Richman, J., 36, 174, *433*
Roberts, M. S., 150, *433*
Robinson, J., 249, *427*
Rochlin, G., 39, *433*
Rohner, R. P., 40, 55n, 276, 288n, 345n, *433*
Roiphe, H., 249, *433*
Rorty, R., 336, 345n, *433*
Rosen, K. S., 42, *433*
Rosen, M. D., 315, *434*
Rosenblatt, A., 39, 198, *422*

448   AUTHOR INDEX

SUBJECT INDEX

449

Benevolent social system, 336–337
    friendship circle's dimensions of,
        337–344
Binge-eating, 88–91
Bowenian Family Systems Theory, 226
Brain development
    emotional abuse and, 43
    environmental factors, 303
    hormones and, 148n
    normal organization of brain sys-
        tems, 55n–56n
    physical and sexual abuse and, 44
    social affiliation and, 286
Bulimia. See Eating disorders
Business ventures, 9
    acts of kindness through, 341
    moving toward real satisfaction in,
        82–83
    sharing of, 372

Child abuse. See also Sexual abuse
    anger and, 139, 304
    coercion used by parents, 316, 318
    emotional maltreatment and, 42
    false memory syndrome and,
        353–354
    occurrence of, 39, 44–45, 273–274,
        288n
    psychoanalysis of, 351
    repetition by parents who were
        abused as children, 37, 40
Child-rearing, 291–310
    analogy to effective psychotherapy,
        291–292
    defense system of parent, 37
        threats posed by child to, 111–
            112, 277–278
    dependency of parents, 42
    disciplinary practices, 41, 49, 304
    factors that impede personal develop-
        ment from, 36–37
    friendship circle constructive sugges-
        tions for, 305–309, 343–344
    guidelines based on sound mental
        health principles, 304–305
    idealization of parents. See Idealiza-
        tion of parents and family
    love-food for children, 45, 60, 293
    nonfeeling physical contact with
        children, 42–43

objectifying of children, 137,
    194–195
parental ability to accept their
    child's love, 113, 294
parental ability to relate to child as
    separate person, 294–295
parental capacity to respond person-
    ally to child, 293–294
parental love, forms of, 67, 345n
parental valuing of their own lives,
    295
possessiveness of parents, 194–195
prerequisites for optimal conditions,
    293–295
projection of self-image on child, 36,
    279–280
psychotherapy for parenting groups
    and parent education, 295–302
sexuality, parental attitudes toward,
    240–241
voice therapy for parenting groups,
    295–302
Children. See also Child-rearing; Family
    relationships; Infants
    abandonment threats of parents,
        318–319
    abuse. See Child abuse
    alcoholic parent, statistics on, 101
    ambivalence of parents, 276, 289n
    anxiety and pain, reaction to,
        113–114
    boundary violations by parents,
        325–326
    condescending behavior toward,
        328–329
    death anxiety and, 53
    difficulty of parents in sustaining
        loving relationships with,
        276–281
    fantasy bond's development by, 17
    father–daughter relationship,
        253–254
    father–son relationship, 252–253
    imitation of parents, 36, 44, 114
    inwardness developed by, 110–114
    mother–daughter relationship, 249–
        252, 269n
    mother–son relationship, 249, 269n
    nightmares of, 53–54
    painful experiences, reacting to,
        40–41

parents' rejection of child's loving feelings, 113, 294

as participants in friendship circle, 81

passivity and victimized stance of, 136–137

socializing of, 332

teenagers, treatment by parents as equals, 329, 343

unlikeable children, 280–281

Circumnavigation of the world, 8–9, 146

Claustrophobia, 138, 192

Coercion in interpersonal relationships, 317–319

parental use of, as child abuse, 316, 318

Cognitive therapy, 120

Compassion, 22–23

Competition

friendship circle's techniques for coping with, 383

sexual rivalry, 265–266

Complexity theory, 85n

Condescending behavior toward children, 328–329

Contingency-contracting, 106n

Contingent threats, 318

Continuum of negative thought patterns, 168, 169

Coping, 131–148

anger, psychotherapy techniques for coping without, 138–144

assuming responsibility, 142–143

child's imitation of parents for, 114

closeness to feelings and, 107

friendship circle's coping mechanisms, 382–383

withholding, psychotherapy techniques for coping without, 159

Core conflict in personal development, 48, 59

categories of fantasy involvement in resolution of, 65

Corrective emotional experience, 86n

Corrective suggestions. *See* Friendship circle; Psychotherapy

Counter-will, 102

Couple relationships, 213–237. *See also* Sexuality

addictive attachments, 88, 94–95, 193–194

distorted view of partner, 214

emerging family and, 274–276

empathy and understanding, 229–230

fantasy bond and, 214–218, 334

effect on children, 274–276

form versus substance, 218

friendship circle, corrective suggestions for, 231–235

defensive patterns of relating, 231–234

group therapy for, 219–224

honesty and integrity, 228–229

idealization of the other, 217

challenging in friendship circle, 81–82

individual rights in, 313–330. *See also* Individual rights

loss of independence, 217–218

nondefensive listening, 228

nonthreatening, nonmanipulative behavior, 230

outward versus inward lifestyle, 67

physical affection and personal sexuality, 229

polarization of parent-ego states, 217

provocation in, 214

psychotherapy for, 218–231

goal setting for relationship, 227–230

group therapy, 219–224

journal keeping, 225–227

revealing destructive thought processes to each other, 225

reliving the past through, 214–215

respect for boundaries of the other, 230, 325–326

respect for partner's freedom, 326

selection of partner, 214

strategy of "unilateral disarmament," 230–231

stubbornness in, 144

vanity in, 75, 193

voice therapy for, 218–224

withholding, effects on, 152–155, 216–217

Creativity, 23–24

Criticality, 37

Cynical attitudes, 334–335

Family relationships, 271–289. *See also*
    Child-rearing
    couple relationship's effect on,
        274–276
    current societal status of families,
        272–274
    defense system of parents. *See* De-
        fense system
    dependency load by assuming full re-
        sponsibility for child, 279
    difficulty of parents in sustaining lov-
        ing relationships with children,
        276–281
    emotional hunger of parents, 306
        confused with genuine love,
        278–279
    extended family, advantages of,
        285–287
    friendship circle's corrective sugges-
        tions for, 281–287
    idealization of parents and family,
        62–63, 271–272
    immortality, children seen as means
        of, 36, 194–195, 280
    individual rights in, 313–330. *See*
        also Individual rights
    projection of negative traits onto
        children, 63–65, 279–280
    sexual withholding related to,
        249–254
    single-parent family, 286
    socializing of child, 332
    unlikeable children, 280–281
Fantasies
    of expectant parents, 279
    sexual, 254, 264
Fantasy bond, 17–18, 45–48, 59–86. *See*
        also Self-parenting process
    categories of, 65–67
    couple relationship and, 214–218,
        334
    effect on children, 274–276
    death anxiety and, 53, 74, 193–194
    dimensions of defensive process,
        61–65
    exposure of discrepancy between ac-
        tions and stated goals, 73
    formation of, 17
    healthy functioning versus reliance
        on, 65

idealization of parents and family,
        62–63
    interfering with creativity and
        achievement, 64
    microsuicide and, 170, 171–172
    negative self-image and, 63
    outward versus inward lifestyle and,
        66
    projection of negative parental quali-
        ties and behaviors onto others,
        63–65, 279–280
    psychotherapy for, 76–80
    purpose of, 17, 60
    realistic feedback to fantasized
        image, 74–75
    resistance to change in psychother-
        apy, 61
    social reinforcement of, 314–315
    threats to, 67–75
    unusual success or satisfaction in a
        relationship and, 73–74
    voice process supporting, 18, 75–76
FAST. *See* Firestone Assessment of Self-
        Destructive Thoughts
FAVT (Firestone Assessment of Violent
        Thoughts), 183n
Fear
    aversive events and, 41
    of change, 361
    overcoming in friendship circle,
        82–83
Feeling-release therapy, 116–118, 120,
        129n, 348
Feelings, 107–129. *See also* Inwardness
    costs of suppressing, 108, 114–120
    friendship and ability to express,
        371–372
    friendship circle methods to enhance
        capacity for, 122–127
    intense feeling-release therapy. *See*
        Feeling-release therapy
    loss of, 108–110
    nature of, 107–108
    psychotherapy to enhance capacity
        for, 120–122, 128, 359–362
    sadness versus depression, 119–120
    social pressure against displays of,
        335–336
    voice process in suppressing,
        118–119

manipulation through, 321
passive–aggression and, 134
sexual, 240, 241, 254

Habits. *See* Routines and habitual responses
Happiness as goal, 334, 381
Hereditary factors, 35, 36
Honesty and integrity, 228–229, 326–328, 341–342
  in friendship, 368, 371–372
  in friendship circle, 382
Human body, views on, 240–241, 260, 264
Human rights. *See* Individual rights

Idealization of parents and family, 62–63
  correlation with bad self-image, 85n
  friendship circle's corrective suggestions for dealing with, 81–82
Identification
  child's identification with aggressor, 49–52, 56n, 114
  process of, 36
Idolization of leader, 195, 197
Imagination, 25
Imitation
  of parents, 36, 44, 114
  social pressure for, 335–336
Immortality and desire for children, 36, 194–195, 280
Incest, 91
Individual rights, 313–330
  couple and family systems and, 315–317
  friendship circle's values regarding, 319–329, 338
    awareness of and modification of behaviors that intrude on others' rights, 321–324
    sense of well-being, developing behaviors to enhance, 325–329
  social systems and, 314–315
Infant–Parent Program at University of California San Francisco, 303
Infants, 40
  aggression of, 131

assimilation of parents' feelings, 110–111
  parental attachment to, 274
  response to caretaker's behavior patterns, 68–70, 85n
Integrity. *See* Honesty and integrity
Intense feeling-release therapy. *See* Feeling-release therapy
Interpersonal psychological pain, 38–39
  formation of defense system, 39–52
Introspection versus inwardness, 109
Inwardness, 108–110
  generosity and, 158
  microsuicide and, 170, 171–173
  origins of, 110–114
  outward versus inward lifestyle and, 66–67
Isolation
  of contemporary society, 16
  fantasy bond and, 65
  microsuicide and, 168, 170, 171–173, 183n
  projection of negative parental qualities leading to, 64

Jealousy
  parental jealousy of child, 279
  sexual rivalry, 265–266
Journal keeping, 98, 106n, 128n
  couple therapy, 225–227
  excerpt from journal, 402–407
Judgmental attitudes, 143

Learned helplessness, 138
Life-affirming potentialities, 21
Life expectancy and generosity, 158
Love
  ability to love, 22
  emotional hunger of parents confused with genuine love, 278–279
  fantasy of enduring love, 94
  genuine love, 23, 60, 94
  parental love, forms of, 67, 113, 345n
  sexual love, 23
  spiritual life and, 383–384
Love-food, 45, 60, 293

Psychotherapy, *continued*
　　therapists
　　　　defenses of, 357–359
　　　　personality characteristics of,
　　　　　355–357
　　　　training of, 357–358
　　　　for victimized point of view,
　　　　　141–142
　　　　for withholding behaviors, 159
Punishment of children. *See* Disciplinary
　　practices of parents

Regression, 180–181, 395–400
Rejecting behavior, 66–67
Religion
　　death anxiety and, 195–196, 379
　　science's inroads on, 377
　　sexuality and, 240
　　social pressure from, 335
Repressed memories of abuse, 353–354,
　　364n
Respect
　　for boundaries, 230, 325–326
　　for children, 328–329, 343
　　in friendship, 370, 371
　　for partner's freedom, 326
Revenge, feelings of, 133
Ritalin, 351
Routines and habitual responses, 92–93

Sadness
　　about death, 400–402
　　adaptive sadness, 129n
　　capability of feeling, 381
　　distinguished from depression,
　　　119–120
Sailing. *See* Adventure and travel
Schizoid personality disorders, 110
Schizophrenia, 76
Search for meaning, 21–22, 380–382. *See*
　　also Spirituality
Seduction theory, 350
Self-actualized existence, 17–18
　　overuse of terminology, 34n, 349
　　risks associated with, 20
Self-control and feelings, 108
Self-denial, 155, 156, 159
　　defined, 172

friendship and, 368
as manipulation, 319, 324
microsuicide and, 168, 170
progressive, 172–173
societal influences on, 174, 335
Self-destructive tendencies, 165–183. *See*
　　also Suicidal tendencies
　　antiself system and, 50
　　continuum of negative thought pat-
　　　terns, 168, 169
　　corrective suggestions for modifying,
　　　176–178
　　couple therapy revealing, 225
　　development of, 21, 131
　　Firestone Assessment of Self-Destruc-
　　　tive Thoughts (FAST), 168, 170
　　as manipulation, 319, 324
　　microsuicidal behavior, 165–166
　　regression, 180–181
Self-disclosure. *See* Honesty and integrity
Self-esteem, 149, 158
Self-hatred, 63. *See also* Negative self-
　　image
　　avoidance of feelings and, 115
　　friendship and, 368
　　parents discouraging children from
　　　adopting, 304–305
Self-image. *See* Negative self-image
Self-nurturing lifestyles, 87–106. *See also*
　　Addictive patterns of behavior
　　compensating for lack of nurturance,
　　　46, 60
　　corrective suggestions for, 97–98,
　　　102–103
　　　resistance to, 99–102
　　development of, 87–88
　　expression of needs and desires, 97
　　projection of negative parental quali-
　　　ties and behaviors onto others,
　　　64, 279–280
　　psychotherapy for, 95–102
　　society's reinforcement of, 333
Self-parenting process, 47, 50, 56n. *See*
　　also Fantasy bond
　　death anxiety and, 53
　　disruption of patterns and routines
　　　of, 68–73
　　extended to addictive attachments,
　　　88, 94–95
　　healthy functioning versus, 65

idealization of parents and family, 62–63

internalized voice in, 75–76

real love and, 60

sexual problems in adult relationships and, 93–94

society's reinforcement of, 333

threats to, 67–75

Self-reflection versus inwardness, 109

Self-righteousness, 133–134, 156

Self-system, 18, 49

emergence after giving up addictive behaviors, 103

Self-talk, 50, 75–76. *See also* Negative thoughts

in friendship circle, 81

Separation anxiety, 52–53

September 11th events, reactions to, 191–192

Sexual abuse

childhood exposure to, 41, 44–45, 56n, 248–249

emotional maltreatment and, 42

false memory syndrome and, 353–354

repetition by parents who were abused as children, 37

statistics on frequency, 45

Sexual addiction, 90–91, 106n

Sexuality, 239–269

competition and sexual rivalry, 265–266

continuum of sexual love, 269n

emotional distance, 254

fantasy, 254, 264

friendship circle and development of healthy perspective on, 258–268

guilt reactions, 240, 241, 254

influences on, 259–263

modes of relating, 242–244

negative thoughts during sex, 254–255

open versus closed relationships, 266–268

parental attitudes toward, 240–241

problems in adult relationships, 93–94

societal attitudes toward, 241–242

stereotyping, 242

views of, 239–240

voice therapy applied to, 255–258

withholding, 244–254, 264

family dynamics related to, 249–254

relationship to sexual child abuse, 248–249

Sexual stereotypes, 76

Single-parent family, 286

Social affiliation, 24–25. *See also* Friendship

need and desire for, 368

Socializing of children, 332

Social systems, 331–346

benevolent social system, 336–337

children and, 343–344

ethics of, 337–339

family's function in socializing of child, 332

friendship circle's dimensions of, 337–344

individual defenses extended into malevolent social system, 331–336

individual in society, 332–334

individual rights and, 314–315

mixed messages of, 334–335

social pressure, 335–336

Specialness. *See* Vanity

Spirituality, 26–27, 377–385

celebration of nature, 378

experience of the sacred, 379–380

love and, 383–384

mystery of existence, 379–380

search for meaning, 21–22, 380–382

Spiritual suffering, 330n

Spontaneity, 82

Stubbornness, 144

withholding and, 150

Substance abuse, 91–92

childhood exposure to, 41

hereditary factors, 36

microsuicide and, 168, 170

psychotherapy after abstinence, 95

Success

fantasy bond and, 73–74

withholding following atypical success, 151–152

Suicidal tendencies

antiself system and, 50

Beck Suicide Inventory, 170

Suicidal tendencies, *continued*
  deserting family as substitute suicide, 97
  hereditary factors, 36
  microsuicidal behavior, 165–166
  prisoners, 166
  progression toward suicide, 173
  women with incestuous relationship with fathers, 91

Terror Management Theory (TMT), 55n, 197–198
Threats. *See* Coercion in interpersonal relationships
Toilet training, 241
Travel. *See* Adventure and travel

Undefended individual's characteristics, 27–28

Vanity, 63
  death anxiety and, 192–193
  male vanity and female control, 322–323
  realistic feedback to fantasized image, 74–75
Victimized point of view, 132–138
  active participation in life as antidote to, 146–147
  friendship circle methods for overcoming, 144–147, 323–324
  giving up, 143
  as manipulation, 323–324
  modification of, through psychotherapy, 141–142
  origins of, 136–137
  paranoia, 134–136
  parents discouraging children from adopting, 305
  passive–aggression, 134
  self-righteousness, 133–134
Violence. *See* Child abuse; Domestic violence
Voice process, 18–19
  addictive behaviors and, 91, 98
  friendship and, 368

microsuicide and, 168, 177
negative self-image and, 63
in self-parenting fantasies, 75–76
sexuality and, 255–258
suppressing feeling, 118–119
withholding, identification of internalized voices that foster, 156
Voice therapy, 18–19, 34n, 76, 77–79, 83–84
  for couple relationships, 218–224
    group therapy, 219–224
  defined, 77
  for parenting groups and parent education, 295–302
  process of, 86n
  steps in, 78

Withholding, 149–163
  couple relationship and, 152–155, 216–217
  defined, 149
  friendship circle techniques for overcoming, 160–162
  identification of internalized voices that foster, 156
  as manipulation, 319
  microsuicide and, 170
  passive–aggression and, 150–151
  precipitated by positive events, 151–152
  psychotherapy techniques for overcoming, 159
  renunciation of personal and vocational goals, 172
  self-denial and, 155
  sexual withholding, 244–254, 264
    family dynamics related to, 249–254
    power of, 322
    relationship to sexual child abuse, 248–249
Women
  homicidal acts by, 148n
  passive–aggression and, 134
  sexuality of, 264–266. *See also* Sexuality
  sexual stereotyping, 242, 322
  threats to couple relationship, 193
  violence of, 318

ABOUT THE AUTHORS

Robert W. Firestone, PhD, clinical psychologist and author, has established a comprehensive body of work that focuses on the concept that defenses formed by individuals early in life often impair their ability to sustain intimate adult relationships and can have a damaging effect on their children. He was engaged in the private practice of psychotherapy from 1957 to 1979, working with a wide range of patients, expanding his original ideas on schizophrenia, and applying these concepts of a theory of neurosis. In 1979, he joined the Glendon Association as its consulting theorist. His major publications include *The Fantasy Bond, Compassionate Child-Rearing,* and *Fear of Intimacy.* His studies of negative thought processes led to the development of an innovative therapeutic methodology described in *Voice Therapy, Suicide and the Inner Voice,* and *Combating Destructive Thought Processes.*

Lisa A. Firestone, PhD, clinical psychologist, is the director of research and education at the Glendon Association in Santa Barbara, California, and an adjunct faculty at the University of California, Santa Barbara Graduate School of Education. Since 1987, she has been involved in clinical training and applied research related to the assessment of suicide and violence potential. Her publications include *The Firestone Assessment of Self-Destructive Thoughts* (FAST; coauthored with Robert W. Firestone), *Voices in Suicide: The Relationship Between Self-Destructive Thoughts and Self-Destructive Lifestyles, The Treatment of Sylvia Plath,* and *Conquer Your Critical Inner Voice.*

Joyce Catlett, MA, author and lecturer, has collaborated with Robert W. Firestone in writing 10 books and has coproduced 37 educational videos for the Glendon Association. She developed the Compassionate Child-Rearing Parent Education Program, a child abuse prevention model curriculum that has been used in six U.S. states, Canada, and Costa Rica. She currently lectures and conducts continuing education workshops at universities and mental health facilities throughout the United States and Canada.